THIRD EDITION

Not for

ESOL
TEACHERS

What every classroom teacher
needs to know about the
linguistically, culturally, and
ethnically diverse student

Eileen N. Whelan Ariza

Florida Atlantic University
Boca Raton, Florida

Kendall Hunt
publishing company

Book Team

Chairman and Chief Executive Officer Mark C. Falb
President and Chief Operating Officer Chad M. Chandlee
Vice President, Higher Education David L. Tart
Director of Publishing Partnerships Paul B. Carty
Senior Developmental Coordinator Angela Willenbring
Vice President, Operations Timothy J. Beitzel
Senior Project Coordinator Michelle Bahr
Senior Permissions Editor Jade Sprecher
Cover Designer Faith Walker

Cover image © Shutterstock.com

This book previously published by Pearson Education, Inc.

Kendall Hunt
publishing company

www.kendallhunt.com
Send all inquiries to:
4050 Westmark Drive
Dubuque, IA 52004-1840

Copyright © 2018 by Kendall Hunt Publishing Company

ISBN: 978-1-5249-4877-1

Published in the United States of America

TABLE OF CONTENTS

Appendices   335

ABOUT THE AUTHOR

Eileen N. Whelan Ariza, Ed.D.

Source: Eileen N. Whelan Ariza

Dr. Eileen N. Whelan Ariza is a professor in the Department of Teaching and Learning, and ESOL Coordinator in the College of Education at Florida Atlantic University, Boca Raton, Florida. She received her doctorate in multicultural/multilingual education at the University of Massachusetts, Amherst; a Master's in Teaching English to Speakers of Other Language (ESOL); MA in Teaching Spanish as a Foreign Language; and a Bilingual/Multicultural Endorsement from the School for International Training, Brattleboro, Vermont. Her undergraduate degree, from Worcester State College, MA (summa cum laude) is in elementary education. She completed her student teaching at the American School in Madrid, where she first learned about bilingual education through English as a foreign language. She holds two levels of certifications by the Cervantes Institute, Ministry of Education, Spain, as a teacher of Spanish as a Foreign Language.

Ariza has over 30 years of experience teaching ESL/EFL to students with varying backgrounds and experience from around the world, including Eurasia, Latin America, Europe, the Middle East, and Asia. At FAU for the last 20 years, she has taught graduate and under-graduate courses with a focus on ESOL training and foreign language methodology to preservice and in service teachers. She specializes in cross cultural and intercultural training for educators who are unfamiliar with "non-mainstream" students and spent several years teaching ESL/EFL, both overseas, and at Harvard University's English Language Institute. She has taught, lived in, presented and/or given workshops in many cultures, including the Philippines, Colombia, Mexico, Ecuador, Thailand, Costa Rica, Brazil, Hong Kong, France, Ireland, and the Commonwealth of Puerto Rico, which has shown her the significance and power of cultural sensitivity. Additionally, she taught English as an additional language to multicultural guests on two transatlantic voyages on the Queen Mary 2, from London to New York.

Ariza is a three-time Fulbright Scholar, first at the Universidad de las Americas in Puebla (Fulbright-García Robles), in spring 2009. Her second Fulbright was in Costa Rica (spring, 2016), working with the American Embassy, the Ministry of Education, and the University of Costa Rica in San Jose. Her third Fulbright is at the University of Malta, spring 2018, where she is involved in the study of mainstream teachers of refugee and migrant students.

Ariza is dedicated to the Fulbright mission and is awestruck by the impact it makes on participants. Her other Fulbright experiences have included: Fulbright-Hayes Seminar, Alternate Reviewer, January 2016; Fulbright Presentation and Public Speaking Certificate, Poynter News University, September 2015; Fulbright Alumni Ambassador, Fall 2013–Fall 2015 (invited); Fulbright U.S. ETA Reviewer, March 2014, 2015; 2017, Fulbright Peer Reviewer (TEFL) 2014–2015; Fulbright Candidate Specialist Roster, 2010–2014; Fulbright Specialist Peer Reviewer, 2006–2009; and is a member of the Fulbright Oversight Committee (Scholar-in-Residence, SIR) at Florida Atlantic University. She also is involved as an external reviewer for English teachers at Nazarbayev University in Kazakhstan, through the Kazakhstan Embassy in Washington D.C.

Over the span of her career, Dr. Ariza has won multiple teaching awards and recognition by her students, teachers, and colleagues (FAU undergraduate excellence; FAU College of Education Distinguished Teacher of the Year; FAU university-wide, Distinguished Teacher of the Year; outstanding alumni award at Worcester State College; and excellence in teaching at Harvard University). She has authored or coauthored 12 well received books and materials that focus on training teachers of English learners (several that are recommended by the Florida Department of Education), authored or coauthored over 62 peer reviewed publications/chapters on TESOL, and has presented several times a year nationally or internationally, on TESOL and language learning issues, since 1998. Her personal life is dedicated to her children, Stefani and Nico, and her professional life is devoted to the constant mission of helping mainstream teachers understand students who are learning through English as a new language.

PREFACE

I entered the field of teaching English to speakers of other languages accidentally, in 1985. As an elementary teacher, I went to teach English at a bilingual American school in Valencia, Spain. My job was to be the "remedial" teacher for the native Spanish speakers who were learning academic content through English. I had never heard or ESL/ESOL/EFL/ENL or any of the acronyms we may use now, but after teaching for a while, I realized that there was nothing remedial about my students. They simply were not proficient in English. I also realized that just because I spoke English, it did not mean I knew how to teach English learners and I needed training to learn how to do that. (I was the remedial student.) I discovered a master's degree program (TESOL -teaching English to speakers of other languages) in Vermont called The School for International Training, and that experience proved to be the door to my destiny. Little did I know that I would never teach in a regular classroom (without English learners) again.

After teaching in several locations (Colombia, Spain, Puerto Rico, and Mexico), I became a bilingual teacher in the USA. Over time, I noticed that my colleagues were usually monolingual (English speaking), and were unfamiliar with students from other cultures. I wanted to share my knowledge and experiences about English learners, which led me to accept a position training preservice and inservice teachers in Florida, where I have been teaching for the last 20 years. My conclusions were simple:

1. Most mainstream teachers in the United States have little familiarity with students from other cultures.
2. It is impossible to fathom the difficulty of learning through a foreign language unless one has experienced the process.
3. Teachers have to look beyond their own cultural lens to understand that their perceptions are not the same as those of students from other countries.
4. Teaching through English to native English speakers has no relation to teaching through English to those who are learning English.
5. We cannot compare academic English language learners with native English speakers, which is what goes on in our classrooms today.
6. My ideas were supported by Shim's (2013) research: teachers form opinions of ELs based on their sociocultural backgrounds and these preconceptions are reflected affectively in their teaching practice. Teachers' pedagogical behaviors are determined through the way they filter and interpret information received in the classroom, but their beliefs are developed long before the teacher gets to the classroom. Teachers make sense of things based on factors before and beyond the context of the immediate classroom. (p.17)

This book is the third edition, but the original one took me three years to complete. It was conceived as a labor of love for the student who is learning through a foreign language, as well as tremendous affection, respect, and compassion for the mainstream teacher who is not a trained teacher of English to speakers of other languages (TESOL) yet takes all of the responsibility for the achievement of these very special students.

The biggest gift I can give to mainstream teachers who do not speak another language is to share what I have learned throughout my own language-learning and teaching career. Not everyone has the desire or ability to go get a master's degree in TESOL, so I put together the basics and background information that I believe are the minimum level of knowledge that teachers need to possess to teach English learners in their classrooms. While the basics of learning through another language are the same, there have been changes in the field and I have tried to include the most critical information.

New to this edition:

In this third edition, we have set up the chapter format to be more uniform in design. The chapters include updated references, key points, final points, more voices from stakeholders, and online resources for further learning.

Chapter 1, "Who are our students?" Maria Coady joined me in writing about today's English learners and the diversity in mainstream classrooms that our amazing teachers are expected to attend to on a daily basis. We talk about students in mainstream classes who may be classified as English as a New Learner (ENL), or second language learners, but are born in the United States. Students may be migrants, refugees, asylees, unaccompanied minors, SLIFE/SIFE (limited or interrupted formal education), or undocumented, and they all have academic, learning, emotional, and other issues that vary widely, but mainstream teachers are expected to provide for all these differing needs. Teachers share their own stories, reflections, experiences, and concerns about providing safe learning environments, while trying to meet required standards.

Maria writes about debunking myths of learning English, while other teachers from various locations across the country share the characteristics of the ELs in their mainstream classrooms. These descriptions show the incredible variety of students that can be found in just one classroom.

Chapter 3, "Cross-Cultural Understanding in Academic Settings," talks about the importance of culturally relevant teaching, and how we should use students' own backgrounds to create more culturally relevant instruction. It also describes an interesting theory about the universal facial expressions of seven emotions—anger, contempt, disgust, fear, joy, sadness, and surprise. There is evidence confirming the idea that these emotions are felt universally, but there are differences in how individuals show these feelings because in some cultures people express these emotions openly, and in others, people do not. This can be confusing if we are judging someone based on the ideas we have about what a display of one of these signs means.

Chapter 4, "Diverse Learning Styles" goes into detail about diverse learners and the need for differentiated instruction, based on individual learning styles, which are often influenced by the home culture as well as home language. Gardner's classification of intelligences are well known, and this chapter offers ideas for the classroom that correspond to and reflect each intelligence and learning style of students. Based on these classroom tips, teachers can modify instruction, which will really help to mitigate the incongruence between instruction and the individual's preferred learning style.

Chapter 5, "What Teachers Need to Know About Language Acquisition," is a tough one because it is like a basic primer of language learning and acquisition principles. Justin White offered his expertise to make modifications in this chapter with me. My primary goal is to make dense linguistic topics more comprehensible for the teacher who has not studied linguistics. Typically, this information is presented in multiple courses if one is studying in a formal TESOL program. However, in this chapter, the information on language learning is abridged, and it might feel overwhelming. It talks about the historical theories, principles, and the prominent theorists like Krashen, Chomsky, and Skinner that are still covered in ESOL courses. Many examples are given with the hope that it will make the content more illustrative.

Chapter 6, "The School Experience for the New English Learner," addresses the landmark decision of *Plyer v Doe* in the Supreme Court in 1982. This law protects and says we cannot constitutionally deny students a free public education because of their immigration status. This information is timely as the current presidential administration is working within an opposing point of view and we have many undocumented students in the US that need and deserve to be educated. Different classifications of literacy levels are defined and explained, as well as the new learner experience in an American school.

Chapter 7 is "Why Integrate Language and Content?" This chapter talks about the WIDA consortium (academic and language development standards) that many states have joined in order to formalize clear, high level content objectives through English. The former NCLB Act, now the Every Student Succeeds Act (ESSA) requires states to include ELs' English language proficiency (ELP) progress as a core component of their Title I accountability plans. The US needs to find more uniform standardization measures and this need dovetails with the problems students have in trying to become academically successful through content, to raise their academic knowledge. Additionally, tips for teaching beginning English learners are discussed in detail because this level of proficiency is usually the most difficult for the mainstream teacher. Intermediate, advanced, and multilevel students will all be in the same classroom and teachers need to modify content instruction for all.

Chapter 9, "Literacy, Technology, and the English learner," written by Susanne I. Lapp, is completely revised. Susanne writes about improving English literacy with the help of technology and apps. She takes older literacy strategies and infuses modern technology into instruction for improving reading and literacy teaching.

Chapter 11, "Teaching Science to English Learners," is a new chapter written by Lindsey Laury, a passionate science teacher. She writes about ways that science can improve content knowledge while improving English literacy, the barriers that English learners face in science instruction, and how to improve science content instruction by using literacy strategies.

Chapter 12, "Teaching Social Studies to English Learners," is also a new chapter, written by Rina Bousalis, who trains educators to teach social studies to English learners. She shows how teachers can teach ELs to distinguish the meaning and importance of social studies and she identifies possible challenges teachers may face in teaching social studies to new English learners. Within the chapter, she identifies successful ways ELs can be taught social studies, and how they can personally benefit by learning about this subject. Meanwhile, the social studies classroom can profit from having EL students share their experiences, outlooks, and adventures in the class as well.

Chapter 13, "Teaching English Learners Literacy Through the Arts," is another new chapter written by art methods professor, Susannah Brown. She describes the connection between arts and literacy concepts and explains how arts integration supports ELs language development. She analyzes creative literacy strategies appropriate for ELs and shows how teachers can use vocabulary building strategies that connect to visual art. Finally, she draws a connection to strategies for other art forms such as music, dance, and drama.

Chapter 14, "Vocabulary Development in a Literacy Curriculum (From Elementary to Older ELs): An Action Plan" is another new chapter written by Kate Mastruserio Reynolds. She discusses how to differentiate levels of proficiency while factoring vocabulary knowledge, integrating research on vocabulary learning into instruction, and utilizing evidence-based, field-tested strategies for vocabulary teaching and learning. She offers some illustrative examples of students with underdeveloped literacy skills, like Dayax, a third grader whose native language was Somali. Although he was born in Minneapolis, he was a student with interrupted formal education due to living in a succession of foster homes. She describes the strategies she used to assess his needs via the WIDA placement test so she could develop an action plan to further Dayax's literacy skills.

In Chapter 15, Samantha I. Uribe writes with me as we refresh and update the chapter, "Traditional Assessment: Why it is Inappropriate." We include new information about assessments for English learners as it relates to the NCLB revision, now the Every Student Succeeds Act (ESSA). WIDA's Can Do Descriptors of levels of language proficiency can support teachers in differentiating instruction within each language domain (listening, speaking, reading, and writing.) Using these indicators, assessment can be more authentic and accurate.

Chapter 16 is a new addition to this third edition. "Working with Parents of ESOL Students" is written by Naomi Hagen and Erin Meuer from Spokane, Washington. They teach in the public schools, work with immigrants and refugees, and train educators to work with parents of these students. They want readers to know that teacher-parent relations are different from country to country; that parents new to the US may not realize they are expected to show a presence in the American school setting, but they are deeply concerned about their children's education, although it might not appear this way. They offer positive steps educators can take to teach and encourage parents how to help advocate for their children.

In Part 6, "The Sampler of Cultural Groups-Teacher as Cultural Observer," I chose to include certain cultural groups that are prominent in the Southeast. Understandably, with the wealth of cultural groups in the United States, I could not address them all. I believe it is critical to know your students' culture for that is the key to understanding the individuals who make up your classroom. Once you discover where your students are from, you can take the time to research the idiosyncrasies of their cultures (beliefs, values, customs, foods, rituals, etc.) but be sure to look at deep culture in addition to the surface culture. It is also important to avoid cliché cultural descriptions of the group as a whole because each person is an individual. However, some commonalities can be attributed to a cultural group in general, with the caveat that people are individuals and once you get to know them, you will be better prepared for differentiated instruction.

Chapter 18, "Hispanics, Latino/as, and Spanish Speakers" contains more information on the different lives and cultures of Spanish speakers from different countries and regions. Again, there are overarching commonalities within these societies, but the individuals are as distinct as any individual in the United States. Voices and reflections of Spanish speakers are shared with hopes that you can see a bit of how diverse their lives are.

Chapter 19, "Jamaicans in the American school system: An understanding of language and culture, "is a new addition to this book. Angela Rhone, originally from Jamaica, notes that students of color in the US are usually presumed to be African-Americans, but there is a vast diaspora of people of color and it is often an incorrect assumption. Students from Jamaica and other cultures have concerns and difficulties with American culture, standard English, and discerning appropriate cultural behavior. Even though students of color may speak English as a first language, teachers may think these students need to study English as an additional language. Students might be referred to remedial intervention if they don't speak standard English, and are from a culture where English is a main language. However, it is important to know that Jamaican, Caribbean, etc. and students from other cultures usually have an extended family that will help one another.

Chapter 20, "Muslims, Followers of Islam, and Speakers of Arabic," has been revised to include voices of parents, teachers, and students who are followers of Islam and live in the US. It is a fascinating chapter, and a delightful read. I hope you enjoy reading it as much as I did. My first vignette is about an American woman I met on a plane who was traveling with her sisters and when I asked her if she was speaking Arabic, she said yes, but she said she would only do that with her sisters (or other females). Then she told me that she was afraid to speak Arabic when traveling with her husband. I felt ashamed to hear that in my beloved country.

Rachida Faid-Douglas offers her personal reflections on being a professor, mother, and Muslim who lives in the US. Her words are powerful as she explains what she wants teachers to know about her children as Muslims. I also asked two students (Afsana Chowdhury and Essam Abdelrasul Bubaker Elkorghli) what they would want educators to know about them as Muslims, and they wrote enlightening, revealing, and very personal answers for you to read. In sum, the chapter highlights the following points:

Muslims may look very different racially, culturally, and in the ways they carry themselves; they can be Caucasians, Africans, Asians, Arabs and in between; unless they are identified by a dress code, there is no way one can associate anyone as Muslim; Arabs, Muslims, and followers of Islam all widely different and should not be lumped into one group; people who are Muslims might not speak Arabic; people who engage in questionable acts might be reacting in accordance with their culture, and not their religion (Islam); Islam is a non-violent religion; terrorists who commit violence are not practicing Islam; teachers should take every opportunity to learn about their students, and use teachable moments to spread understanding of a gravely misunderstood religion.

Chapter 21, "Chinese, Japanese, South Korean, and Indians," is a totally revised chapter. Linglan Cao and Ke Xu, English instructors in New York, join me in explaining cultural and linguistic features of these four cultural groups. They explain which people are considered Asians, where they are from, and give background information they think would be helpful to educators. They write a comprehensive overview of the intricacies of each culture that will help explain Asian students, their cultures, languages, and issues students might have learning English.

Chapter 22, "Haitians," has been updated to include more voices of Haitians and what they would like educators to know about them. Success Innocent (French teacher), and Evan Noel (preservice teacher working on a math education degree) contribute to this chapter. Both have been educated in Haiti and moved to Florida. Success is an older gentleman who is a French teacher, and has been in the US for a long time. Evan moved to the US when he was a teen and went to high school here.

I hope that these chapters and narratives offer a brief picture of individuals from diverse cultures and the struggles they encounter living in the mainstream, English speaking cultures of the United States.

FOREWORD

Increasingly, mainstream teachers rather than specialist language teachers are expected to work with English language learners (ELS) in their classroom. In fact, ELs continue to outpace the non-ELL population in K-12 school enrollment (Shin & Kominski, 2010; Uro & Barrio, 2013 as cited in de Jong, 2013, pp. 40). This phenomenon combined with research that 'new destination states' like Georgia, North Dakota, and South Carolina have experienced a 200% increase in their EL population has put huge demands on schools. These enrollments, plus other political, economic, and educational demands mean that many ELs are placed either full time or most of the day in mainstream rather than in specialist language programs.

Much of the research in this area to date has focused on what mainstream teachers should know and be able to do when working with ELs. Eileen Ariza's *NOT for ESOL Teachers* (now in its 3rd edition) covers a huge array of this content in a very accessible, non-technical, and practical way. Mainstream teachers who encounter ELs in the classroom are by definition ESOL teachers and they need a basic understanding of how best to educate these students. Especially important is knowing how to teach the same curriculum to both native and non-native English language speakers through modifying, adapting, and extending their materials.

This volume took shape from the author's own personal experiences as an 'accidental teacher' or one who found herself in a teaching position, liked it and then decided to make it her career, and from an empirical one. Heavily influenced by Shim's (2013) research, which found that teachers form opinions of ELs based on their own sociocultural backgrounds, these preconceptions are reflected in their teacher practice. Ariza has dedicated herself to providing a resource that mainstream teachers could use to educate themselves about their new students and how best to serve them.

Divided into five sections, Section 1 is relegated to helping mainstream teachers become familiar with the 'Classrooms of Today'. The excellent introductory chapter by Coady & Ariza provides critical information about who our students are and where they come from. Other major topics in this section include cultural diversity, cross cultural understanding, and diverse learning styles in modern day classrooms.

Section 2 focuses on the 'Perplexity and Complexity of Learning Another Language'. Chapters catering to both major stakeholders (teachers and students) are found here. The author has provided a 'what teachers need to know about second language acquisition' for teachers and one about 'the school experience for the new English learner' so that teachers can acquaint themselves about what kinds of issues their learners are going through as they join US schools.

The major concentration in Part 3 is through the integration of academic content and how best to exploit it in classes with ELLs. An introductory chapter on why it is critical to use an integrated language and content approach is included and is followed up with a chapter on differentiated learning. Further chapters feature input on teaching mathematics, science, social studies,and literacy through the arts in English.

Parts 4 and 5 focus on assessment and ELs and the Wider Community respectively, while Part 6 features a 'sampler' of cultural insights into various groups of learners. These chapters are designed to educate teachers on culturally-responsive teaching and how the different cultural backgrounds of their students might have an impact on their learning.

This new edition features updated references and resources for further learning. In each chapter, the author(s) make the content of the chapter accessible by providing key points to consider and case studies of real teachers (and students). Readers are then asked to reflect on the chapter contents through sets of reflection questions. At the end of each chapter, there are extension activities and discussion questions that readers can engage with to extend their knowledge about the contents of each respective chapter.

Although this book is intended for those educators who teach ELs but do not have substantial previous TESOL training, personally I feel that Ariza's *NOT for ESOL Teachers* is relevant to all educators who teach and interact with ELs. As a TESOL-trained teacher with more than 30 years of teaching both in the US and in three countries worldwide, through this book I learned a great deal about ELs and the particular challenges they face in classrooms today.

Filled with relevant non-technical content (both academic and practical) and authentic voices from stakeholders, *NOT For ESOL Teachers* provides everything the mainstream teacher needs to know about how to function effectively with ELLs in their classrooms.

Dr Christine Coombe

TESOL President (2011–2012)

Reference

De Jong, E. (2013). Preparing Mainstream Teachers for Multilingual Classrooms, *Association of Mexican-American Educators Special Invited Issue*, Vol. 7, Issue 2: 40–49.

PART 1

CLASSROOMS OF TODAY

CHAPTER 1

WHO ARE OUR STUDENTS?

Maria Coady and Eileen N. Whelan Ariza

Diverse Learners in the United States

KEY POINTS

- Students in classes in the United States (as in many other places) are no longer all White, English speakers.
- Many students in mainstream classes may be English as a New Language Learner, (ENL) or second language learners, but are born in the United States.
- Students come from a diverse range of linguistic, racial, ethnic, and socioeconomic backgrounds, and all have their own history of educational continuity.
- To successfully instruct diverse learners, teachers need to learn about the cultures their students come from and as much as they can about their linguistic backgrounds.
- Students may be migrants, refugees, asylees, unaccompanied minors, or SIFE/SLIFE, (students with limited or interrupted formal education) or undocumented.
- Students may need resources for academic support as well as emotional support.

Simply peer into any classroom window in a public school today, and it is easy to see that classrooms are comprised diverse learners, including students who were born in the United States, but may speak a language other than English at home, and those who are new arrivals to the country. In fact, of the approximately 50 million students in PK-12 public schools across the United States, about 10% are English learners, or ELs (Hussar & Bailey, 2014). In addition, about 11.4 million identify themselves as Hispanic, 8 million as Black, and about 26 million as White. Hispanics comprise the fastest growing group. Importantly, many of our public school students, almost one in four, are living in poverty (National Center for Children in Poverty [NCCP], 2013).

Teachers in today's classrooms must respond to the wide range of learning needs of the students that they teach. For example, a *refugee* student from Bhutan who has had interrupted formal schooling (SLIFE—Student with interrupted or limited formal education) while awaiting resettlement to the

United States has much different learning needs from an immigrant, *sojourner* (temporary stay) student from India whose father is enrolled in a graduate education program. A SIFE or SLIFE early or elementary student will have different needs from the middle or high school student because of the age and academic disparity. Another student might have come to the United States as an unaccompanied minor trying to escape gang activity, poverty, or crime. Some students are considered asylees as their families are seeking *asylum* from their home countries for any number of reasons. Yet, all of these students will be required to follow the same curriculum and will likely take a similar standardized test to demonstrate their learning. Working with all of these students and ensuring that their learning goals are met, as well as offering a safe, nonthreatening environment is a challenge that teachers face across the United States.

REFLECTION QUESTIONS

- How do you think the demographic data above affect education?
- What differences will you find as the teacher of these dissimilar students?
- How do you think those data [will] affect you as a teacher?
- What would you have to do to prepare to instruct these types of student with multiple types of issues?
- In what ways do you think your instruction will differ for a refugee Bhutanese student with interrupted schooling, and a sojourner Indian student? What would you need to know about these students and what type of support would you need to have in place?
- How will you prepare for instruction for a SLIFE students who has only attended school for two years, or is semiliterate in the native language?

Teachers' Voices

The teachers' voices you will read in this chapter reveal the experiences of many lower elementary, upper elementary, and secondary (high school) teachers working in schools around the country today. We hear from first year teachers as well as seasoned veterans who discuss their immediate concerns about teaching.

Immigrant—a foreign, non-US born person, typically receiving a special visa (permission) to live and work in the United States. (https://www.merriam-webster.com/dictionary/immigrant)

Refugee—a person who seeks asylum based on the actual or potential persecution due to religious or ethnic discrimination. In the United States, a refugee receives a special immigration and visa status. The United Nations high commission on refugees determines what conditions qualify for refugee status. (http://www.unrefugees.org/what-is-a-refugee/)

Sojourner—a temporary relocatee or immigrant; typically someone whose stay is short term and length of stay is predetermined. (http://www.dictionary.com/browse/sojourner)

Migrant—in the United States, this is a special designation for people working in agriculture, fishing, and dairy industries who typically move frequently (migrate) as a result of seasonal harvest. (http://www.unesco.org/new/en/social-and-human-sciences/themes/internationalmigration/glossary/migrant/)

Asylum—when a refugee requests to stay in another country based on claims of danger in the homeland, he or she is an asylee. (http://www.unhcr.org/en-us/asylum-seekers.html)

Undocumented—when people are living in the United States without current papers that give legal status, they are called "undocumented." (http://www.nolo.com/legal-encyclopedia/who-is-undocumented-immigrant.html)

DACA—an acronym that stands for *Deferred Action for Childhood Arrivals*. President Obama passed this law for children who were brought to the United States before their 16th birthday that allowed them to legally work or go to school. (http://www.immigrationequality.org/get-legal-help/our-legal-resources/path-to-status-in-the-u-s/daca-deferred-action-for-childhood-arrivals/)

TPS—temporary protective status for eligible nationals who need protection for a certain amount of time. (https://www.uscis.gov/humanitarian/temporary-protected-status)

Unaccompanied Minors (UAC)—children who enter the United States without adults. (http://www.migrationpolicy.org/article/unaccompanied-immigrant-children-growing-phenomenon-few-easy-solutions)

Mr. Patrick Morehouse and Mr. John Saball, First Year Teachers

As a first year teacher, in a middle school Montessori Magnet Program, it is difficult to keep up with all of the requirements of teaching, including but certainly not limited to, lesson planning, grading, instruction, and behavioral management. One thing that I have personally struggled with as a first year teacher is addressing all of the standards that we are required to have our students "master" by the end of the academic school year. I am realizing very quickly, as I teach four different "preps" (classes), that it is nearly impossible to address all of these standards effectively with all my students. The Florida middle school that I work for is currently following Florida State standards that resulted from the implementation of Common Core Standards (CCS) in the classroom. We are in the transitional phases of understanding how we will be addressing both of these sets of standards in the classroom.

My opinion of both of these sets of educational standards is generally the same. It is quite a lofty goal for teachers to ensure that their instruction covers every single standard adequately enough for students to perform well on the assessments that do not always accurately measure their understanding. The nature of the system is that we are governed by instructional pacing guides that leave very little "wiggle room" for remediation before moving onto the next topic. At best, we strive to provide the highest quality of instruction possible, in hopes that the majority of students have learned what they need to know. While I can appreciate that the Common Core Standards are designed to integrate students' academic knowledge with real-world applications to build a generation of critical thinkers, they are very broad and vague. Like a first year teacher needs any more of that! This is why additional exposure to these standards through clarification guides, workshops, and practice will be necessary for teachers learn how to effectively incorporate these into our classrooms.

Teaching Culturally Diverse Populations

Working in this county has allowed me to see first-hand just how culturally diverse our student population actually is. In my own classroom, I have students that come from every walk of life, including those of Haitian, Asian, Indian, Romanian, Western European, Latino, and Hispanic descent. These cultural and linguistic differences make instruction and behavioral management even more challenging for a first year teacher. My veteran co-teacher and I often discuss the challenges and surprises that we have encountered dealing with culturally diverse students, especially our Haitian students, which represents a large percentage of our student population. For example, I have learned that in the Haitian culture, children are taught that making eye contact with authority figures (especially during disciplinary matters) is disrespectful. As a first year teacher of mainstream English-speaking U.S. students, I lacked prior knowledge about behaviors of students from other cultures so, it was easy for me to misinterpret this behavior. I had been taught that not making eye contact is disrespectful, and I expected my students to have the same perspective. This has taken some adjustment on my end. Helping students retain their cultural identity means that we must understand these cultural differences that have the potential to lead to miscommunication. I only wonder what else I am innocently misjudging due to my unfamiliarity with other cultures.

We both feel that it is extremely important for teachers to know both the surface cultures and deep cultures of their students; knowing holidays, ethnic foods and languages, for example, is not enough. Being knowledgeable about students' religious and moral beliefs, personal space and body language definitions, mannerisms, and customary greetings, for example, is far more beneficial to the educator. The better the understanding the teacher has of these deeper cultural differences, the easier it is to tailor the instruction to meet the individual needs of that particular student. Teachers also need to know what is valued in their particular students' cultures, so as not to offend them or misunderstand something that has been said, or done, in the classroom. We believe that the number one rule in teaching, whether it is with a culturally diverse group or not, is to know your students and know them well. We are not teaching math, science, reading, language arts, and social studies—we are teaching individuals. This is a conscious mindset and requires additional effort, but we believe that by knowing our students and their cultural backgrounds, we can create more culturally relative, and therefore, more effective, lessons that provide unique opportunities for students that positively identify with their cultural heritage.

Sharing Cultural Misunderstandings

Ms. Keelyn Meselsohn is an elementary teacher in the South Florida school system. Once we met, we began to share stories of our students. I shared my story about my Chinese student new to my classroom in Massachusetts, who was a lovely little girl and very shy. She made eye contact with me, and pointed to the restroom, and I nodded my head for her to go. She was taking quite a long time, so I went in to check on her. Her door was open and I saw that she was squatting on the seat, facing the back of the toilet. I gently showed her how to put some toilet tissue on the seat, so she could sit on it. She did not appear very comfortable, but I left her alone and when she came out, I went through the rest of the ritual of showing her how the soap comes out automatically, and how to put her hands under the water faucet and it runs by sensor. The paper dispenser was operated by sensor as well, but it was a little tall for her. We managed together, but I made a note to make sure some paper towel was always accessible.

Then while talking to Keelyn, she shared a similar story with me about something her Hungarian student went through last year!

Half way through the school year, an 8-year-old Hungarian girl entered my second-grade class literally right from the airport. They changed her into her school uniform that her parent's friend picked up for her in the hallway bathroom before they brought her to my room. The interpreter they brought with them said that the student had been practicing saying "Hello, teacher" the entire flight from Hungary. She wanted her first English words on American soil to be to her new teacher. She came in confident with a big bright smile as she greeted me. Everything was going well, until she had to go to the bathroom. She let me know she had to go in a typical second-grade way . . . by bouncing up and down with that "have to go and have to go now" look on her face. I showed her the bathroom in my classroom. She pulled my hand over to the toilet, still smiling . . . I realized she didn't know how to flush it. I showed her and when it flushed, she screamed! She started to cry and shake. She refused to use the bathroom after that, but she would desperately have to go! She would shake and repeat, "no, no, no!" I called a conference with her mom and the interpreter. We found out that she thought that the toilet was going to suck her down the pipes! She had never experienced the industrial flush of a toilet like this before. She was used to a similar toilet to those your Chinese student used and any flush toilet was a much gentler flush. Poor thing would not drink all day because she didn't want to have to use the restroom! I downloaded a $10 mobile app on my smartphone that translated my voice to her language so that I could talk to her and reassure her that the toilet would not swallow her up if she used it. (Unlike my usual students who come from Brazil or other central and South American countries, I didn't have another student or teacher to help me communicate so the app was my best option.) During my formal observation, my principal used my app to ask my student how she liked the United States. She spoke into the app in Hungarian and in English it loudly gave the interpretation, "America sucks. The toilets are scary." The look on my principal's face was priceless! He still tells that story at every leadership meeting! I guess I didn't realize that our industrial bathrooms could be such an unusual and scary place for some of our new students. I can only wonder what other things could be so misconstrued to a newcomer.

Another thing that I really feel is important for teachers to know is that a student's academic abilities may be hidden by the language barrier. I am a gifted endorsed teacher. At our school, we loop (i.e., keep the same teacher with the same class each year.) I teach the second/third loop so I have my students for two years. My class is partially gifted and partially general education. My gifted students leave for half-day pullout in a self-contained gifted class. We had a student move from Brazil last year. He was gifted, and was in gifted classes in Brazil. He did not speak any English. The class he was put into here was a class that had a larger number of ELs in the classroom. The teacher is not trained to recognize the traits of a gifted student. It took a very long time, much longer than it should have, to recognize this student's gifted abilities. Once the teacher realized this, it took even longer to get an EL psychologist (in his native language) to come test him since the district does not allow EL students to be tested by the on-staff psychologist. The student was finally moved to my room and given an EP (educational plan) to go to the self-contained half-day gifted classroom. He is a brilliant third grader who is currently in fifth-grade math. I can only imagine where he would be if he had been placed in my room originally or with a teacher trained to recognize a gifted child rather than just see the language barrier. Moreover, in the same loop, I struggled with the opposite problem with another child. I believe she has a learning disability. I have tried for 2 years to get this child tested and qualified for ESE (Exceptional Student Education) pullout; I was told that her issues were due to a combination of language barrier and attendance. This child travels with her migrant parents who travel around Florida working on farms. It may not be the only problem, but I am sure the lack of academic continuity and time missed from school exacerbate her academic problems. She has not shown the progress in reading I know she should have shown. In math, she does much better. Moreover, she has shown "some" progress, so our child study team will not put her through the RTI (Response to Intervention) process. I have had to get the district EL department and our school's EL teacher to fight this fight with me. So far, I still have not had this child tested. Any teacher with an EL student in their classroom needs to look beyond the language. You can try for a very long time, but it could be over a year to find out results.

Ms. Kollitides' Fifth Grade Class—a Microcosm of the World

Ms. Kollitides is a departmentalized fifth-grade math and science teacher in Hollywood, Florida. Her school is Title 1 because approximately 80% of the student population qualifies for free or reduced lunch. Ms. Kollitides teaches a total of 45 fifth-grade students. Her morning class is a mainstream inclusion class with three EL students and seven ESE (exceptional needs) students. Her afternoon class is a gifted/high achieving class with four students who are labeled gifted.

Ms. Kollitides' students are racially and ethnically diverse. Approximately 60% of her students are Hispanic, 20% are White, 10% are African American/Black, 6% are Native American, and 4% are Asian. Ms. Kollitides reflects on the diversity of her classroom and school community:

The majority of my students are Hispanic. Many of them are either bilingual or proficient only in Spanish. This year, I have three EL students. All three students are either advanced or fluent English speakers. My school does not have a formal pull-out program for EL students. Instead, EL students are mainstreamed and teachers provide support and accommodations in the classroom. Next school year, our school will be adding a dual English/Spanish language program for kindergarten and first grade. Students will be taught half the day in English and half the day in Spanish.

My three EL students—all of whom are boys—were either born abroad, have one parent who does not speak English, and/or spent a formative period of their lives living in a majority Spanish-speaking country. I've observed that, despite the linguistic barriers, the parents of my EL students are active participants in their child's education. Even if they speak only Spanish, the parents still attend every teacher conference we schedule. We either secure an interpreter, who is usually another teacher at our school, or the parent brings an older child or relative to translate. (I understand having a child translate is not the best practice, but sometimes it is the only option we have.)

The parents of my EL students want to know how they can help their child. They are very focused on making sure that their children complete all homework and assignments. They value education highly and want their child to succeed in school. I've also observed that my EL students generally interact well with their peers and make friends easily. However, last year I had an EL student with a speech disorder who was new at our school and had difficulty communicating in both English and Spanish. He had just moved to our community from Ecuador and struggled to make friends in the beginning of the year. During recess time, I encouraged him to join in with others. I would start up games of Ultimate Frisbee to foster social interaction between him and other students. Interestingly enough, this student eventually befriended a student who also had a speech disorder and a student with ASD (autistic spectrum disorder). I think my EL felt a sense of belonging and acceptance with these two other students.

Beyond my EL students, my classroom is very racially and ethnically diverse. Our school borders the Seminole Indian Reservation of Hollywood and, as a result, we have a small population of Seminole students. My Seminole students all live on the reservation and take great pride in their cultural traditions. For example, one of my students this year only wears traditional Miccosukee skirts to school. Other Seminole students I've taught wear traditional black, red, and yellow beads to represent the colors of the Seminole Tribe.

Last year, a representative from the Seminole Tribe came to our school to provide information about our Seminole students and their traditions. This gave us a great deal of context for many things we had observed in the classroom, such as the avoidance of owls, as they are considered a bad omen in Seminole culture. (This is critical knowledge because, ironically, my Colombian students believe owls are good luck.) In order to be culturally responsive teachers, we need to understand our students and their cultures. If we are not aware of this information, we run the risk of isolating our students and creating negative experiences for them in the classroom.

A Note to Mainstream Teachers: Debunking Myths of Learning English

- Learning the language of the country is essential for success in the adopted country; it empowers the newcomer and facilitates achievement of goals in life. That said, there are several misconceptions regarding English learners in the United States. First is the misconception that immigrants do not want to learn English. In fact, data from the U.S. Census, analyzed by James Crawford, indicates that the vast majority of immigrants can and do speak English, and most immigrants have a strong desire to learn the language (Crawford, 2002, 2008). A bigger issue related to learning English is that there are frequently not enough programs available to immigrants, especially to adults.
- A second misconception is that immigrants should give up the home language in order to learn English. In fact, the opposite is true. Families who speak a language other than English in the home have a rich resource, both oral and written, upon which to draw to learn a second language. The more native language use and communication that occurs in the home, both oral and written, the stronger the foundation for learning English. Many of the language skills acquired in the first language also transfer to English (or a new language). Imagine a mother not saying, "I love you," to her child

in her first language? It is difficult to express those feelings and to build relationships in a language one does not speak or know well. Teachers should encourage their students and families to engage in language-rich communication practices in the language they share. These build a foundation for literacy development.

- The third misconception is that just because a student seems to understand and speak English, he or she is "proficient" in the language. Today's classrooms require high degrees of both oral and written language, in addition to conversational language and "academic language" or the specialized language of schooling that is used in the content areas (Cummins, 2009; Schleppegrell, 2004; Townsend, Filippini, Collins, & Biancarosa, 2012; Valdés, Menken, & Castro, 2015). It is important for teachers of all students to not only teach content but also the language associated with that content. In that regard, all teachers are actually language teachers. This job is especially important for students in the process of learning English as a second language.

- It becomes increasingly apparent that all teachers need to learn effective instructional strategies to successfully teach English learners, even though the teacher might not speak the students' native language. Today's teachers need help in the classroom without having to get a master's degree in ESOL (English to Speakers of Other Languages). They need immediate answers and basic guidelines to follow for success in our multicultural, multilingual, and global climate.

Ms. Cook's First Grade Classroom

Ms. Cook is a first grade, mainstream classroom teacher in a semirural area in Florida. Per state requirements limiting classroom size, her class consists of 18 students in a mainstream, inclusive classroom setting. This means that Ms. Cook teaches students with multiple and varied learning needs, and the students follow the same curriculum in her room. In fact, of the 18 students that she teaches, three are English learners (or ELs), one is designated Exceptional Student Education (ESE) and is pulled-out of the classroom for the Language Arts block each day, and another student has Attention Deficit Hyperactivity Disorder (ADHD). A special aide assists her in the classroom with that child. The school has been designated a Title I school, which indicates that a significant percentage of the student population receives free or reduced price lunch. In 2011, Ms. Cook was the school's Teacher of the Year.

> I have been a teacher for 30 years. I spent 18 years as a teacher of adult English Learners teaching English as a Second Language (ESL). Two years ago, I returned to the public school classroom and was placed in first grade. The classroom has changed! I have three English learners, two of whom were born in the United States and one born in Mexico. My students are at the beginner (knows very little English) and Speech Emergent (two- or three-word phrases) levels. This is very challenging because I cannot assume that my ELs understand words or have the background knowledge needed to follow the curriculum like my native English speakers do. In addition, coming from a home where a language other than English is spoken means that my students will likely have little homework help, even if their parents value education, which they all seem to do.
>
> I understand and speak some Spanish, which is really important, especially for my beginning level English learners. I try to find books from different countries and that represent different cultural backgrounds, so that my students see themselves reflected in the books. Some of those books are in other languages; I believe that my classroom reflects the rich diversity all around us!

My classroom is designed for ease of learning. I continually model the kinds of behavior and activities I want my students to engage in while either working with me or at the different literacy stations [learning centers] that I have set up around the classroom. I sometimes have students model their learning task for other students to see. I also use a lot of visual aids in the classroom to assist my students, especially the ELs.

One challenge that I face is the pacing of the curriculum and the sheer number of tests that I have to administer to my students each week. I am constantly planning in order to match the curriculum and learning objectives to my individual students' learning needs. And I have had to incorporate technology (Smart Board, computer literacy skills) into my instruction as well. I spend a lot of extra time preparing for my students' learning, but I love those children and won't let them down, no matter what!

Ms. Chursenoff's Fifth Grade Class

Ms. Chursenoff is a seasoned fifth-grade mainstream teacher in Las Vegas, Nevada, in the Clark County School District (CCSD). Along with her native-English-speaking students, her class is comprised of many ELs. She shares her experiences with Hispanic families as they relate to the U.S. educational system.

With regard to interdependence of the family, I have always been pleasantly amused during conference times. My Hispanic students are always accompanied by a parent, frequently both, and also a grandparent or two, who all appear at the student's conference time, along with all the siblings! This is very different for me, as my American parents almost never bring children to a parent-teacher conference. I welcome the family, and I have learned to respond to this situation by making sure I have crayons, paper, and picture books available to keep the little ones busy. The student who is being conferred about frequently is expected to "take care" of the brothers and sisters, particularly if the student is a girl. The family members who have attended these conferences are unfailingly polite to a fault and appear very proud of their children, even when their children's academic performance is suffering.

I have noticed another important clue to effective instruction, which is recognizing how a cooperative learning style culturally complements the Hispanic child. I could be wrong, but my Hispanic students do not seem to openly want to show what they know for fear of embarrassing those who do not know. For my students, it appears that a Hispanic family does not encourage children to excel over or compete with their siblings or peers; rather, they might prefer that their siblings help each other, or otherwise it may appear to be considered bad manners.

The teacher of Hispanic EL students should become familiar with a variety of cooperative learning strategies (Padrón, Waxman, & Rivera, 2002). My experience has always been that most Hispanic students are not competitive with one another and love to "partner up" in completing tasks. They are generally very gracious toward each other and are congenial and well mannered in class.

In the classroom, my Hispanic students demonstrate a distinct pattern of interaction when I am lecturing and posing questions for discussions and comprehension. They are frequently very quiet and look somewhat intimidated at the thought that they might be called upon individually; consequently, they will often freeze and get confused or embarrassed as they try to answer. One student last year began crying the first time she was asked to come to the board to solve a simple math problem. She was exceptionally bright and motivated, knew the answer, but "fell apart" when singled out for any interaction. Her shyness was painful to watch. Even the gentlest interaction she and I had in private was difficult for her. With respect for her "silent stage" of language acquisition, I did not push her. By the end of the year, she actually performed in a skit for a social studies unit and could almost be heard by the audience!

Based on my experience as classroom teacher, it appears that Hispanic students feel much more comfortable responding in groups and helping each other. Often, I see that it appears girls may not feel comfortable responding when boys are in the group; therefore, the teacher might not know that the girl really does know the answer. I always try to find out if this is the case, or if it is lack of comprehension.

As each Hispanic family is unique and/or from a different culture, I am not sure if I am seeing a typical behavior, or a family trait, or the individual. I am merely reporting what I am seeing.

Through implementing instructional strategies that are congruent with Hispanic cultural traits, such as cooperative learning situations in the classroom, teachers can help students upgrade their social and language skills. By listening, encouraging them to support each other, giving constructive feedback, and checking understanding, teachers can take steps to ensure success. Providing teaching and culturally relevant learning approaches that embrace Hispanic tradition and culture will encourage recent Hispanic immigrants to participate more comfortably, because they can express themselves as a group and not as individuals, thus promoting interdependence yet forcing them to become individually accountable.

Table 1.1 shows an example of the variety of educational backgrounds students bring with them from their home countries. Ms. Chursenoff creates a table such as this one every year for her ELs because it provides a guide to the educational histories of her students (see also Igoa, 1995). Ms. Chursenoff can use this information to guide the instructional strategies she must use with her ELs.

The school is in a very low socioeconomic area of North Las Vegas and is designated as Title I, "At Risk," by the Clark County School District. The desks are arranged in two "E" shapes facing each other. The room is a small portable at the far end of the campus. The classroom size does not lend itself to the arrangement of desks in small groups. The student numbers fluctuate between 24 and 28, unusually low this year; the number also changes frequently as students move in and out of this transient area of Las Vegas. The class is comprised of 70 percent Hispanic, 30 percent African American, and no Caucasian students this year.

Carol Chursenoff contributed material for this chart.

Grade	Karina	Anahi	Maria	Jose	Alejandro	Juan
TABLE 1.1 Educational Backgrounds of Students in Ms. Chursenoff's Fifth-Grade Class						
5	CCSD*	CCSD	CCSD (arrived in spring)	CCSD	CCSD	CCSD
4	CCSD	CCSD	none	CCSD	CCSD	CCSD
3	CCSD	CCSD	Mexico (retained in 2nd)	CCSD	CCSD	CCSD
2	CCSD	CCSD	Mexico	Mexico	CCSD	Mexico
1	CCSD	Mexico	Mexico	Mexico	CCSD	Mexico
K	CCSD	Mexico	none	Mexico	CCSD	Mexico

*CCSD denotes Clark County School District.

Backgrounds of Profiled Students

Karina is a bright and motivated girl who has recently asked to be tested for the gifted program. She has been in the CCSD system since kindergarten. Although her speaking skills are good, she still has below-grade-level grammar and writing skills despite having been in this system for six years. Her reading level is also below fifth grade. She loves school and her teacher, and she always strives to understand academic concepts and to improve her English.

Anahi also loves school, is hard working, and is exceptionally polite and helpful. She began her education in Mexico and entered the CCSD system at the beginning of third grade. Like Karina, she speaks fairly well, but has great inconsistencies in her reading and writing ability. She and Karina, along with several of the other Hispanic girls, are good friends and excellent role models in class. This group of girls helps each other with assignments, which helps reinforce the use of English in the classroom, except when occasionally explaining concepts in Spanish.

Maria was enrolled in the class in late spring, but she did not show up for school until several days after I received notification of her matriculation. She arrived with her mother one morning after class had begun. Maria was crying. I immediately called on several of my sweet, Hispanic girls who settled her in between them at their desks. Maria had not been in school for a year (since fourth grade), and her mother explained that her daughter had medical and emotional issues. Maria had been retained in the second grade. The Mexico school system she attended required that students pass a proficiency test before entering the next grade. Clearly, my school inappropriately placed her in my fifth-grade class. My immediate attempts to rectify this situation fell on deaf administrative ears. I referred the problem to our ESOL facilitator, but instinctively I knew Maria would remain in my classroom for the duration of the year.

Jose has been in the CCSD school system for almost three years. He is a good math student but is working at a second-grade level in reading and language arts, which proves the importance of academic language for reading comprehension. He can calculate and perform algorithms successfully; however, because of his poor reading comprehension skills, he fails all story and word problems in math. He is affable and well mannered. He understands more English than he can speak. His attendance record is very poor, and by the end of the school year, he has missed forty-eight days. He simply did not or could not come to school, and even with repeated calls to his mother, it appeared that no home supervision was forthcoming. (There could be many reasons for this that might be beyond his control: babysitting, transportation, lack of gasoline, family issues, caretaking issues, illness in the family, and so on.) On the decision of my principal, he was not retained in fifth grade, despite our district's requirement that students not miss more than twenty unexcused absences. Jose was nonchalant when asked why he didn't come to school. He just shrugged his shoulders and smiled. Currently, we see more and more absences because of the fear of deportation.

Alejandro has been in the CCSD system since kindergarten. He is exceptionally bright; when I requested that he be tested for G.A.T.E. (our gifted program), he was accepted. His skills are very good, and he is extremely motivated. He rarely smiles and is always obsessed about completing his work as quickly as possible. He does not take criticism easily, but with cajoling will finally accept positive feedback. Alejandro is still designated by CCSD as a "limited English" speaker and has not been tested in two years, which is the only way to change the label in his cumulative file. Efforts on my part to intervene on his behalf have not worked because the EL facilitator is extremely backlogged. I'm hoping this problem won't affect Alejandro's placement in middle school or beyond. Alejandro loves to work hard and complains that the work isn't challenging enough. Unfortunately, I have too many students to attend to all of them in the way they deserve and should be served.

Juan has been in the school system for three years. He is quite immature in his peer relationships, and his academic performance is poor. He will sit doing nothing, unmotivated, even when it appears an assignment is clear and simple. He actually seems to like school and says that he does, but his actions belie his words. He is not well liked by the other students. His parents are both non-English speaking, and he appears to make little attempt to try to better his understanding of English. He doesn't seem to have a great curiosity about learning or to demonstrate recognition of the need to work on improving English acquisition. I am not sure if it is because he does not care or because he does not know how to go about learning English better. My guess is that it is difficult to be interested in things that are incomprehensive to this child.

In looking at these six children, one sees a range of ability and motivation. Although those who have attended CCSD throughout elementary school appear better adjusted, their academic skills are not necessarily reflective of where they should be with regard to literacy. With possibly the exception of Alejandro and Karina and her group of friends, who have been at this same school for a number of years, the others don't appear to me to be at an appropriate level of English acquisition. They are all below grade level. This is partly due to the problems and programs at this school, as well as the school's changing the bilingual literacy issue every year or two, before any programs can really be assessed. The girls seem to like school very much, but the two boys, Juan and Jose, are far less motivated. Although this may be a gender-based response, it may also be due to not doing well in school and therefore not wanting to try. It also might be due to other expectations at home for boys. Any number of reasons could be the cause of these problems, and I wish I could do more to help.

In addition to the factors of gender and motivation, these brief profiles note both the receptive and expressive skills of the English learners. Receptive skills include listening and reading, essentially language skills that reflect the "input" of language; expressive skills refers to speaking and writing, or language skills that outputs or linguistic production. Teachers of ELs must be aware of these four modalities of language (listening, speaking, reading, and writing) and the development of those skills in the classroom.

A corollary seems apparent between liking school and the enjoyment of learning English. This may possibly be attributed to human nature; we usually like what we can do well. The Hispanic child in my class is most often below grade level, has been retained one or two times, and frequently "fails" assignments and other academic work. A fifth grader who is reading on a second-grade proficiency level knows it. Jose was a big boy, fairly mature for his age, and already hanging out with his older brother's gang-related friends. Why would he want to come to school?

In addition to all the other issues mentioned, the Clark County School District has now instigated a new and "profound" system whereby any student not working at grade level cannot receive a grade higher than a D. This system, of course, affects my African American students in this low socioeconomic area, as all of them in my classroom last year were unable to do fifth-grade work. When we turn to my Hispanic second language students, with few exceptions, none of them could begin to master the fifth-grade curriculum, let alone pass the state standardized tests. Try and explain to hard-working Anahi that she was receiving all Ds, even though she buried herself in her attempts to complete assignments, because she tested at only a third-grade level in reading. Prior to this mandate, English learners were

Receptive Skills—language "input" skills that include listening and reading.

Expressive Skills—language "output" or production skills that include speaking and writing.

designated as such in their cumulative folder (CUM) and on report cards so that teachers could grade according to effort. One can only imagine what parents must think when their child comes home with grades below satisfactory. Would they think that Anahi did not even try?

Although attempts are being made on national and state levels to solve issues such as not passing students who don't meet grade-level requirements, the efforts are entirely missing the point and do not address the problems we face in the classroom. Interesting, too, is the fact that teachers have been disregarded as the individuals who have the clearest understanding of what needs to be done to successfully educate students in today's world.

Since 2014, Nevada has been involved in the CCSS (Common Core State Standards) and WIDA Nevada ACCESS for ELs 2.0 was incorporated in 2016–17. Hopefully, the focus on academic content and vocabulary will make a marked increase on students' academic ability.

Mrs. Sarah-Christensen-Sharpe is a gifted class teacher. She should have more ELs in her class but they are underrepresented in her school. She explained her thoughts:

> Working with English learners is truly a gift. They bring so much to the table including culture differences. It's important to understand how to properly help your students that are learning English. One year, I had a student that was so kind and sweet. He would respond when attendance was called and I didn't think twice of the thought that he didn't speak English. The next day another student asked me if he could translate for the student. I immediately contacted our ESOL coordinator, who informed me that he was a new student and they had not completed testing him yet, so he stayed in my class for a few days until his schedule could be adjusted. During those days, I did the only thing I could think of . . . use Google translate on my computer. I could immediately see a sense of relief on his face because he could finally understand me. My biggest piece of advice is to learn about your students and their culture and do everything in your power to help them learn!
>
> This year I only had one EL student out of all of my 120 students, and once he was tested, he was pulled from my class. Our principal usually keeps our EL students in the same class, because an EL teacher will push in with that class to help all of them. Level 1 and 2 students have an EL/ELA course, taught by our ESOL coordinator. In the past, I would maybe only have 1 or 2 EL students per class and they were usually level 3 and up. Since my class is gifted, students have to be on grade level and it is not unusual for my ELs to be under grade level. However, there is a big problem with identification of gifted students. Oftentimes, gifted students are labeled as behavior problems because they are bored and are not challenged. Also, gifted students are identified by IQ scores (by American criteria) and typically the EL or diverse student may never be identified or tested.

Ms. Pérez—A Puerto Rican Spanish Teacher and Her Mexican Students

Viodelda Pérez is a high school Spanish teacher from Puerto Rico. She arrived on the U.S. mainland in the late 1980s and has taught Spanish as a foreign language for 22 years. The students she teaches live in a rural area, and their parents are employed principally as seasonal pickers (migrant workers) in the peanut and watermelon industries. In addition, some of her students' parents are also employed on local dairy farms. Because of the nature of their seasonal work, many of the students are considered "migrant," meaning that they move frequently to follow seasonal harvests.

Most of Ms. Pérez's students in her high school Spanish come from Mexico. Although the students speak the "same" language, Spanish, as she does, Ms. Pérez realizes that the variety of Spanish that her

Mexican-background students speak is different from her own form of Puerto Rican Spanish. And although they speak the language, their literacy skills in Spanish are less developed, probably due to less academic consistency. Yet most importantly, Ms. Pérez understands that her cultural background is very different from that of her Mexican students. She has realized the only way she could help her students to become successful in learning was by learning what she did not know about their culture.

When I first started teaching students from Mexico, I realized immediately that our background knowledge and experiences as Spanish-speakers were quite different. It's a misconception that just because we speak the same language we share the same background. Moreover, some of my Mexican students don't even speak Spanish! They speak indigenous languages such as Mixtec and Otomí. So, when I was a new teacher, I began to understand that I needed to connect with the students that I teach and to learn about their particular customs, religious beliefs, foods, and values. I also needed to understand their histories in the United States. For example, as a Puerto Rican, I am considered an American citizen and can travel effortlessly between Puerto Rico and the U.S. mainland. However, many of my students have come to the United States via walking through the desert in fear of being caught or, worse, dying. To learn about their country and experiences, I immersed myself into the study of their culture by reading historical accounts, biographies of famous Mexicans, and familiarizing myself with news via the Internet. I then engaged my students in conversations about those topics. Another thing that we did was to compare and contrast different words and terms between Puerto Rican Spanish and Mexican Spanish. We laughed at some of the different ways that we name things!

In their journal entries, they wrote about the different aspects that they thought would be of interest to me. We spoke about their favorite holidays and foods. We had group discussions about their culture and how it is different from the American culture. These activities brought class unity and formed a class community. I also shared with them many things about my Puerto Rican culture that are different from the Mexican culture, which I hold dear to my heart. I learned about their cultures as they learned about mine, which taught us to respect each other's values. I invited the students' parents to come into our class to share their experiences, too. One insightful event was why the students had such difficulty saluting the flag every day. Initially I assumed they were in conflict about saluting the American flag because of their allegiance to the Mexican flag. What a shock to learn that it was due to a religious reason, not political. I had no idea that by saluting the American flag, my Mexican students thought they were praying to something other than the Virgin Mary. Because they were so far away from their homelands, they were trying to maintain their cultural belief and heritage. The more we learned about each other, the closer and more cohesive we became as a united classroom. The impact on me confirmed my aspiration to refrain from judging others through my own cultural lens.

Wilma Diaz's Reflection on Learning English

In my experience, learning the language of the country is essential for success in the adopted country; it empowers the newcomer and facilitates achievement of goals in life. However, if the children of non-English-speaking parents do not embrace the idea that English is necessary for achievement, no impetus to try to learn the language exists. I learned that if students believed that the family could be successful without knowledge of the English language, the students assumed they would be successful without English, too. With no motivation on the students' part, it is very difficult to teach them the language. The following examples illuminate the rationale behind my students' resistance to learning English:

- Students believe that if their parents own small companies that they too could be business owners without mastering the English language.
- The English language is not necessary for survival, especially if they live in an ethnically similar neighborhood where everyone (from shopkeepers to houses of worship) speaks the heritage language.
- Lack of second-language comprehension is not an obstacle to finding a job, nor does it interfere with completion of their tasks as employees.
- Family residency in the United States is temporary. The family plans on returning to the homeland. Students want to return to Mexico (or their home country) and do not see urgency for learning the English language.
- The family fears cultural amalgamation.
- Parents fear young children will lose the native language.

Therefore, acquisition of the second language may not be regarded as a necessity for survival in the United States for these newcomers. This attitude may or may not prove true, however. Generally, not knowing the language of the host country makes it very difficult to advance oneself. The responsibility then falls upon the shoulders of teachers to ensure that both native language and English are supported. In school, modifications to language-learning strategies must be made for these students, while at home, parents should be encouraged to provide a rich first-language experience both verbally and through literacy.

These teachers are not alone in their assessment of today's classroom. In addition to the myriad of administrative duties, the population is ever changing, numbers of students have swelled, funding has been reduced or eliminated, and high-stakes standardized tests have been implemented in many states. One of the toughest obstacles for the mainstream teacher to face is that of teaching students who do not speak English or have limited knowledge of English. According to the National Clearinghouse for English Language Acquisition (NCELA) (2006, as cited in Crawford & Krashen, 2007), about one in ten American students is an EL, which represents a 65 percent increase of this segment of the student population in the last decade. According to Crawford and Krashen (2007), "If these trends continued at current rates, by 2043 one in three of the nation's students would be ELs" (p. 13). Monolingual teachers who have limited exposure to cultures outside their own may have difficulties understanding and meeting the needs of these diverse students. Bilingual education is rapidly losing ground, but federal laws such as *Lau v. Nichols* (1974) still mandate that all students have the right to comprehensive instruction and equal access to the curriculum (Crawford, 1999; Crawford & Krashen, 2007). Additionally, the *Plyler v. Doe* (1982) law, (a supreme court case saying that schools must not deny students entrance to school based on immigration status) is of critical importance and implications, especially in today's political climate.

It becomes increasingly apparent that all teachers need to learn effective instructional strategies to successfully teach English learners, even though the teacher might not speak the students' native language. Teachers need help in the classroom without having to get a master's degree in ESOL (English to speakers of other languages). They need immediate answers and basic guidelines to follow for success in our multicultural, multilingual climate.

This book is a roadmap for general K-12 educators who have "nonmainstream" students. Teachers will learn the very least they need to know to teach students from other cultures and will learn to understand what they can expect from non-native English learners. By increasing critical knowledge of their own American cultural values, the reader will better understand the different cultural values of their students, especially as they relate to schooling and the classroom. By correctly interpreting the cultural cues and body language of their students, teachers will understand why students of other cultures might behave differently. Raising our cultural consciousness leads us to understand different behaviors and helps us to adapt classroom instruction according to the language acquisition process English learners undergo. Only after much exposure to the issues and language acquisition process of ELs will the teacher be able to correctly distinguish learning disabilities from problems in simple language acquisition. Finally, the reader will learn how to implement appropriate and effective strategies that ensure comprehensible instruction and assessment for the student who is not yet academically fluent in English.

FINAL POINTS

- Today's students who need to learn English often have additional emotional and physical concerns as well as academic issues.
- English learners are in mainstream classrooms all over the country.
- Teachers are responsible for far more than academic teaching.
- Teachers need to provide culturally relevant lessons.
- Instructors make great efforts to get to know their students so they can provide instruction that is more comprehensive.

Discussion Questions and Activities

1. Individually or with a group, decide how you would teach ELs even if you cannot speak other languages. List ten strategies, methods, or approaches you might use. Use mobile apps, websites, and other technology.
2. Discuss how the United States should attempt to solve the problem of students who do not meet grade-level requirements due to lack of language proficiency, but are nonetheless passed on to the next grade.
3. Based on what you know so far, discuss what you believe to be the most challenging issues for mainstream teachers who have ELs in the classroom today.
4. How will you be prepared to deal with students who are afraid to go to class because they are afraid of deportation? What can you do in your classroom to provide a safe and nonthreatening environment?

Resources

For Teachers of English Learners (ELs) and parents, especially Spanish-speaking students www.colorincolorado.org—this website offers a wide array of materials and information for teachers. The site is fully bilingual (Spanish–English) and has downloadable and printable guides for parents, in addition to links to experts in the field.

For Educators Working With Refugee Students
http://www.refugees.org—this website is from the U.S. Committee on Refugees and Immigrants and provides excellent background-building for teachers and profiles of refugees and immigrants in the United States.

Grouping ELs for Instruction
http://www.colorincolorado.org/article/how-should-ells-be-grouped-instruction

World Relief Jacksonville is based in Jacksonville, Florida, a mid-sized city in the southeast United States that is a large recipient of refugees. Their information offers multiple suggestions for working with refugee families.
http://worldreliefjacksonville.org

Teaching refugees
http://teachingrefugees.com/instructional-programming/resources/

Unaccompanied children and youth
http://www.colorincolorado.org/ell-basics/special-populations/unaccompanied-children-youth

Across the border and into school
https://www.theatlantic.com/education/archive/2016/08/across-the-border-and-into-school/496652/

Integrating ELs into General Education
https://www.edutopia.org/blog/integrating-ells-general-education-classes-dorit-sasson

Teaching in the Multilevel Classroom
http://www.pearsonlongman.com/ae/download/adulted/multilevel_monograph.pdf

Cult of Pedagogy
https://www.cultofpedagogy.com/supporting-esl-students-mainstream-classroom/

Using Flexible Grouping for Instruction
http://www.learnalberta.ca/content/eslapb/organizing_for_instruction_using.html

References

Crawford, J. (2002). The role of materials in the language classroom: Finding the balance. *Methodology in language teaching: An anthology of current practice*, 80–91.

Crawford, J. (Ed.). (2008). *Advocating for English learners: Selected essays* (Vol. 69). Multilingual Matters.

Cummins, J. (2009). Multilingualism in the English-language classroom: Pedagogical considerations. *TESOL quarterly*, 43(2), 317–321.

Hussar, W. J., & Bailey, T. M. (2014). Projections of Education Statistics to 2022. NCES 2014-051. *National Center for Education Statistics*.

NCCP | Home. (2017). *Nccp.org*. Retrieved 13 November 2017, from http://www.nccp.org/

v Doe, P. (1982). 457 US 202, 102 S.

Padrón, Y. N., Waxman, H. C., & Rivera, H. H. (2002). Educating Hispanic Students: Obstacles and Avenues to Improved Academic Achievement. Educational Practice Report 8.

Schleppegrell, M. J., Achugar, M., & Oteíza, T. (2004). The grammar of history: Enhancing content-based instruction through a functional focus on language. *TESOL quarterly, 38*(1), 67–93.

Townsend, D., Filippini, A., Collins, P., & Biancarosa, G. (2012). Evidence for the importance of academic word knowledge for the academic achievement of diverse middle school students. *The Elementary School Journal, 112*(3), 497–518.

Valdés, G., Menken, K., & Castro, M. (Eds.). (2015). *Common Core, bilingual and English language learners: A resource for educators*. Philadelphia, PA: Caslon Publishing.

CHAPTER 2

CULTURAL DIVERSITY IN THE MAINSTREAM CLASSROOM—WHO AM I

Eileen N. Whelan Ariza

KEY POINTS

- Everyone has his or her own world view and it might be that they think their language, culture, country, people, or food are the best in the world.
- If you think you are the best, you might believe that everyone else is inferior.
- Cultural identify identifies who we are, what we believe, no matter where we are.
- We may also identify with a third culture as a result of intermarriage, birth, or growing up in a country but not feeling the nationalism inherent with being a native of the country. We may relate to another culture, or both cultures.
- Some people cannot consciously relate to their country.

I was born in Marlboro, Massachusetts, but I heard every day of my life, "You are Irish, you know." It was drilled into me daily. "Your great grandfather built this house. He was from Waterford County, Ireland. He came here when he was 17. He fought for Abraham Lincoln, on the USS Constellation. His wife was Julia, from Cork. All their siblings, their parents, their cousins, were all born in Ireland but died in the United States. My father's mother, Rose Monahan, had five siblings, three of whom were baby triplets. All of the triplets died, one month after another, from unpasteurized milk, and then their father died a month later. They were all born in Ireland, but they all died in Marlboro and I visited their graves frequently. Did I inherit the strength of that poor mother, Catherine Deasy, who lost three babies and her husband within 6 months?

I was raised by a man who was raised by everyone who was born in Ireland. I did not grow up hearing I was Marlboronian, or even Bostonian, or American. I was Irish. Is it any wonder then, that even though I was born in America, my cultural identity is of being Irish? I grew up with Irish attitudes, for example, any work, as long as it was honest, was noble. And going to mass was mandatory, and corned beef and cabbage were for dinner on St. Patrick's day, and Irish Step Dancing were natural parts of my life. All this, and yet I had never left the United States. These cultural roots run deeply, so you could probably take the person out of the culture, but you can never take the culture out of the person. You might add parts of other cultures (and then that becomes the third culture) but those cultural beliefs from birth form us as human beings. Is this ethnocentricity? Actually, I don't think so because I did not hear that we were better . . . only what we were. Ironically, I did hear all my life that America was the best country in the world. Now that might be ethnocentricity.

Ethnocentricity

This chapter addresses the concept of *ethnocentricity,* which is common to every cultural group. Ethnocentricity is usually the belief that our nation or our cultural group or family is intrinsically superior. (http://www.dictionary.com/browse/ethnocentricity). We usually base our perceptions on our own cultural perspectives; thus, we judge others according to what is familiar. This applies to cultural beliefs as well as "foreign accents." Many people may not have much experience with other cultures or foreign languages; as a result, miscommunication occurs both inside and outside the classroom. This perspective stays with us wherever we go; therefore, when we go outside of our country we tend to interpret what we see through our own comfortable, cultural lenses.

I have experienced the odd feeling in a few countries that even though I was trying to speak the language, the person I was speaking to was deliberately trying not to understand me. In a bar in Spain I asked for a napkin (una servieta) but he gave me a beer (una cerveza). Once in Mexico in a bakery, I pointed to a pastry and asked the lady, "Que hay adentro?" (What's inside?) She looked at me and said, "No hablo ingles." (I don't speak English.) I think she did it deliberately but I can't be sure.

> Luis, from Brazil, a high school student who is going to school in the United States, works part-time as a troubleshooter for a large telecommunications company. His job includes working with small businesses and unhappy people who call him when their telephone lines are malfunctioning. He has to defuse the potentially volatile situation, track down errors, and get the lines up and running as soon as possible. One very busy day, Luis answered the phone, "Luis Rocha, Small Business Repair. May I help you?" The man on the other end of the phone barked at him, "Get me someone who speaks English. I don't want to deal with any outsider!" Luiz answered him politely, "But sir, I am speaking English. I just have a Portuguese accent."

I think we need to make a deliberate effort to understand others who are speaking English. Just a little "twist" of our ears could help our understanding of someone who is trying to speak English.

Many Americans believe that the United States is the best country in the world. People from other countries may feel the same about their homelands as well. This type of thinking is called **ethnocentrism**, and it colors our outlook on the rest of the world, including our interactions with immigrants, refugees, migrants, or newcomers to the United States, with people who speak English as their second (or third, or fourth . . .) language, and how we feel about "foreigners" or people with "foreign accents" in general.

The schools in the United States are grounded in beliefs shaped by the mainstream, dominant culture that is White, European, and English speaking. Therefore, the hidden curriculum in schools reflects the underlying values of the mainstream culture, thus unwittingly creating barriers for minority students (George & Aronson, 2003; Pennycook, 2014). Newcomers to the country are bound to encounter cross-cultural conflicts in every area of life, especially in the classroom. All components of their culture, such as language, behaviors, beliefs, and values, may be incongruent with the host country.

Nonnative speakers of English automatically are marked as newcomers. Instinctively, people who have no conspicuous accent are understood and may be accepted as "one of us." Someone who has an accent, no matter how good his or her English is, may never be accepted as an "American." One who speaks English well is also expected to know the rules of the American culture. We may "forgive" the person with the accent when making an inappropriate social or cultural blunder, but the person who speaks native-like English is expected to behave like a native English speaker within the American paradigm and cultural rules.

Cultural Misunderstandings

While in Spain, Mark, an American study-abroad student, is invited to visit his Spanish friend's family at a restaurant for a 7:00 p.m. dinner. Excited to feel a part of the Spanish culture, he goes to the train station for information about the train schedule. The clerk shrugs his shoulders and tells him that the train will be there when it arrives. Uncertain about what he should do but not wanting to arrive late for dinner, he decides to leave at 6:00 p.m. He believes an hour should be plenty of time to traverse the city. As it turns out, Mark's train is stopped on the track for quite a while, and Mark doesn't arrive until 8:30. After finding the correct address, he enters the restaurant to find no one there. He can't believe his bad luck; the dinner party is over already, and he is so disappointed to have missed his new friends. He decides to sit down and order a bocadillo de tortilla (egg omelet sandwich on long, white bread). Surprisingly, wine is included with his meal, but he has to pay for the glass of water he orders. He lingers over an infusion (herbal tea), and at around 10:00 p.m. he gets up to leave. As he is leaving, his friends arrive and exclaim, "Ya comienza la fiesta!" (Now we can start the party!) Mark is dumbfounded!

Can you make sense of what happened here?

Looking at Our Own Culture—U.S. Values

We may not truly know our own culture until we leave it or until our cultural values are challenged. Mark's experience above shows how he is trying to navigate Spain using the only cues he knows, those from an American perspective. His belief system does not apply to situations he encounters in another country. Let's analyze what has happened to him. When invited to a dinner in the United States, it is important to arrive on time. Common knowledge dictates that if you are very late for dinner, it is rude and you might miss the meal. In Spain, if an invitation is for a certain hour, everyone operates under the assumption that the affair won't start until several hours after the specified time. Obviously, Mark did not know this. Time is treated differently in many other cultures. In the train station, when Mark asked what time the train was going to leave, the clerk couldn't even tell him a schedule. In the United States, public transportation operates on a scheduled time, and the schedule is something to which people must adhere. Time is money, as the adage goes, and American life is geared to that mindset.

Returning to Mark's not-so-excellent adventure, he discovers that not only had he not missed the party, it hadn't even started yet. When he ordered a *tortilla,* he expected a Mexican tortilla, which he had eaten in Mexican restaurants in the United States. (If he had ordered a taco, the waiters would have been stumped because in Spain the word *taco* means foul language.) The wine was free; this surprised him, as alcoholic beverages are usually quite expensive in the United States. But there was a charge for the water. At home, water can be ordered in unlimited quantities, but cocktails are costly. Then, just as Mark was heading home, his friends arrived and were ready to start the party.

I had a similar experience with a New Year's Eve party with Colombian friends. We were invited to a family party and I was really happy for the invitation because our Colombian friends always had great parties, music, and food. We arrived at 11 p.m. and I thought we had missed the party for sure because no one was there. In fact, our friends were still cooking so I appreciated learning how to cook rice using their recipes. Around midnight, everyone arrived, we were all given 12 grapes, and the party began. It continued throughout the night, long after I was ready to leave.

Kohls's (2001) popular book *Survival Kit for Overseas Living* mentions traits that are ascribed to typical Americans by cultural outsiders (Table 2.1).

Other books and articles are readily available about American culture. Each cultural group is known for its own personal traits and characteristics. However, individual idiosyncrasies, capriciousness, or uniqueness of character can account for the distinctive behavior of some people. We have to be careful not to incorrectly assume or stereotype individuals. Several books are in existence that talk about American customs and culture and you might be surprised at what they say. As I mentioned before, you might not realize what customs and beliefs you have until they offend or threaten your beliefs. (See Stewart and Bennet, 2011, and https://www.press.umich.edu/pdf/9780472033041-101AmerCult.pdf) for an interesting list of 101 American Cultural Traits. See how many you agree with.)

If you are a teacher in a U.S. mainstream classroom, you will see many of your cultural beliefs challenged on a daily basis. For example, if you expect your students to be on time for school and your students function on the principle that being late is not a negative thing, clashes are bound to occur. You may have carefully scheduled appointments with parents, only to have them arrive late, cancel without

TABLE 2.1 U.S. Cultural Values	
1.	Personal control over the environment/responsibility
2.	Change seen as natural and positive
3.	Time and its control
4.	Equality/fairness
5.	Individualism/independence
6.	Self-help/initiative
7.	Competition
8.	Future orientation
9.	Action/work orientation
10.	Informality
11.	Directness/openness/honesty
12.	Practicality/efficiency
13.	Materialism

Source: Kohls (2001).

notice, not show up, or arrive with the entire family with whom you must try to carry on a conference. Other examples of cultural miscommunication will be presented throughout this book.

If a teacher has students from many different cultures, it is difficult to have in-depth knowledge of them all; however, at the very least, a general understanding is a must for successful intercultural communication. **Cultural sensitivity** can level the diversity playing field. If a teacher is from the mainstream population, those students who are not from the majority population may be forced to play by, and be judged by, rules of which they might not be aware. **Cultural proclivity** will guide the teacher's approach to teaching, just as it will guide the student's approach to learning. What steps can the teacher take to mitigate misunderstanding and promote cultural understanding? Some of the following recommendations emanate from Brown University's Education Alliance for Culturally Responsive Teaching (Richards, Brown & Forde, 2007):

- Get to know the culture of your students by researching their backgrounds, the countries they are from, their languages, values, behaviors, beliefs, holidays, traditions, customs, and foods. In other words, learn about their **surface culture** (e.g., food, dress, and music) as well as the **deep culture** (values, family roles, expected behaviors, male and female roles, etc.). When teachers possess profound cultural information about their students, they are better able to discern behaviors and to provide effective instructional strategies.
- Try to make home visits to get to know the family and the students' living circumstances. Usually, the family appreciates the interest the teacher shows, and the dynamic among the teachers, students, and family becomes more of a partnership. The knowledge gained from the home visit can be translated into effective instructional practice.
- Attend neighborhood and local cultural events. Get to know cultural insiders; ask questions and conduct your own research on the culture in question. Ask your students probing questions about their own cultural practices: Their consciousness will be raised to recognize and reflect on their own habits and beliefs.
- Teachers can focus on inquiry-based and discovery-oriented thematic units on topics that relate to the interest of the students and are socially and culturally relevant to student's lives. Relate teaching scenarios, questions, and problem solving to real-life interests and issues pertaining to the students.
- Offer a challenging curriculum and enough time to complete tasks, but provide scaffolding for students to succeed by activating prior knowledge as much as possible, or provide schema to make the unknown familiar for all students. Provide an equal and equitable academic playing field for all students regardless of linguistic, cultural, or ethnic background.
- Provide ample feedback and call on all students, regardless of English proficiency. Modify your questioning strategies according to the level of the language proficiency of the student. Give them plenty of wait time to let them think of an answer.
- Integrate multicultural viewpoints and histories into the daily curriculum.
- Learn about diverse **learning** and teaching **styles** and culturally appropriate classroom behaviors that are associated with each culture. Teach students to recognize and actively participate in their own learning.
- Try to encourage learning within appropriate sociocultural and linguistics situations. Don't hesitate to incorporate the students' native language within the class learning situations. Become aware of the classroom management styles that your students are familiar with, and help them to adjust to the American classroom styles and routines. Recognize diverse ways of achieving developmental benchmarks.
- Seek to understand parents of English learners and help them to understand school routines that may be unfamiliar to them. Let them know what services the school offers.
- Develop higher order knowledge and skills within a modified curriculum. Utilize a variety of learning strategies, and establish high expectations for all students.

- Use cooperative, collaborative, and community-oriented instruction as well as individual work within a nonthreatening classroom environment.
- Continuously aim to increase academic language proficiency as well as oral proficiency. Expand oral discourse by modeling and helping students to develop verbal expression.
- Be conscious of your own ethnocentric attitudes. Hone your cultural negotiation skills. Know that language and culture play a vital part in identity formation. Be empathetic, open, and flexible, and demonstrate caring for all your students' well-being and individual differences.

Culture Shock

Diana was excited to go to France to learn French. She had taken basic French and was intrigued by the language. After learning about a French language institute, she decided to matriculate. Her excitement grew as she planned her trip. She would be there for two semesters, live with a family, and be able to practice the language every day. On the day she arrived, no one was there to meet her at the airport, and she had to navigate the bus system to the university. She didn't know how to get the bus tokens from the machine since she had no Euros, and she tried to make herself understood. The machine did not take her credit card. She didn't have a SIM card for that country, so she could not call Uber or Lyft, and even if she had the ability, she didn't know how to make a call anyway. Finally, she found someone who understood English, and she was able to get some change for the bus.

The trip to the university took hours; she'd had no idea how lost she was. To find the university, she had to changes buses twice, and once a strange man insisted on paying her fare. Her next problem was trying to tell the secretary at the university that she was there to register, then to find out who her host family was, and then to get to their house. Even the smallest task was becoming a tremendous obstacle. She sat down and cried. She couldn't speak French; she was there to learn, but everyone kept talking to her in French as if she understood. She felt she had made a terrible mistake. She hated her situation, and she wanted to go home.

Cultural patterns are deeply ingrained in an individual. As I said earlier, you can take a person out of his or her culture, but you may have problems trying to take the culture out of the person. When individuals move from one culture to another, very often they suffer from what is called "**culture shock**" (Hall, 1959; Ward, Bochner, & Furnham, 2005; Zhou, Jindal-Snape, Topping, & Todman, 2008). In your own culture, you are a functional individual who knows how to do all the things necessary to survive. Suddenly, the "bottom falls out" when all your familiar patterns are skewed. What works at home does not work for you now. You can't ask for what you need; you try to shop and realize you don't know how to ask for a half pound of cheese, sliced very thin. You have to read the money before you use it, and negotiate the price of a taxi ride before you even get into the vehicle. The easiest task at home is insurmountable in the new country. You ask for milk, and it doesn't taste the same. You can even go into McDonald's, a mainstay of the United States, and the hamburger tastes different. "For here or to go," takes on new meaning, as you can't ask the counterperson to wrap it to go. Perhaps they give you only one napkin or don't have artificial sweetener. Even the milk, meat, chocolate, or beer that you are accustomed to will not taste the same. Consider different agricultural reasons for this-grass, soil, and ingredients are different, so our taste buds will discern the different flavor.

Newcomers to the United States suffer the same fate. Culture shock (Brown, 1994; Brown & Holloway; 2008, Oberg, 2006; Pedersen, 1994; Ward, Bochner, & Furnham, 2005) typically starts with the honeymoon stage, when (and if) the traveler is excited about the trip. Next comes the *hostile* or *aggressive* stage, as the newness of the situation diminishes. Being frustrated, anxious, and angry about the inability to function are symptoms of this stage, which can last an indefinite amount of time. During this time, the newcomer will want to go home, criticizes the host country, the food, the language, and the people, and blames the country for any problems encountered. If this period becomes intolerable, the individual might return to the home country before adaptation occurs.

Recovery is the next period; the newcomer adjusts to the language and the host culture, as well as the new environment. The last stage is a period of *adjustment* when the individual accepts the new culture as just another way of life; anxiety is minimal, the new language, food, culture, and habits of the country are acceptable, and adjustments have been made. Sometimes people never recover or get to the next stage, and sometimes they never experience the negative stages.

Newcomers of all ages can suffer from culture shock. Teachers may see symptoms of reactions to culture shock, such as irritability, exhaustion, upset stomach or headaches, poor sleep, impatience, and great concern over minor pains. Learning a language is exhausting, and students might fall asleep in class from sheer fatigue. Just be aware of any unexpected symptoms.

Implications for the Classroom

It is important for the classroom teacher to know and recognize the symptoms of culture shock and to expect to see manifestations of each stage. The teacher can help students adjust by maintaining a positive attitude about themselves and celebrating the noticeable cultural differences. Teach students expected classroom and societal behaviors, and show sensitivity by protecting the newcomer from unkind behavior from other students and by highlighting the newcomer's culture. Use the opportunity as a learning experience for the whole class. Express positive values in whatever appears "foreign" to the other students. Present the newcomer's music, food, dress, and other surface values that can be seen, while learning to appreciate the deep cultural values that can present potential conflicts. See all situations as "teachable moments," and exploit the circumstances in the best light possible. Try to get to know the families, and invite them to the classroom so the other students can see them as family instead of strangers. This is culturally relevant instruction (Gay, 2010; Ladson-Billings, 1992). When you incorporate culturally responsive teaching, it is student centered because the teacher has identified cultural strengths that will promote student achievement based on those unique cultural strengths. Finally, try to introduce the family to American expectations while appreciating the richness of the culture they bring to us.

Recommendations for Culturally Relevant Classrooms

Ms. Bingham was scheduled to teach fourth grade in Pompano Beach, an area highly populated with recently arrived Haitian children. She had taught English learners in her practicum and was prepared to modify her instruction with ESOL strategies. She entered the classroom, and her students stood up as if on command. "Please sit down," she suggested. They did as she asked. Deciding to use one of the boys to model how they should salute the flag, she called out, "Pierre, please come up to my desk." Pierre stood up and walked toward the teacher, his head hung low, averting his eyes from the teacher. When he approached her, he held out his hand expecting the punishing slap of a ruler. She had not expected this and didn't know what to make of this misunderstanding.

Students who come from other countries bring their expectations and understanding of classroom behavior with them. The students mentioned above come from a rigid school system where they must respect the teachers by standing when they enter and where corporal punishment is the norm. Naturally, Ms. Bingham was shocked to learn that the student was expecting a slap for some alleged discretion.

It is surprising how many cultures teach their children to avert their eyes away from an adult as the polite way to behave (e.g. Puerto Ricans, Asians, Black, or certain Hispanic groups.) It is wise to investigate any action or behavior that you see that you do not understand. It may be a cultural norm that you are unfamiliar with. Many students in the classroom may behave in a way that confuses the teacher. Miscommunication can occur because a student may appear to show defiance instead of respect, but that could be actually anxiety, or confusion about what the instructor expects (Burdick-Will, 2013; Henkin & Nguyen, 1981; Nine-Curt, 1976).

Competitive Classrooms may be the wrong climate for the student who is noncompetitive and needs a more cooperative learning style. This could be the preferred climate for Native Americans, or Blacks, or Hispanics or Asians, since it is an individual style preference. (Alasya, 2011; Brendtro, Brokenleg, & Van Bockern, 1991; Grossman, 1984). The classroom that has students who are accustomed to help one another (especially when the work is expected to be done individually) will be criticized in the U.S. classroom, and the students may withdraw from trying to help one another again (Dobao, 2012; Grossman, 1984). Culturally based discipline may not work well for students who respond better to touch (like Hispanics) but may be offensive to Asians, who, due to Confucianism, view the head as the place where the soul resides and therefore, should not be touched, or patted on the head (Ariza, 2010)

Teachers might want to avoid touching certain Hispanic, Arab, and Black students in ways that may appear to be playful, like black slapping or hair mussing (Ariza, 2010; Yao, 1979). Finally, there may be a disconnect time wise in the sense that the deadlines are not exactly fixed, or school tasks may be delivered late, or they may not feel as rushed to begin the next academic task (Ariza, 2010).

A well-known habit of Asian students (and others) is for them to say yes when asked if they understand. The teacher may believe that the student is being dishonest when all the student is doing is trying to "save face," not wanting show conflict or public embarrassment, which also extends to shaming the family (Ariza, 2010; Woo, 1985).

Some boys may resist responding to teachers because they are females, which means a cooperative attitude will work better than demanding compliance (Horvat & Lewis, 2003; Mills, Martino, & Lingard, 2004; Grossman, 1984).

One enormous problem in many schools is the attitude that certain youth face when they are under pressure **to not succeed** in school. Gollnick and Chin (1990), Hanna (1988), Horvat and Lewis (2003), and Ogbu (1990) talk about African American, Mexican-American, Native Hawaiian and Native American youngsters that face peer pressure to **not** reject their culture by abiding by the rules, or are accused of acting "White" if they are successful, and therefore must hide their academic efforts. The same can be said for certain types of resistance to acting White if students are acting positive (Fordham, 1988; Ogbu, 1988, 1990). Even attending school can be seen as a rejection of their culture. Trying to appeal to the individual's good nature and positive (appropriate) reinforcement is far more productive than being confrontational with students (Bendtro, Brokenleg, & Van Bockern, 1991).

Criticism by the teacher may be seen as personal insult to Arab-American students, Native Americans, and Hispanics. An attitude of encouragement and indirect critique may be the best way to deal with trying to cultivate higher expectations and corrections of errors (Nine-Curt, 1976; Nydel, 1982; Wingfield, 2006).

The same principle applies for Arab-American students. As in the Hispanic and Native American cultures, frank criticism may be perceived as a personal insult (Nine-Curt, 1976; Wingfield, 2006). Best practice includes indirect criticism, mixed with encouragement and praise regarding any positive points or expectations that were met.

In the Haitian classroom in Haiti, things were different for Jean Paul. Had he looked into Ms. Bingham's eyes, members of his culture would have considered him rude. In his country, the classroom desks are connected, side by side, so the rows are horizontal instead of vertical. Students learn by rote memorization, and they repeat chorally. They are expected to memorize whatever material they are assigned, and they are punished if they have not done so. Multiple-choice tests are unheard of, and tests in Haiti always consist of essay questions. Much pressure is placed on tests, and the scores of individuals are published and announced on the radio so the entire village knows how everyone has done. American classes are very different, and the students will eventually learn the customs of the American classroom. They will learn that students can question the teacher, that students are expected to work independently (otherwise they might be suspected of cheating), and that taking initiative is usually rewarded. Expectations that are in direct opposition to rules of their home will cause discord. For example, American children are usually taught to tell the teacher of another youngster's trouble making instead of fighting. However, a male child from Mexico is taught that "men" never tell on each other, no matter what, and they will fight to defend a sister's honor.

In Japan, often students are seated by the best student being first, and the worst student being last, so everyone knows who the smart and slow ones are.

These discordant behaviors can cause miscommunication if not understood by the teacher. Knowing the expectations of the student's culture can demystify the most complex situations.

FINAL POINTS

- The idea of culture is all consuming and we really cannot fight it.
- Creating a culturally responsive culture in your classroom can make all students feel comfortable.
- Ask students what they miss most and what they would like to see in their classroom to make them feel at home.
- Be prepared to make and use other strategies to reach your students if you find that your traditional ways are not working.

Discussion Questions and Activities

1. You can experience culture shock by going to another country, by going to another region, or even by changing jobs or schools. For example, moving from the north to the south or from the east to the west, one can feel disoriented. Have you ever experienced culture shock? Where? Discuss how you felt and what you did to orient yourself to the new culture.

2. In trying to help your students, what signs of culture shock will you look for? Plan five activities to help your students recover from culture shock.

3. Look at news headlines, advertising, textbook content, classroom and school rules, and so on. Do you notice any obvious American values? For example, a poster in a store window shows a dog licking his owner's face. This would be contrary to many other cultures in which animals are considered not as family members but rather as animals that should not be in the house. A dog sitting on the owner's bed or furniture might be bizarre to people who think animals are not family members. Think of five examples to share with your group.

4. If the teacher in a mainstream classroom discovers that students in the class have divergent cultural beliefs, what methods should be used to alleviate cultural miscommunications?

5. Create a diagram of how you think your own or a student's cultural shock would look like. How could you help a student get over culture shock?

Resources

NEA Diversity toolkit
http://www.nea.org/tools/30417.htm

Community Tool Box
http://ctb.ku.edu/en/table-of-contents/culture/cultural-competence/culture-and-diversity/main

Cultural Differences—The lost boys from Sudan
http://video.nationalgeographic.com/video/movies/god-grew-tired/cultural-differences-ggtu/

Blame in different cultures
https://www.wsj.com/articles/SB10001424052748703467304575383131592767868

Culture shock (teens)
http://teenshealth.org/teen/your_mind/emotions/culture_shock.html

Deep culture/surface culture
http://quizlet.com/10871376/iceberg-surface-culture-vs-deep-culture-flash-cards/

Deep culture and surface culture
Examples
http://education.csm.edu/students/abolen/surface_culture_&_deep_culture.htm

The iceberg concept of culture
http://www.msdwt.k12.in.us/msd/wp-content/uploads/2011/10/iceburgofculture.pdf

Strategies for Managing a culturally diverse classroom
https://www.teachervision.com/strategies-teaching-culturally-diverse-students

Teaching tolerance—Culture in the classroom
http://www.tolerance.org/culture-classroom

TEFLNET
http://edition.tefl.net/articles/home-abroad/cultural-differences/

References

Alasya, M. (2011). *High school students' learning styles in North Cyprus* (Doctoral dissertation, Eastern Mediterranean University (EMU)).

Althen, G. (1988). *American ways.* Yarmouth, ME: Intercultural Press, VA: American Association for Counseling and Development.

Ariza, E. N. W. (2010). Not for ESOL teachers: What every classroom teacher needs to know about the linguistically, culturally, and ethnically diverse student. Boston, MA: Pearson Education.

Brendtro, L., Brokenleg, M., & Van Bockern, S. (1991). The circle of courage. *Beyond Behavior, 2*(1), 5–12.

Brown, L. & Holloway, I. (2008). The initial stage of the international sojourn: excitement or culture shock?. *British Journal of Guidance & Counselling, 36*(1), 33–49.

Burdick-Will, J. (2013). School violent crime and academic achievement in Chicago. *Sociology of education*, 0038040713494225.

Dobao, A. F. (2012). Collaborative writing tasks in the L2 classroom: Comparing group, pair, and individual work. *Journal of Second Language Writing, 21*(1), 40–58.

Fordham, S. (1988). Racelessness as a factor in Black students' school success: Pragmatic strategy or pyrrhic victory? *Harvard educational review, 58*(1), 54–85.

Gay, G. (2010). *Culturally responsive teaching: Theory, research, and practice*. Teachers College Press.

Gollnick, D. & Chinn, P. (1990). Multicultural education in a pluralistic society. Columbus, OH: Merrill.

Grossman, H. (1984). Educating Hispanic students: Cultural implications for instruction, classroom management counseling, and assessment. Springfield, IL: CC Thomas.

Grossman, H. (1990). Trouble-free teaching: Solutions to behavior problems in the classroom. Mountain View, CA: Mayfield.

Horvat, E. M. & Lewis, K. S. (2003). Reassessing the "burden of 'acting White' ": The importance of peer groups in managing academic success. *Sociology of education*, 265–280.

Hall, E. T. (1959). *The silent language* (Vol. 3, p. 1959). New York: Doubleday.

Hanna, J. L. (1988). *Disruptive school behavior: Class, race, and culture*. New York: Holmes & Meier.

Henkin A. & Nguyen, L. (1981). Between two cultures: The Vietnamese in America. Saratoga, CA: Rand.

Kohls, L. R. (2001). *Survival kit for overseas living: For Americans planning to live and work abroad* (4th ed.). Intercultural Press, Incorporated.

Ladson-Billings, G. (1992). *Culturally relevant teaching: The key to making multicultural education work*. In C.A. Grant (Ed.), *Research and multicultural education* (pp. 106–121). London: Falmer Press.

Mills, M., Martino, W., & Lingard, B. (2004). Attracting, recruiting and retaining male teachers: Policy issues in the male teacher debate. *British Journal of Sociology of Education, 25*(3), 355–369.

Nine-Curt, C. (1976). Non-verbal communication in Puerto Rico. Cambridge, MA: National Assessment and Dissemination Center for Bilingual/Bicultural Education.

Nydel, M. (1982). *Understanding Arabs*. Yarmouth, ME: Intercultural Press.

Ogbu, J. (1988). Class stratification, racial stratification, and schooling. In L. Weiss, *Class, race, and gender in American education, 163*, 182. Albany, NY: State University of New York Press.

Ogbu, J. U. (1990). Minority education in comparative perspective. *The Journal of Negro Education, 59*(1), 45–57.

Oberg, K. (2006). Cultural shock: Adjustment to new cultural environments (Reprint 1960). *CURARE-BERLIN-, 29*(2/3), 142.

Pedersen, P. (1994). *The five stages of culture shock: Critical incidents around the world*. ABC-CLIO.

Pennycook, A. (2014). *The cultural politics of English as an international language*. Routledge.

Richards, H. V., Brown, A. F., & Forde, T. B. (2007). Addressing diversity in schools: Culturally responsive pedagogy. *Teaching Exceptional Children, 39*(3), 64–68.

Zhou, Y., Jindal-Snape, D., Topping, K., & Todman, J. (2008). Theoretical models of culture shock and adaptation in international students in higher education. *Studies in higher education, 33*(1), 63–75.

Stewart, E. C. & Bennett, M. J. (2011). *American cultural patterns: A cross-cultural perspective*. Hachette, UK.

Ward, C., Bochner, S., & Furnham, A. (2005). *The psychology of culture shock*. Routledge.

Wingfield, M. (2006). Arab Americans: Into the multicultural mainstream. *Equity & Excellence in Education, 39*(3), 253–266.

Woo, J. (1985). *The Chinese-speaking student: A composite profile.* New York: Bilingual Education Multifunctional Support Center at Hunter College.

Yao, E. L. (1979). Implications of biculturalism for the learning process of middle-class Asian children in the United States. *Journal of Education, 161*(4), 61–72.

Zhou, Y., Jindal-Snape, D., Topping, K., & Todman, J. (2008). Theoretical models of culture shock and adaptation in international students in higher education. *Studies in Higher Education, 33*(1), 63–75.

CHAPTER 3

CROSS CULTURAL UNDERSTANDINGS IN ACADEMIC SETTINGS

Eileen N. Whelan Ariza

Try to use your students' backgrounds to create more culturally relevant instruction.

Education is supposed to be the great equalizer that will offer every student and equal opportunity for learning. But research shows that teachers are often at odds with students from other cultures because the students' ways of life are discordant with the values and behavioral expectations of the teacher, who is typically White, English speaking, and middle class, which exacerbates the disconnect of teacher and student discord (NCES, 2012; Owen, 2014). This incongruence can lead to miscommunication as teachers unwittingly inflict their own perception of reality upon students who interpret life through a different paradigm (Feuerborn & Chinn; 2012). The miscommunication occurs not only verbally but also through body language, gestures, facial expressions, personal space, and movement (Burgoon, Guerrero, & Manusov, 2011). Trying to decipher what another individual is truly conveying without knowing the "rules" to the other's cultural "game" is difficult. Everyone, including teachers, reacts consciously and unconsciously to preconceived notions of which they are probably not even aware, but these feelings drive our behaviors, acceptances, and treatment of others.

According to Matsumoto (2001), there is strong evidence for the universal facial expressions of seven emotions—anger, contempt, disgust, fear, joy, sadness, and surprise. This idea is very old as it was based on Darwin (1872) who was the first to suggest the idea that these emotions are felt universally, the very lynchpin of his theory of evolution. But the differences among people are the extent to which they show these feelings because in some cultures people express them openly, and in others people do not. They are also expressed differently and this is the part that is confusing, when you are judging someone based on the ideas you have about what a display of one of these signs means. To further compound the complexity, expressions of shame, pride, and guilt were studied also and there were differences between the way East Asians and Westerns (Jack, Garrod, Yu, Caldara, & Schyns, 2012) display these emotions. Their findings showed that Western Caucasians showed basic emotions with a distinct set of facial muscles, while East Asians showed more overlap for surprise, fear, disgust, and anger. That means we might easily misread an expression. Succinctly, their findings show that facial expressions of emotions exist, so the emotion is universal, but not for the same people at the same time, for the same reasons. This would remind us to be cautious in assuming how someone feels by our perceptions. For example, Asian students may smile or giggle but not from humor; it could be from embarrassment. We are not going to be able to know all of our students' cultures, but if we are at least aware that we might be misinterpreting some action or reaction, it will give us encouragement to investigate further about how our students are feeling.

Banks (2015) uses the metaphor of an iceberg to describe culture. Looking at the part of an iceberg that is not submerged, one can see only about one-tenth of it. This fraction depicts surface culture, or the outward vestiges of culture, such as clothing, food, and music. The other nine-tenths of the iceberg reflect the components of deep culture, which includes values, gender roles, and religious beliefs. We are often unaware of how profound and deep-rooted our values are until they are unexpectedly challenged. At that point, major misinterpretations can occur, which often wreak hurt feelings, outrage, anger, and disbelief that someone else could be so "wrong."

While the tip of the iceberg represents the individual's conscious understanding of his or her culture, the submerged part symbolizes the larger, subconscious influence of culture in one's life. Coming to an understanding of this subconscious influence requires some inner exploration.

> Mr. Thomas, a Caucasian American teacher from Minnesota, is young and shows a natural zest for life. He feels great respect and fascination for Native American cultures, and he leaps at the opportunity to begin his teaching career in a school located on the Native American reservation in Oklahoma. He prepares his classroom to look friendly, warm, and intellectually interesting. On the first day of class, he feels ready and well prepared. He introduces the concepts he is going to teach with a **KWL chart** (what you know, what you want to know, and later, what you learned). He asks a young girl, Little Flower, a comprehension question, but she does not know the answer. In an effort to engage the class, Mr. Thomas asks someone else, but the student lowers his eyes and remains silent. Again and again, Mr. Thomas gets the same response from the rest of the children. He does not understand the defiant attitude, and he is truly baffled by their behavior.

The explanations for the above scenario are simple. The Native American students in Mr. Thomas's class hail from a cultural lifestyle that is more group oriented, where learning takes place in a method that is more self-directed and exploratory than is found in his own Anglo-cultural background. Because one student does not know the answer, the other students will not answer in an attempt to "save face," or not embarrass Little Flower. Even if they really know the answer to the question, they will not answer to try to "outdo" each other. The value of this noncompetitive principle is reflective of the belief that no one should be singled out because the group as a whole is the most important identity. The tribal elders sit in a group, sometimes not speaking, and are comfortable in their silence. If children are raised within this environment, they demonstrate these behavioral patterns. Problems arise in the classroom only when the cultural styles of the students counter those of the teacher.

Teachers who are not from the same culture as their students may find difficulties understanding the beliefs, behaviors, or values demonstrated in their classrooms (Farris, 2016; Ogbu, 1988; Pajares, 1992). Knowing the learning and cultural styles of your students helps to explain behaviors that can cause misunderstandings. Although on the surface this appears to be a simple explanation, in reality the situation is quite complex. Teachers need to understand diverse learning styles in the classroom. However, as useful as this information might be, mere knowledge of learning styles is not a panacea for the myriad of issues found in the classroom of today (Bennett, 1990; Yildirim & Tezci, 2016). The students' home language, culture, heritage, family beliefs, previous education, and experience are only a few of the components necessary to consider in creating an effective formula for instruction. In addition, as students begin to overlap with other cultural groups, behaviors begin to mix, students might end up using one cultural practice at home, and then another at school.

Nonverbal Communication

Making assumptions of cultural meanings based on your own perception of cultural reality can result in incorrect interpretations of another's intentions. Using Banks's iceberg metaphor again, this chapter further discusses surface culture as well deep culture and nonverbal communication, which can be misinterpreted if we apply significance from our own cultural values to the actions of others.

First, it is important to know your own culture. If you are from the United States, look up your own culture to see what overarching ideas and principles that Americans abide by (either loosely or strictly). You will find some ideas that you might never have noticed. For example, my Colombian niece told her family back home that Americans always hang flags for the holidays outside their houses. Personally, I have never done this, and I never noticed that there are many people who do hang flags around their houses (e.g., for Easter, Halloween, Christmas, and Thanksgiving).

But we do have cultural values in the United States. To think of some examples, as a society, we value time and expect things to start and end on time. When invited to dinner at a certain hour, we are expected to show up pretty much at that hour. An appointment at 3:00 p.m. is usually an appointment at 3:00 p.m. We are expected to call if we are running late. We apologize a lot for anything: excuse me; I am sorry, please, and thank you are very important in the American culture.

Other typical values we might expect to find have to do with size. Americans like large size portions, as a rule. Our cars are usually bigger than those in other countries. Our personalities overall are more outgoing than people from many other societies We are surprisingly friendly, generally speaking, and will make small talk to strangers. We typically promote independence. When people stand too close to us, we are uncomfortable, whereas people from other cultures may stand closer to each other, and even "share breath." Privacy is a very important issue and we usually do not want to interfere in other people's business. Self-sufficiency and independence are very important to Americans. Once you start thinking, you will come up with some other things, but the most obvious ones you will recognize are those things that people do that offend you or make you feel comfortable.

Mrs. Sato, an American-born teacher of Japanese descent, has relocated with her husband and children to Framingham, Massachusetts, a city with a high population of Brazilians. Being from Hawaii, Mrs. Sato has had much experience with students from diverse cultures, so she is welcomed into the public school system as a high school teacher. Mrs. Sato is teaching a lesson on economics and is trying to describe the inflated housing pricing in Hawaii. After giving an example, she concludes by saying, "So, you need to have a lot of this (making the "OK" sign with her thumb and forefinger) to get a house in Hawaii." Her American students look puzzled, her Brazilian students gasp with embarrassment, and Mrs. Sato is wondering what has just occurred.

In fact, the difficulties of communicating with someone from another culture arise not only from language differences but from cultural differences as well, including **body language**. When we talk about nonverbal communication, the problem compounds because each cultural group has its own set of symbols, and the meanings of the same symbols may and often do vary across cultures. Although Mrs. Sato was born in the United States, she was raised with much Japanese influence. From the Japanese reference point, the "OK" symbol refers to money. To Brazilians, this gesture is obscene and vulgar, referring to something sexual; in the mainstream American culture, this widely recognized symbol just means "OK." Unfortunately, not until Mrs. Sato accidentally discovered this difference in meanings did she realize how badly misconstrued nonverbal communication can become.

Renowned anthropologist Edward T. Hall is best known for his seminal works in nonverbal communication. *The Silent Language* (1959) (see Neuliep, 2014) depicts culture as having its own system of communication with different meanings. Teachers can better understand their students from other cultures if they have knowledge of the underlying significance of nonverbal communication. Eye contact is an interesting matter. In the Western culture, such as the United States, we believe that making eye contact is expected and respectful, because it shows that we are attentive and honest. In cultures such as Asian, Middle Eastern, some Hispanic, and Native American cultures, it is seen as rude. It can be actually dangerous in some Eastern cultures because it might give an incorrect impression such as unintended sexual interest. Gestures, touch, facial expressions, body movement, and so on are all parts of the "silent language."

Nonverbal communication can be classified into categories known as **kinesics** (the study of body language), **proxemics** (conscious and unconscious use of personal distance), **paralinguistics** (vocal effects that modify speech; elements of speech), **haptics** (communication through touch), and **chronemics** (perceiving and using time). Additionally, cultural beliefs can be further subdivided into categories of surface culture and deep culture (beliefs about how families should function, attitudes about religion, health, life, and death) (Gregersen, 2005; Kang, 2000).

A note on kinesics: Each culture demonstrates body language in a different way. When greeting each other, Asians bow, Americans shake hands, the French kiss each cheek three times, and Hispanics kiss on one cheek or two, depending on the country. In Asia, the custom of bowing has more subtleties that are decipherable to the unsuspecting Western eye. The person with the higher rank in society (the employer or an elder) will be bowed to by someone younger or by someone who holds a subordinate position. A Thai will press hands together, steeple style, and bow the head. If a Thai is bowing to a higher-status individual, the hands will be raised higher. Americans appear informal to more formal cultures. Newcomers to the American society may have difficulty judging whether the situation is formal or not because Americans appear informal when actually an unspecified hierarchy does exist. Teachers who are cognizant of potential cultural clashes in the classroom are better equipped to deal with everyday issues that can cause misunderstandings.

Even in the business world, the simple act of exchanging business cards carries cultural significance. How a card is presented to a new acquaintance (e.g., Asians proffer the card with two hands) or whether the card is looked at immediately or pocketed without a glance can represent respect or rejection.

Now let's look at some examples of how each culture determines its own rules of behavior, both in and outside the classroom.

> In an adult ESOL class, Ms. Walsh, the teacher, invited her students to her wedding. She told her students that dress was not formal. The students were excited to go to their first American wedding. Ms. Walsh's Colombian student, Henry, who usually dressed quite formally, arrived an hour late. He walked into the function in the middle of the ceremony, wearing jeans, a T-shirt, and tennis shoes. He was mortified and insisted on going home to change. When the teacher said the wedding was not formal, she was implying that tuxedos were not required. Henry believed that the word "informal" meant sports clothing. He did not have the background knowledge to distinguish the degrees of formality implied in the American culture.
>
> Ryoko, a Japanese student, was thrilled to go to Disney World on her first visit to the United States. Stopping in front of a roller coaster, she stared up in surprise as she watched a grown man shouting excitedly. She said, "It is shocking to see a grown man yell on the ride! In Japan, men do not shout out."

Display of emotion is unique to each culture. Many individuals must hold their grief inwardly because it is not for public display. However, in other cultures people may openly keen (wail) when in grief. This is obvious in televised American trials: When the accused does not openly demonstrate grief or remorse, it is well noted according to media, and it appears, almost as an indication of guilt. The individual is judged according to "typical" American response to grief. Smiles can be deceiving, too. In the United States, we often smile at strangers just to be polite. As mentioned previously, if Asian people smile, it may be their attempt to cover up embarrassment, pain, or grief. Some people look on us suspiciously for smiling at them. Individuals display grief, shock, or happiness openly, while others are expected to hide their feelings.

Kinesic differences are evident in the classroom in many ways. How? When a teacher tries to affectionately pat an Asian student on the head, the student may recoil because many people believe that the head houses the soul and must not be touched. For individuals from many cultures, to show the bottom of the feet is an insult because they are the dirtiest part of the body. If a teacher requests the students to remove their shoes for any reason, this might cause conflict for some students. Sitting on the floor is another area of potential conflict for students.

For certain Arab cultures, offering your left hand for a handshake is an insult because this hand is considered "unclean." The right hand is preferred for eating, while the left hand is used to clean the body after going to the toilet. In many Arab or Islamic countries, the crime rate is low because in accordance with to the Koran, punishment is very severe. For example, if someone picks a pocket in Morocco and gets caught, the right hand might be cut off, ensuring that the person, left with only an "unclean" hand, will be shunned for a lifetime.

> Eileen and Mary, teachers from Massachusetts, were in Morocco touring the labyrinth of street markets. From all sides, vendors yelled out invitations to buy their wares. One vendor, upset that the ladies were ignoring him, began to curse them in English. (Remember that non-native speakers of English will use words that hold no deep meaning for them but will be offensive to native speakers). The leader of the tour group chastised the vendor and told him

to apologize to the women. The vendor replied, "Of course," and held out his left hand for a handshake with Mary. She quickly refused, saying, "I know what that means."

In the classroom, children from cultures that maintain a closer physical proximity may crowd around the teacher and will not know it when they have crossed the personal boundaries of the teacher. If the teacher backs up, which may be an unconscious response, the students may feel rejected or think that the teacher does not like them. Hall (1966) coined the term **proxemics** to describe the use of personal body space. For example, Americans have a certain personal space surrounding their bodies that others must not penetrate. It is unspoken, but everyone knows that to get too close to an American is an uncomfortable declaration of intimacy and may even be considered a threat. The American will become uncomfortable, or even hostile, and will back off. If Americans touch each other accidentally, they immediately say, "Excuse me" or "I'm sorry" (Felder & Henriques, 1995).

At the end of the summer session at the English language institute, Ms. Clark held a goodbye party for her students from Korea, Taiwan, Peru, and Brazil. As the teacher, she had enjoyed learning about the cultures the students came from. When the party was in full swing, she scanned the room and looked at the group of students in wonder as she realized how different they were from each other. The Brazilian girls were trying to get everyone to dance. Two Korean young men were sitting on the floor, backs against the wall, with their arms draped around each other, and the Peruvian and Taiwanese students were deep in discussion. The Peruvian girls stood very close to the Taiwanese students, and it appeared that the Taiwanese boys were shying away from the girls. Ms. Clark noted with amazement and delight the students were behaving naturally, according to their individual cultural patterns, which is what they had discussed in their cross-cultural communication classes.

The Teacher's Role in Creating Understanding

The ways in which an individual characteristically acquires, retains, and retrieves information are collectively termed the individual's learning style. Learning styles may be a mismatch between the student and teacher. As a result, the quality of learning and attitude will be compromised. A teacher can prepare to have a culturally responsive classroom. The curriculum should not try to be a one size fits all plan, so the culturally relevant curriculum can focus on relevant information on many issues so with proper preparation, that address diverse issues.

Culturally relevant teaching draws on the experience of the students. Stories of their experiences learning English, and what their lives are like in the new country will validate their experiences. Personal narratives can include and incorporate actual learning standards such as questioning strategies, interpreting stories, analyzing ideas within the context of meaningful issues. Typical assignments that are found in the curriculum can be adapted to the individual learner's experiences. Sonia Nieto (1996) stated that sociocultural consciousness means that diversity must be affirmed. Affirming one's identity is crucial to one's well-being and positive self-identity.

Learning about your students will affirm their identities. Find out what they know, and what is important to them. They will probably have life stories that will sound very difficult. It takes quite an effort to move to another country, especially if it was under unpleasant circumstances, but draw on your students' knowledge, and find out what they don't know as well. Use one method to build on another. Embed new ideas, skills, and instructional strategies within meaningful projects with your guidance.

Teach your students to utilize aids such as dictionaries, technology, reading materials, instructional units with scaffolded vocabulary, and simplified language. Be sure to use visuals, graphic organizers, hands-on activities, and modeling so that students can totally understand the lessons and vocabulary. Try to connect what is being taught with the background of the student. It is important that the teacher is sensitive to each student and each student's story. There will be cultural differences among all the students and you may inadvertently offend or hurt the student's feelings. Allowing your students to have the ability to learn in a nonthreatening atmosphere will give them permission to make mistakes and to learn within a safe environment.

> "Teachers' biases or assumptions about students' capabilities and behavior can have both major and subtle implications for students' social and academic outcomes" (Parks & Kennedy, 2007, p. 938).

Have high expectations for your students, but be sure to modify and scaffold for them along the way so they will have the chance to be successful. Have students help each other, especially if your class is crowded. Collaborative learning will be helpful, especially if your classroom has out-of-date resources, or a limited number of materials.

It is very important to recognize that everyone has his or her own perception of culture, reality, and life view. Be open to the cultures of your students and try to use the contexts that they bring to class because it is all around you. Share your own culture with them, but be aware of the cornucopia of riches to choose from right from your own students. Try to see what you can use within your own classroom scenarios, but above all, be super conscious and sensitive to what your students have gone through and what you can use to construct learning based on their previous experiences.

The one last and highly important item to remember is the family lives of your students. Parents and family members of your students may not speak English and your students might not have the best situations at home to do their homework in (space, light, computers, technology, resources, time, job responsibilities, non-English speaking family members, etc.). This could be mitigated by offering special services to help students become successful by offering extra help after school, or during class time, offering buddy tutors in class, providing a template of what the work should look like (during class time and sending home for family members to see), translating directions, or additional practice. Helping students to help themselves will promote satisfaction because they will find pride and solace in themselves as viable, valuable, contributing human beings who have much to offer, in spite of previous dilemmas and plights.

FINAL POINTS

- Communication is oral, verbal, and nonverbal. It is up to the teacher to try to decipher what the real meanings are. Try to teach your students what American cultural values in the classroom are as well.
- Help provide your students and parents with strategies to promote instruction both in the classroom, with help to make up for possible difficulties for students who cannot study at home.
- Have high expectations but be sure to provide accommodations (visuals, graphic organizers, and extra measures to increase comprehension) so the students can be able to actually complete the task.
- Use your own students' narrative to create culturally relevant instruction.

Discussion Questions and Activities

1. Plan four questioning strategies that you can use to make sure all students have a chance to contribute to the class discussion, despite their different cultural backgrounds. If students do not know what to say, what will you do to make sure they don't feel embarrassed in class? Show examples of:
   A. Kinesics
   B. Proxemics
   C. Chronemics
   D. Paralinguistics
   E. Haptics
   F. Surface Culture
   G. Deep Culture

2. Imagine you are in a classroom with students who come from different countries. What can you do to get to know their beliefs? How can knowing their beliefs make you a more informed teacher?

3. Brainstorm possible cultural misconceptions your students might display in the classroom. Refer to the situation with Henry wearing the wrong clothing at the wedding. Give five examples of situations where students might misinterpret situations in the classroom.

4. One student leans so close to you when you are sitting at your desk that it makes you feel uncomfortable. Another student recoils when you pat her on the head. A third student stands so close to you, he "shares his breath" with you. How would you handle these situations?

5. As you correct a student from Japan, she keeps smiling at you. What would you think this student is feeling? How can you find out?

6. Survey your students in your class and come up with a list of their: Beliefs; Attitudes; Values; Culturally comfortable classroom organization; Classroom management; Behavior modification(s); Delivery of curricular content; and Cultural relevance.

7. Plan how you could have students write their own stories and narratives. Based on what they write, create a culturally responsive lesson plan. Allow your students to share their own stories with each other. Embed culturally relevant content in your academic instruction.

Resources

Nonverbal communication/body language (kinesics)
http://www.youtube.com/watch?v=uEbtRt00HVU

Hand gestures
http://www.youtube.com/watch?v=PYcID4KWKe4

Body language and world culture: Different countries
http://www.youtube.com/watch?v=IQuFNvkPjik

Edward Hall proxemics
http://www.afirstlook.com/docs/proxemic.pdf

Understanding body language
http://psychology.about.com/od/nonverbalcommunication/ss/understanding-body-language_8.htm

Edward Hall
http://www.csiss.org/classics/content/13

Proxemics in the ESL classroom
http://www.au.af.mil/au/awc/awcgate/state/proxemics.htm

Monochronic and polychromic cultures
http://blogonlinguistics.wordpress.com/2013/10/23/chronemics-monochronic-and-polychronic-cultures/

Haptics: Touch
https://sites.google.com/site/nonverbalcommunicationportal/forms-of-nonverbal-communication/gestures-and-touch

Paralinguistics in the classroom
http://www.culturesintheclassroom.com/5_paralinguistics.shtml

Surface culture and deep culture
http://extension.oregonstate.edu/metro4h/sites/default/files/understanding_esl__learners-_moving__toward_cultural__responsiveness--__a_guide_for_teachers.pdf

Lessons that explore culture and identity
http://www.cmef.ca/downloads/ExploreCultureandIdentity.pdf

References

Banks, J. A. (2015). *Cultural diversity and education*. Routledge.

Barry, N. H. & Lechner, J. V. (1995). Preservice teachers' attitudes about and awareness of multicultural teaching and learning. *Teaching and Teacher Education, 11*, 149–161.

Burgoon, J. K., Guerrero, L. K., & Manusov, V. (2011). Nonverbal signals. *The SAGE handbook of interpersonal communication*. London: SAGE.

Darwin, C. (1872). *The expression of emotion in man and animals*. New York: Oxford University Press.

Felder, R. M. & Henriques, E. R. (1995). Learning and teaching styles in foreign and second language education. *Foreign language annals, 28*(1), 21–31.

Ferris, D. M. (2016). *Missed opportunities and connections in teacher learning* (Doctoral dissertation, Florida Atlantic University).

Feuerborn, L. & Chinn, D. (2012). Teacher perceptions of student needs and implications for positive behavior supports. *Behavioral Disorders*, 219–231.

Gregersen, T. S. (2005). Nonverbal cues: Clues to the detection of foreign language anxiety. *Foreign Language Annals, 38*(3), 388.

Jack, R. E., Garrod, O. G., Yu, H., Caldara, R., & Schyns, P. G. (2012). Facial expressions of emotion are not culturally universal. *Proceedings of the National Academy of Sciences, 109*(19), 7241–7244.

Kang, C. I. (2000). Nonverbal communication skills in the EFL curriculum. *Find us on the web!*, 3(1), 13.

Matsumoto, D. (2001). Culture and Emotion. In D. Matsumoto (Ed.), *The handbook of culture and psychology* (pp. 171–194). New York: Oxford University Press.

Matsumoto, D., Keltner, D., Shiota, M. N., Frank, M. G., & O'Sullivan, M. (2008). What's in a face? Facial expressions as signals of discrete emotions. In M. Lewis, J. M. Haviland, & L. Feldman Barrett (Eds.), *Handbook of emotions* (pp. 211–234). New York: Guilford Press.

National Center for Education Statistics. (2012). Beginning K-12 teacher characteristics and preparation by school types, 2009. Retrieved from http://nces.ed.gov/pubs2017/2017153.pdf

Neuliep, J. W. (2014). *Intercultural communication: A contextual approach.* Sage Publications.

Nieto, S. (1996). "I Like Making My Mind Work": Language minority. *Education reform and social change: Multicultural voices, struggles, and visions,* 147.

Owen, Z. (2014). *The relationship between pragmatic language competence and school exclusion: An interactionist perspective* (Doctoral dissertation, University of Birmingham).

Parks, F. R. & Kennedy, J. H. (2007). The impact of race, physical attractiveness, and gender on education majors' and teachers' perceptions of student competence. Journal of Black Studies, 37(6), 936–943. doi:10.1177/0021934705285955

Pennycook, A. (1985). Actions speak louder than words: Paralanguage, communication, and education. *TESOL Quarterly,* 259–282.

Villegas, A. M. & Lucas, T. (2002). Preparing culturally responsive teachers rethinking the curriculum. *Journal of teacher education,* 53(1), 20–32.

Villegas, A. M. & Lucas, T. (2007). The culturally responsive teacher. *Educational Leadership,* 64(6), 28.

Yildirim, S. & Tezci, E. (2016). Teachers' attitudes, beliefs and self-efficacy about multicultural education: A scale development. *Universal Journal of Educational Research,* 4(n12A), 196–204.

CHAPTER 4

DIVERSE LEARNING STYLES

Eileen N. Whelan Ariza

KEY POINTS

- Every student has a different learning style.
- Students' cultural backgrounds influence their learning style.
- Home cultural styles may be incongruous with the school style of learning.
- If teachers can get to know their students, they can create culturally relative instruction that is differentiated for individuals.

This chapter's focus highlights the reflections of **home cultures** on learning styles. Teachers are better prepared to understand their students' instructional strengths when they are conscious of the influences that cultures have on how students interact in an educational setting. With this knowledge, teachers can plan the most effective instructional practices.

Howard Gardner's (1999; 2008) seminal work on learning styles has made us aware that every student has strengths in different areas of learning. (See examples at the end of the chapter.) Learning style inventories (Dunn & Dunn, 1978; Dunn & Griggs, 2003; Kolb, 2005, 2007; Park, 2002; Rita & Dunn, 1993) are available to determine what kinds of learners we are; as a result of this awareness, we can learn how to modify teaching and learning strategies for all our students.

Students' learning styles often reflect their cultures as well as how they are treated in their homes. Since **personal independence** often is a salient characteristic of the American culture, American children may be encouraged to be more independent than children from some other cultures. The example below illustrates a different cultural outlook on what children should and should not do for themselves at a given age.

> As an English/Spanish bilingual teacher in the first grade, Ms. Zelden was amazed at the behaviors of some of the parents of her Hispanic students. She noticed that some parents would carry their children into class, hand-feed them, carry their books, take their boots off, and some children even had pacifiers and baby bottles. She noticed that this heightened dependence was also reflected in the way the children approached their assignments. The teacher would give a set of multiple directions, and the children would check with the teacher at each step. For example, if the directions were (1) go to the crayon box, (2) choose the

crayons, (3) choose the drawing paper from the bin, and (4) draw a picture of your favorite play place, the children would question the teacher after doing each task. They would ask questions like, "What color crayons should I pick?" and "What should I draw?" or "Teacher, can you draw a horse for me?" On the other hand, the American children seemed to act more comfortable with choice and took the initiative to proceed independently, which apparently was a direct reflection on how they were treated at home. In fact, Ms. Zelden found that the American children were so accustomed to doing things their own way; they often crossed over the acceptable boundaries between teacher and student. Ms. Zelden often had to tell the children, "This is not how we act with a teacher," or "You need to ask permission first before you get up from your seat," or "This is not how we talk to the teacher," because they truly did not know they were overstepping their limits.

Generally speaking, Americans promote and cherish independence. It is looked at as an inalienable right. The country was founded by people searching for the right to be independent. We teach children to care for themselves at a very early age. They contribute to the household by being responsible for chores; they learn how to dial 911 and report an emergency; they are allowed and even encouraged to make choices; and they order their own food in a restaurant. American mothers are expected to wean babies from nursing and bottles as soon as it is feasible.

We might not be aware how we are conditioned to accept our cultural values as the right way of life, but it is evident from infancy and early childhood. U.S. pediatricians often encourage new mothers to wean babies from bottles or nursing to drinking from a cup after about 1 year of age. Mothers in other cultures might nurse or feed their babies from bottles until they are 4 or older. In the U.S. society, we believe that is too old. We look askance at the child who is sucking on a pacifier if the child looks too mature to indulge in that habit. The value placed on independence applies even in our slumber patterns, as U.S. children are usually encouraged to sleep alone instead of being with the parents or the mother in a "family bed." These expectations will enforce the ideas and values of independence. Later, this inculcated behavior will reflect in classroom behavior and the conduct of children in the everyday business of living.

The U.S. values described here are contrary to the values of a culture where dependence on parents and elders is the norm. Again, the students who are more dependent on teacher interaction and direct instruction are usually a reflection of societies that do more for the child, which delays independence.

Field Independence and Field Dependence

As we have read, teachers from the **mainstream culture** in the United States will reflect the values common in U.S. society. Students from **nonmainstream cultures** possess their own value systems, which often lead to incongruence and misinterpretation of behavior, expectations, and learning styles in the classroom. **Cognitive styles** of individuals differ in processing and analyzing information, acquiring knowledge, and reacting to the teaching styles and assumptions of the instructor (Dunn & Griggs, 1990; Riding & Raynor, 2013). How we approach problems, address issues, ask questions, and interact with the teacher and our peers may be very different from culture to culture. This can be due to the ways of thinking or behaving that have been modeled for us (Banks & Banks, 1993, 2009; Garcia & Malkin, 1993), or it can be due to cognitive or physical disabilities (Grant & Sleeter, 1989). However, within each culture, general characteristics of cognitive similarity can be found (Grant & Sleeter, 1989; Philips, 1983; Ramirez & Castaneda, 1974; Rentsch, Small, & Hanges, 2008; Willis, 1993).

Field-independent and field-dependent learners do not differ in intelligence or cognitive ability; however, they differ in learning strategies and the approaches they take to problem solving and interacting with others. Once students enter school, they approach each situation at hand in the way they have been taught at home. If the process at school is incompatible with the way the student has been raised, misinterpretation and conflicts will occur (Baruth & Manning, 1992; Li & Li, 2008; Riding & Rayner, 2013). U.S. schools typically have favored an Anglo-European educational style, which reflects the mainstream learner who may need to articulate perceptions but does not pay much attention to social clues. Learning is impersonal. The field-independent approach to education may not be compatible with the nonmainstream minority student, and it may even appear that the minority student is in need of special education due to the perception of different behaviors (Harry & Klingner, 2014; McIntyre, 1993; Rueda & Forness, 1994).

Mainstream European Americans tend to be **field-independent learners** (Angeli & Valanides, 2004; Mestre, 2006; Witkin et al., 1975). The tendency is for them to be motivated by impersonal, analytical activities that do not necessitate a group-type approach. They may like competition, individual recognition, show a rational, intrinsic appeal for the task without consulting others, and do best with learning the history or theory of the activity before attempting the assignment (Angeli & Valanides, 2004; Anderson, 1988; Banks & Banks, 1993, 2009; Diaz, 1989; Ishii-Jordan & Peterson, 1994).

Field-dependent learners (Altun & Cakan, 2006) usually hail from nonmainstream cultures and like to work with others to achieve a common goal, very often while interacting with the teacher (DeTure, 2004; Ramirez & Castaneda, 1974). These learners are more sensitive to the feelings, opinions, and ideas of others and may like to assist one another in a group effort. They like to practice and learn by experimentation as opposed to engaging in conceptual discussion before attempting the task (Anderson, 1988). Students from cultures that are African American (Banks & Banks, 1993, 2009), Arab American (Nydell, 1987), Hispanic (Banks & Banks, 1993, 2009), Native American (Utley, 1983), and, often, Asian American (Hvitfeldt, 1986) tend to be field dependent and are greatly influenced by the teacher (Zhou, Jindal-Snape, Topping, & Todman, 2008). This type of learner may prefer a global perception and be more attentive to social clues.

When the cultural mismatch occurs, teachers may assume students are less competent than they really are, which can result in cultural bias or students being labeled as having behavioral disorders (Gollnick & Chinn, 1990; McIntyre, 1995; Rueda & Forness, 1994; Stephens & Townsend, 2015; Zhou et al., 2008).

With differing ideas of appropriate behavior, it is easy for teachers and students to misunderstand each other. For example, the field-dependent student comes from a culture that may appreciate helpfulness and cooperation between members. A student may try to help another student by sharing work or answers or letting a friend copy his or her answers. This is perceived as cheating in the individualist-oriented mainstream American culture.

Mainstream teachers usually expect silence, while people from other cultures, such as those that are Arab or African American, may demonstrate a more contributory, vocally responsive or physically oriented style of behavior (McIntyre, 1995; Nydell, 1987; Ogbu, 1988; Riding & Rayner, 2013). Other issues, like the importance of being task oriented, time conscious, and prompt can also be misconstrued. The student who is rushed may not finish work on time, or the student who needs to finish work at his or her own pace is definitely not appreciated by the teacher who is obligated to stick to a strict schedule. Additionally, consider the student who is not accustomed to asking questions or is not comfortable participating verbally in class. For example, a teacher may ask an Asian student if he or she understands a concept. To "save face" and avoid public embarrassment for the teacher for not explaining it well enough, or because the student was not capable of understanding the concept, the student will say "yes" (Li & Su, 2007; Wei, 1980; Woo, 1985). That student may fail the assessment, which indicates that he or she did not really understand the assignment, and the teacher might think the student was lying. Alternatively, often the student might say "yes," then go home and try to figure it out alone.

Modifying Instruction for All Learners

Although students may be prone to one style of learning, they can be taught to be **bicognitive** (Alfaro, Durán, Hunt, & Aragón, 2014). That is, the field-dependent student can learn to be more field independent and the more field-independent student can learn to become more field dependent. Although we must not categorize all individuals according to their ethnic groups, it is essential to keep in mind what type of learner the student is more likely to be. For example, in a list of characteristics that determines what a "gifted" student is, one of the measures mentioned was taking initiative to begin a task without being prompted. That is a typically "American" value, and a gifted minority student might not behave according to that "American" gifted-student criterion. Success for both types of learners greatly depends on the teacher, who should keep in mind that the instructor's own teaching style usually reflects his or her own learning style.

Field-dependent teachers are usually student centered and try to use positive reinforcement as opposed to negative feedback. They often use a hands-on, participatory approach with student discussion as opposed to lecture or discovery methods of teaching (Chao, Huang, & Li, 2003). Field-independent teachers may focus more on the subject, use a negative evaluation approach, and prefer inquiry or problem-solving methods of instruction, and the teaching situation may be more impersonal (Zhang & Sternberg, 2002).

To reach all students, a mix of both styles should be taught so that instructional methods can complement the cultural style. For those students who would thrive in more physically oriented tasks, implement activities that incorporate group work that depends on a hands-on activity, a project-based task that necessitates active participation, perhaps with a kinesthetic objective. Students can role-play a courtroom scene or a session in Congress or put on a play that portrays a historical event that they have researched and written about themselves.

For students who are more comfortable with field-dependent types of learning, introduce them to a more field-independent task by taking a systematic process using the discovery approach, or create a competition using groups instead of an individual contest. Know which approach your students seem to prefer, and incorporate that as much as possible.

Once cognizant of the differences in learning styles, teachers should reflect upon their own teaching and learning styles to see if they need to adjust their instructional practices to include a wider variety of strategies. Teachers can provide various opportunities for their students to experiment with more diverse instructional styles. At the same time, teachers can guide students to discover for themselves what types of learners they are, which can lead to their becoming more autonomous learners.

Differentiated Instruction Using Learning Styles

Differentiation of Learning

Different students have different learning styles. Gardner (1999) identified at least eight styles of learners:

- **Linguistic**—word enthusiast
- **Logical/Mathematical**—inquirer
- **Visual/Spatial**—visualizer
- **Musical**—music enthusiast
- **Bodily/Kinesthetic**—mover

- **Interpersonal**—socializer
- **Intrapersonal**—loner
- **Naturalistic**—nature lover

Different styles can be exacerbated by language differences as well. Some students prefer writing with paper and pencils, and reading with books that have pages to turn. Some students will prefer a Kindle, Nook, or iPad. However, there are some students who are so frightened or put off by using a computer, it will deter them from taking an online test (like the GED test) or it will take away the joy of feeling, touching, smelling, or writing on the paper found in a traditional book.

The first approach to determining what your students are like is to observe as they interact with one another, and by exposing them to different techniques. Experiment with a variety of teaching techniques and activities to get a comprehensive overview of your classroom culture and general learning preferences. As always, remember to maintain the flexibility of teaching strategies so you can learn together what will work best. Try to get your students to tell or show you which learning styles they prefer.

Students will have different levels and ranges or reading and academic skills. Within the different levels, teachers must control the content as well as the time it takes to present the material, and provide differing ways that students can demonstrate what they know. Formative assessment along the way will help teachers adjust learning and regulate how to share what they know, whether there is a written task or a presentation or a model.

It is of primary importance to know your student's level of ability, so you can correctly gauge the level of performance to expect, within the students' capacity. Allowing the student to show how he or she has mastered the content is true differentiated learning.

When it comes to learning, we all receive and process information differently. It is wonderful to teach students to be metacognitively aware, which means that when students are able to think about their own learning, they are better able to communicate about what they like to do when they have a choice of academic tasks, according to their preferences. Some students prefer to work alone while others prefer collaborative work. Others don't mind working within either style.

Instructional strategies should be varied for several reasons. Students will be able to choose their favorite modalities of learning while they will be practicing all the skills of language learning (reading, writing, listening, speaking, pronunciation, etc.). Learning only one way is not obligatory. For example, a combination of learning styles may include a visual representation (modeled instruction), with a lecture (auditory), and then a presentation of what was learned (which could be linguistic or kinesthetic). Use all the learning styles possible.

Another strategy that is a benefit of differentiated instruction is to work with culturally relevant content. The more the teacher learns the essence of the student as an individual, the more interesting the individual becomes and the teacher can use this knowledge to create relevant curriculum. Every student has their own abilities, such as an affinity for their native music, sports, dance, musical ability, or art. Incorporate these qualities within the curriculum according to the interest of the students so that they become more valuable to the learner. If the language level is not proficient enough to be called fluent, allow the student to be creative (such as within a project) by other means (charts, models, or graphics, etc.)

Below are some ideas to use with individual types of learners (note that some overlap).

Linguistic Learners

Some students must learn through words, either written or spoken. They will listen and speak, with repetition and practice repeatedly. They might enjoy the traditional teacher-centered classroom with lectures, explanations, overhead/PowerPoint presentations/whiteboard, pictures on the walls, speaking with partners, discussions, and new vocabulary.

Ideas for the Classroom

- Grammar and language games
- Reports made to the class
- Dictionary and thesaurus activities
- Reading selections
- Oral readings
- Creating and asking questions
- Spelling games
- Creating word games, crossword puzzles, riddles, jokes, puns,
- Writing and narrating plays
- Creating a newsletter, or magazine
- Mock interviews
- Speeches on current topics, or impromptu affairs
- Writing descriptions and then reading them to the class
- Debates
- Creating a game show
- Role-plays
- Creating commercials and slogans
- Treasure hunts and scavenger hunts
- Costumes and acting in scenes, shows (of any length, written by students or prewritten shows)
- Readers theater
- Acting out well-known stories
- Acting out stories that the students have written about themselves and their cultures
- Acting for parents; invited audiences
- Vocabulary word banks
- Singalongs; using songs from movies or popular well-known songs, or from their own cultures
- Talent shows, with students being the judges
- Writing menus and recipes; acting out ordering food
- Writing diaries, journals (teacher/student journal)

Logical/Mathematical Learners

These learners enjoy questioning, finding answers, and trying to solve problems.

Ideas for the Classroom

- Charting data
- Mystery solving
- Money games
- Sequencing games, activities, and worksheets
- Puzzles
- Case studies (logical reasoning)
- Problem solving
- Multistep activities, tasks, and projects
- Graphing
- Solving word problems (make sure students know the vocabulary in the problem, that they can have multiple meanings, like table, quarter and teach attack skills)
- Analyze language, grammar, and sentence structure
- Grammar rule study
- Recognition of errors

Visual/Spatial Learners

Visual learners might be the most common style of learners. They need something that engages the eyes, such as visuals, images, learning media, pictures, models, graphs, and other visual representations to connect learning to what is being taught. They may enjoy being involved in displays, projects, posters, story boards, writing on paper, or white board, or computers. Visual learners will understand the instructor better because they can see the face, body, expressions and gestures. They may make their own notes or pictorials to indicate what they are learning.

Fun Tip—to see how many people are visual learners, tell the class to stand up and watch you. Everybody should face you. Point your finger toward your cheek and say: Everybody touch your chin. Watch how many people do what you do and touch their cheek. Almost everyone will touch their cheek because visual commands take priority over auditory commands. This is a good lesson for the instructor. You can say something several times, but until the students see it and embed it in the brain, they may not follow your directions.

Ideas for the Classroom

- Silent reading
- Reading out loud
- Make and use mind maps
- Watch a video or play to encourage discussion
- Playing a type of game with an academic undertone
- Board games that will practice any topic, such as spelling, matching, number facts, grammar, etc.
- Comics made by the students, written by the students, and acted out by the students

- Reading any kind of trade books
- Use photos to promote an assignment
- Watch videos that complement areas of study
- Use diagrams, and teach students how to make diagrams with graphic organizers
- Use multimedia to create projects
- Play Scrabble, Pictionary, etc.
- Use tools such as highlighters to highlight text, indicate vocabulary, or word functions

Musical Learner—music enthusiast

Music can help with learning in several ways. It helps with rhythm and makes a connection in the brain with the language.

Ideas for the Classroom

- Singing
- Chorale or group singing
- Jazz chants
- Listening to music
- Playing instruments

- Drilling
- Clapping
- Creating
- Create dialogue for rap songs

Bodily/Tactile/Kinesthetic Learners (learners who connect by touch or physical movements)

Ideas for the Classroom

- Simon says, and other physical games
- Dance
- Tag games
- Building models
- Hands-on learning
- Tapping, clapping, banging
- Jazz chants
- Rap/physical
- Whole body/exercise/movement
- Building models/construction/graphic structures

- Maps/maps drawing (tell each other what to draw on the map)
- Touching games/moving around
- Crafts
- Vocabulary games (touch items in a bag)
- Spatial games
- Legos
- Physical expression games/with rules
- Charades
- Pantomime
- Sports

Interpersonal Learners—socializer

These students are interactive, talkative, sociable, and might appear boisterous at the wrong time.

Ideas for the Classroom

- Assign meaningful activities that **teach social awareness**
- Introduce peer editing
- Group discussion
- Team work and competitions
- Have them make presentations on an interesting topic such as current events or cultural topics
- Allow them to peer teach
- Have them create a lesson and teach it to their peers
- Role play
- Dialogues of conflict solution
- Create effective communication activities

Intrapersonal Learners—loner

This type of learner will be quiet, appears to be introverted, and teachers need to pay attention to make sure the student comprehends the instruction. They may appear to be able to work alone, with minimum supervision. They may dislike group work and prefer to work alone.

Ideas for the Classroom

- Assign writing in journals, logs, and diaries
- Assign activities that promote personal expression
- Create projects that are interesting to the student, but assign individual jobs or roles within the project
- Use the student's interests to write self-narrative
- Assign an auto-photography project
- Create a family book and have the student write about his or her own family
- Use real-world issues in your assignments
- Use appropriate prompts for these students
- Promote interactive games
- Promote interactive technology games
- Assign a study buddy for these students

Naturalistic/Environmental Learner

These learners have an excellent understanding of the world, and the environment about us.

Ideas for the Classroom

- Use the environment to learn the appropriate vocabulary
- Create outdoor explorations with scavenger hunts
- Research the findings from the scavenger hunts
- Take field trips with students who collect data that can be classified
- Collect plants and flowers and discover the vocabulary associated with them
- Using the Internet, explore museums, arboretums, libraries, places around the world, nature gardens, zoos, and other countries
- Create activities based on the above trips
- Examine butterfly farms and species

Auditory Learners

An auditory learner appreciates sounds and will learn by hearing. Music may be a great addition to enhance auditory learning. Auditory learning is defined by sensitivity to sounds, speech, tones, pitch, and accent. However, there is a great deal of overlap between the styles of learning and linked together they can enhance learning.

Classroom Ideas for Auditory Learners

- Read-alouds
- Audio books
- Songs
- Raps about content
- Lecture
- Discussion
- Debate
- Presentations
- Songs
- Raps/verbal
- Chorale readings
- Poetry
- Story
- Music
- Language listening games
- Jazz chants with a clapping rhythm
- Karaoke singing
- Cloze passages
- Jigsaw listening
- Madlibs (the word game; you choose a word randomly and it becomes a funny sentence)

FINAL POINTS

- Differentiated learning is important and helps to be culturally relevant.
- The home culture can be mismatched with the school culture.
- Instruction should be modified for all learners so that content is comprehensible.
- The more you know about your students, the better you will be able to reach them.
- Be sure to break down vocabulary so your students will be able to understand enough to do the work.

Discussion Questions and Activities

1. Describe your preferred learning style. What kind of teaching and learning situation are you most comfortable with? Why?
2. Create five activities you could incorporate in your class to help field-dependent learners become more independent, and vice versa.
3. Gardner's (1993, 2008) multiple intelligence learning styles are as follows:
   - Visual/spatial intelligence
   - Musical intelligence
   - Verbal intelligence
   - Logical/mathematical intelligence
   - Interpersonal intelligence
   - Intrapersonal intelligence

- Bodily/kinesthetic intelligence
- Naturalist intelligence

Determine the objectives that you would like to teach. Keeping in mind cultural and age differences, create one activity that utilizes each intelligence that will reach your objectives.

Resources

Field-independent/dependent learning styles and L2
https://pdfs.semanticscholar.org/6515/905ba3cd3015c39ea29413e637237c54028e.pdf

Diverse learning styles
http://www.bcps.org/offices/lis/models/tips/styles.html

Field-dependent learners/field-independent learners
http://www.houghton.edu/academics/academic-resources/center-for-academic-success-and-advising/study-advisement/general-study-information/learning-styles-field-dependency/

Diverse learning abilities
http://www.bing.com/search?q=diverse+learning+styles&src=IE-TopResult&FORM=IE10TR

Diverse teaching
http://www.brighthubeducation.com/teaching-methods-tips/79153-examples-of-diverse-learning-styles/

Modifying instruction for ELs
http://www.colorincolorado.org/article/differentiated-instruction-english-language-learners
http://www.edmentum.com/sites/edmentum.com/files/resource/media/0272-27_DifferentiateInstructionESL_081415.pdf
http://journals.library.wisc.edu/index.php/wej/article/viewFile/378/479

References

Alfaro, C., Durán, R., Hunt, A., & Aragón, M. J. (2014). Steps toward unifying dual language programs, common core state standards, and critical pedagogy: Oportunidades, Estrategias y Retos. *Association of Mexican American Educators Journal, 8*(2).

Altun, A. & Cakan, M. (2006). Undergraduate students' academic achievement, field dependent/independent cognitive styles and attitude toward computers. *Journal of Educational Technology and Society, 9*(1), 289.

Angeli, C. & Valanides, N. (2004). Examining the effects of text-only and text-and-visual instructional materials on the achievement of field-dependent and field-independent learners during problem-solving with modeling software. *Educational Technology Research and Development, 52*(4), 23–36.

Banks, J. A. & Banks, C. A. M. (2009). *Multicultural education: Issues and perspectives.* John Wiley & Sons.

Chao, L., Huang, J., & Li, A. (2003). A study of field independence versus field dependence of school teachers and university students in mathematics. *Perceptual and motor skills, 97*(3), 873–876.

DeTure, M. (2004). Cognitive style and self-efficacy: Predicting student success in online distance education. *American Journal of Distance Education, 18*(1), 21–38.

Dunn, R. & Griggs, S. (2003). Synthesis of the Dunn and Dunn learning styles model research: who, what, when, where and so what–the Dunn and Dunn learning styles model and its theoretical cornerstone. *St. John's University, New York.*

Gardner, H. (1999). Intelligence reframed: Multiple Intelligences for the 21st century. New York, NY: Basic Books.

Gardner, H. E. (2008). *Multiple intelligences: New horizons in theory and practice.* Basic books.

Harry, B. & Klingner, J. (2014). *Why are so many minority students in special education?* Teachers College Press.

Kolb, A. Y. (2005). *The Kolb learning style inventory—version 3.1 2005 technical specifications.* Boston, MA: Hay Resource Direct, *200,* 72.

Kolb, D. A. (2007). *The Kolb learning style inventory.* Boston, MA: Hay Resources Direct.

Li, J. J., & Su, C. (2007). How face influences consumption. *International Journal of Market Research, 49*(2), 237–256.

Li, Z. X., & Li, S. S. (2008). Research on the relationship between field independence/dependence cognitive style and L2 teaching and learning in China: A Review [J]. *Journal of PLA University of Foreign Languages, 5,* 013.

Mestre, L. (2006). Accommodating diverse learning styles in an online environment. *Reference & user services quarterly, 46*(2), 27–32.

Park, C. C. (2002). Cross-cultural differences in learning styles of secondary English learners. *Bilingual Research Journal, 26*(2), 443–459.

Rentsch, J. R., Small, E. E., & Hanges, P. J. (2008). Cognitions in organizations and teams: What is the meaning of cognitive similarity? In D. B. Smith (Ed.), *LEA's organization and management series. The people make the place: Dynamic linkages between individuals and organizations* (pp. 127–155). New York: Taylor & Francis Group/Lawrence Erlbaum Associates.

Riding, R. & Rayner, S. (2013). *Cognitive styles and learning strategies: Understanding style differences in learning and behavior.* Routledge.

Rita, D. & Dunn, K. (1993). Learning styles/teaching styles: Should they . . . Can they . . . be matched. *Educational leadership.*

Stephens, N. M. & Townsend, S. S. (2015). The norms that drive behavior: Implications for Cultural Mismatch Theory. *Journal of Cross-Cultural Psychology, 46*(10), 1304–1306.

Witkin, H. A., Moore, C. A., Goodenough, D. R., & Cox, P. W. (1975). Field-dependent and field-independent cognitive styles and their educational implications. *ETS Research Report Series, 1975*(2), 1–64.

Zhang, L. F. & Sternberg, R. J. (2002). Thinking styles and teachers' characteristics. *International Journal of Psychology, 37*(1), 3–12.

Zhou, Y., Jindal-Snape, D., Topping, K., & Todman, J. (2008). Theoretical models of culture shock and adaptation in international students in higher education. *Studies in Higher Education, 33*(1), 63–75.

PART 2

THE PERPLEXITY AND COMPLEXITY OF LEARNING ANOTHER LANGUAGE

CHAPTER 5

WHAT TEACHERS NEED TO KNOW ABOUT FIRST AND SECOND LANGUAGE ACQUISITION

Eileen N. Whelan Ariza and Justin White

KEY POINTS

- Learning another language is incredibly difficult.
- Learning to speak another language to converse, and leaning another language to do academics, calculating, math, science, writing, and other things of that nature, are entirely different.
- What you know in one language can help you (or hinder you) in the new language.
- Your native language can confuse your second (or additional language/s) learning but eventually you will overcome the difficulties.
- Learning more than one language can help your brain in numerous ways.

Charlie, a three-year-old boy, exclaimed, "Mommy, the doggie wented round back front." Charlie's mom knew that he was trying to tell her that Tinker, their German shepherd, had gone into the backyard. Charlie created his own verb tense and description of the backyard, even though he had never heard this language before.

Scenario one (mother and child in conversation):

CHILD:	"Mommy, take me a bath."
MOTHER:	"You mean **give** you a bath."
CHILD:	"Yes. Take me a bath."

Scenario two:

MOTHER:	"We have to go to Miami."
CHILD:	"Then after we go to your ami, can we go to my ami too?"

Scenario three:

CHILD:	"I want to wear my Batman jamamas to bed.
MOTHER:	"You mean pajamas."
CHILD:	"Yeah, **jamamas**."

A young man lost his passport overseas. When he went to the U.S. consulate to apply for another, the consul wanted to test his cultural knowledge to see if he was really an American. Instead of asking him to recite the Pledge of Allegiance or to sing the U.S. anthem, the Consul asked him one question. He told the young man to finish this sentence: "M&Ms melt in your mouth . . ." The young man answered correctly, "Not in your hand," thus proving that he indeed was from the United States.

> Lina, my niece from Colombia, was working at a store on Martha's Vineyard Island when a customer asked her, "Is this a dry town?" Lina answered, "No, the beach is just down the street." (He was asking if they serve alcohol, as some towns do not sell alcohol (aka: "dry.").) Lina took him literally and was pointing out where the ocean was.)

Researchers used to believe that children learned their first language by listening and repeating what adults said. These beliefs are based on a **behaviorist theory**, made famous by Skinner (1957; Gleason & Weintraub; 1978; Staddon, 2014) who argued that language learning is culturally determined and is a behavior learned by imitation of adult speech. Skinner based his *behaviorist* theory of language acquisition on the current wave in psychology at the time, which included *operant conditioning*. You may recall learning about the physiologist, Ivan Pavlov, who is most known for his experiments with dogs and stimuli. The experiments he conducted showed how dogs were trained to expect some sort of reward (such as food) when they heard a bell "ding" and they would salivate when hearing the bell even if there was no food in sight. Language researchers believed that this type of behavioral training was the same for children learning languages; when they imitated adults, they got attention, people cheered, smiled, clapped, waved, tickled, and they received all other sorts of positive feedback, and because of that, children kept imitating adults. Behaviorists thought that language was actually acquired through this imitation.

As we know, children say many words and verb forms that adults around them do not use (i.e., 'wented'). Therefore, there came a point at which linguists questioned the belief that children merely imitated adult speech because they observed children producing novel utterances (sentences) they could not possibly have heard before. (See the end of this chapter for more scenarios.) In fact, there is even a saying coined by television personality Art Linkletter that states "kids say the darndest things," which alludes to this phenomenon.

The Language Acquisition Device (LAD) (Chomsky, 1979)

In 1979, a **nativist** theorist named Noam Chomsky offered an explanation that accounts for children's creative language use. Chomsky claimed that children are born with a basic innate language learning capacity, called the Language Acquisition Device (LAD) (Krashen, 1987; Komarova & Nowak, 2001). The LAD is often thought of as a type of prewiring in the brain that makes us, from birth, capable of learning any language that we are exposed to. Chomsky's theory of *Universal Grammar* (Chomsky, 1998; Cook, & Newson, 2014; Yang, 2004) espoused that all languages in the world operate on one set of rules, which he referred to as principles. Children are born with these codes in their (brain): LAD. According to this theory, all languages abide by these principles. Of course there are differences among languages, but these differences are explained by that fact that these rules have sub-rules and languages can differ in the sub-rules that apply. These sub-rules are referred to as parameters. Again, these principles account for all of the possible variations of languages and although these principles apply to all languages in the world, children begin to set parameters that restrict what is possible in the language that is around them. Let's draw a loose analogy; we can say that it's like going to a Subway restaurant for a sandwich. You can choose from all kinds of types of sandwiches (which would be the "principles") but you are going to pick and choose based on how you want your sandwich to be, so, the "fixins" you choose would be the parameters. The analogy is loose, but I think you get the idea; all the possibilities are there, you just choose what you want your sandwich (language) to be like. The Universal Grammar theory posits that based on whatever language the children are exposed to (English, Spanish, Swahili, etc.), they begin to set the specific parameters to how this particular language functions (i.e., what is linguistically possible and what is not possible). It is not possible (correct, that is) in English to say "Red is the barn." The child might mistake the barn for a house and say, "The house is red." But instinctively the child will never say, "Red is the house."

As we know, children don't *choose* the language they want to acquire (unlike in a sandwich shop) as their native language; they acquire the one that is around them as children. Imagine a child with Russian-speaking caretakers, only having been exposed to Russian, saying, "you know what, I don't want to grow up speaking Russian, even though that is the only language around me. I think I want to be a native French speaker' and then acquiring French instead. This does not happen. In turn, the language the child is exposed to will determine what language is acquired. According to Chomsky, this acquisition takes place via the "LAD" using the general principles of how languages function and setting the parameters of the specific language in their environment. As shown in the scenarios at the end of the chapter, the children do not respond to error correction, but correct themselves in their own developmental time frame, as if it were an internal syllabus. The nativist and behaviorist theories are compared and contrasted in Figure 5.1.

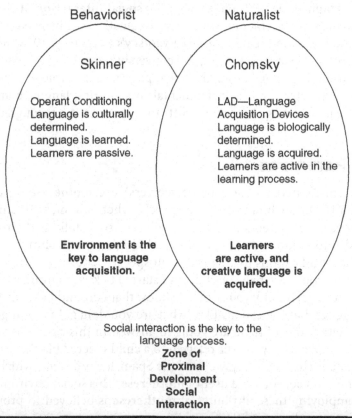

Figure 5.1 Theory Comparison Chart (Ariza, 2002)

Early Speech

If we look at how children start to speak, we can see that crying, cooing, and babbling are the first signs of speech because their purpose is to communicate a message. During the first stages in a child's life, they are trying out their vocal apparatus and preparing themselves for a lifetime of language production. Eventually, children begin to produce one-and two-word utterances like "Mommy go," "Doggy bye bye." They begin producing negative sentences by adding "no" to an utterance as in, "Mommy no go." Children start forming questions by incorporating rising intonation like, "Baby sleep?" Children progress naturally through these developmental stages and as time goes by, they actively construct more advanced speech forms. The language acquisition process develops in predictable stages at the children's own speed, but their understanding is usually grounded within the immediate context of their environment. Some children progress through these stages more quickly than others and although the rate at which children acquire language may vary from child to child, the route of acquisition remains the same. In other words, children follow the same developmental sequence in acquisition even though the speed at which they progress from one developmental stage to another may differ slightly.

Have you ever seen a child's first utterance include the passive tense (e.g. The cookie *was eaten* by the dog.) or the present perfect (e.g. I *have eaten*)? No, of course not, these types of grammatical forms appear much later in a child's repertoire of possibilities and they have to go through the developmental stages in order to get to that level. We are witnesses to this phenomenon when we see that some children start speaking "sooner" and seem to be using "more advanced" constructions. Eventually, all children will reach the same stages, however, some get there more quickly than others.

Another theory of language acquisition is called the **social interactionist theory**; which claims that children develop language by interacting with more linguistically advanced adults in a give and take interface. It reflects the Russian psychologist Lev Vygotsky's (Vygotsky, 1978) ideas primarily that children play an active role in their own learning by conversing, receiving a response, and then speaking again. The child's surrounding linguistic environment plays a central role in how they acquire language. According to this theory, interaction is instrumental in acquiring language and because humans are social creatures and we use language to communicate to each other, it is through interaction that we learn language.

Motherese or Parentese

In some cultures, a child's parents (or other caregivers) use *motherese* (also known as *parentese*, child-directed speech [CDS] or infant-directed speech) when talking with children. This is a certain type of modified speech that parents or other caregivers use to talk to their children and it usually includes exaggerated intonation, slower rate of speech, higher pitch, shortened and simplified words among other types of modifications to a typical adult speech pattern.

Think of the last time you saw a baby or child and started talking to him or her. Did you instinctively change your tone of voice, or simplify your words? I know that I do, and I usually talk to puppies the same way; my voice gets higher, I ask questions like "what are you doin'?" "are you going to the park?" even though I know that neither one of them are going to answer. In this case, I use a type of child-directed speech. Or another example: have you ever referred to a child's sacred blanket as a "*bankey*" or the word that the child has created? (In our family, we used the Spanish word "*tete*" which was short for *tetero,* or a baby bottle, in Spanish.) If so, you are a user of **motherese**. This social environment of speech between a parent and child employing these attributes of **motherese** is believed to promote active negotiation of meaning as they interact. For example, the child sees that you have juice in your hand and she says "*wawa*." Negotiation of meaning happens when you say "no, not *wawa*, juice."

These same types of conversational strategies can be seen between a native and non-native speaker (*foreigner talk*) as they use language and paralinguistic devices (i.e., nonverbal elements such as body posture, hand gestures, and facial expressions) intentionally to promote meaning. Vygotsky (1962, 1978) describes this type of development as the *zone of proximal development* (ZPD), which infers that what learners can accomplish today with help, they can do alone (without help) tomorrow. By using strategies and materials that target students' individual zones of proximal development, teachers can move them from their actual developmental level to their potential developmental level. An example of this expansion is when a child makes a simple statement, such as "*Doggie.*" The mother expands the statement by saying, "Yes, see the doggie. What a big doggie! What does the doggie say? Does the doggie say 'Woof, woof'?" Although some cognitive theorists (Bialystock, 1978; Gredler, 2012; McLaughlin, 1980) maintain that Vygotsky's ideas are too simplistic, Krashen (1981) incorporated a similar hypothesis into his theory of second language acquisition, which is discussed in more depth later.

Theories of Second Language Acquisition

Throughout the years, many theories of language acquisition have produced information and conjecture about how we learn language. This chapter will explore some of the first and longstanding theories that have developed, and we have tried to simplify some ideas that could be very complex.

Learning a language is complex and includes more issues than just cognitive functions. There are numerous factors influencing language acquisition. One of the early language researchers, Stephen Krashen, developed ideas about factors that contribute to language acquisition including age, motivation, comprehensible input (language information that is understood), affective conditions (emotional states), and the methods used in teaching and learning.

However, Swain (1993, 2005) made a great point by proclaiming that **output** (when the learner was forced to produce language) was necessary for language learners to recognize what they do or do not know. Swain said this evidence would motivate the learner to realize what the learning gap really is. So input must be clear and comprehensible, but output must be the language practice that will teach the language learners what they know, and what they have to work on.

As a second language learner myself, I experienced this personally when I first went to Mexico to study Spanish. I had studied Spanish for about 10 months in the United States and thought I was quite proficient until I had to make a phone call. I asked for my friend, Victor, and the answer I received was totally unintelligible to me. His mother answered, "No se encuentra." I had no idea what that meant, because I had learned, "No esta." I quickly realized that I could not speak Spanish and the rest of my studies did not get any easier as I went along. It has taken me years to become proficient.

Krashen's Monitor Model

Krashen's (1978) theory of second language acquisition proposes five hypotheses (Figure 5.2):

> **Acquisition versus Learning Hypothesis** (learning the language naturally versus actively studying)
> **Natural Order Hypothesis** (language functions are learned in a specific order, though not at the same pace for everyone)

Acquisition versus Learning Hypothesis	Learning the language naturally versus actively studying.
Natural Order Hypothesis	Language functions are learned in a specific order, though not at the same pace for everyone
Monitor Hypothesis	A natural editor within ourselves that self corrects when we make mistakes
Affective Filter Hypothesis	The emotional level of the learner must be positive and free of stress and anxiety
Input Hypothesis	This concept is also known as (i + 1) theory, i being the input (language data that learners are exposed to that carries a message) and (+1) being the message a bit beyond the learner's level of language proficiency (Krashen, 1981).

Figure 5.2 Krashen's Model

The **Monitor Hypothesis** (a natural editor within ourselves that self corrects when we make mistakes)

The **Affective Filter Hypothesis** (the emotional level of the learner must be in positive and free of stress and anxiety)

> The **Input Hypothesis.** This concept is also known as (i + 1) theory, i being the input (language data that learners are exposed to that carries a message) and (+ 1) being the message a bit beyond the learner's level of language proficiency (Krashen, 1981).

Krashen argues that creating comprehensible input that is slightly challenging (one level beyond learners' current level) will push the learner further on the language development continuum. With this comprehensive theory in mind, Krashen and Terrell created the Natural Approach for learning a second language. As a result of their work, the direction of classroom teaching has been altered to include methods that aim to provide comprehensible input for second language learners and promote acquisition of the language.

The chart below might make the Krashen hypotheses clearer.

Implications of Krashen's Work for Classroom Learning

According to Krashen's theory, classroom instruction contributes to acquisition only if it provides *comprehensible (understandable) input* that entices students' interest. (Students must understand what they are hearing.) Optimal input in the classroom is especially important for students who live in literacy-deprived environments in which they may not have other opportunities for exposure to input (i.e., newspaper, books, TV, radio). Listed below are some implications arising from each of Krashen's hypotheses:

> **Drill and practice promote learning, while communication promotes acquisition.**

> **The *Acquisition Versus Learning* hypothesis implies that learners create two systems of language: a learned system and an acquired system.**

The language system consists of prescriptive (taught) grammar rules that are created by instruction about how language works. For example, instruction of Spanish language tenses, such as "the preterite (past) is formed by adding the following endings," or "the subjunctive is used under the following conditions . . .", are examples of instruction that contribute to learning the system of language. On the other hand, learners create an *acquired* system of language via exposure to input, much like how children create their language system. The acquired system, or acquiring the language naturally, does not consist of explanations of rules.

(Take the example of the phrase: *might as well*. How can you explain what this means? Well, perhaps people can only learn it by hearing it in context again and again, without having a precise definition. Personally, I would not know how to explain this expression with just one word.)

According to Krashen, when you talk about *learning* the language, it refers to picking up the language by studying it.

The *acquired* system consists of examples and uses of how the language is formed just by being around it.

Have you ever asked a native speaker when to use a certain grammatical point, such as the subjunctive (e.g., If I were . . . I wish I were . . .) and gotten the answer, "Uh, what's the subjunctive?' That is because they have an *acquired* system of language, whereas if you ask learners in a language class, likely they will respond with a lengthy discussion of a set of grammar rules. This is information created by a *learned* system.

> **Grammar need not be the center of instruction. Acquisition of correct language will evolve gradually and naturally within the school curriculum.**

> **The *Natural Order Hypothesis* suggests that the acquisition of grammatical structures takes place in a predictable order based on developmental stages.**

Although, some students will acquire structures faster than others, they still all move through the same stages, just at different rates. Take, for example, the English present-tense third-person "s"; it is one of the first grammatical structures to be taught, but yet one of the last to be acquired with proficiency for some learners (e.g., the child says "he go" instead of "he goes").

> The *Input Hypothesis* implies that when learners are exposed to language that is both at their current level of comprehension and one level above ($i + 1$), maximum language acquisition takes place.

Input is made more comprehensible when the teacher uses scaffolding (learning support) through visuals, realia, graphic organizers, less complex language structures, modifying curriculum, paraphrasing, clear and slower pronunciation, buddy tutoring, and so forth. Krashen also posits that just as very young children take time before they produce any verbal output, second language learners go through a silent stage. Teachers should be patient with students who are still in their silent period because "real language acquisition develops slowly, and speaking skills emerge significantly later than listening skills, even when conditions are perfect" (Krashen, 1982, p. 7).

> *The Monitor Hypothesis refers to an error-correcting mechanism in the brain that edits the language learners' own utterances by using their grammar rules*

The function of the monitor is to help learners to edit their language production with focus on correct form, but this can only occur when the learner explicitly knows the correct rules of the language. In other words, if the student does not know the correct grammar system, then they don't have anything with which to monitor. This type of self-correction and monitoring serves a different function from that of error correction in the forms of feedback by teachers and native speakers. Feedback from these members of the speech community may not have an effect on students' language skills until the learner is developmentally ready. In this vein, because errors are a part of the natural order of acquisition, second language teachers should not overemphasize them during instruction. To try to correct every error is the fastest way to impede a learner's natural inclination to communicate. Remember, the individual is already competent in his or her native language and excessive error correction may inadvertently make the learner feel stupid because of one's inability to communicate and it can be demoralizing. For children, the correction won't be internalized until they are ready to learn it, no matter what you do.

At the point where learners are thinking about what they are saying instead of how they are saying it, mistakes will be made, even though the learner really knows the correct words (e.g., saying He instead of She, when the person really knows the difference).

> *The Affective Filter Hypothesis means that the learner must feel secure and "unthreatened" in the learning environment.*

When stress and anxiety levels rise in the classroom, so does the *affective filter*, which can impede language learning. An optimal learning environment keeps learners' affective filters low so that acquisition can be maximized. Affective filters can be lowered when teachers identify and include topics with which students can relate positively, sustain their interest, and engage in naturally. A collaborative and noncompetitive environment is ideal for students to receive input and to produce language output (Krashen & Terrell, 1983). Language teachers should strive to motivate students, and include nonthreatening practices that will lessen their anxiety. As mentioned previously, the learner will "mangle" the new language until he or she "dominates" it; allow that to happen since it is a natural process.

Understanding Social Language and Academic Language

I learned my second language relatively late in life, so I have experienced how painful the process of language learning can be for an adult. As a bilingual teacher of ELs and a teacher educator, I still learn from my students, from the teachers I train, and from reading new books in the field. When I was where you may be now, first learning the difference between **Basic Interpersonal Communication Skills (BICS,** or social language) and **Cognitive Academic Language Proficiency (CALP,** or academic language) (Cummins, 1981b), it was an epiphany for me. At this stage in my career, and at the time already a bilingual/ESOL teacher, I was one of those teachers who asked, "This child speaks perfect English; why is he in ESOL?" Understanding the reasons why students should not be advanced from the transitional bilingual class to the mainstream class answered many of my questions. Simply, it is better to learn as much as possible in the native (home or heritage) language because then you can just transfer the knowledge to the new language instead of trying to learn the concept through the new language.

Many teachers make what appears to be the logical decision of trying to push their English learners into more advanced classes, which may prove to be a mistake due to their unawareness of these important language differences. It is because these students have a solid foundation in social language (and the younger they are, the more native-like they may sound), teachers are under the impression that the students know more English than they actually do and that they are capable of performing tasks that they are actually not able execute successfully. Although these learners might be accomplished (social) speakers, sound native-like, and be able to successfully complete the cognitively undemanding tasks, academically they might be years behind the native speakers. This lag may be explained by weak or interrupted schooling in the students' home countries, by months of not comprehending academic instruction delivered in English, or by the combination of both factors (Freeman, Freeman, & Mercuri, 2002).

Before I became a bilingual/ESOL teacher, I did my internship with a wonderful third-grade teacher of a mainstream class. One student had difficulty with his spelling tests and appeared to spell the words phonetically:

- apul (apple)
- skul (school)
- bar (bare)

Beginning writers commonly do what is called Inventive Spelling, but this situation was odd because the student was a bright third grader who excelled in many tasks. My cooperating teacher was baffled and she firmly believed the boy had some sort of disability attributable to these spellings. It suddenly dawned on me that maybe he spoke Spanish. So, I asked him in Spanish if he spoke Spanish at home. He answered, "Sí. Señora. Mis papás son de Puerto Rico." ("Yes, ma'am. My parents are from Puerto Rico.") Gabriel's parents spoke perfect English and no indication of a second language background was noted in his cumulative folder. Just as it was evident in this case, it is possible that teachers (including yourselves) will have second-language learners in their classes without even realizing it. Again, when children learn languages early in life, they are able to speak with accents that are native sounding and display no discernible signs that they speak another language at home. The lesson to be learned is that accent-free speech is not an indicator that a child is a monolingual or native English speaker. The assumption that children have a "critical period" (Lennenberg, 1974) of language learning that enables them to gain native-like fluency before puberty is often a cause for mistaking it for academic ability in the second language.

To reiterate, learning about Cummins's work on the distinction between social language and academic language was pivotal for me as an educator. In one of Cummins' studies (1984), they looked at standardized scores of ELs and compared them to native English speakers. He found that the ELs acquired social English within about two years while their acquisition of academic language took five to seven years. This difference in learning rates of social language and academic language may be influential in the child's learning experience in school. Consider a child that has no noticeable accent and is progressing with his or her social language skills at a normal rate. Now, hypothetically pair this child with a teacher not aware of the differences in learning rates of these two distinct types of English. If the teacher is not aware of this distinction and assumes that this child is developmentally (regarding language) the same as native speakers, what do you think he or she would assume is the "problem" with the child if they begin to demonstrate poor academic performance? Likely they would suspect that the child has a learning disability. Once aware of these distinctions, teachers are better prepared to make these preliminary assessments. Remember, when the child is young enough to learn the language without an accent, the teacher may never even suspect the student might have a problem with the language.

> Cummins (1984) later developed a theoretical framework titled the **Common Underlying Proficiency (CUP)**.

The CUP encompasses both the BICS and CALP ideas and assumes that knowledge and literacy skills learned in the native language will transfer to the target language. This is the foundation for the main argument for bilingual education: When a learner receives academic knowledge in the first language, it can be transferred to the second language. The CUP theory is contrasted with what is referred to as the Separate Underlying Proficiency (SUP) theory, which posits that this transfer would not take place. According to the CUP, if a student has a strong academic foundation in a native language, it is accepted that the transfer of knowledge to the second language is more a question of language learning than of knowledge learning (Figure 5.3). With that in mind, a child who has learned to read in his or her native language already understands the concept of reading. The difficulties they encounter when learning to read in their second language are attributable to fact that the texts are in their second language. For these children, the concept of deciphering print is already understood; only the new language needs to be learned. This is a particularly difficult road for those students for whom this language-based issue is never addressed as such. In fact, Cummins' idea of Common Underlying Proficiency also accounts for why an international high school student with a strong academic background from the native country might fare better academically in an American school than a second language learner who was brought up in the United States. Although the U.S. student will sound more "American," the foreign student could conceivably achieve a higher level of academic success.

Picture an iceberg and the top half of the iceberg shows what teachers can see. Underneath the bottom half of the pyramid is the information the student has, but we cannot see. Now underneath the pyramid there may be an intersection of what the student knows in the native language, and that can be transferred into the second language. That is considered the CUP, or common underlying proficiency, which can transfer from the first language to the other.

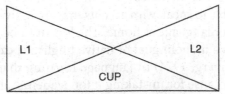

CUP (Common Underlying Proficiency)
It is the base of knowledge that the student can transfer to English. When you have knowledge in the L1 and that knowledge can transfer into L2, this is CUP.

Figure 5.3 Comparison of Social language, Academic language, and the Common Underlying Proficiency CUP (adapted from Cummins' theory, 1984)

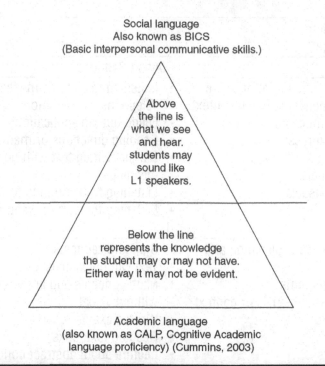

Social language
Also known as BICS
(Basic interpersonal communicative skills.)

Above
the line is
what we see
and hear.
students may
sound like
L1 speakers.

Below the line
represents the knowledge
the student may or may not have.
Either way it may not be evident.

Academic language
(also known as CALP, Cognitive Academic
language proficiency) (Cummins, 2003)

Figure 5.4

Additive bilingualism versus subtractive bilingualism (Cummins, 1994):

Cummins encourages us to continue to develop the additive bilingualism where the second language is being taught. We can't let the first language diminish as we grow the additional language (1994), which is called subtractive bilingualism.

Content Objectives in Language Learning

Cummins tried to show an Figure form (in quadrants) of what he meant by academic and social language. See the picture of the quadrant below in Figure 5.5.

Quadrant A of Figure 5.4 list tasks that are simple, and the English learner can use context to determine meaning by using paralinguistic cues such as facial expressions, hand gestures, and other forms of nonverbal behavior.

If an English learner (EL) cannot understand the words themselves or deduce meaning based on context, the speaker can modify or repeat the utterance.

Cognitively Undemanding (BICS) Social Language	
Context Embedded	Context Reduced
<ul><li>Talking on the playground or at playtime</li><li>Social face-to-face conversation in context</li><li>Follow directions if modeled</li><li>Understand facial expressions</li><li>Reading or following a map with comprehensible visuals</li><li>Telling stories with visuals</li></ul> A	<ul><li>Listening to a phone message</li><li>Telephone conversation</li><li>Filling out job applications with no model to follow</li><li>Reading directions or menus without illustrations</li><li>Simple written text with no visuals to enhance meaning</li><li>Listening to recordings for informational purposes</li><li>Listening to news or weather with no context clues</li></ul> B
<ul><li>Taking notes with visual explanation and support</li><li>Project-based assignments</li><li>Verbal instructions with visuals or context clues</li><li>Demonstrations</li><li>Science experiments</li><li>Use manipulatives to solve math problems</li></ul> C	<ul><li>Standardized tests</li><li>Text without visuals</li><li>Math concepts and applications (word problems without visuals)</li><li>Written exams</li><li>Reading textbooks</li><li>Lecture about abstract concepts with no visuals</li></ul> D
Cognitively Demanding (CALP) Academic Language	

Figure 5.5 Social and Academic Language

Source: Adapted from Cummins (1981b)

> Quadrant B includes a different type of situation, ones in which the EL has no way to negotiate meaning from the context even though the tasks are cognitively simple. In these cases, comprehension is more difficult because they cannot rely on the paralinguistic cues to deduce meaning.

Taking a further look, context clues are **embedded** in quadrant A but not evident in quadrant B.

For the situations in quadrant A, social conversation can take place, but students' true academic ability cannot be determined because they sound as if they possess proficient language skills.

Compound this social conversation ability with a native-like accent and the teacher has no idea of the student's true academic skill level. Take, for example, a student who has had exposure to English before puberty and has a native-sounding English-speaking accent. The teacher will assume that the student has the same language abilities and background knowledge that the native English speaker possesses. If the student does not have the same abilities and proficiency, the teacher will have no idea that the student needs more academic scaffolding for successful instruction to take place.

In quadrant C, notice that the tasks involve more advanced cognitive abilities, but context clues are embedded with the task, making comprehension clear. Students are able to perform the academic tasks because of visual and graphic scaffolding.

In quadrant D, no context clues are embedded within the activities; students will begin to fail because they lack the academic language necessary to complete the academic task. The longer they are in school, the more they fall behind; these particular types of students are long-term English learners who are at a high risk of failing and dropping out of school. This phenomenon is very common with English learners who go through the U.S. school systems (Thomas & Collier, 2002).

The ideal for teachers is to have more visuals and context-embedded materials with in the cognitive demanding realm. Please see quadrant C. This is the goal so students can receive rigorous academic content with comprehensible input.

With regard to language proficiency, each organization has its own way of determining language proficiency. Figures 5.6 and 5.7 show common designation of the stages of language proficiency.

The American Council of the Teaching of Foreign Languages (ACTFL) (https://www.press.umich.edu/pdf/9780472033041-101AmerCult.pdf) has their own guidelines of language proficiency in "terms of speaking, writing, listening, and reading in real world situations in a spontaneous and non-rehearsed context." 2017, p. 1) For each skill, there are five levels of proficiency:

Preproduction	Silent stage
Early production stage	Six months to one year of English learning
Speech emergence	Beginning speech
Intermediate fluency	Students are able to speak with fluency but will still have errors
Advanced fluency	Students speak quite well and appear to understand most information

Figure 5.6 Stages of Language Proficiency

Distinguished	High	Mid	Low
Superior	High	Mid	Low
Advanced	High	Mid	Low
Intermediate	High	Mid	Low
Novice	High	Mid	Low

Figure 5.7

Additionally, WIDA now has its own set of English language proficiency standards (Bauman, Boals, Cranley, Gottlieb, & Kenyon; 2007; Gottlieb, Cranley, & Cammilleri, 2007) so you can chose which set best represents your students' needs.

Implications of the First Language on the Second

For a classroom teacher, it is important to know how a student learns a language so we can align our teaching according to the developmental stages of language acquisition. Although you may not know the student's language, if you understand how language is learned, you can adjust and correlate your instruction to the student's level of proficiency. Often you will hear, "All you have to do is immerse yourself in the language, and you will just pick it up." If that is true, I can say the following words to you all day, and you should eventually understand them.

> Круговорот воды в природе является одним из грандиозных процессов на поверхности земного шара. Вода находится в постоянном движении. Испаряясь с поверхности водоемов, почвы, растений, вода накапливается в атмосфере. Рано или поздно, она выпадает в виде осадков, пополняя запасы в океанах реках, озерах и т.п. Таким образом, количество воды на земле не1 меняется—она только меняет свои формы—это и есть кругов орот воды в природе.

According to the submersion theory, you should be able to understand it now, especially after hearing it several times. I could also put this concept in another written form, which you might be able to understand better if you are literate. Try reading this:

> Известно, что 90% всех испарений воды поставляют океаны. Испарение также происходит в преснов одных озерах и реках. Водянои пар, поднимаясь в атмосферу, конденсируется в облаках и возвращается на землю в виде осадков. Осадки—это дождь, снег и град. Когда выпадают осадки, вода пополняет водоемы, проникая через почву, питает подземные воды земли. В итоге, вода вновь возвращается в океан речным и подземным стоком. Растения, питаясь дождевой и грунтовой водой, затем листьями выделяют воду в атмосферу в виде пара. Так продолжается круговорот воды в природе.

Is there anything in the above text that gives you a clue to what is being said? Unless you read Russian, you probably will not understand any of the above text no matter how many times I read it to you. According to Krashen (1981), unless it is accompanied by comprehensible input, it does not matter how many times you hear a message in another language. If you hear someone talking "at" you, it is just noise. Once there is something to connect meaning to the words, we can begin to learn the language. Babies are immersed in the sounds of their native languages for at least a year before they are expected to speak. Yet the newcomer to a language is expected to repeat words without being given the chance to internalize the sounds.

Language researchers such as Fillmore and Snow (2000) believe that teachers who know educational linguistics, that is, how language impacts teaching and learning, will make a greater impact on the learning achievement of English learners. This idea makes sense because the teacher will understand why the English learner is having difficulty, and she or he will be better prepared to engage in proactive teaching, thus facilitating literacy development.

Morphology	the study of word formation
Syntax	refers to the word order in a language
Semantics	the study of meaning, words, and phrases
Phonology	the study of the sound system of a language
Pragmatics	the study of how people use language within a certain context and why people use language in a particular way

Figure 5.8 Definitions of Language Functions

> **Basics of Language Components: Morphology, Syntax, Semantics, Phonology, Pragmatics: A mini course**

Following is a short summation of the basics of language characteristics or functions. If you were interested in further study of TESOL, each of the following categories would be an individual course. However, I believe you need to know at least the basics of language acquisition so I have written brief definitions of each component (Figure 5.8).

Morphology

Morphology is the study of word formation. Certain languages do not have the same word tenses or words that denote gender. For example, in Haitian Creole "he" might be used to refer to a female or an inanimate object because "she" does not exist. The English verb to be in "to be hungry" is conjugated "I am hungry," "You are hungry," and so forth. In Haitian Creole, the morpheme (smallest unit of meaning) "be" is not utilized, and the Creole speaker would say, "I hungry," instead of "I am hungry."

In my (Eileen) experience teaching English as a new language, one of the most difficult concepts for students to learn is how we use "do" in all its forms. Picture the conversation between two native speakers:

Do you **do** your homework?

Yes, I **do do** my homework.

Do you really?

Yes, I **do**.

No, you **don't**.

I **do** so.

You **didn't do** it last night.

I **did do** it last night. I just didn't do it the night before.

Imagine trying to explain how to use "do" correctly. Did you ever wonder how English-speaking children pick this up naturally? Test your English learners to see how much they know about the usage of "do" by asking them, "Ask me what I did on my birthday last year." Chances are, they will give you an answer like this, "What you did on your birthday last year?" The native speaker will instinctively ask, "What did you do on your birthday last year?"

Another problem across English morphology is the use of prepositions. In Spanish, for example, the word en means "in," "on," "at," and "inside." Trying to decipher which preposition is the correct one to use in English takes a long time, especially with such nuances as "**in** the morning" but "**on** Monday morning." Additionally, in French, Spanish, and some other languages, the same verb is used for "to make" and/or "to do." The result of this confusion winds up with the student saying, "I made my homework."

Syntax

Syntax refers to the word order in a language. In English, the writer or speaker must be clear to express what he or she really wants to say. In every language, a word pattern exists. In English it is subject, verb, object (SVO): For example, *John has a black car*. In a language such as Spanish, this sentence is not stated in the same order. The order would be translated to *John has a car black*, or *Juan tiene un carro negro*. Additionally, English speakers must avoid ambiguity within sentences, as shown in the following examples:

Dr. Weaver inspects documents in the Department of Education.
There is nothing odd about the number of students who fail.
John and Bob took the exam, but he failed.
To be served shirts must be worn.
The boys fed the snakes rabbits and mice.

And my personal favorite:

Woman, without her, man is nothing. (By changing the punctuation, the meaning changes.)
Woman, without her man, is nothing.

Semantics

Semantics is the study of meaning, words, and phrases. The idea of semantics is complex to a native speaker, but can be confounding to a non-native English speaker. The new language learner needs "the appropriate cultural knowledge to process language that contains special connotative meanings, idiomatic expressions, and ambiguous sentences, as well as the relevant real-world knowledge to comprehend messages in a second language" (Ariza, Morales-Jones, Yahya, & Zainuddin, 2002, p. 89). Words, idioms, or metaphors hold special meaning for each culture. If the teacher says, "It looks like we're not in Kansas anymore, Toto," only the person who is familiar with the Wizard of Oz is going to relate to the true meaning of this phrase. How many other expressions do we use that are culturally pertinent that an outsider may not understand? "Let me say this about that . . . I am not a crook" (former President Richard Nixon). "Read my lips . . . no new taxes" (former president George Bush). We get "paid under the table," driven "up a wall," and give someone a "piece of my mind." How many non-native speakers can finish this: "Jack fell down and broke his _____"? What do we mean by saying, "It's not over til the fat lady sings"? Would a non-native speaker know these phrases? Would a younger person know these phrases? Watch a movie such as *Good Morning, Vietnam* with a group of students. Older students who lived through that era will laugh hysterically in places the younger ones will not, because the older ones have background knowledge and schema. Or if you have the opportunity to see a movie in English with subtitles in another language, you will find yourself reacting differently than the non-native-English-speaking audience because your background knowledge gives meaning where simple words will not. Our common knowledge of background meaning is pervasive and colors our understanding whether we realize it or not.

Teachers must be vigilant in their speech and oral instructions to be sure no special, culturally specific, or nonliteral meanings are necessary for understanding. This attention to nonliteral significance must also include instructional materials.

Always ask yourself if the meanings of the topics are perfectly clear. Will your student understand that "lid" is another word for "top or cover"? Some of our native English speakers won't even know that. What about "teacup and saucer"? Maybe they use a mug. Language use also varies depending on the geographical location within the United States and in some cases, the same object is referred to with entirely different words. For example, "garbanzo beans" and "chick peas" are the same food; they only differ with words used to refer to them. What word do you use to refer to the gaseous refreshment drink available at fast-food restaurants? Do you call it "soda," "pop," "soda-pop," "cola," "coke," or even "tonic"? These terms vary in their use among regional dialects. In some cases, words may be common in certain regions and unfamiliar in others. Let's look at the uses of the following words:

> *a fire escape on a city building in New York* (the stairs on the side of the building that can be accessed by the windows),
> *tonic* (soda or soft drinks in Boston),
> *sleet* (hard, frozen snow falling in very small pellets),
> *lanai* (a porch in Hawaii),
> *porch* (the landing outside the front or back door of a house such as those found in New England),
> *hearth* (the flat surface in front of a fireplace),
> *basement* (the underground room in a house),
> *attic* (the room or space in the highest part of a house),
> *dungarees* (jeans),
> *cobbler* (one who fixes shoes or a dessert made with fruit),
> *bubbler* (water fountain),
> *Florida room* (a sitting room in a house that is sunny and usually faces the outside),
> *mudroom* (the first small room you walk into in a house located in a state with snowy or inclement weather, where you will take off your boots or shoes before entering the house), and
> *dumbwaiter* (a small elevator within a wall that you utilize with a pulley to deliver dishes, trays, etc., between floors of a house).

These words are all culturally pertinent, and without prior knowledge, you or your students (both native and non-native English speaking) will not know what they mean. Imagine an assignment such as this:

Write about what the cobbler did after he went to the bubbler in front of the mudroom. Without knowing the meanings behind these words, the student is set up to fail.

Phonology

Phonology is the study of the sound system of a language. The English pronunciation of learners will be imperfect because the sound system of the first language gets in the way of the second language. Unless the person has learned English at an early age and has no accent, the new English speaker will approximate the sounds that are the closest to the native language. The speaker can neither "hear" nor "form" the same exact sound because it does not exist in the native language. For example, in Spanish *B* and *V* are pronounced the same. The speaker can be understood but still can get into linguistic trouble. Imagine the Spanish speaker saying, "It is hard for me to be in this class because I really have trouble with my bowels," when he really means "vowels." Stress and pitch are also included in this troublesome area. One of my students tried to tell me he was "unique" but he stressed the first part of the word, so he really said "eunuch." He was quite embarrassed when I explained what a eunuch was.

Pragmatics

Pragmatics is the study of how people use language within a certain context and why people use language in a particular way. Would you approach your minister, the Reverend John Simmons, with "Yo Rev"? If we apply for a job, we dress as nicely as we can and put our best foot forward. When we are asked what our weaknesses are, we probably will not tell them that we are lazy, even if we are. We know what the employer is looking for, and it is probably not a lazy employee. We know we need to impress the interviewer, and we usually learn how to do this within our U.S. cultural experience. If people from other cultures (such as Asian societies that encourage humility) were asked questions such as the above, they would be modest and self-effacing. Americans are trained and encouraged to promote themselves, whereas the humble person might be perceived as insecure or inexperienced. These are culturally learned behaviors that work in one culture but are incorrect behaviors in another. Picture these verbal scenarios, and decide where they occur:

- ❏ How many in your party?
- ❏ For here or "tago"?
- ❏ Will that be thin, thick, or traditional?
- ❏ Regular or black?
- ❏ One lump or two?
- ❏ Paper or plastic?
- ❏ Say, "aaahhh."

Answers:

- ❏ Seating in a restaurant.
- ❏ "Will you be eating your food at the restaurant or do you want to take it out?"
- ❏ "Do you want your pizza with thin, thick (stuffed with cheese), or traditional crust?"
- ❏ "Do you want cream in your coffee or would you like it black?"
- ❏ "Do you want one or two lumps or sugar in your coffee?"
- ❏ "Do you want your groceries in a paper or plastic bag?"
- ❏ The doctor is looking at your throat.

How do you know what these phrases mean? You know because they are all common phrases used in U.S. culture. We learned the right thing to say at the right time because we have grown up within the context and have the background knowledge to know what is correct. If you came from another country, you would have to learn the background to understand this "cultural code."

If a small child hears an obscenity and repeats it, adults may react with shock or embarrassment. The child does not know the meaning of what he has said; he only responds to the listener's reaction. He will probably repeat the obscenity at the most appropriate time, so it looks as if the child knows what he is doing and understands what he is saying. If an English learner says a vulgar word in English, chances are it means only that he or she has heard it within a certain context and has repeated it. It holds no meaning for the non-native speaker; the meaning is held within the native English speaker. In the classroom, a teacher must deal with this situation but take into consideration that the student is only repeating what he or she has heard. This is a pragmatic interference; the newcomer has not learned the pragmatic rules of the target culture.

From culture to culture, pragmatic rules differ. In English, very often we use indirect speech. When the teacher says to the student, "Do you want to sit down now?" it is really not a question but a command couched within a question. But the student might answer, "No," without realizing that it was not a question. The U.S. teacher says to the student who is doing nothing, "Have you finished your work?" Although the question appears to ask if the student has finished, the true implication is that the student should be doing something else to stay on task or to keep busy. Doing nothing in the classroom is **not** a value in the U.S. culture. In another culture, it might be a true question. But until students learn what the teacher really means, cultural miscommunication can occur. In the home culture of the student's country, perhaps the teacher would be praising the student for finishing the assignment.

Bilingual Basics

The newcomer to the class with no English ability at all is at an obvious disadvantage, as is the teacher who must provide the same curriculum for the non-English speaker as well as the fluent speaker. Yet the home language needs to be supported as well, because bilingualism is an asset that should be cherished and is not in any way a liability. Being bilingual has cognitive, social, cultural, and economic advantages (Bialystok, 2011; Engel de Abreu, Cruz-Santos, Tourinho, Martin, & Bialystok, 2012; Hakuta & Pease-Alvarez, 1992; Mehisto & Marsh, 2011). Very often young children lose the ability to speak their native language when they begin schooling in English. Baker (2014), Linton (2004), and Wong-Fillmore (1991) point out that children who do not maintain their bilingualism are in jeopardy of losing the ability to communicate well with their parents and grandparents. Although promoting bilingualism will enhance the richness of their students' lives, teachers should be aware that bilingual individuals may not be balanced bilinguals, and language can be lost quickly if it is not used (Fishman, 1997; Wong-Filmore, 1991). Typically for a bilingual, each language is used in one domain; for example, English in school and the native language at home.

At times, it may look as if a child is limited in both languages (Ariza, 2010). If the child does not use the home language enough, it may stunt the richness of native language knowledge, thereby affecting what could then be transferred to the second language. In effect, if the child does not know the age-appropriate amount of their second language, it may then appear that the child is proficient in neither language. Rest assured, eventually the language will become more balanced. However, it is in the best interest of the child if the teacher does everything possible to help the child maintain the home language. This means exposure and usage in sufficient amounts. As a teacher, you can encourage the parents to speak the native language at home, even if the child seems to resist.

Additionally, it is helpful if teachers (and parents) know that "**code-switching**" is a normal occurrence even though it may appear that students are getting their languages confused. Sometimes students will be speaking English and will interject a word from the native language or vice versa. For example, Spanish speakers might say:

❑ *I am going to averiguar to see if I can go.* (*Averiguar* means "to find out.")
❑ *Yo tengo un part time.* (I have a part-time job.)
❑ *He wants to aprovechar the time and get his homework done now.* (*Aprovechar* means to "take advantage of.")

Code-switching is actually a sophisticated communicative device that follows rules and demonstrates meaning (Auer, 2013; Pease-Alvarez, 1993). Even though code-switching may seem like it is haphazard use of both languages, research offers evidence contrary to popular belief. Research indicates that speakers who employ code-switching actual follow a unique set of rules particular to code-switching.

Language Interferences

Although the native-English-speaking teacher will notice the errors English learners make in speaking and writing, learning *why* they make these mistakes lends great insight into understanding the processes of second language acquisition and to realizing that the students can still make academic gains, even with language errors.

When bilingual learners are acquiring their second language, they may use rules or patterns from their first language. As we know, sometimes this leads to producing a correct utterance free of grammatical errors, and sometimes it does not. When learners transfer from the first language a construction that is also possible in the second language, this is referred to as **positive transfer**. In this case, the teacher will not recognize that a process of transfer has taken place given that the construction was grammatically sound. However, when the student transfers to the second language a construction that is possible in the native language but not possible in the second language, then we say that **negative transfer** has taken place. In this case, the errors we see the new language learner making are traceable to the first language. Knowing that these processes take place will help teachers understand why the first language often interferes with the second language (Table 5.1).

Translanguaging

The last topic I want to talk about in this chapter is translanguaging. When you have multiple language speakers in your classroom, it is helpful to all students to work within their own language groups. Although this obviously makes sense for young learners because they are not feeling so lost, I have found with my older English learners that they are very grateful and relieved to use their home languages as well as English to be able to get through their assignments, talk about their feelings, and even journal. I have used this strategy with younger learners when I wanted to let them know the rules of the classroom, and what expectations and clarifications we made for the classroom instruction. For the older learners, I have been able to use this when I can speak my only other language (Spanish) with them, but when I don't speak their language, I am able to work through the other students who speak that language.

TABLE 5.1 Language Interferences		
Positive Transfer	horrible	horrible
	terrible	terrible
Negative Transfer	Actual	now, currently
	carros rojos	cars reds

Translanguaging is dynamic and allows students the benefit of comprehension. García and Li Wei (2014) note that this is not the same type of code-switching in the sense of using words from each language, but it allows a more in-depth opportunity to understand what is taking place in the new language, through understanding via the home language. We are using both languages with equal status.

In fact, lately I have been using a form of translanguage to help people who have to take exams (TOEFL, or the Florida Teachers Competency Exam). Against all previous advice from people who tell ELs to think in English, I have suggested that the learner read the writing prompt (and hope the vocabulary is understandable), think about how they would approach the writing in their native language, write notes, or bullets, and after thinking about the outline of the essay points, then start writing in English. In this way, the learner only has to think about writing in English instead of trying to organize their thoughts in English. It seems clearer to me to do each task in the individual language.

With this use of original thought, before transferring the writing to discourse in English, the brain is able to think clearly, and focus on one domain, and cognitive task, at a time. We are allowing them to use a more complete repertoire of the language ability.

Translanguaging is potent and it has allowed my students to extend the knowledge they already possess, and then transfer to English (García & Kleifgen, 2010, p 63.) I encourage them to think in their home language, to hear and read in one or both languages, but they can develop project, paper, or essay based on their basic knowledge, and then just work on the mechanics in English.

FINAL POINTS

- One language can interfere with another, but eventually these problems can be sorted out.
- Having knowledge of one language can help you learn another language.
- Students will learn concepts at their own pace, given input that is comprehensible to them.
- Output (practice) of the language allows the leaner to practice, rehearse, and rephrase to make sense of the language.
- There is a huge difference between social language and academic language. Social language is just being able to converse in the new language but academic language proficiency is being able to study and do academic tasks in the academic part of the new language.

Discussion Questions and Activities

1. Create your own 2×2 grid based on Cummins's (1981b) Social and Academic Language theories. Brainstorm individually or with your group and come up with at least four activities that reflect the language abilities depicted in each quadrant.

2. Positive transfer happens when the language learner tries to use a construction from the native language (L1) and successfully applies it to the second language (L2). Negative transfer occurs when the learner tries to relay a word or idea from the first language to the second, but it does not apply. (For example, *embarazada* in Spanish does not mean embarrassed in English. It actually means "pregnant."

   With your group, research and come up with 10 examples of interferences that can happen as a result of language learners applying the principles from their L1 to their L2. Show morphological, phonological, syntactic, and pragmatic examples of positive and negative transfer.

3. Think of examples of idiomatic expressions that might be difficult to translate, such as the examples below:

   I'm going to give you a piece of my mind.

   He drives me up a wall.

   He took off like a "bat out of hell."

   How might these expressions confuse the English learner?

4. Think of a subject area and a topic of a lesson. Create examples of comprehension questions you can ask the new language learner at each proficiency level (you may use your own preferred proficiency level scale, such as WIDA or ACTFL:

   ❑ Preproduction
   ❑ Early production
   ❑ Speech emergence
   ❑ Intermediate fluency
   ❑ Advanced fluency

5. Think of some ways you could translanguage in your own instruction or classroom setting.

6. How can you teach students to draw on their complete language repertoires when learning (not just English language learning)?

Resources

ACTFL (American Council on Teaching Foreign Language)
http://www.actfl.org/advocacy/discover-languages/what-the-research-shows#academic_achievement

Omniglot
http://www.omniglot.com/language/

An introduction to the work of Stephen Krashen
http://esl.fis.edu/teachers/support/krashen.htm

Center for Applied Linguistics
http://esl.fis.edu/teachers/support/krashen.htm

Judie Haynes EverythingESL website
https://ellresourceideas.weebly.com/everything-esl.html

Stephen Krashen
http://www.youtube.com/watch?v=jaCdNTurH1k

Stephen Krashen on Comprehensible Input
http://www.youtube.com/watch?v=a3pipsG_dQk

Video on Krashen's Theory on Language Acquisition
http://www.youtube.com/watch?v=jobpF4c-1NI

The Natural Approach
http://www.youtube.com/watch?v=eTVbdstastI

Stephen Krashen: How do we acquire language
http://www.youtube.com/watch?v=NiTsduRreug

References

Auer, P. (Ed.). (2013). *Code-switching in conversation: Language, interaction and identity.* Routledge.

Bailey, A. L. & Carroll, P. E. (2015). Assessment of English language learners in the era of new academic content standards. *Review of Research in Education, 39*(1), 253–294.

Baker, C. (2014). *A parents' and teachers' guide to bilingualism* (Vol. 18). Multilingual Matters.

Bauman, J., Boals, T., Cranley, E., Gottlieb, M., & Kenyon, D. (2007). Assessing comprehension and communication in English state to state for English language learners (ACCESS for ELLs®). *English language proficiency assessment in the nation: Current status and future practice,* 81–91.

Bialystok, E. (2011). Reshaping the mind: The benefits of bilingualism. *Canadian Journal of Experimental Psychology/Revue canadienne de psychologie expérimentale, 65*(4), 229.

Celic, C. & Seltzer, K. (2011). Translanguaging: A CUNY-NYSIEB guide for educators. *CUNY-NYSIEB. New York.* http://www.nysieb.ws.gc.cuny.edu/files/2012/06/FINAL-Translanguaging-Guide-With-Cover-1.pdf

Chomsky, N. (1998). *Minimalist inquiries: The framework* (No. 15). MIT Working Papers in Linguistics, MIT, Department of Linguistics.

Creese, A. & Blackledge, A. (2010). Translanguaging in the bilingual classroom: A pedagogy for learning and teaching?. *The Modern Language Journal, 94*(1), 103–115.

Cook, V. & Newson, M. (2014). *Chomsky's universal grammar.* John Wiley & Sons.

Cummins, J. (2003). BICS and CALP: Origins and rationale for the distinction. *Sociolinguistics: The essential readings,* 322–328.

Engel de Abreu, P. M., Cruz-Santos, A., Tourinho, C. J., Martin, R., & Bialystok, E. (2012). Bilingualism enriches the poor: Enhanced cognitive control in low-income minority children. *Psychological science, 23*(11), 1364–1371.

Fishman, J. (1996). What Do You Lose When You Lose Your Language?

Fishman, J. A. (1997). Language and ethnicity: The view from within. *The handbook of sociolinguistics,* 327–343. Oxford: Blackwell.

García, O. (2011). *Bilingual education in the 21st century: A global perspective.* John Wiley & Sons.

García, O. & Kleifgen, J. A. (2010). *Educating emergent bilinguals: Policies, programs, and practices for English language learners.* Teachers College Press.

Garcia, O. & Kleyn, T. (Eds.) (2016). *Translanguaging with Multilingual Students: Learning from Classroom Moments.* New York: Routledge.

García, O. & Wei, L. (2014). Translanguaging and Education. In *Translanguaging: Language, Bilingualism and Education* (pp. 63–77). Palgrave Macmillan UK.

Gleason, J. B. & Weintraub, S. (1978). Input language and the acquisition of communicative competence. *Children's language, 1,* 171–222.

Gottlieb, M., Cranley, M. E., & Cammilleri, A. (2007). Understanding the WIDA English language proficiency standards: A resource guide. *Board of Regents of the University of Wisconsin System.*

Gredler, M. E. (2012). Understanding Vygotsky for the classroom: is it too late? *Educational Psychology Review*, *24*(1), 113–131.

Hornberger, N. H. & Link, H. (2012). Translanguaging and transnational literacies in multilingual classrooms: A biliteracy lens. *International Journal of Bilingual Education and Bilingualism*, *15*(3), 261–278.

Komarova, N. L. & Nowak, M. A. (2001). Natural selection of the critical period for language acquisition. *Proceedings of the Royal Society of London B: Biological Sciences*, *268*(1472), 1189–1987.

Krashen, S. D. (1987). *Principles and practice in second language acquisition* (pp. 1982–1982). New York.

Linton, A. (2004). A critical mass model of bilingualism among US-born Hispanics. *Social Forces*, *83*(1), 279–314.

Mehisto, P. & Marsh, D. (2011). Approaching the economic, cognitive and health benefits of bilingualism: Fuel for CLIL. *Linguistics Insights. Content and Foreign Language Integrated Learning*, *108*, 21–48.

Staddon, J. (2014). *The new behaviorism*. Psychology Press.

Stewart, E. C. & Bennett, M. J. (2011). *American cultural patterns: A cross-cultural perspective*. Hachette UK.

Swain, M. (1993, October). The output hypothesis: Just speaking and writing aren't enough. *The Canadian Modern Language Review*, *50*(1), 158–164.

Swain, M. (2005). The output hypothesis: Theory and research. *Handbook of research in second language teaching and learning*, *1*, 471–483.

Vygotsky, L. (1978). Interaction between learning and development. *Readings on the development of children*, *23*(3), 34–41.

Yang, C. D. (2004). Universal Grammar, statistics or both? *Trends in cognitive sciences*, *8*(10), 451–456.

CHAPTER 6

THE SCHOOL EXPERIENCE FOR THE NEW ENGLISH LEARNER

Eileen N. Whelan Ariza

KEY POINTS

- Your new English learner and characteristics of the differing literacy backgrounds.
- The Home Language Survey determines whether a student needs ESOL or not.
- Examples of school registration scenarios and the difficulties of negotiating a new school system.
- Hints to help the teacher get to know the type of English learner at hand.

In today's presidential administration's anti-immigrant climate, a fact that is hugely important to remember is that the Supreme Court made the landmark decision of *Plyer v. Doe* in 1982. This law protects and says we cannot constitutionally deny students a free public education because of their immigration status. The Court felt that that it was far more harmful to the undocumented students to deny them an education than to save the resources that would be spent on the students to educate them.

The *Plyler v. Doe* law is now feeling threatened because some states are trying to enact laws that will demand school administrators to determine the immigration status of newly enrolling students, causing fear and great absenteeism. So far the courts have blocked any challenges.

Although the law is well established, some school districts have felt that this law hasn't stopped some school districts from imposing obstacles to prevent many of the approximately 770,000 undocumented school-aged children in the United States from registering for school ("How Undocumented Students Are Turned Away From Public Schools—NEA Today", 2017)

The New Learner

When non-native speakers of English enter your classroom, you need to know as much background as possible about them. In the publication *Reading and Adult English Learners: A Review of the Research* (Burt, Peyton, & Adams, 2003; Schwarzer, 2009), the authors offer a chart of the types of native language **(L1)** literacy and their effects on second language **(L2)** literacy. Although it specifically mentions adults, it is as revealing as the types of English learners that are described in the publication by Freeman,

Freeman, and Mercuri (2002), *Closing the Achievement Gap: How to Reach Limited Formal Schooling and Long-Term English Learners*. Both depict the very special characteristics and levels of language proficiency in L1 and L2 that English learners bring with them when they begin their studies through English in the United States. Educators who are aware of the specific characteristics of these groups of learners will be better prepared to construct effective instruction to meet these learners' needs (see Table 6.1).

Compare Table 6.1 with Freeman, Freeman, and Mercuri's (2002) chart in Table 6.2 (which they based on Olsen & Jaramillo, 1999) that describes types of English learners (children as well as older English learners), and you can begin to appreciate the range of students and literacy issues you will encounter in your classes.

TABLE 6.1 Literacy Characteristics

L1 Literacy	Explanation	Special Considerations
Preliterate	L1 has no written form. Indigenous, African, Australian, and Pacific languages.	Learners need exposure to the purposes and uses of literacy.
Nonliterate	Learners have no access to literacy instruction.	Learners may feel stigmatized.
Semiliterate	Learners have limited access to instruction.	Learners may have had past negative experiences with literacy learning.
Nonalphabet literate	Learners are fully literate in a language written in a nonalphabetic script.	Learners need instruction in reading and alphabetic script and in the sound–syllable correspondence in English.
Non-Roman alphabet literate	Learners are literate in a language written in a non-Roman alphabet (e.g., Arabic, Greek, Korean, Russian, or Thai).	Learners need instruction in the Roman alphabet to transfer their L1 literacy skills to English. Some, such as readers of Arabic, will need to learn to read from left to right.
Roman alphabet literate	Learners are fully literate in a language written in a Roman alphabet script (e.g., French, German, or Spanish).	Learners need instructions in the specific letter-to-sound syllable correspondence. They read from left to right, read English, and recognize letter shapes and fonts.

Source: Burt, Peyton, & Adams (2003).

TABLE 6.2 Types of English

Learners	
Newly arrived learners with adequate formal schooling.	■ Recent arrivals (less than five years in the United States).
	■ Adequate schooling in the native country.
	■ At grade level in reading and writing.
	■ Able to catch up soon academically.
	■ May still score low on standardized tests given in English.

Newly arrived learners with limited formal schooling.	■ Recent arrivals (less than five years in the United States).
	■ Interrupted or limited schooling in native country.
	■ Limited native-language literacy.
	■ Below grade level in math.
	■ Poor academic achievement.
Long-term English learners.	■ Seven or more years in the United States.
	■ Below grade level in reading and writing.
	■ Mismatch between student perceptions of achievement and actual grades.
	■ Some get adequate grades but score low on tests.
	■ Have had ESL or bilingual instruction, but no consistent program.

Source: Freeman, Freeman, & Mercuri (2002).

Understanding Your English Learner

Typically, students who come to the United States with a strong academic background have had the economic or political means to have received a thorough education that readily transfers to English (Cheng, Klinger, & Zheng, 2007; Cummins, 1982, 1994; Krashen, 1981, 2002b). However, with the variety and diversity of political, financial, and educational backgrounds of students entering the United States, there is no guarantee that any students will bring an uninterrupted, complete education. The idea that basic knowledge in the native language can transfer to the target language makes educating ELs less difficult, but that is the best-case scenario and is just not the reality in many cases.

In recent years, in addition to refugee and immigrant newcomers, we are seeing an influx of students who arrive with limited, interrupted, or no previous education (SLIFE-students with limited or interrupted formal education, or SIFE, which refers to students with interrupted formal education). We also see an influx of unaccompanied minors (under 16) who are arriving alone in the United States, with severe problems and traumatic histories (who may be very fearful of sharing their personal stories.) Students come from bordering countries (e.g., Mexico), who may be returned to the home country, and are processed into the system immediately, but wind up staying with family of friends for a long while, or students who enter through bordering countries (but are from countries and just passed through Mexico to get into the United States). They are not repatriated immediately and may get lost in the system. These students require academic, social, and emotional resources, and very often will be in the mainstream classes (English Literacy Development, 2014).

The world's refugee situation has caused a situation that exacerbates the usual issues and concerns that come with the newcomer to the country. Many refugee students have experienced violent conflict, loss of home and country, and the interruption of their education (MacNevin, 2012; Stewart, 2011). They have a host of issues such as PTSD (post-traumatic stress disorder) and serious emotional and psychological problems that may show up in the classroom for the teacher to respond to.

The time required for students to acquire social language (up to two years) and academic language (five to ten years) greatly affects academic achievement (Cummins, 1981a, 1982; Larsen-Freeman & Long, 2014). Students who arrive in the United States with strong educational foundations easily transfer that knowledge to English; therefore, they are apt to perform better academically. Students who come to the United States with limited or interrupted educations will have a more difficult time catching up to their English-speaking peers academically.

To classify students further, another group of students called **Generation 1.5** (Harklau, Losey, & Siegal, 1999; Roberge, Siegal, & Harklau, 2009) are described as non-native English speaking students who sound native-like and may have been in the United States educational system for many or most of their scholastic years but are still unsuccessful academically because they lack the academic language needed to be successful. Actually, they might have been born in the United States but relate to family members from other countries who they are raised by. These students usually have better English proficiency than their first-generation immigrant parents, and they may sound like native speakers because they learned English at an earlier age. They may not be true native English speakers, yet they are more than international students. They are bicultural with the traits of both the first- and second-generation immigrants. They don't fit the profile of the typical ELs: therefore, they may not have had the benefit of ESOL classes and, consequently, are still not prepared to do academic work in English. They may not have a strong connection with the homeland, yet are not quite "American" enough to fit in with the native speaker. Since the ESOL class, or a remedial or developmental class, has a negative connotation for them, they may resist taking those classes. The further they go along in school, the more at risk they are of failing and of dropping out of school. Although orally fluent, bilingual, or multilingual, they lack adequate competence in academic reading and writing. This is the "hidden" population of students that may go unnoticed as their teachers might think they are intentionally lazy or avoiding their work. These are the students who cause a teacher to say, "If Tony would just apply himself, he could do much better in school."

School Registration

In an effort to determine placement of a new student, many schools provide a Home Language Survey for parents to complete when registering their children. Another scenario depicts a non-English speaking parent who tries to register her children at the neighborhood school. As she approaches the counter, she begins to tell the secretary what she is there for, but the secretary does not speak German. Imagine what the parent must be feeling.

PARENT: Frau des gutenmorgens. Ich bin hier, meine Kinder für Schule zu registrieren.

SCHOOL SECRETARY: Hello folks. Welcome to our school.

PARENT: Verzeihen Sie mir bitte. Ich verstehe nicht Englisch, aber ich muss meine Kinder für Schule immediatelz registrieren.

SCHOOL SECRETARY: Yes, well here are the forms you have to fill out. You need their birth certificates, social security numbers, proof of residency, and the grades from their last school. Please answer the questions that ask about the children's home language. That will tell us if they need to be tested for the ESOL program or not.

PARENT: Verzeihen Sie mir bitte, aber ich sehe, teh Formen aber kann nicht sie lesen, weil sie auf englisch sind. Ich kann nicht sie übersetzen. Haben Sie jemand hier, wer mir auf Deutsch helfen kann?

SCHOOL SECRETARY: I am sorry, I can't understand a word you are saying and no one here speaks German. You will have to get someone to help you because I can't. I am truly sorry. I wish I could speak your language.

PARENT: Lieber Gott im Himmel. Was ich annahmen, um jetzt meine Kinder zu tun sind, die Neigung zur Schule gehen und sie müssen i Nocken zu diesem Land für ein besseres Leben erlernen, aber meine Kinder können nicht eine Ausbildung sogar erhalte.

The parent walks away dejectedly. No one has asked the children if they can speak English. If they did, they would have learned that the children understood what the secretary was saying. However, in many cultures, the familial hierarchy would be disrupted and the parents would lose face if the child were to interpret for the parent. Children who are "language brokers" act as linguistic, cultural, and emotional mediators, and this role reversal is detrimental to the familial roles, and the hierarchy. Children are not capable of understanding more adult matters, vocabulary, and consequences of what they are saying. This is an undue burden on the child who may not interpret correctly, especially since many English words or concepts cannot be exact translations, or the concept does not exist in the newcomer's home language. This could be especially dangerous in a medical situation.

Picture yourself entering a school in any non-English-speaking country to register your children, but you don't understand the language. You would not be able to fill out forms or ask about the teacher, proper placement of your children, or school procedures. What would you do?

For many schools, at registration, there will be procedures to try to categorize the student's ability. For example, in a school in Florida, the student would be classified into one of the following categories, after the initial screening. The code in the school that denotes what category the student will be placed in is for the purpose of tracking and trying to place the student into the correct level. The state requires careful record keeping for purposes of funding, school grading, analyzing the success of the students and the school programs, and also for changing the students' language classification from one level to another.

E   English for Speakers of Other Languages
H   Home Language/Bilingual Education
L   English for Speakers of Other Languages and Home Language/Bilingual Education
N   Newcomer/New Beginnings Program (Primarily grades 6–12)
Z   Not applicable

The Florida state Consent Decree uses the definitions and the codes given below, which indicate the status of the student who has been identified as an English learner (EL) student. An EL is one who:

- Was not born in the United States and whose native language is other than English; or
- Was born in the United States but who comes from a home in which a language other than English is most relied upon for communication; or
- Is an American Indian or Alaskan Native and comes from a home in which a language other than English has had a significant impact on his or her level of English language proficiency; and
- Who as a result of the above has sufficient difficulty speaking, reading, writing, or understanding the English language to deny him or her the opportunity to learn successfully in classrooms in which the language of instruction is in English.

When speaking with the newcomer family that is trying to register for school, be sure to have multiple language translations for the family. There is a possibility that the family is illiterate in the home language. Technological translations and apps are very helpful when individuals do not read or write in their home language or English.

Speak slowly and clearly. Point to items, and try to have visuals or other non-linguistic clues to help make the forms clear. In Florida, as of the 2012–13 school year, there were more than 277,000 ELs, the most common languages spoken by ELs are Spanish, Haitian, Portuguese, and Arabic (Migration Policy Institute, 2015). Therefore, any materials should be written in these languages.

English learners: Instructional Model—the type of instructional strategy provided to English learners in each course. The types of instructional models are:

E Sheltered—English

S Sheltered—Core/Basic Subject Areas

I Mainstream/Inclusion—English

C Mainstream/Inclusion—Core/Basic Subject Areas

O Maintenance or Developmental Bilingual Education

T Dual Language (Two-way Developmental Bilingual Education)

Z Not applicable

English learners, PK-12 Codes

The Home Language Survey

When students are registered for school, a Home Language Survey, such as the one in the Florida schools, asks simple questions such as the following:

1. Is a language other than English used in the home?
2. Does the student have a first language other than English?
3. Does the student most frequently speak a language other than English?

These questions reveal the most rudimentary information, yet this does not help the teacher very much. The teacher needs to know more comprehensive and detailed information, such as that asked by the Home Language Survey distributed by the state of Maine. It asks the parents more pertinent questions:

1. What language do you most often use when speaking to your child?
2. What language did your child first learn to speak?
3. What language does your child most often use when speaking to brothers, sisters, and other children at home?
4. What language does your child most often use when speaking to you and other adults in the home? (referring to grandparents, aunts, uncles, guests)
5. What language does your child most often use when speaking with friends or neighbors outside the home?

As a result of learning this information, teachers are provided with more background information to help determine language dominance and proficiency. However, we are still unable to ascertain crucial information about literacy levels. Can the students read and write in their native language(s) and, if so, up to what level?

Schools or individual teachers can create their own Home Language Survey, keeping in mind that the more information the teacher has, the more appropriate the instruction can be for the student. For example, students from Haiti possess a rich oral literacy tradition but may be illiterate in writing. Notice how students of any age hold a book or a pencil, or where they begin to write on the paper. By being observant, teachers can determine much of the student's literacy background. Some students will not know how to hold a book, use a pencil, or turn a page. That would tell us that the person lacks familiarity with books and with writing. A transient student from a family of migrant workers might never have owned a book, or may have experienced interrupted schooling because the parents move around the country to find work. Each student arrives in school with a history. A student may come from abroad, and the parent may have papers that indicate a birth date that is very different than is indicated by the appearance of the child. The following is a true story shared by a fifth-grade teacher.

Background and Basis

The Civil Rights Act of 1964 Title VI, Language Minority Compliance Procedures, requires school districts/charter schools to identify limited English proficient students (language minority students). The Pennsylvania Department of Education has selected the Home Language Survey (HLS) as the tool to identify limited English proficient students. The purpose of this survey is to determine a primary or home language other than English (PHLOTE). Schools have a responsibility under federal law to serve students who are limited English proficient and need ESOL or bilingual/bicultural instruction in order to be successful in academic subjects. Given this responsibility, school districts/charter schools have the right to ask for the information they need to identify these students. If not given to previously enrolled students, the HLS must be given to all students enrolled in the school district/charter school and then can be given at the time of each new student's enrollment. The HLS is placed in the student's permanent record file and remains there through the student's graduation.

Suggestions

The school needs to maintain a reasonable balance between the family's privacy interests and the school's need to know information about the child in order to carry out its responsibilities. After a student is identified as a PHLOTE (primary or home language other than English), the school may request additional information about only the student for whom it is needed.

Home Language Survey Questions

The questions listed below are in logical order. The first three questions are necessary to determine minimum information.

What was the student's first language?

Does the student speak a language other than English?

If yes, specify language _____.

(Do not include languages learned in school.)

What language(s) is/are spoken in your home?

If identified as a PHLOTE, a student with a primary home language other than English, additional questions may be asked to get information about the student's academic experiences.

Additional Questions (Optional)

What language(s) does your child read?

What language(s) does your child write?

What language(s) has your child studied in school?

What language(s) do you use when speaking to your child?

Does your child understand, but not speak, a language(s) other than English?

What language(s) do you (parents/guardians) read? *This is important for determining the language of documents you send home and the need for a translator.*

Do you (parents/guardians) read English? *Some parents/guardians may have a good command of written English, but are not able to speak it fluently. They may want documents sent home in English.*

What language(s) do you (parents/guardians) write?

What language(s) do you (parents/guardians) speak? *This will determine if the school needs to use an interpreter for parent conferences, telephone calls, etc.*

Parent/Guardian Signature: _____

> I teach fifth grade, and I have a little Haitian boy in my class who is much smaller than his classmates. I wonder if he is developmentally delayed because I can't even seem to teach him how to write his name. He hangs on my leg; I know there is something wrong with this situation, but his father will not talk to me. The boy does not speak much English at all, but I sense that there is something else going on with him.

As is turned out, the youngster should have been in first grade but had arrived in the United States using an older child's papers and birth certificate. The father was afraid to be truthful for fear of being deported. After much deliberation and talk with a Haitian Creole interpreter, they convinced the father to let the boy go into third grade and they would retain him at the end of the year. By that time, school personnel hoped the boy would be caught up enough with his classmates so that he could function at the correct grade level.

What the Teacher Needs to Know to Teach the EL

One of the most baffling ideas is to imagine how a teacher can teach a student when neither one knows the other's language. Yet with the elimination of bilingual education and the advent of the No Child Left Behind Act of 2001, legislators, who are almost never educators, demanded that mainstream teachers instruct students who don't speak English and then hold the teachers accountable for the students' academic success. This act stresses a number of federal requirements that many states have already readjusted.

- Now we have the mandated 2015 Every Student Succeeds Act (ESSA), which has replaced the *No Child Left Behind Act*. How this works determines how ELs are reclassified according to language proficiency. English learners are classified and reclassified into English proficiency groupings but as it stands now, every state and district is functioning differently. It will be critical to have all educational institution EL assessments standardized and uniform. This way, teachers, administrators, and students can go from district to district knowing that there is consistency between schools and unvarying standards. It is important that all students be graded on the same criteria and schools will have authentic data when students graduate (or do not graduate). Classification can also dictate suitable settings, academic instruction, and appropriately serving student needs.
- It is impossible to judge true progress if all benchmarks are not actually equal. It will also be more equitable to judge graduation rates and program success if there is academic and assessment consistency. It is also important that all programs maintain a high academic standard, and if all programs are following the same benchmarks and standards, all schools will be on a level playing field for assessment. Some institutions will have lower standards because it makes the school look like students are more successful than the really are. Classification is important also because of funding. If students are reclassified out of ESOL too quickly, students lose both in funds as well as learning gains.

Given the plethora of research (Collier, 1989, 1992, Cummins, 1981a, 1982; Zhang, 2016) that indicates a period of five to ten years is required for non-native English speakers to approach or equal the academic abilities of native English speakers, ESOL educators have serious concerns about the prospects of success for this plan.

The teachers who are responsible for the task of educating ELs must know teaching strategies that integrate language within content. Unlike older methods of foreign language teaching, researchers today emphasize that a natural approach to language learning can be accomplished by learning English through the content area. Most of us remember wearing headphones in the high school foreign language lab, trying to learn by repeating words that the speaker was saying, usually at too rapid a pace, and feeling the frustration of not being able to complete the phrase. Personally, I always hoped the teacher would not be listening in on my booth because I could never complete the entire sentence and would just mumble along. We were supposed to repeat the speaker's words and, by some miracle, learn the language. Currently, when I ask my university students how many years of a foreign language they have taken, many will indicate two to four years. Then when I ask them how many can speak the language today, not one will answer affirmatively. What happened to those two, three, or four years of language learning? The fact is, that is not the way we acquire a language. Not one of us learned English by memorizing: *I am, you are, she is, he is, you are, we are, they are.* Yet that is how our schools tried to teach us foreign languages.

Learning rules of reading, writing, listening, speaking, grammar, and pronunciation, one structure at a time, is not necessarily the best way to become communicatively competent in the target language. **Communicative competence** (Brumfit, 2017; Hymes, 1972) means the speaker knows how to use the language and address individuals appropriately throughout all settings and situations and within the correct context. There is a difference between **linguistic competence**, which means knowing about language forms, and communicative competence, which recognizes that social and cultural contexts of language are just as important to successful communication (Bachman, 1990, Canale & Swain, 1980; Gleason & Ratner, 2016). Background meaning, or schema, is critical. Anyone who has studied a foreign language has experienced this situation: After studying the foreign language, you think you know how to speak it, only to visit the country or talk to native speakers of the language and not understand a word the native speakers are saying. As an example of how one can formally study a language but not become proficient, I share my experience below.

> I first decided to go to Mexico because I liked Spanish. After studying Spanish for two years in college, I was ready to go study Spanish formally at the Universidad Nacional Autonoma de Mexico in Mexico City. Upon my arrival, I immediately called my friend, Victor, who could speak English. I was proud of myself for having mastered the telephone procedure with foreign coins and all. When someone answered, I said, "Por favor, puedo hablar con Victor? (Can I please speak to Victor?). The woman replied, "Victor no se encuentra." I was clueless as to what that meant because, if he wasn't home, I thought she would have said, "No está", or "No está en casa." I tried again, "Victor, por favor?" Again she said, in a rush of words, "Lo siento. No se encuentra." I was in serious trouble now. I didn't know what she was saying, and all I understood was the word, "No." I decided to negotiate an alternate communicative route with the memorized phrases I knew. Taking a guess that I might get more information I could understand, I asked another question I was sure of: "A que hora esta en casa?" (What time will he be home?). Finally, I hit pay dirt! She said, "A las tres." (At 3:00). Wow, and I thought I could speak Spanish! I finally understood how people who come to the United States feel when they study English in their home countries yet can't communicate when they encounter native English speakers.

The focus should be on learning a language through authentic texts and situations, in other words, through the use of materials that have not been specifically produced for the purposes of language teaching (Nunan, 1989; Thornbury, 2016). A more "communicative approach" offers a natural emphasis where learners are actively engaged in "comprehending, manipulating, producing, or interacting in the target language" (Nunan, 1989, p. 10; Thornbury, 2016). By using authentic materials, more genuine communication can take place.

Many of the older methodologies of language teaching, such as the Audio Lingual Method, are based on structure and form, error correction, native-like pronunciation, and eliminating any use of the native language, rather than on meaning. The Communicative Language Teaching approach concentrates more on meaning within the authentic context, with fluency, acceptable language, and communication being the immediate goal, rather than speaking the language perfectly.

Having established the point that language should be acquired in the most natural and authentic manner, how do we approach this task? First, the teacher has the crucial responsibility of making the learner feel comfortable in taking language risks. New language learners will make mistakes; this is inevitable and expected. Teachers have the responsibility of facilitating language learning in the classroom by planning for interaction to take place and for assisting the learner to move from "total dependence to relatively total independence" (Brown, 1994a, p. 162; Brown, 2006). Eventually, students will learn language appropriate to the classroom settings as well as outside the classroom.

FINAL POINTS

- Languages should be taught with authentic material.
- A Home Language Survey is really an approximation of what the student knows linguistically so it should be used as a guide.
- The Every Student Succeeds Act (ESSA), which currently replaces the *No Child Left Behind Act*, determines how ELs are reclassified according to language proficiency. However, every state defines the data differently.
- Communicative and linguistic competence are the goals of competent language learning.

Discussion Questions and Activities

1. Individually or with a group, create your own Home Language Survey. What important questions do you need to ask to obtain information about your new student? What do you need to know to be able to teach this student?
2. Does your school collect data on newcomers? How do you think you can successfully classify ELs? Why? What recommendations would you give to administrators?
3. Does your school have a program for newcomers? Think about what resources your students would need after they arrive in your school? What will they need, and how would you meet these needs?
4. Your new students have different backgrounds. One studied extensively in her homeland, and another was uprooted from his school when war broke out in his country. What differences do you think you will encounter? How will you address the needs and issues of these two students?
5. Have you studied a foreign language? How well did you learn it? Describe your experience. What would have been a better way for you to have learned the language?

Resources

Your English learner's background
http://www.colorincolorado.org/educators/reachingout/backgrounds/

WIDA K-12 English Development Standards
https://www.wida.us/standards/eld.aspx

American history for English learners
http://www.manythings.org/voa/history/

Guide for EL Educators, Broward County
http://www.nasponline.org/resources/culturalcompetence/ell_educators.pdf

Watch and learn
http://www.colorincolorado.org/multimedia/learn/

EL parental involvement in the schools
http://suzannepanferov.faculty.arizona.edu/sites/suzannepanferov.faculty.arizona.edu/files/Increasing%20ELL_0.pdf

Home Language Surveys for multiple languages
http://www.k12.wa.us/MigrantBilingual/HomeLanguage.aspx

Home Language Survey, Pennsylvania
http://www.education.state.pa.us/portal/server.pt/community/measurements,_standards___policies/7531

Listening to teachers of ELs
http://files.eric.ed.gov/fulltext/ED491701.pdf

References

Brown, H. D. (2006). Principles of language learning and teaching.

Brumfit, C. J. (2017). The communicative approach to language teaching.

Cheng, L., Klinger, D. A., & Zheng, Y. (2007). The challenges of the Ontario Secondary School Literacy Test for second language students. *Language Testing, 24*(2), 185–208.

Gleason, J. B. & Ratner, N. B. (2016). *The development of language.* Pearson.

How Undocumented Students Are Turned Away From Public Schools—NEA Today. (2017). *NEA Today.* Retrieved 15 November 2017, from http://neatoday.org/2016/04/22/undocumented-students-public-schools/

Larsen-Freeman, D. & Long, M. H. (2014). *An introduction to second language acquisition research.* Routledge.

MacNevin, J. (2012). Learning the Way: Teaching and Learning with and for Youth from Refugee Backgrounds on Prince Edward Island. *Canadian Journal of Education / Revue Canadienne De L'éducation, 35*(3), 48–63. Retrieved from http://www.jstor.org/stable/canajeducrevucan.35.3.48

Roberge, M., Siegal, M., & Harklau, L. (Eds.). (2009). *Generation 1.5 in college composition: Teaching academic writing to US-educated learners of ESL.* Routledge.

Schwarzer, D. (2009). Best practices for teaching the "whole" adult ESL learner. *New Directions for Adult and Continuing Education, 2009*(121), 25–33.

Stewart, J. (2011). *Supporting refugee children: Strategies for educators.* University of Toronto Press.

Thornbury, S. (2016). Communicative language teaching in theory and practice. *The Routledge Handbook of English Language Teaching,* 224.

Translating a Problem Into a Bill. (2017). *Los Angeles Times.* Retrieved 6 May 2017, from http://articles.latimes.com/2003/jul/18/local/me-interpret18

Zhang, L. (2016). Developing students' cognitive/academic language proficiency: genre and metacognition in interaction. *Epoch-Making in English Teaching and Learning.*

PART 3

LEARNING ENGLISH THROUGH INTEGRATION OF ACADEMIC CONTENT

CHAPTER 7

WHY INTEGRATE LANGUAGE AND CONTENT?

Eileen N. Whelan Ariza

KEY POINTS

- Language and content should be integrated using academic language and instructional strategies.
- Strategies for beginning language learners will make instruction more comprehensive for the students.
- Methods for making progress in beginning to intermediate learners are included in this chapter.
- The WIDA consortium of several states has developed an excellent example of academic and language development standards for teachers to follow.

Two exchange students from Italy came to the United States to study English. They lived together in a homestay situation. When the director of the language school asked them if their living arrangements were satisfactory, they said that they loved the family, but they were glad they were living together so one could guard the other when they went to the bathroom, because there was no door. The director was horrified and called the host family. The mystery was solved when the host mother told the director that their house had pocket doors that slide into the wall. How could the students be expected to figure out something about which they had no prior knowledge?

This is similar to the situation about students who are expected to complete academic tasks, yet don't have the language facility to apply to the content task. Earlier I mentioned in this book about a Haitian gentleman who was teaching French on a temporary certificate. He had to take competency tests to be a teacher, and he passed every one of the tests, except the writing. I knew, as his teacher, he did not really have a problem with writing, but I asked him why he thought he did not pass? He explained to me that he did not understand one of the words in the writing prompt, and he could not make a correct guess based on the context. The test offers two writing prompts, but the same thing happened with the second prompt. The vocabulary referred to something that he had no familiarity with and therefore, the writing assessment could not be done.

This same reasoning can be applied to all students, English learners or not. If students do not have the schema, or background, the question cannot be answered, but this does not measure knowledge or ability. Native English speakers cannot do well on reading or writing essays if they don't understand the vocabulary. An English-speaking student was given a math problem that required knowledge about paycheck terminology. For example, a word problem like this: Fredericka makes $10.00 an hour. She works 40 hours a week. What would her gross salary be? And what would the net salary be if it is taxed 10%? There is no way she could answer without knowing what that terminology meant.

WIDA: The Quest for Academic and Language Development Standards

As mentioned in the last chapter, ESSA requires states to include ELs' English language proficiency (ELP) progress as a core component of their Title I accountability plans. Dr. Tim Boals, WIDA executive director, states "ESSA really has done away with state accountability to the federal government" (Boals, 2017, p. 1). This means that the United States need to find more uniform standardization measures and this need dovetails with the problems students have in trying to become academically successful through content, to raise their knowledge. More states needed to band together to come to a consensus of how to reach these goals. For that reason, multiple states have joined the WIDA consortium. Now there is better communication between the SEAs (state education agencies) and about three-fourths of the states are affiliated with the consortium, which has created resources for teachers and school system.

Recognizing the problem between academic language development and achievement of ELs, WIDA was started as a grant, with the Center of Applied Linguistics as WIDA's test development partner. The goal was to create high quality standards, assessments, research, and professional development for educators of culturally and linguistically diverse students across the country ("WIDA: Mission & History," 2017). In 2008, WIDA EL Can Do Booklets were published for each grade-level cluster and a new testing format called ACCESS for grades 1–12 was published. In 2011, WIDA ELP Standards for Common Core State Standards alignment report was published, and ACCESS for ELs 2.0 2014, and Early English Language Development Standards were released in 2014. Now the states that have bought into this plan have a more standard and uniform field to base teaching and assessing learning upon (https://www.wida.us/aboutus/AcademicLanguage/) ("WIDA: Mission & History," 2017).

Integration of Language and Content

Language and content must be integrated—you cannot wait until the student knows enough English to start studying academic content. The law says teachers must provide the same curriculum for the new EL as for the native English speaker, in a manner comprehensible to the student and at his or her level of proficiency, without diluting the curriculum. The Council of Chief State School Officers (CCSSO, 1992) determined that success for English learners "hinges upon gaining access to effective second language learning opportunities and to a full educational program" (p. 4). In an effort to ensure that ELs have the same opportunities as English-speaking students, CCSSO recommended that, although supportive language-assistance programs may help develop language proficiency, schools must provide a way for English learners to "continue to learn and expand their knowledge of new content and, therefore, not fall behind peers whose native language is English" (p. 6). Consequently, this attitude corresponds to federal laws that insist all students, regardless of native language, receive comprehensive curriculum in a manner that they can understand.

In many states, bilingual education is not an option; language teachers and subject area teachers have begun to collaborate to prepare curricula that will include ELs in the mainstream classroom and keep students on grade level while developing English proficiency. Several approaches have offered teachers resources for integrating language with content, such as books, training workshops, courses for ESOL endorsement, teacher development inservice programs, professional conferences, presentations, seminars, and training in ESOL techniques. Content-based instruction does not focus on discrete-point language training such as grammar rules and memorizing vocabulary lists. Rather, teachers use regular content topics as the framework for instruction that complements language learning. Another approach, Sheltered English or Sheltered Instruction, is geared for intermediate-level (of language proficiency) students who are all ELs; the teacher adjusts the instructional level to that of the students' capabilities. ESOL techniques are utilized to make the content understandable or "**scaffolded**" to make learning understandable to the English learner.

In the integrated language and content class, the focus is on communication through reading, writing, listening, and speaking. More concrete instructional techniques such as visuals, demonstrations, graphic organizers, prewriting, and prereading skills are utilized. Students are taught **cognitive processes**, such as how to think and how to develop study skills, which actually helps all learners (Brinton, Snow, & Wesch, 1989; Crandall, 1993; Gregory. & Burkman, 2011; Short, 1991) A buddy system for peer support is offered for companionship and translation if possible, and authentic and meaningful situations are provided for communication to take place through social interaction and contextualized communication. In other words, meaning can be constructed because communication takes place as it is embedded within the situation.

More detailed information about language and content lessons will be discussed later in this book. In the Appendix is a sample of a lesson plan format that integrates language and academic content. This approach is called **Sheltered Instruction Observation Protocol (SIOP)** from the book *Making Content Comprehensible for English Learners: The SIOP Model* (Echevarria, Vogt, & Short, 2004).

Strategies for Teaching EL Beginners

Teaching the English beginner calls for certain strategies. The students who are in the **silent stage** or the emerging language stage may appear to understand or pretend to understand when they do not. More proficient students might act the same way, so it is imperative that the teacher constantly check for understanding. If you say, "Do you understand?" the student very often will say yes. The best comprehension check is to have the student show you that he or she understands by acting out what he or she is supposed to be doing. Fillmore and Snow (2000) recommend a list of strategies for the teacher to use with the beginning English learner. These strategies will be referred to and expounded upon throughout this text.

- ❏ Use demonstrations, modeling, and role playing to teach the appropriate language to make polite requests, apologize, express thanks, and so forth for particular circumstances. For example, a real telephone can be used to show how to use appropriate telephone language, a table can be set with real cutlery to practice authentic language, and so on.
- ❏ New information should be presented within the context of a situation (**context clues**) the student already knows. Themes and materials for reading and other instructional activities should

be appropriate to the students' cultural background and are best presented embedded within the context of the here and now (Cummins, 1982). For native and non-native speakers, vocabulary should never be presented in isolation. Present words in context so the students can better determine their meanings.

❏ Paraphrase and extend language utterances as you would with a native English speaker learning a first language. Whatever the student says, repeat the utterance but elaborate and extend upon it. Model correct language when errors are made. For example, the student might say, "She name Susie." Then you could say, "Her name is Susie? Susie is a lovely doll. She is very pretty. What a beautiful face she has."

❏ Use simple language structures and avoid complex sentences. When paraphrasing, we often use more complex grammatical construction. I remember listening to a teacher give an orientation to a new group of English language students. In trying to explain the rules, she said, "This is a fire extinguisher. If you want to play with it, it will cost you 50 bucks." I interjected, "Mrs. Johnson wants you to know that it is illegal to play with fire extinguishers in this country because the firemen will come, and you will have to pay a fine or penalty of 50 dollars." If I say, "The boy, who is from Morocco, is going to buy a book," I really am saying two sentences because one is embedded within another. I am saying: *The boy is from Morocco. He is buying a book.* It is easier to understand simple sentences than ones with clauses. Stories and language can be just a little bit above the students' language ability, but not so much as to be frustrating.

❏ Use repetition of sentence patterns and routines. Songs and rhymes are wonderful for promoting language development because students will learn what to expect within the repetitions. Classroom routines with predictable language are good for students to attach meaning to the words. Common classroom imperatives are repeated again and again, and students can look around them to see what classmates are doing if they don't understand the words. Some examples:
Take out your book.
Close your book.
Take out your pencil.

❏ Ask questions according to the language level and participation of the student. If he or she is in the silent or preproduction stage, tailor your questions to correspond with his or her ability. In the order of simplicity, the easiest language forms are yes/no or one-word answers, which are great for beginners. According to the levels of difficulty, the order of questions will range from *what* to *where, when, how,* and *why,* with *why* questions being the most difficult to answer. Teacher response will train the learners in the appropriate protocol for questions and answers.

❏ Finally, be tolerant of students' mistakes. They may be developmental and will self-correct with time. Understanding the message initially is more important than perfect speech.

Methods for Teaching EL Beginners

One of the most useful approaches to teaching the beginner is using the **Total Physical Response** method (Asher, 1972). Asher, a psychologist, conjectured that people learn better when they are incorporating physical and mental processes. TPR is quite fun for students, as it satisfies their kinesthetic needs; they are not expected to speak, only to obey and to respond to physical commands. Think of the game "Simon Says." Imagine the teacher giving a command in English and the students responding. The teacher can model the behavior first, then students follow. After a few times, the teacher may stop modeling and just state the commands. Students who do not understand will look around at other students and follow their actions. With much repetition, all students will eventually understand what is being said, yet they are not expected to say a word. The following commands are an example. Commands can be built upon little by little:

Stand up.
Sit down.
Turn around.
Raise your hand.
Touch your head.
Pick up the book.
Put down the book.
Walk to the door.
Walk to the door, touch the door, turn around, and then sit down.

After much practice, not only will students respond to the command, but they might want to play being the teacher. As they begin to utter their own commands, their language proficiency develops. It is easy for me to discern how much exposure to the language the students have experienced prior to being in my class; those students with little or no exposure seemed to merely "approximate" the pronunciation of the word, and it sounded similar to how a deaf person sounds. In my experience, it appears to me that young children who are not native English speakers but have been raised listening to *Sesame Street* and *Barney* in English have internalized the sound system and will sound more native-like in their pronunciation.

Visuals, pictures, objects, realia, pointing out, choosing, organizing, classifying, grouping, and regrouping, and rearranging pictures are only some of the other components that can be used within TPR. Teaching prepositions (put the book ON the table, put the pencil UNDER the table) is easier when the students see the concrete meaning for the word. Although TPR is focused on listening comprehension for those students in the silent or preproduction stage of language proficiency, the teacher can introduce reading and writing the commands as well. From positive statements, you can go to negative statements and even to questioning formats.

After the students are very certain of the commands the teacher has chosen, they can be written on the board so that the students can see what the spoken words look like in written form: for example,

Give me the book.
Paul, give Helen the book.
Paul, give her the book.

Seeing the written form of the pronounced word will help reinforce reading, pronunciation, and writing. With writing, the next stage of grammatical development can be teaching negatives by seeing the action; this can then develop into a question format by watching the expression and action of the teacher.

Paul, give Helen the book. (Give the book to Helen.)
Do not give Helen the book. Give the book to Juan.
Give Tran the book. Do not give the book to Tran. Give the book to Manolo.

Pictures work well within TPR. Comprehension is shown after giving a command and the correct actions are done.

Vocabulary can be expanded by giving the students an array of pictures and saying:

Raise (or hold up) the picture of the apple.
Put the picture of the orange on your desk.
Stand up if you have the picture of the watermelon. Walk to the bulletin board and hang the picture.

With a little imagination, you can create any type of activities for your ELs and include their class-mates as buddy tutors. Collect and laminate pictures of every type of vocabulary a new student is likely to need to know. *Bathroom, faucet, desk, locker* (most students from other countries do not have lockers or cubbies in their schools), *pencil, pen, hall, closet, chalk, eraser, computer, computer keys*, and so forth are all common vocabulary words that your students will need to know for survival. I used to take my students on unconventional "field" trips into the bathroom, the kitchen, the cafeteria, the playground, the students' lounge, and name whatever I was doing. On a trip to the bathroom, I would talk my way through what I was doing: for example,

- ❑ *I am opening the door.*
- ❑ *I am entering the bathroom.*
- ❑ *I am sitting on the toilet.* (I act as if I am going to sit down. This might seem obvious to you, but as I explained in a previous chapter, a little Chinese girl I know used to sit in the reverse position on the toilet because no one had ever told her the right way to sit.)
- ❑ *I am taking the toilet paper off the roll.* (Show the student how much to take. Use your own dis-cretion, and consider the age of the student. At times I pantomime what to do.)
- ❑ *I am flushing the toilet paper down the toilet.* (Many students do not know that it is permissible to flush paper down the toilet. Numerous countries do not have a septic system that can support flushing toilet paper. On the other hand, you must also indicate what is not permissible to flush down the toilet.)
- ❑ *I am turning on the faucet.* (Show and let them feel the hot and cold water. Depending on the country, they might not expect the hot water. Actually, in many bathrooms around the world, you cannot even find paper or soap. Everyone knows to bring their own toilet paper, or there may be an attendant who sells toilet paper by the piece.)
- ❑ *I am wetting my hands.*
- ❑ *I am washing my hands with soap.* (Have you ever noticed that every soap dispenser is different?)
- ❑ *I am rinsing my hands.* (Every faucet is different as well. How would someone know that all you have to do is stand in front of the sink and the water would go on?)
- ❑ *I am drying my hands.* (Again, this may be with individual paper towels, a warm air blower, or a towel on a roll.)

Being prepared before the first day of school ensures that you will not be caught off guard when your EL comes into the classroom. It is a lonely feeling to sit in a class and have nothing to do because the teacher cannot speak to you or is too busy with the other thirty kids in the class. That is why visuals, TPR, and buddy systems are wonderful methods to use for the EL. Language master machines (machines that show a picture as a voice pronounces the name of the picture) and computer programs are also excellent tools for beginning language speakers. Do not assume, however, that the new student will know how to operate a computer. Have an assigned buddy help guide the student if you cannot get to the student indi-vidually. Teachers can utilize partner work, group work, or entire class work to maximize opportunities for language practice.

I have focused on beginning learners because I believe they are the most challenging for the classroom teacher. If a student has intermediate language skills, at least there is some English to draw upon.

Tips for Intermediate Learners and Advanced Learners

"On grade level content" is the best scenario for teaching academics to English learners (or any student, actually). In this book, we offer chapters on math, social studies, science, arts/literacy, and English language arts using technology to advance learning for all, but particularly intermediate and advanced learners. In creating a lesson plan, it is best to plan for the "average" or "typical" student. However, that is a very wide field because you may have a beginning learner who can whip through your lesson in 5 minutes, or you can have the intermediate or advanced learner take hours to complete the assignment. We are dealing with people, so we can't assume they can all fit in the same little square. You make your lesson plan for the "average" student in the class, but you must have other options ready, like other more advanced lessons for the students who are ready for more, or you must be able to accommodate for faster or slower learners.

For teaching multilevel learners, try to make your lessons interesting and exciting. Visuals and vibrant topics will catch their attention. Whatever you show that is interesting will spark their attention. From that point, you must present material that is accessible to them. You probably know all the obvious strategies.

Visuals
Models
Songs
Graphic organizers that break down the material into reasonable, manageable chunks.
Videos
Puppet shows

Whatever the content you are teaching, the grammatical objective should be inside the context. Show videos, pictures, music, documentaries, or whatever it is, with students who look like they do, or are from countries that they are from. Inside your content area, pull out the grammar or other point you want to make, but within the context will make much more sense to the learner.

Think out of the box, but remember to help students make connections to what is "in the box."

FINAL POINTS

- TPR is a great way to teach beginning speakers.
- Language learners need to be learning the same types of academic material so learning is standardized, uniform, and can be measured state by state.
- Lesson plans have to be thought out carefully, according to the level of the learner. However, you must think out the plan carefully, determine what you want to teach, and then determine the best way to get to that end.
- Older or more proficient learners still need scaffolding to be able to keep up with mainstream learners.

Discussion Questions and Activities

1. Write a script using TPR (Total Physical Response) for a beginning-level student: for example,
   Stand up.
   Sit down.
   Pick up your pencil.
   Go to the door.
2. Show by role playing how you could teach prepositions, nouns, and verbs using TPR.
3. Take the dialogue you have used for question 2 and manipulate the language to write sentences, questions, and negatives. Show how you would turn a TPR activity into a writing lesson. Using the sample lesson plan in Appendix I, create modified lessons for ELs in
   ❏ The silent stage.
   ❏ The emergence stage.
   ❏ The intermediate stage.
4. How can states get on the same page to assess language learners? What would be the reasons why it is not a good thing to have every state and district with their own standards? How can this hurt the student? How could this hurt the school?
5. Think about what you want to present or teach. What do you want them to learn? Now, what is the most interesting way you can show your students what you are trying to teach? How will you get to the end, or the objective? Find videos that represent your ideas. Wear a costume that represents your idea. Let them choose their own ways (out of the box) to present their own idea. Anticipate what their problems might be and provide a template or a word bank with illustrations. Think about what you want to teach, and how you will get there. It is like a blueprint. If possible, show your students what the ending will or should look like. Give positive feedback for the little steps they did correctly.

   Based on the above ideas, make a plan (like a lesson plan) of what you want your students to do, and then show step by step how you will get them there. Share your idea with your classmates, and be critical in the sense of keeping one another on track: What should come next? Did you forget a step? Can the student get to the objective based on the steps you gave?

Resources

Center for Applied Linguistics (CAL)
http://www.cal.org/resources/archive/rgos/content.html

Making content comprehensible for ELs
http://digitalcommons.nl.edu/cgi/viewcontent.cgi?article=1002&context=wsli

British Council, teaching content and language
http://www.teachingenglish.org.uk/article/content-language-integrated-learning

Teacher skills to support English learners
http://www.kckps.org/teach_learn/pdf/group2/t_l9_teacher.pdf

Effective practices
http://sites.edvantia.org/publications/arcc/effectiveellpractices031109.pdf

Diane Larsen-Freeman TPR
http://www.youtube.com/watch?v=YuS3ku-PSL8

Omniglot
http://www.omniglot.com/language/articles/langlearning.htm

Stages of Language Acquision
http://www.colorincolorado.org/article/language-acquisition-overview

References

Boals, T. (2017). *ESSA's impact on English Language Learners: What we know so far. Blog.ellevationeducation.com*. Retrieved 15 November 2017, from http://blog.ellevationeducation.com/essa_impact_ells

Gregory, G. H. & Burkman, A. (2011). *Differentiated literacy strategies for English language learners, Grades 7–12*. Corwin Press.

WIDA's Executive Director, Dr. Tim Boals. (2017). Retrieved 7 May 2017, from https://www.newamerica.org/education-policy/edcentral/wida-essa/

WIDA: Mission & History. (2017). Wida.us. Retrieved 7 May 2017, from https://www.wida.us/aboutus/mission.aspx

CHAPTER 8

DIFFERENTIATED INSTRUCTION FOR ENGLISH LEARNERS

Eileen N. Whelan Ariza

A native English-speaker and ESOL teacher, Ms. Silva fell in love with the Spanish language while she was visiting Mexico. After completing her elementary education program, she decided she wanted to be a bilingual teacher. She taught in Puerto Rico, Spain, Colombia, and Mexico before feeling comfortable enough with the language to teach native speakers of Spanish in the United States. With the influx of Spanish speakers into the U.S. school systems, she was quickly hired as a bilingual first-grade teacher. The principal thought he had struck gold by finding a teacher with ESOL, elementary, Spanish, and bilingual certification.

Ms. Silva learned much during her first year of teaching in the United States. She learned how to handle the situation if no supplies were available for her young charges; she learned how much she loved the Hispanic children in her class; and she learned about politics. She quickly discovered that being able to speak two languages did not make her feel "bilingual." Even though she had studied Spanish for years and could live in a Spanish-speaking culture, the 6- and 7-year-old children often knew more Spanish than she did. She also did not feel comfortable teaching writing in Spanish. They laughed at jokes she didn't understand, even though she knew every word. Simply, she realized how much she did not know. She could converse well, but when it came to underlying meanings and understanding jokes that required previous schema, she knew she was at a loss. Speaking Spanish and knowing pedagogy of bilingual teaching and the second language learner were two very different issues. Fortunately, she had a native Spanish-speaking assistant who could help her with the nuances of the language.

Ms. Silva did her best throughout the year. She believed that if she said everything in Spanish and then again in English, the children would understand and learn the language at the same time. By the end of the year, she switched to only English, as the children understood everything she said; they even sounded like native English speakers, even parroting Ms. Silva's Boston accent. At the termination of the school year, she recommended that thirty-four of her thirty-seven children be mainstreamed into monolingual. The principal was shocked and told her that would be impossible.

Ms. Silva did everything she could to differentiate instruction for her children. She always paid attention to how they responded to her instruction, and changed her style, materials, and instructional practices so her students would understand. Sometimes no matter what she did, her students did not do well.

What Is Differentiated Instruction?

Tomlinson (2000) describes differentiated instruction simply. Whenever a teacher varies teaching to create the best learning experience possible, or reaches out to address a student in the best way the students learns, that is differentiating instruction. Further, teachers can differentiate the content, the process, the product, and the environment to create a better learning experience. It is critical to differentiate instruction especially when states are obliged to use Common Core State Standards ("The Common Core State Standards and English Learners," 2017). The TESOL International organization offers a wonderful page of resources and strategies for English learners where teachers can find valuable information while using CCSS at:

https://www.tesol.org/advance-the-field/standards/the-common-core-state-standards-and-english-learners

The standards are rigorous and are not easy for English learners. Teachers will need to research strategies to make the standards comprehensible to ELs so students will be able to produce high quality academic achievement (Bunch, Kibler, & Pimentel, 2012; Coleman & Pimentel, 2012; Echevarria, Vogt, & Short, 2004, and van Lier & Walqui, 2012).

Research and recent legislative mandates dictate that students need to learn English through the content area, and teachers must have the ability to modify mainstream content textbooks. Overall, bilingual education may no longer be an option. Therefore, teachers must be skilled in modifying lessons that will scaffold learning subject matter through another language. Language-integrated approaches to teaching must provide opportunities for cognitive growth as well as language practice. This chapter provides examples of lesson modifications, shows how to critically analyze mainstream textbooks for appropriateness, and gives guidelines for adapting materials.

Ms. Silva's scenario at the beginning of this chapter is embedded with issues. First, she doesn't realize that, although the children may speak flawless English, they are not ready to be mainstreamed. They need academic support and modifications with ESOL strategies to continue to be successful. Even though you may hear, "Why is this child in ESOL? He speaks perfect English," research shows a great cognitive difference between social language and academic language (Bailey & Butler, 2003; Cummins, 1981b). In fact, Ms. Silva found the same thing happening to her: She could speak Spanish very well, but had difficulties when abstract concepts where involved. Her social language was excellent, but understanding language is more than just possessing an extensive vocabulary.

Ironically, when the principal said it would be impossible to mainstream thirty-four children the next year, he was not referring to language issues at all. His main concern was political; he did not want to lose the position held by the second-grade bilingual teacher. If the children went to the mainstream class, they would not need a bilingual teacher, and she would be out of a job. No other mainstream teacher was available. Probably more important to the principal was the fact that he received funds for each student who was in his bilingual program. If the children were exited, so was his funding. It was a hard but valuable lesson for a new teacher to learn.

With bilingual education losing favor, more mainstream teachers bear the responsibility of teaching English learners in the classroom. Although some schools have English for non-native speakers as a pull-out program or even bilingual programs, the short time these specialized teachers spend with English learners is not sufficient enough to grasp the social language, never mind the academic language of the subjects taught in schools.

Students from other countries come with a kaleidoscope of varying abilities in academics and language proficiency. I see a recurring pattern of students who seem to fall into the following categories:

- Strong academic background in their native language, ready to transfer this knowledge to English
- No previous school experience or interrupted schooling, with poor language and academic proficiency in their heritage language
- American citizenship or residency, but speaking a language other than English
- Fluent English, born in the United States, but with poor academic skills

Regardless of the academic language or diversity of your students, they will be in the same classroom with all the other students of varying abilities, languages, and individual issues.

The mainstream teacher is mandated by law to teach all students in a comprehensible manner. This means that the teacher will have to integrate language learning through the content area. The most important phenomenon about language learners I have ever learned was that it takes five to ten years to become as proficient as native speakers in a given academic area (Cummins, 1981b; Thomas & Collier, 2002). If this is the case, a teacher may see students enter the class in first grade and go through until eighth-grade graduation without ever seeing them gain sufficient English proficiency to become academically successful. This fact also begs the question: Why are we forcing students to take standardized exams without English language proficiency? It is ludicrous, yet every year we hear more and more about the government's stand on "raising the bar" for teaching and learning through the ubiquitous, if not misguided, standardized test, the "cure all" for "poor teaching." Teachers are faced with incredible odds, including poor pay, long hours, students who are not motivated, parents who are ready to sue if the child is chastised for improper behavior, and lack of administrative support, which robs the teacher's power to maintain discipline in the class.

From the thousands of preservice teachers who have passed through my classes, one constant remains: Teachers are drawn to the profession because they have a burning desire to teach. Quite often, teaching is the last thing educators get to do in the classroom. Class sizes have swelled, students with behavioral problems must be monitored, students with exceptionalities and limited English proficiency are mainstreamed, and it seems like every new teaching and learning fad that comes along is adopted before proven successful. Yet, teachers still desire to teach because of their passion for helping students.

Federal laws mandate that all students must receive an education that is comprehensible to them, regardless of native language. Deciding that separation of races in schools was not really "separate but equal," ***Brown v. the Board of Education of Topeka, Kansas*** (1954) guaranteed equal protection under the law for all races, students with handicaps, and the linguistic and culturally diverse populations. In the case of ***Meyer v. Nebraska*** (1923), the Supreme Court determined that instruction in the native language was not immoral or injurious and should be allowed. Consequently, the landmark case ***Lau v. Nichols*** (1974), where 1,800 Chinese children filed a class-action suit in California, established a precedent stating that having the same textbooks and curriculum did not imply equality of education, because the students could not understand instruction in English. At that time, special language programs were developed across the nation. Therefore, this chapter is dedicated to teaching educators how to modify the curriculum for English learners so they can learn language through the content area.

A language-integrated approach to teaching content will allow teachers to use the same curriculum that is used for the mainstream class; however, scaffolding with ESOL strategies is necessary. Many publishing companies are now providing strategies for language learners and students with disabilities in the teacher's edition, but it is not probable that every bit of material will come with these provisions. Additionally, in an effort to provide authentic resources, teachers will have to modify their own materials. Today though, the Internet is a treasure trove of resources, websites, translation apps, interactive sites, and you can find almost anything you need. In my university's ESOL-infused teacher education program, we emphasize a list of common teaching strategies that is by no means comprehensive but is recommended by Broward County Schools (see Appendix A). There are also classification and descriptions of language proficiency levels to determine how much modification is necessary (see Appendix B).

As in teaching any students, the teacher must nurture the development of cognitive skills and provide avenues for student participation for language practice. Researchers have studied language immersion programs and determined that students can attain high levels of language proficiency while learning content matter (Fortune, 2012; Lambert & Tucker, 1972; NCBE, 1990). Students understand the material because the teacher uses visuals, realia, demonstrations, hands-on learning, manipulatives, and cooperative strategies where students have to participate in their own learning. Instead of traditional foreign language learning that focuses on isolated classes of grammar, reading, writing, listening, and speaking, learning language through content allows background knowledge, or **schema,** to be built on. The students then can process the information more holistically, top down (Ajideh, 2003; Carrell, 1983; Schleppegrell, Achugar, & Oteíza, 2004) instead of bottom up, or piecemeal.

Hoover and Collier (1989) and Islam and Mares (2003) have created a list of suggestions for selecting and adapting materials for ELs. However, these strategies work well for all students with special needs.

- Be aware of each student's language abilities.
- Make sure appropriate cultural experiences are reflected in the material.
- Ensure that the material progresses at a rate that is commensurate with the needs and abilities of the student.
- Document the success of selected materials.
- Experiment with the materials until you find the most appropriate for your particular student.
- Make a smooth transition into the new material.
- Follow a consistent format or guide when evaluating material.
- Be sure to become knowledgeable about the cultures and heritages of your students to ensure appropriateness and compatibility of the material.
- Evaluate the success of adapted or developed materials as the individual language and cultural needs of the students are addressed. (p. 253)

Many teachers want guidelines for adapting materials. Although this chapter shows actual examples of how to adapt text, other tips are included in the following section (Echevarria & Graves, 2007; Harris & Schultz, 1986; Lewis & Doorlag, 1987; Mandell & Gold, 1984; Reiss, 2005).

- Develop your own supplemental materials.
- Record directions for the material so students can replay for clarity. (You can use your phone, mobile apps, your computer, or recording machines.)
- Provide alternatives to responding verbally to questions (e.g., use prearranged signals, white boards, a card to hold up, individual name tags, a flag, or any indicator they can use instead of speaking).
- Rewrite sections of the text to condense the reading for those with lower proficiency levels.

- Outline the material for the students before they read.
- Teach students the meaning of using bold headings, italicized words, subheadings, and transition words (*first, last, however, although,* etc.).
- Use graphic organizers for preinstruction.
- Reduce the number of pages or items to be completed by the student.
- Break tasks into smaller subtasks.
- Provide additional practice to ensure automaticity and mastery of the material.
- Substitute a similar, less complex task.
- Develop simple study guides, rubrics, graphic organizers, and templates for uniform assignments.
- Develop study guides for all students.

After presenting the content to be learned, the teacher can focus on individual concepts such as grammar or obvious language interferences. Students demonstrate competence on a daily basis within authentic situations as they interact with class members. Using this method challenges students and teaches them how to use learning strategies.

Preparing to Teach the Standard Curriculum

Ms. Aldrich was frustrated and annoyed. Henri, from Haiti, had been sitting in her classroom all year, and she could not seem to motivate him to produce work. He barely uttered a word, and she wondered if there was something wrong with his hearing or if he had other problems of which she was unaware. She knew he would not be able to take the test on the Civil War with the other students. She passed out the test to the rest of the class. When she got to Henri, she tossed a piece of paper on his desk, and said, "Here, draw a picture." He took out his colored pencils and began to doodle. When the bell rang, he shyly put his paper on her desk. When she picked it up, she was speechless. Henri had drawn a gorgeous pictorial of the entire Civil War, from start to finish. He had grasped the lessons, but did not participate in the class work because he was unable to write in English.

All classroom teachers are going to face the same types of problems; therefore, it behooves teachers to collaborate with each other. A thematic approach will unify content throughout the grade levels, and all teachers will be focusing on the same topics. Initially, look at the content you are expected to teach. What are the objectives? Note the language used. Look at the pictures, if any. What realia can you use to enhance the concepts being taught? Will your students be able to understand what is written? Note the language proficiency levels in Appendix B. If a student cannot speak because he or she is in the silent stage of language acquisition, it will be up to the instructor to modify the content to make it comprehensible. What key terms are the students expected to know? You will have to simplify and adapt the text to fit the appropriate language level of the student, from beginner to intermediate to advanced. Using the strategies found in Appendix A, teachers can present information clearly and systematically, so the learners can count on daily structure and format that does not change. Routines will make the ELs comfortable, and soon they will be able to follow the predictable class schedule.

Begin your lessons by writing objectives on the board so students can see what they are expected to know, to do, and to learn. Then, as in good teaching everywhere, list the steps they need to follow to complete the assignments. Use visuals wherever possible, with lists, charts, diagrams, templates, concept maps, and concrete examples. Review frequently; finally, have the students show you what they know through verbal discussion, in a drawing, or in any other acceptable way.

We are often advised to incorporate multicultural factors in our daily academics. Familiarity with your students' culture will allow you to include and refer to situations, matters, and issues that are important to them. All students feel more valued when their teacher knows what is important to them and their families. In the United States, we are taught that it is our job as teachers to reach out to the students, to determine their preferred learning styles, to appreciate the diversity of our learners, and to modify what we can to ensure academic success. The educational culture in the United States stipulates that we adopt a student-centered approach that allows the students to be more responsible for their learning, while the teacher is more of a facilitator. A constructivist method of teaching allows the students to form their own opinions in a type of inquiry approach to learning. Students from other cultures may see this as not really teaching, and will comment to their parents that they are "waiting for the teacher to teach." Thus, learner training is encouraged so the students are cognizant of the class objectives and will understand that the teacher does know how to teach, even though the students might have been asked their opinions about what or how they wanted to learn.

In many countries, going to school means that the teacher lectures while the students sit and copy notes to be used for a test later. In American classrooms, the ideal approach is to allow students to speak to facilitate interactive language practice. With ELs, language has to be very clear and direct. They need time to think, to process what is being said in one language, and then to find an answer. The typical English speaker may speak too fast to be understood by the EL. When we ask one question, we need to make sure it is one question. We have a tendency to ask a question in this way: "So what would have happened if we had not won World War II? What would life be like today? How would we be living, and who would be controlling our country? How would you feel if some other country were controlling the United States?" The student does not know which question to answer.

We need to reduce the amount of teacher talk, ask one question at a time, give plenty of wait time for the question to be processed, rephrase the question if necessary, and create authentic opportunities for students to speak interactively. Know that language learners will make many mistakes; I always tell my students that language learners are going to mangle the language before they dominate it, so do not expect perfection. Expect and encourage trial and error, and take this into consideration when grading. Think globally. Can you understand what the student is trying to say? If the ELs are making themselves understood, that is something to celebrate. Beginners should not be corrected unless the mistake interferes with understanding. For example, "That is a nice chair," when it is really a table, needs to be corrected. "He like she; she pretty" is very clear. You can correct this by saying, "He likes her? Yes, she is pretty," which is a good modeling strategy.

Asking pertinent questions is an art form. It is tempting to ask cognitively lower level questions, such as, "How many people were in the play?" A more profound learning experience can be elicited by asking, "What can we learn from this play?" Think out loud so the students can see your cognitive process. According to Bloom's (1984) taxonomy, critical thinking skills such as hypothesizing, analyzing, predicting, inferencing, reasoning, summarizing, and justifying will help with comprehension of reading and academic content. Always keep in mind that cognitive skills have nothing to do with language skills.

Preparing students for instruction is an important element of effective instruction. Help them become successful by giving them tools to sharpen study skills. Ensure your students will grasp the concept of the lesson by motivating them before instruction begins. Start at the students' level of listening and speaking ability before transitioning into reading and writing. Teach them what steps to follow to solve problems and how to infer meaning from a textbook through the bold print, subtitles, illustrations, graphs, table of contents, and index. Teaching study skills will help all your students, regardless of native language. Develop questioning techniques that will assist students to develop a higher level of cognitive skills instead of expecting them to answer lower level questions. Watch your students closely, and analyze their learning styles. Remember that students from different cultures will reflect a variety of learning preferences. Experiment with a variety of alternative activities, and note the methods students prefer. Check comprehension by using methods such cloze tests (where they fill in the missing word), completing a template (an outline that the student completes with missing information), filling out a timeline, drawing a picture, or any other method that shows comprehension of the subject matter.

Review vocabulary and key concepts with a graphic organizer, a **KWL chart**, a semantic web, or a concept map. (Look up free graphic organizers on the Internet.)

Concept maps will help direct and categorize thoughts, while providing schema or background knowledge for your students. KWL charts will give you the opportunity to see what students already know about a topic.

To complete the KWL chart in Table 8.1, ask the class what they think they know about rainforests, and fill in the first (K) column. Ask what they want to know, and fill in the details in the middle (W) column. At the end of the lesson, to review and summarize, ask students what they have learned. This summation will go in the last column (L). You will be astounded to learn what preconceived notions students have about a topic.

All students will be able to engage in the topic if they possess some background knowledge that will connect concrete concepts to abstract ideas. Teachers can make a subject come alive by offering an enticing initiating activity to open a lesson. Imagine the interest students may show when they enter the classroom and encounter a large, artificial tropical tree, hanging "vines," tropical "animals" hung around the room, and music of the rainforest and wild animals playing. The teacher is decked out in a safari hat with rations of food to carry around the room. The book *The Great Kapok Tree* is displayed and read from, and everything in sight is labeled. Students are surrounded by vocabulary of the rainforest as pictures, collages, maps, and evidence of realia is everywhere.

An opening approach like the one described above is apt to whet the interest of even the most intransigent student. Vocabulary is easily demonstrated by looking at the labels, pictures, and models. When the teacher initiates the KWL chart, students will be eager to offer what they know; their memories are prodded as they understand what the rainforest includes and transcend into the "rainforest" mood. The teacher can start with a group task, engage students in discussions, invite them to share previous knowledge, and examine tactile artifacts found in a rainforest. The Internet can be utilized to find pictorials of "live" rainforests, and students can be invited to engage in various activities to begin the thematic unit.

Although language learning techniques are used in the language learning class, the same or similar methods can be incorporated in the content class. Typically, the younger the student, the more realia are used. However, as the students get older, less embedded information that gives clues to understanding is

TABLE 8.1 Example of KWL Chart		
Rainforests		
K	W	L
What I know:	What I want to know:	What I learned:

present in the text. Unless students have extensive vocabularies, they will soon become lost. Therefore, even the older students will appreciate the scaffolding built in to enhance understanding.

We have offered other strategies in this book but Short (1991) and Troncale (2005) also offer ideas taken from traditional ESOL techniques for content teachers to incorporate in their classes. They recommend the following:

- Realia.
- Demonstrations with action (e.g., science experiments, model language functions in context).
- Filmstrips, video and audio recordings with books and headphones, computer programs.
- Hands-on activities (e.g., role play, TPR, laboratory experiments, art, story sequences, comic strips, creating math word problems, creating templates to be filled in).
- Incorporating Big Books (social studies, science, stories) into lessons.
- Using jazz chants, music, dance, rap songs, poetry; have students write their own rap and poetry about subjects or people being studied.
- Sustained silent reading (SSR), where students are allowed to read material of their choice.

Teachers must provide comprehensible content matter for students. The regular classroom curriculum can be used if modified for the EL. Echevarria, Short, and Powers (2006) and Short (1991) provide excellent strategies for simplifying and adapting materials and encourages teachers to begin with presenting the main point of the text in clear, simple, and understandable language:

- Decide what should be learned by comparing text information with the curricular objectives.
- Eliminate unnecessary details (start by presenting concrete references to abstract ideas).
- Try to relate information to students' backgrounds.
- Use visual representations.

Rewrite the text using these guidelines (Short, 1991):

- Topic sentence, then supporting detail.
- Reduce words in the sentence, and sentences in a paragraph.
- Use subject-verb-object word order.
- Simplify vocabulary, while retaining key concepts and technical language.
- In the text, avoid using many synonyms, which can confuse the reader.
- Use clear vocabulary definitions repetitively, while giving clues by connecting new vocabulary with known vocabulary.
- Use simple verb tenses (present—*I eat*; past—*I ate*; simple future—*I am going to eat*).
- Use the imperative form. (Sit down, please. Take out your books, please. Stop talking, please.)
- Use active, not passive voice. (*Active*: John hit the ball. *Passive*: The ball was hit by John.)
- Use pronouns only when you can tell to whom they are referring. (John went to the store. Tom went to the game. He got lost on the way.)
- Avoid *there*, *it*, or *that* at the beginning of the sentence. They are ambiguous words. (*Don't use*: There are many cars in the garage. *Do use*: Many cars are in the garage.)
- Avoid relative clauses with *who*, *which*, or *whom* in sentences. Make the clause into a sentence, since it creates an embedded sentence. (*Example*: John, a man who is from Texas, is a doctor. *Better*: John is a man from Texas. He is a doctor.)
- Use negative judiciously, especially when testing. (*Avoid*: Which of the following does not belong . . . try to use the form of negation that includes the verb, as in *don't cry*.)
- When the students' language level warrants readiness, teach sequence markers (*first, second*), transition words (*although, however*), and terms that prioritize (*most important, best of all, the least likely*).

Content Area Analysis and Evaluation

In many classrooms, the required texts do not arrive with modifications for diverse learners. This will be up to the teacher. Examine the text to ascertain the adaptability of the text for your class. Figure 8.1 shows an example of how a high school text can be examined to determine how it should be modified. An elementary text would be scrutinized in the same way. Examine the sample of the text analysis in Figure 8.1, developed by Jennifer Peffer. As a result, the teacher can determine whether the book is appropriate and how the book needs to be modified for the ELs.

Short's (1991) training manual is an excellent resource that offers steps to develop lesson plans, adapt material, and incorporate ESOL strategies and techniques for integration of language through the content area. Her model is used in A

Name of Textbook: United States Government—Democracy in Action

Publisher: Glencoe/McGraw Hill—Congressional Quarterly

Content Area: American Government/Civics/History

Grade Level: High School Grades 9–12

*Contributed by Jennifer Peffer.

1. Content Objectives of the Book—Scope and Sequence:

United States Government—Democracy in Action introduces the key concepts required to understand the history and composition of the American governmental system. These concepts include Federalism, Separation of Powers/Checks and Balances, Civil Rights and Liberties, Constitutional Law, Political Processes, Comparative Government, and Economics. The book also highlights a variety of critical thinking, writing, and technology skills used to study American government. Examples include understanding cause and effect, decision making, interpretation of poll results, taking notes, outlining, writing reports, and using computers for research.

   The teacher's edition begins each chapter with a "Bell Ringer." This activity is used to motivate students and to get them involved in the chapter. It introduces the key concepts to be discussed. The book is organized into nine units and twenty-six chapters. The student is guided through the book beginning with the origins of American Government. The next three units focus on the three branches of government: Legislative, Executive, and Judicial. Unit Five spotlights the Constitution and civil rights. This appropriately leads into government participation and policy. The book finishes with an overview of state and local government and a comparative look at different political and economic systems that exist throughout the world.

   Every section begins with a series of questions designed to focus the reader's attention to the important ideas present in the reading. The sections end with vocabulary and key people reviews as well questions about the reading. Critical thinking questions are also placed at the end of each section. Each chapter has a review of facts, key terms, and concepts. There are also critical thinking exercises, technology activities, and government participation assignments.

   A. Chapter: The Constitution

   Four sections:

   1. Structure and Principles

   2. Three Branches of Government

   3. Amending the Constitution

   4. The Amendments

   B. A large number of concepts are covered in this chapter because the Constitution is the basis of the entire American Government, which is a conglomeration of many interrelated concepts. Each chapter reviews many of the concepts that were previously introduced, solidifying the reader's comprehension.

Figure 8.1 Analysis of a Textbook to Be Modified* (See appendix for sample lesson.) (*Continued*)

Thirty new ideas and vocabulary terms are to be mastered in Chapter 3. Some of these are jurisdiction, popular sovereignty, judicial review, checks and balances, federalism, impeachment, ratification, probable cause, due process of law, and warrant. After completing the study of Chapter 3, students will be able to

❑ Summarize the historical origins of the Constitution.

❑ List the major parts of the Constitution.

❑ Define the major principles involved in the formation of the Constitution.

❑ List the three branches of government and the expressed powers of each.

❑ Define implied powers and give examples of each by analysis of the Constitution.

❑ Explain the concepts of checks and balances and why the system is important to a stable government.

❑ Outline the amendment process and explain why it was designed to be a difficult one.

❑ Identify the ten amendments that make up the Bill of Rights.

❑ Differentiate between a right and a privilege.

❑ Classify the amendments into ones that affect governments, personal rights, and societies.

❑ Explain the concept of judicial review and give examples of its effect on citizens today.

2. Unfamiliar Cultural Assumptions:

The study of American Government presents concepts that might be unfamiliar or even uncomfortable to some people from other nations. Notions such as freedom of speech, women's rights, popular sovereignty, and capitalism are all concepts that are foreign to many nations. These concepts are addressed from a very basic level. Most of the exercises require at least a basic understanding of the concepts after they are covered to fully answer the questions. The author's examples are well explained and are accompanied by a good amount of background information, which allows the student who might be unfamiliar with the material to answer the questions and participate fully.

One area that would prove difficult for some ELs would be the political cartoons. Much of the humor is characteristically American and might not be grasped by students from another nation who do not have schema pertaining to American popular history.

A group of women in a museum are standing around a portrait of men. The caption on the cartoon reads, "Founding Fathers! How come no Founding Mothers?"

Students might be from countries where women are not expected to play a role in government and therefore might not understand the significance of this cartoon.

For the most part, this book is free from cultural assumptions in the testing and review questions. The role of the text is to portray the culture of American government and the history that led to its development. After teaching the core concepts, students should understand the evaluation exercises, despite their initially unfamiliar ideas.

3. Higher Order Thinking Skills:

Many exercises in this textbook require higher order thinking skills (see table):

Example	Skill
What is the relationship between the principles, concepts of federalism, and the separation of powers as detailed in the Constitution?	Analyzing the two concepts of federalism and the separation of powers as detailed in the Constitution. Relating two concepts to another.
Have students keep a journal of their daily activities for two weeks. At the end of the period, ask students to name activities that would have been restricted or impossible under a repressive government or a government that does not have a constitution based on the major principles discussed in section one.	Analyzing the Constitution to draw a conclusion of what rights are protected as they relate to students today.
Which principles or provisions of the Constitution allow students to carry out their daily activities without fear or punishment?	Making predictions. Drawing conclusions. Relating applicable concepts.
How would the federal system of government be affected if the Supreme Court did not have the power of judicial review?	Making predictions. Drawing conclusions. Relating applicable concepts

Figure 8.1 Analysis of a Textbook to Be Modified* (See appendix for sample lesson.) (*Continued*)

a. Modification of Question: These exercises are appropriate for ELs. The wording may be a little advanced, but simple rewriting of the question would assist the students by clarifying what is being asked.

An example would be another version of question 1: *How are federalism and separation of powers the same? How are they different?* This would make the question easier to understand and would allow the student to focus on the concept and not the language.

The second question also would be appropriate for ELs, with language modification to ensure comprehension. This task allows the students to practice writing in a nonacademic arena and also to take time to analyze and formulate their answers, free from the language issues.

4. Text Evaluation:

This text is visually oriented, which makes it comprehensible. Over eighty maps and charts complement the text, as well as pictures on nearly every page, a boon for teaching students of other languages and the visual learner. The book is also in tune with issues that are pertinent to today's society. Many news stories and illustrative examples highlight relevance of the subject matter to the students' lives, including censorship, civil rights, and equal protection under law. The text also establishes important vocabulary and terms at the beginning and end of each section. Important words are highlighted in bold when they are introduced within the text. What would help would be making review answers available to the students to allow self-checks for understanding as they continue to study.

The teacher's addition has many supplemental activities that are appropriate for different academic levels. The author also focuses on multiple learning styles and has activities that focus on the different intelligences. Many resources are available to accompany the book such as a DVD that contains video and audio material to complement each chapter, Internet sites, and computer software with review activities. The text also offers supplemental materials that would be particularly helpful to ELs, including lecture notes that outline the chapter content and guided reading activities with graphic organizers to help convert the reading into comprehensible input.

The text was well organized and appropriate for ELs as well as the general student population. The variety of activities that are available to solidify the concepts being taught is impressive and will allow the teacher to reach students of all levels. The activities are labeled by difficulty (levels 1–3, with 1 being basic for all students and 3 being advanced) in the teacher edition. The text is sensitive to students who need more vocabulary assistance and focuses on concept building and relating those concepts to concrete, real-life situations. This book will be a valuable tool in teaching the ESOL population as well as English-proficient learners.

Note: See Appendix for template.

Note: In the appendix, Honey Smith shows how she adapted text from a book on government. She created a PowerPoint presentation with pictorials and modifications for the English learner in the mainstream class. Because of copyright issues, I am unable to include the visuals she used. However, I have included the text slides along with the websites with wonderful clipart that can accompany the text. To make your own visuals, you can use public domain and sites that give permission to use for learning purposes.

Figure 8.1 Analysis of a Textbook to Be Modified* (See appendix for sample lesson.)

FINAL POINTS

- Consider the level and ability of your English learners. They will be different, but all students will benefit from differentiated instruction.
- Remember that students may not have the schema that will allow them to do their work. Be sure to provide vocabulary instruction before attempting to give a lesson.
- Make sure your materials will be comprehensible for your students.
- Although you may gear your lessons for grade-level proficiency, be sure to include modifications for the more advanced level student, as well as the more limited proficient student. You may be surprised to see an unexpected outcome.

Discussion Questions and Activities

1. Describe the steps you would take to discover what background knowledge your students possess. What activities would you offer to connect their prior learning with the lesson you are going to present?
2. Choose three books. Using the Content Area Textbook Analysis form provided in Appendix F, analyze the main objectives of the books. What unfamiliar cultural assumptions do you find? (Remember that your students will not come from an American mind frame. Everything might be different.) Name three higher order thinking skills that are present in the text. What is your overall evaluation of the books for English learners?
3. Choose a paragraph from a text. Using the methods prescribed in the chapter, simplify the language for beginning, intermediate, and advanced language proficient English learners. Create an alternative assessment for each level of language proficiency (beginning, intermediate, and advanced). Why do you think these assessments are valid?
4. Create a lesson plan based on one of the CCSS objectives. What types of modification will you use to modify the language in the lesson plan?

Resources

Colorin Colorado differentiated instruction
http://www.colorincolorado.org/article/41025/

Strategies for teaching English learners
http://www.csun.edu/science/ref/language/teaching-ell.html

Teachers first-differentiating instruction
http://www.teachersfirst.com/di.cfm

Scaffolding and differentiating instruction in mixed ability ESL classes using a round robin activity
http://iteslj.org/Techniques/DelliCarpini-RoundRobin.html

Classroom strategies and tools for differentiating instruction in the ESL classroom
http://minnetesol.org/journal/vol25_html_pages/17_Dahlman.htm

Differentiated instruction and testing accommodations for ESOL students
https://www.montgomeryschoolsmd.org/departments/development/documents/ell/Accomm_and_Differen.pdf

Teaching ESL in Mainstream classes
http://www.youtube.com/watch?v=TT_-kXUE2xo

Teaching English learners across the Curriculum
http://www.youtube.com/watch?v=-nBvnk8_1F8

References

Ajideh, P. (2003). Schema theory-based pre-reading tasks: A neglected essential in the ESL reading class. *The reading matrix, 3*(1).

Bailey, A. L., & Butler, F. A. (2003). An evidentiary framework for operationalizing academic language for broad application to K-12 education: A design document. CSE Report.

Bunch, G. C., Kibler, A., & Pimentel, S. (2012). Realizing opportunities for English learners in the common core English language arts and disciplinary literacy standards. *Stanford, CA: Understanding Language Initiative.* Retrieved March 25, 2013.

Coleman, D. & Pimentel, S. (2012). Revised publishers' criteria for the Common Core State Standards in English language arts and literacy, grades 3–12. Retrieved from the Common Core Standards Initiative at www.corestandards.org/assets/Publishers_Criteria_for_3-12.pdf

The Common Core State Standards and English Learners. (2017). *Tesol.org.* Retrieved May 8, 2017, from   https://www.tesol.org/advance-the-field/standards/the-common-core-state-standards-and-english-learners

Common Core State Standards. *http://www.corestandards.org/*

Echevarria, J., & Graves, A. W. (2007). *Sheltered content instruction: Teaching English language learners with diverse abilities.* Los Angeles, CA: Pearson Allyn and Bacon.

Echevarria, J., Short, D., & Powers, K. (2006). School reform and standards-based education: A model for English-language learners. *The Journal of Educational Research, 99*(4), 195–211.

Echevarria, J., Vogt, M., & Short, D. (2004). *Making content comprehensible for English learners: The SIOP model.* Boston: Allyn & Bacon.

Fortune, T. W. (2012). What the research says about immersion. *Chinese language learning in the early grades: A handbook of resources and best practices for Mandarin immersion,* 9–13.

Howard, J. & Major, J. (2004). Guidelines for designing effective English language teaching materials. *The TESOLANZ Journal, 12,* 50–58.

Islam, C. & Mares, C. (2003). Adapting classroom materials. *Developing materials for language teaching,* 86–100.

National Governors Association. (2010). Common core state standards for English language arts & literacy in history/social studies, science, and technical subjects. *Common core state standards.*

Reiss, J. (2005). *Teaching content to English language learners: Strategies for secondary school success.* Longman.

Schleppegrell, M. J., Achugar, M., & Oteíza, T. (2004). The grammar of history: Enhancing content-based instruction through a functional focus on language. *TESOL quarterly, 38*(1), 67–93.

Tomlinson, C. A. (2000). Differentiation of Instruction in the Elementary Grades. *ERIC Digest.*

Troncale, N. (2005). Content-based instruction, cooperative learning, and CALP instruction: Addressing the whole education of 7–12 ESL. *Working Papers in TESOL & Applied Linguistics, 2*(3).

van Lier, L. & Walqui, A. (2012). Language and the common core state standards. *Commissioned Papers on Language and Literacy Issues in the Common Core State Standards and Next Generation Science Standards, 94,* 44.

CHAPTER 9

LITERACY, TECHNOLOGY, AND THE ENGLISH LEARNER

Susanne I. Lapp

KEY POINTS

- Curriculum planning is heavily influenced by the standards movement.
- Personally relevant information inspires student learning.
- Technology applications enhance phonics and word skills.
- Applying appropriate literacy strategies inspires student learning.
- Sharing ideas inspires student learning.

Upon entering Ms. Draginoff's actively engaged and dynamic second-grade classroom, visitors are instantly aware of the positive academic forces in play. Scrolled across one of the classroom walls, Ms. Draginoff has posted a brightly colored Professional Pledge to her students: As your teacher, I will strive to provide you with a safe learning environment where you will learn something new and exciting about our world and the people in it . . . **Every Single Day**! Clearly, Ms. Draginoff's paramount concern for her students is that they become successful learners, equipped to succeed in an academically charged environment, surrounded by positive learning outcomes. To establish this learning environment, Ms. Draginoff followed several fundamental rules about creating and embracing a student-centered, active learning environment where students are:

❏ recognized for their varying levels of literacy knowledge and unique experiences using literacy concepts and skills,
❏ immersed in academic activities, which encourage them to read, write, and discuss ideas,
❏ engaged in meaning-making inquiry, action, imagination, invention, interaction, hypothesizing and personal reflection (*Cranton & Taylor, 2012*).

Ms. Draginoff eagerly shared how she came to the above instructional conclusions while working with a young English learner, Katerina, who had been placed in her classroom. Katerina had recently arrived in the United States from Russia. Expecting the child to have significant academic challenges learning in an English-speaking classroom, Ms. Draginoff seated Katerina close to her teacher's desk. During the first few days of class, Katerina demonstrated hesitation engaging in daily activities with her classmates, preferring to sit at her desk, and draw using one of the classroom iPad tablets. She was particularly interested in the app 123 Color HD, Premium Edition for Kids, which allowed children to complete freestyle and paint by numbers and paint by letters drawings.

Observing Katerina's natural interest in expressing herself through drawing, Ms. Draginoff realized that Katerina was a talented artist. She quickly seized the opportunity to validate Katerina's creative efforts and asked her to add words to her drawings, which the app allowed. Ms. Draginoff assumed that Katerina might use Cyrillic script in her writing, but to her surprise, Katerina actually attempted to use English words to describe her drawings. In Russia, Katerina had attended a bilingual Russian-English preschool and elementary school. Katerina had spent her school days speaking English and Russian with her teacher and classmates, and was actually learning to read and write in English.

Although Katerina demonstrated confidence as an illustrator, she still manifested difficulty with the English language. Katerina understood some complicated speech but only after Ms. Draginoff repeated herself several times in the conversation or gave alternate examples. Katerina frequently asked her teacher for *the right word* and she seemed challenged by some of the phonic rules of the English language.

Ms. Draginoff noted that the child was at the "Developing stage of English proficiency" (WIDA classification) where she successfully understood some complicated speech, but required some repetition. Katerina used English spontaneously with classmates at lunch. During instructional time, however, she experienced difficulty expressing her thoughts due to her restricted English vocabulary, opting instead to speak in simple sentences, which were frequently marked by grammatical errors. Ms. Draginoff wanted to encourage and challenge Katerina to become more spontaneous in her attempts to use English for academic purposes.

Ms. Draginoff's instructional goals were to encourage Katerina to become a more confident English reader, writer, and speaker in the academic classroom. She believed that as Katerina became more inclined to participate in daily classroom lessons and activities, she would be exposed to even greater and more complex literacy processes. Several literacy activities and strategies are discussed below.

Strategy: Word Walls
The use of Word Walls has long been considered an effective instructional tool for early literacy and language learners. Entering (or beginning) proficiency level through developing-level English learners benefit from Word Walls that include the students' names in the alphabetical listing. These Word Walls need to be conveniently posted at the students' eye level, thus encouraging them to identify their names, and those of their classmates. Gradually, students begin to recognize the "power behind the print." Letters and words begin to take meaning, and printed names indicate individual personalities. Students understand the phonic generalizations and word analysis skills that come into play when creating words (CCSS.ELA-Literacy.RF.2.3). Over time, with encouragement, modeling, and opportunity, students will become interested in placing words from songs, poems, and stories on the Word Wall. Students are invited to add new words to the wall from their own literacy experiences, and together in small group instruction, students chorally read the words on the word walls (Peregoy & Boyle, 2012).

The Word Wall strategy can also be used with older, more advanced EL students. Words Walls allow Bridging and Reaching level EL students to make critical connections between new vocabulary and existing items, while adding to and strengthening their developing content knowledge (Daniels & Zemelman, 2014). Word Walls enable students to engage with language and to refer to their thinking about relevant words. Word Walls are capable of providing crucial support for students' comprehension as they look at the key vocabulary terms before reading, check their understanding while reading, and review and reflect on the vocabulary and concepts once they have completed their reading (CCSS.ELA-Literacy.L.6.4).

Personally Relevant Information Inspires Learning

As Katerina's teacher began to incorporate these instructional changes in her classroom, she noticed the student's level of enthusiasm and interest increase. Ms. Draginoff included English words on the Word Wall that were important to Katerina. Curiously, these new vocabulary words began to appear in her writing such as *flowers, trees, sunshine,* and *sky.* She also included more personally relevant words such as *father, mother,* and *child* (CCSS.ELA-Literacy.L.2.6). Katerina was also encouraged to share some Russian words and phrases with her classmates and they were also added to the classroom Word Wall including Мама (Mama), папа (Papa), Ука́тери́на (Katerina), and МеНЯ ЭоВуТ Ука́тери́на (I am called Katerina.).

Katerina's classmates were amazed that her name was pronounced differently in Russian with the additional (/y/ + /ĕ/) sounds at the beginning of her name (CCSS.ELA-Literacy.RF.2.3.f). Soon, all of Katerina's classmates were eager to learn more about the Cyrillic alphabet and wanted to know how to pronounce their names in Russian. Ms. Draginoff, along with the assistance of Katerina, found a wonderful opportunity to teach the rest of the class about the differences in the written scripts and orthographic representations of words in the Russian and English languages. Ms. Draginoff told the children that Katerina learned to write and read using the Russian script, Cyrillic, when she lived in Russia, just as they had learned to use the English script in the United States (Rayner et al., 2001; O'brien et.al. 2011).

Technology Applications and Phonics and Word skills

Since Ms. Draginoff's classroom possessed a number of iPad tablets, she was able to provide students with opportunities to practice important phonic generalizations. During center time, students used two apps (Endless Alphabet by Originatorkids.com, and Pocket Phonics Apps by My Pocket Ltd.). Endless Alphabet allowed students to see, manipulate, and hear letter/sound relationships (CCSS.ELA-Literacy.RF.2.3). By dropping and dragging letters, students were able to hear letter sounds and begin to create new words. Once students created a word, the word became animated, and students were able to watch a mini video clip featuring that new vocabulary word. Students also used Pocket Phonics to experiment with segmenting and blending skills and forming letters into words (CCSS.ELA-Literacy.RF.2.3.a). This mobile app allowed students to focus on letter–sound relationships. Students listened to and pronounced the sounds, and then traced the letter(s) made by the sounds and began to spell words. Each time a student spelled a word correctly, a picture appeared to go along with the correctly spelled word. (This simple technique can be used from very young learners to older learners as well.)

Students were delighted when they were given the opportunity to explore the two apps. Ms. Draginoff reported that some students, including Katerina, added the newly formed words to the classroom Word Walls. Students' interest and positive reactions to phonics and word attack skills encouraged

Ms. Draginoff to provide additional opportunities for contextualized literacy experiences and she incorporated student-centered reading, writing, and listening activities using authentic literature.

Older, more advanced EL students (bridging to reaching-level) must constantly strive to increase their academic vocabulary. Apps such as NPR (npr.com) and Kindle (AMZN) are equipped with text annotation features, which allow users to access online dictionaries, pronunciation guides, and thesaurus, as well as specific annotation features such as highlighting reading passages and allowing students to take notes on the digital texts (CCSS.ELA-Literacy.L.6.4.c).

Strategy: Read Alouds

The Read Aloud strategy can be used to help students at any age or English proficiency level. However, it is most effective with students who enjoy listening to stories read aloud. Read alouds introduce students to the aesthetic pleasures and functions of print. They are exposed to the literary notions about story plots and characters, and they have the opportunity to observe teachers model the reading process. Although read-aloud activities appear to be aesthetically pleasurable, they do in fact create a heavy cognitive–linguistic demand on listeners, particularly in terms of attention, comprehension, and memory. Teachers need to compensate for these challenges by frequently pausing to discuss illustrations and graphic representations as they relate to print, make predictions, and reconfirm predictions that support comprehension. Repeated readings of the text will also enhance comprehension. Once the text has been read aloud to students, it is likely that they will want to have access to the text to practice some of the techniques that they have seen modeled by the teacher. It is advisable for the teacher to have multiple copies of the text so students can access it for individual reading. In addition, a great way of increasing understanding is to provide each student with a text so he or she can follow along silently with the teacher's words. This will model pronunciation while the student visualizes how the word appears.

Read aloud strategies also appeal to more advanced EL readers. Typically, read alouds are introduced before students actually begin to read the text and are used to build an enjoyment of reading. Teachers can select from a number of print-related materials including short stories and brief passages of interesting material or books related to the content area. Read alouds can be used with individual students, pairs, or small groups. Although effective read alouds engage students in a critical analysis of the reading content, another benefit to read alouds is that it creates a powerful listening experience for the audience. Read alouds help listeners grasp the big ideas, formulate questions and make content more meaningful to listeners (Daniels & Zemelman, 2014).

Using Appropriate Literacy Strategies Inspires Learning

Ms. Draginoff continued to focus on ways to engage Katerina in classroom conversations. She decided to implement the read aloud strategy during whole class instruction and almost immediately, Katerina's interest in literacy began to blossom. As soon as the children returned from lunch, Ms. Draginoff read from one of the classroom library books. Katerina put down her iPad and listened attentively to the story being read. Ms. Draginoff frequently drew students' attention to the beautiful illustrations that appeared throughout the book. One picture in the book depicted a busy street with many trucks and busses. Katerina looked at the picture and claimed that it looked like her home in Russia, "I lived in the town of *MOCKBa* (pronounced *Muskva*) but you Americans say it [sic], you make it sound like this /mosk-kooww/ . . . *like a cow at the end!!!*"

Katerina was engaged in the story that her teacher read aloud to the class and found a way to personally connect to the content within the story. As she listened to the story, she used her background knowledge from her first language, Russian, and compared it to the pronunciation differences in English

(CCSS. ELA-Literacy.SL.2.1.c, http://www.corestandards.org/ELA-Literacy/SL/2/1/c/). Ms. Draginoff was impressed that not only did Katarina listened closely to the story, but she actually felt confident enough to share her thoughts with her classmates. Many of Katerina's comments about reading and writing appeared to come from previous experiences with the Russian language. In Russia, where she spent the school day attending a bilingual Russian/English school, students sang Russian and English songs, listened to bilingual literature, and played games. At home, Katerina's mother spoke Russian and read Russian stories to her. Katerina was immersed by the Russian language and culture. This exposure appeared to be reflected in her second-language literacy experiences as she consistently integrated Russian language in her English writing.

As teachers prepare to implement read aloud strategies with their students, it is incumbent on teachers of all English proficiency levels to select books that are age and topic appropriate as well as comprehensible to students. If the vocabulary is too difficult for students, teachers need to clarify, define, and add the new vocabulary to the classroom Word Walls. Introducing unfamiliar vocabulary in a comprehensive context will help scaffold reading comprehension. Since students in the classroom have a variety of literacy experiences, teachers need a well-stocked classroom library complete with an assortment of books and technology applications that will suit a variety of reading levels.

Technology Applications Supplement Reading Strategies

Several mobile learning apps can also be used by beginning level students to enhance the read aloud experience. *MeeGenius* by Houghton Mifflin Harcourt is a storybook mobile app that reads books aloud to students and then allows students to independently read the books to themselves. Students can select from several classic stories that are supported by illustrations to assist with comprehension. Another popular mobile app, *Speakaboos* (www.speakaboos.com) provides readers with stories on a variety of themes. Readers can read along or have stories read to them. Both apps can be used in one-to-one iPad settings or they can be used within a single iPad classroom where the iPad can be projected onto a Smartboard for the entire class to view.

As Katerina engaged in the literacy and learning activities of the classroom, she continued to embrace her love of art and incorporate her illustrations of animals and landscapes in many of her writing assignments. Ms. Draginoff decided to capitalize on Katerina's interests and abilities by encouraging her to continue constructing meaning from texts, which focused on her interest in the environment, as well as her passion for drawing and introduced her to the *Sketching My Way through the Text* strategy.

Strategy: Sketching My Way through the Text

The *Sketching My Way through the Text* strategy helps students visualize meaning and conceptualize ideas from their reading. Students create a sequence of sketches, drawings, or cartoons to illustrate ideas described in the reading. The strategy can be applied easily to a wide range of English language proficiency levels. Developing (language) level students, such as Katerina, are most successful constructing meaning from texts when they are permitted to use their background knowledge. Katarina had expressed an interest in the environment, particularly with plants. During a science lesson, she used this strategy to sketch simple drawings of the germination process of a seedling as it grew to a plant (CCSS.ELA-Literacy. RI.2.3). *Bridging and Reaching* level EL students, who are transitioning into mainstream English content classrooms, can use the strategy to describe the relationship between plants and the soil ecosystem. Students sketch the linear changes of plant life from sowing seeds to the advanced stages of seed germination (CCSS.ELA-Literacy.RST.6-8.3). The strategy can also be useful in social studies content where students are expected to know historical events or how a bill becomes a law (CCSS.ELA-Literacy.RH.6-8.3) and students in English language arts classrooms use the strategy to explain complicated plots in a novel (CCSS.ELA-Literacy.RI.6.5). *Sketching My Way through the Text* is recognized as one of the most effective thinking strategies that proficient readers employ as a means for expansive thinking revealing processes of change, development, or multiple perspectives around the topics (Daniels & Zemelman, 2014).

Sharing Ideas Inspires Learning

Teachers with access to tablets or mobile devices can encourage students to sketch out their drawings using a number of apps including *Drawing Desk by 4 Access Solutions Limited* (drawingdeskapp.com) and *123 Color HD, Premium Edition for Kids*. Students with limited access to technology can quickly complete their sketches on an 8 ½ ×11 blank piece. The goal is to encourage students not to break the flow of reading by dwelling on their artistic masterpieces for too long. In small groups, students can share their digital or hand-drawn sketches and compare them to see the many ways that ideas might be represented. Students have the opportunity to review and revisit their comprehension of new material. Teachers may also choose to take students' paper sketches, tape them up on the walls, and create a gallery walk where small groups move from one set of drawings to the next, noticing and comparing how their classmates sketched images from various aspects of the reading. Teachers with mobile devices could photograph sketches and place them in document-sharing web tools such as *Edmodo* or *Google Docs*, thus encouraging students to view each other's work in an electronic gallery walk (CCSS.ELA-Literacy.RI.6.7 and CCSS.ELA-Literacy.RH.6-8.7).

FINAL POINTS

- Standards can drive curriculum, especially when students are immersed in academic activities that encourage students to read, write, and discuss ideas.
- Personally relevant information inspires student learning, and teachers can plan unique experiences through a variety of activities that promote literacy concepts and skills.
- Technology applications enhance phonics and word skills when students engage in meaningful learning.

Discussion Questions and Activities

1. As a teacher who encounters an English learner in the classroom, how would you initially work with your student to gradually introduce the student to English reading and writing activities? Create a plan and share it with your group.
2. How might you incorporate your English-language-learning students' first language or culture in your English literacy activities? Describe the activities you could incorporate.
3. Identify five other literacy strategies that would be effective to use with primary-grade English learners.
4. Provide three examples of software or mobile apps that might enhance the literacy development of EL students.
5. Using one of the standards, create a project using one of the mobile apps you discovered. Teach your group how to use the app for a lesson to meet the standard.

Resources

123 Color HD, Premium Edition for Kids by Steven Glinberg (iOS devices) and found in the iTunes Store

Drawing Desk by 4 Access Solutions Limited (drawingdeskapp.com)

Endless Alphabet by Originatorkids.com and Pocket Phonics Apps by My Pocket Ltd

Kindle. AMZN Mobile LLC amazon.com

MeeGenius by Houghton Mifflin Harcourt

NPR npr.org

Speakaboos (www.speakaboos.com)

References

Common Core State Standards Initiative. (2012). Retrieved from http://www.corestandards.org

Taylor, E. W., & Cranton, P. (2012). *The handbook of transformative learning: Theory, research, and practice.* John Wiley & Sons.

Cranton, P. & Taylor, E. (2012). Transformative learning theory: Seeking a more unified theory. In E. Taylor, P. Cranton and Associates (Eds.), *The handbook of transformative learning: Theory, research and practice* (pp.3–20). San Francisco, CA: Jossey-Bass.

Daniels, H. & Zemelman, S. (2014). *Subjects matter: Every teacher's guide to content-area reading.* Heinemann.

O'Brien, B.A., Wolf, M., Miller, L.T., Lovett, M.W., & Morris, R. (2011). Orthographic processing efficiency in developmental dyslexia: An investigation of age and treatment factors at the sublexical level. *Annals of Dyslexia, 61,* 111–135.

Peregoy, S. B. & Boyle, O. F. (2012). *Reading, writing, and learning in ESL: A resource book for teaching K-12 English learners* (6th ed.). Pearson: Boston, MA.

Rayner, K., Foorman, B. R., Perfetti, C. A., Pesetsky, D., & Seidenberg, M. S. (2001). How psychological science informs the teaching of reading. Psychological Science in the Public Interest, *2*(2), 31–74.

CHAPTER 10

TEACHING MATH TO ENGLISH LEARNERS— MYTHS AND METHODS

Sally Robison

KEY POINTS

- Language misunderstanding causes mathematical misunderstanding as well.
- Math is not necessarily a universal subject. Every culture has its own way of doing math.
- Be sure to assess your EL student for math concepts that is not mistaken for language concept.

Many teachers tell me that mathematics should be easy for English learners (ELs) because the concepts translate across languages. This idea appears to make sense because many ELs do well in math, even when they are functioning at a rudimentary level of language proficiency. However, language misunderstandings eventually emerge, as mathematics is a subject that has its own vocabulary, double meanings, and idiosyncrasies seen nowhere else. I invited Dr. Sally Robison, a teacher educator in mathematics, to write a chapter highlighting the issues and problems we can expect to find when we teach ELs math in the mainstream classroom. She guides us to the best ways of teaching mathematics to students who are newcomers to English.

> Gloria, a third grader and a native Portuguese speaker, has been in a Florida school for two years. She is bright and apt in math and knows her basic addition and multiplication facts. However, the math vocabulary is different in English, and when Gloria has to show her work, it is always marked wrong, even though she gets the right answer. The same problem happens to Noel Evan, from Haiti. He gets the answer correct, but he does not show his work so his problem is marked wrong. In his country, he has to do math in his head and only show the answer.

One of the greatest misconceptions about mathematics is the idea that, since it is a universal concept, English learners will have no problems transferring mathematical knowledge to English. Although this might be true with simple, concrete number algorithms (2 + 2 = 4), many other aspects of mathematics might prove difficult because of the language differences. Additionally, the assessment of conceptual understanding of important mathematical concepts may prove inaccurate if the primary method of assessment is the standardized test or the analysis of answers to word problems. Any teacher knows the difficulty that even native English speakers have with wording such as this: "Five times a number is two more than ten times the number." "A number" and "the number" are referring to the same number, yet many students will not decode the sentence this way. Look at this phrase: "The sum of two numbers is 77. If the first number is 10 times the other, find the number." How do students know if the second sentence refers to two numbers or the same number? (Campbell, Davis, & Adams, 2007; Dale & Cuevas, 1992). Therefore, teachers must demonstrate the meaning of these problems with pictures and models as concretely as possible, and explain the semantic differences between "a" and "the."

Modifications for language learners must be provided in mathematics instruction as well as every other content area. However, ELs need many opportunities to learn all aspects and complexities of mathematics while obtaining academic and communicative competence in English. Lessons must contain both content objectives and language objectives that help students learn language through specific subject matter rather than through isolated activities (Cantoni-Harvey, 1987; Hill & Miller, 2013; Short, 1991) In other words, students do not have to learn English before they commence learning mathematics.

Critical framing encourages learners to evaluate what they have learned, to constructively critique that learning, and to creatively extend and apply it to new contexts (NLG, 1996; Skovsmose & Borba, 2004). Critical framing directly applies to the concept of problem solving in mathematics. Teachers cannot provide every possible scenario in mathematical problem solving, but teachers should provide connections to key problem-solving strategies that assist the students during their mathematical challenges.

Teaching students to make connections within the subject, and in the real world, to reason mathematically and verify their findings, to solve real-world problems, to communicate their thinking about mathematics, and to represent their findings in a meaningful way, formulate the five process standards that encourage "mathematical confidence" as defined in the National Council of Teachers of Mathematics (NCTM) (2000) *Principles and Standards* document.

Diaz-Rico and Weed (1995, p.137) explain that the major difficulties English learners have with the language of mathematics are in the area of "vocabulary skills, syntax, semantics, and discourse features." To mitigate these problem areas, Schleppegrell (2007) offers answers to linguistic challenges, and Zemelman, Daniels, and Hyde (1998) outline the best practices for teaching mathematics in their book entitled *Best Practice: New Standards for Teaching and Learning in America's Schools*. These practices include

- Using math manipulatives to make math concepts concrete.
- Teaching students to do cooperative group work.
- Discussion of math.
- Questions and making speculations.
- Justifying the thinking processes.
- Writing how they think and feel about math and problem solving.
- Using problem-solving approaches as the most effective type of math instruction.
- Integrating content with math.
- Using calculators, computers, and other types of technology.
- The teacher is a facilitator of learning.
- Using assessment as a learning tool during instruction.

It is evident that many strategies exist for teachers to use that facilitate the learning and application of mathematical concepts by all students, including those who are language enriched. The many strategies mentioned in this chapter have been categorized into the following areas: literacy development, cultural harmony, and effective instruction/assessment. Although the strategies are often intertwined in the teaching process, for ease in explanation of each strategy, the breakdown is beneficial. These strategies will prove helpful in teaching ELs.

Literacy Development Strategies in Math

The spoken word and the written word require students to be literate in the vocabulary and fluent in their reading so they are capable of comprehending what is read. This is easily said, and though it can be difficult, students can be successful with the proper strategies and support. By incorporating the following strategies, students will improve their academic vocabulary, comprehension, and mathematical skills.

Review Concepts

The teacher will need to review important key concepts whenever necessary, such as mathematical terms that may be abstract or confusing to students. For instance, a lesson on multiplication of two-digit numbers may require an explanation and review or teaching of pertinent vocabulary, such as **product, sum, carry, exchange,** and **equals,** in a contextual setting. Don't automatically assume students know these terms or any others or their synonyms.

Generate a concept table, asking students to identify words that have similar meanings. For example, start off with the word **add** and ask students to create three to five more words that mean basically the same thing. Let them brainstorm on their own, and then bring small groups together to compare their answers.

Add
Combine
Sum
Plus

When reviewing these concepts, it is also important to consider the varied proficiency levels of EL students. While students with a higher language proficiency may benefit from an explanation of necessary academic vocabulary prior to a lesson, students with a beginner/low level proficiency will need a visual representation to help make the input more comprehensible.

Vocabulary Building

Introduce pertinent vocabulary in each lesson using realia, photographic representations, and demonstrations whenever possible. Before covering a section in the textbook, examine the material to identify terms that will be new to the students or words that will need further explanation. Present any symbols or words that may create problems for the students. The new vocabulary should be repeated often in a meaningful setting, context, and/or paraphrased so that students will retain and use the concepts that are related. Use any synonyms that will assist in their understanding. Capps and Pickreign (1993) and Loomis (2012) recommend a minimum of six exposures to a new word during the lesson and at least thirty additional exposures throughout the following month. Mathematics has often been referred to as a foreign language, possessing its own vocabulary and meanings that have another connotation outside the subject. For example, **simplify** means making something less complex; yet in mathematics, the process of **simplifying a radical expression** may generate a cumbersome process that results in a final answer that appears much less simple.

Teachers need to clarify expressions, words, and symbols that have multiple meanings. For example, the word **reciprocal** is similar to the word **reciprocate** but does not imply the same meaning. The word

rationalize has a meaning in normal context, yet has a very different meaning in the realm of mathematics. Remember that the repertoire of methods and activities used to teach vocabulary in other areas, such as writing words and definitions, spelling tests, and providing pictures of words, are just as appropriate when teaching a mathematics lesson. Mathematics often includes technical words such as **denominator,** **quotient,** and **coefficient** or other words with multiple meanings, such as **column** and **table.** Encourage students to talk about their conception of mathematics and to verify and justify their thinking. Verbalizing what they are thinking will give the teacher great insight into the misinterpretations and confusion students may have. Physical examples are extremely helpful to show concrete examples of abstract concepts.

Another helpful tool to use as students begin to explore the text and/or vocabulary in the text is using a color system of some sort to annotate the text. This could include, but is not limited to, highlighting important parts of the text in a specific color, using colored sticky notes, or page markers for key pages/paragraphs/chapters throughout the text, color coating by categories, vocabulary sets, using colored flash cards and so on when exploring and reading through the text.

Modeling Mathematical Terms

Model the correct use of appropriate math vocabulary when interacting with students, and encourage students to discuss and use the new concept and role of the word. For instance, *subtraction* is often called *take away, minus,* or *difference.* Help students recognize that the same process can be explained with various phrases. Once again, the use of a concept table will help them identify the relevant connections between the terms.

Accepting the inaccurate phrases students produce will require both patience and flexibility. Teachers should recognize that the written word develops slower than the spoken word. It will be more likely that students learn to speak correctly, although they might be able to approximate mathematical words long before they are able to write correctly about mathematics. Although the process is slow, teachers should work toward requiring the mathematically correct use and form of the terminology. In addition, teachers should ask students to explain how they found the "difference" when discussing an example on subtraction. Repetition of the phrases while modeling the action will encourage automaticity of the mathematical process.

Simplify the Words

The typical textbook may be written at the appropriate grade level, yet the EL may be reading at a lower grade level in the English language. Assist students by reading the textbook with them to ensure they understand the wording. Asking students to rephrase what was just read will encourage writing and communication skills and will prove to be a valuable assessment tool.

Breaking the material down into smaller chunks so that only a small piece is presented at one time will also benefit ELs tremendously. Depending on the proficiency level of your ELs, this may require condensing paragraphs into short phrases and sentences or chunking chapters into small paragraphs. Though it may take the students longer to get through the text, presenting smaller chunks will lower the cognitive load and lower their affective filter (i.e., they will feel less pressure affectively). Whether one reads with their ELs as it appears in the text or chunks the material in the text, having students use a graphic organizer before, during, or after reading can also be a beneficial way to assess their comprehension.

Help students to rewrite word problems in simpler terms and in their own words. Ask probing questions that help them simplify each section they read as well as each portion of the word problem. Read each sentence in the word problem carefully, one at a time, to decipher the meaning and the key elements from the sentence.

Restate complex instructions using simple English that cannot be misinterpreted. The English vocabulary is laden with clichés and slang words that should be avoided. For example, the expression, "You hit the nail on the head," implies the use of a hammer and nail, when the term actually means the person correctly analyzed the situation.

Symbolism and Abbreviations

Abbreviations and symbols can create much confusion. Capps and Gage (1987) and Adams (2003) call attention to the fact that abbreviations and other mathematical symbols create difficulties in a student's ability to understand. For example, teachers should avoid using traditional symbols without providing an interpretation, such as—for similar shapes or the use of the apostrophe for indicating feet. Avoid using abbreviations such as *pt.* for pint, *ft.* for feet, or *lb.* for pound until the students have been introduced to this new symbolism. Repeated use of the symbols and abbreviations will assist them in their proper mathematical usage of these standard items of protocol found in every mathematics textbook and assessment instrument.

The need for teaching the abbreviations and explaining the specific symbolism is a vital part of the instructional process for all students. This consideration is also important to keep in mind when it comes to their ability to take adequate notes and keep up with note taking during any given lesson. Make vocabulary charts that include the abbreviations and symbols, and place them strategically around the room where they are clearly visible to the students. Once again, flexibility is in order. If students use *pd.* for pound, which is actually more logical than the traditional *lb.*, identify the error but accept their answers.

Realia

Learning becomes easier when the material being taught is culturally relevant and viewed as personally necessary. The level of concentration and focus are heightened when our interest is aroused. Therefore, selecting vocabulary and performance tasks that relate to the student's own real-world exposure will enhance learning. Common foods, names, items, and traditional holidays can be used in making up word problems and examples. For instance, when teaching about fractions, refer to common items such as egg cartons, pies, or pizzas to concretely illustrate the values of halves, fourths or quarters, thirds, and sixths. Follow these activities with the usual mathematical manipulatives used in the traditional classrooms. However, be aware of cultural biases.

Select real situations that include local settings for your instructional lesson. Have students handle money in the school store, identify the time, locate the date on the calendar, and measure their own heights and weights. In addition, use the correctly pronounced names of the students in examples used during instruction. Select everyday activities such as cooking and carpentry that the students will see as pertinent to their existence.

Writing About Math Concepts

Once again, it is important to recognize that the spoken word develops before the written form. To encourage the process, teachers should give students the opportunity to write about their new math concepts. Writing can be used to explain solutions, rephrase instructions, generate word problems, decode existing word problems, and express feelings.

Examining students' written work can be a useful assessment technique. Journals are an excellent way to determine the degree of understanding and to provide the opportunity for students to express their concerns and issues without peer pressure inhibiting their interactions with the teacher. For instance, have them rewrite a textbook sentence in their own words to help them clarify their own thinking.

Encourage them to write their own definitions to words, and have them draw pictures to create their own math dictionary. Students should create word problems to share with classmates. This will be a useful way for the students to develop their own interests and understanding.

Encourage students to write often, approximately three times a week, by providing prompts and an audience for whom they should write. If possible, find another class that can become pair partners in reciprocating correspondence with your English learners. Additionally, the teacher should model writing during instruction and class discussions. Above all, allow students to make both grammatical and pronunciation mistakes; however, teachers should be sure to model the correct response back to the students.

Talking About Math

When addressing ELs, use clear, basic English for all questions and explanations, and enunciate clearly. Give short, concise directions one step at a time, and repeat them as often as needed. Adapt the lesson to simplify each step if complex explanations have been typically used to explain the concepts. For example, expressions such as "one dog, two cats" may be confusing to an EL. They may not associate the word you use with number of items, but rather with the type of item referred to.

As previously noted, students may not be reading at the same level as the instructional materials being utilized. Speak slowly and clearly so students can follow along with the instructor. This method will assist in vocabulary building, sentence structure, and comprehension of the material.

Read Slowly

Students should to be taught to read their math books slowly and carefully. They often skip past the words and look specifically at the diagrams and examples without utilizing the valuable dialogue that explains key steps and concepts. Teachers should encourage students to use the textbook guides, such as boldfacing, underlining, and the glossary in the back of the book. However, when these tools fail, they should be encouraged to ask for an explanation of a word or sentence they are having difficulty understanding. Persuade them to search for meanings of new mathematical terms by providing a mathematics dictionary, as well as the typical English dictionaries, but avoid routine assignments of looking up words and writing down definitions. Such activities, along with the excessive use of drill exercises, do little to excite or encourage mathematical development.

Pacing

It is very important that teachers recognize that ELs acquire verbal skills faster than writing skills. This is a normal process in learning a second language. Flexibility and acceptance of mistakes are key factors in helping students move forward in their writing. Allow students to write and rewrite their mathematical understanding. First, second, and third drafts should be encouraged to help the students learn the proper way to express their mathematical thinking. Think alouds about what they want to say in their writing can also be very beneficial in this process.

Mathematical Literature Books

Many excellent mathematical resources exist that promote and develop mathematical concepts. In fact, some books are specifically designed to teach mathematical concepts through the use of dialogue and pictures. A good example of teaching math concepts through literature would be *Grandfather Tang's Story* (Tompert, 1990), which uses a theme unit depicting the culture of China. The book incorporates favorite animal characters, concept mapping of the storyline, and stimulates the imagination as the students learn about geometric transformations and tangrams. Connecting literature with mathematics provides an obvious interrelation among subjects that helps students recognize that math is much more than a set of isolated facts.

Math Centers for All Learners

Traditionally for younger learners (and manipulatives work well with older students as well), math centers are an excellent way to teach math to those who are learning English as well as those who need more concrete examples to comprehend the subject matter. Centers can include a vocabulary component, a review of basic skills for those who need review, individual and group tasks to reinforce the math content, and mathematical enrichment. Centers will encourage students to utilize hands-on activities that are self-paced and student focused. The teacher becomes more of a facilitator of learning while being a guide on the sidelines. A wide variety of activities are available that help to extract theoretical mathematical concepts from textbooks and to translate them into practical use by students.

Centers can be theme driven or relevant to a specific topic or standard; they are an excellent way to encourage the use of manipulatives, especially when the teacher does not have enough items for every student. Centers should include an assessment and recording worksheet for easy maintenance, self-checking options, and a choice of the activities. Centers are also called "shoebox math" in some areas.

Culturally Harmonious Strategies in Math

Teachers should identify the background and prior experiences of the students so they are able to apply this information during instruction. For example, in certain cultures, dominoes and card games are a regular activity in the home. Cards and dominoes are excellent mathematical manipulatives and can be uniquely mathematically related, especially those that show one side as a mathematical expression and the answer on the reverse. Conversely, some cultural groups, such as Haitians, may not be familiar with dice. Instead, they will use bones (such as bones from a goat's knee) to count and make certain significant patterns.

Most of the historical figures in mathematics are famous individuals from other countries. Students can explore their own cultural history for significant key personalities who contributed to mathematics or science; they will feel a sense of pride in their culture when they share this information with their classmates.

Cultural differences can interfere with learning as well. For example, pizza and peanut butter are not eaten in every culture, so vary your models to be sensitive to cultural differences. Try using pita bread or moon pies that are equally round to represent fractions. Search for foods that are specific to the cultures of your students and utilize them in your instructional examples.

Acceptance

Make sure the curriculum provides for cultural awareness. Some countries focus heavily on computational skills, and others utilize work that is more individual. The methods used in the United States may seem foreign to some students. Differences in semantics apply as well. For instance, be aware that 7 and 0 may be crossed through at times, 4 may be opened or closed at the top, 2,500 may be written as **2.500**, and division may be performed in a reverse order. Subtraction may be done with the indicators of borrowing written on the bottom instead of the top. Adapt, individualize, and modify your classroom while considering the student's level of content, language ability, mathematical expertise, and study skills.

Academic Ability Levels

Teachers will find diversified levels of mathematical knowledge in ELs. Students may arrive with limited or interrupted mathematical education, or they may possess superior mathematical skills. Prescreening will provide valuable information about the academic abilities of your ELs. Teachers must consider this diversity in ability levels in their instruction and assessments, and assignments must be varied to meet these diverse levels. Formulate lessons that include a variety of levels so students can obtain some form of success, or individualize homework assignments for your students. For instance, include problems such as **121–34** as well as **12–8**. It is important for the student to feel challenged yet successful and productive.

Process Oriented Versus Product Oriented

In some cultures, the *process* of finding the answer is not as valued as the final answer, so students coming from those cultures will have a difficult time appreciating the teacher's need to see the work process. Teachers should discuss the importance of process as well as product. It might be a contrary concept to some students when their U.S. teachers require them to show their work, as their grades would have been penalized in their home countries if they did not calculate mentally. Additionally, in many standardized high-stakes tests, showing the process of mathematical calculations is mandatory.

Finally, in some countries, students can only use graph paper instead of lined paper. This method of writing a number in each box keeps their work quite organized, both vertically and horizontally. Sloppiness leads to many mathematical errors that are avoided by the use of graph paper. Although it is a very good practice, teachers in the United States might accept regular lined paper as well.

Technological Differences

Technology is often readily available and inexpensive in the United States; however, the use, variety, and quality of technology used are disparate in classrooms both in and outside the United States. Globally, philosophical dissention regarding the use of technology has generated huge chasms within curriculum. Just as in a typical mainstream classroom, some EL students may lack any experience or exposure to using technology, and others may excel in their use of technology. No matter what the circumstances, the teacher should never regard the use of technology as prior knowledge in an EL class.

Unlike U.S. students, students from other countries usually are forced to memorize mathematical formulas. Aids such as calculators and computers are gaining in acceptance in the United States, but not all students are able to afford these devices. Teachers will need to recognize the diverse financial situations of their students. Some students will possess all the modern conveniences at their homes, and others may not. Adequate time and access to technology, both inside and outside of the classroom, must be provided.

Effective Instructional Strategies

Effective instructional strategies in the classroom should include encouraging all students to put forth their best efforts. Varying instructional delivery, activities, and assessments while maintaining a regular routine will maintain and heighten student interest. Recognizing that not everyone learns in the same way, and that teaching styles can inhibit or enhance student learning, teachers can provide a classroom environment that is conducive to learning. *Prior planning prevents poor performance* applies to instructional delivery of the mathematical lesson. The following specific strategies are discussed to encourage success for the ELs.

Visualization

Teachers should always accentuate the visual side of mathematics, because the majority of students may not be auditory learners. Incorporating prompts, cues, facial expressions, body language, and visual aids during instruction will help students to visualize the concept and to form a mental image. Concrete manipulatives, such as base-ten blocks, geoboards, algebra tiles, and snap cubes, and an assortment of models, such as Gummy Bears and M&M candies for children and Popsicle sticks or other countable items for older learners, can be used to develop mathematical concepts. Students will begin to like math when they see it as more concrete and less abstract.

   Multiembodiment (Edge & Ashlock, 1982; Hull, Balka, & Miles, 2009) is important when teaching concepts. Multiembodiment is using different devices or instruments to teach the same concept. For example, teaching addition of fractions with fraction tiles, fraction circles, and fraction bars will all help students to recognize the need for finding a common denominator before adding the unlike fractions.

Concept Charts

The teacher should generate a preinstructional concept map to relate the new topics and words to things students may already know and understand to encourage scaffolding and interconnections within mathematics. For example, the base-ten metric system is easier to learn than the customary units taught in the United States, especially when it comes to converting from one unit to another. By developing a concept map, students make the connections between what they know and what they need to learn for mathematics taught in the United States.

Alternative Algorithmic Methods

A lesson on an *algorithmic process*, such as division or subtraction, may require the teacher to cover the methods used in the United States that may or may not be similar to the students' former knowledge of division. Acceptance of the various algorithmic processes should also be encouraged. However, this will require the educator to become familiar with a variety of alternative algorithms not taught as "standard methods." For example, in Brazil and Haiti, a division problem may be reversed and look like this: $\overline{50}(2,$ as opposed to the American stylistic arrangement: $2\overline{)50}$ It is extremely difficult to "think backwards," and yet we are expecting students to do a cognitive reversal.

   Recognize that it is extremely difficult to replace what appears to be a logical approach with what seems completely illogical at the time. This does not mean you should avoid teaching the standard algorithmic approach used in the United States. Rather, until the students can learn the "American" style of mathematics, allow them to feel comfortable performing math the way they were originally taught. Teachers might eventually discover that some of the methods from other countries prove to be more logical.

Modeling the Process

Be sure to model problem-solving strategies through real-life situations so students can "observe" your thinking process through a concrete problem that has an authentic purpose for the math learning in which they are involved. The typical problem-solving approach includes reading the problem, understanding the problem, planning a strategy, solving the problem, and verifying the answer.

During instruction, teach and model the many problem-solving strategies while working through mathematical problems. Strategies include acting out the problem, working backwards, guessing and checking, making a table, looking for a pattern, solving a simpler problem, changing your point of view, making a drawing, and systematically accounting for all possibilities so students become critical thinkers in mathematics and develop confidence in their problem-solving abilities. Be careful not to make the problem-solving process appear too easy for you. They need to realize that it is natural to attempt, think through, adjust ideas, and try other approaches when one approach proves unsuccessful. Confusion is bad only when it is terminal.

Heterogeneous Grouping

The benefits of using groups to teach and learn concepts are innumerable. Pairing students into groups of two, three, or five helps them both socially and academically. However, just as it would be inappropriate to group low students together, it is just as inappropriate to group students according to language preference or ability. Heterogeneously arranged cooperative groups can facilitate discussion and peer teaching if incorporated and monitored properly. However, if necessary, be sure to ask a more fluent English speaker (often called a "bilingual buddy") to assist in interpreting instructions and questions if learning will be impaired otherwise.

Hands-On Learning

Everyone learns through different modalities; however, many students are tactile learners. These students will learn best with the use of **hands-on activities** involving concrete or mechanical aids that reinforce learning. Manipulatives, computers, calculators, and tape recorders are good devices when selected and used appropriately to reach your academic objective.

Many evaluative instruments can test students to determine their learning styles. Teacher observation can identify learning preferences as well. Understanding diverse learning styles and incorporating students' learning preferences will benefit both the teacher and the students. Regardless of preferences, varying instructional approaches will keep the curriculum interesting and exciting to your students. This is good practice for any teacher.

Assessment

Alternative assessments such as thinking aloud, presentations, interviews, observations, checklists, reflective writing, self-assessment, drawings, and portfolios will help teachers adequately assess and evaluate students' work. Considering the delay in writing as opposed to speaking proficiency, this is especially helpful in assessment. Encourage students to formulate drawings that translate and visualize the problems.

Students should be encouraged to think aloud and to pair–share their ideas with others as they work through a problem. Open expression is encouraged as students give an oral explanation of their thinking process while solving a problem in a nonthreatening environment. Remember, a traditional test that requires competent English proficiency may not truly test the student's mathematical abilities.

Often an English learner may be improperly placed in the math class due to an apparent lack of English proficiency. This placement will result in either a high level of boredom or frustration. Proper assessment must be a vital part of the ESOL program to avoid inaccurate placements. Just because a student is reading and writing two grades below level does not signify that the mathematical aptitude is also below grade level. Often students from other countries are learning algebraic concepts that far surpass those being taught to their American counterparts.

Minimize Anxiety

Stephen Krashen's seminal work from the 80s is still applicable today. In his work on second language acquisition (1982), he discusses the Affective Filter Hypothesis and notes that anxiety (along with self-confidence and motivation) is one of three categories (with many factors falling into each category) that influence one's ability to successfully acquire a second language. As with any academic content material, this is certainly applicable to mathematics content. The most important goal for any teacher should be to create a comfortable, nonthreatening environment for all students. Anxiety and frustration directly affect academic learning. A lack of success in any subject will generate a dislike and avoidance of that subject. In the United States, it has become culturally acceptable to profess one's dislike for the subject of mathematics. Yet, this openness indicates a lack of successful teaching of the subject matter and should not reflect mathematical ignorance. Too often, the subject has been taught primarily as a set of procedures to follow with little conceptual understanding. Eventually, this approach leaves students in a quandary about the use and purpose of mathematics and with the feeling that it is insignificant in their personal lives.

Sensitivity demonstrated by the teacher and the students will go a long way in helping all students feel accepted and comfortable in the classroom, regardless of mathematical or linguistic capabilities. This attitude will minimize the anxieties within the classroom and will create a more conducive environment for learning mathematics.

Myths about certain cultures and genders being more mathematically capable proliferate in the educational arena. It is true that certain cultures emphasize the importance of mathematics and education in general, but that does not mean that individuals from that culture are more mathematically inclined. This type of stereotyping should be addressed within the classroom. Teachers need to be aware of the cultural and gender factors that have permeated the mathematics classroom. Ensuring gender and cultural equity include providing the same wait time after asking questions, asking the same number and level of questions from all students equally, and encouraging all students to achieve. All students can learn mathematics.

Questioning ELs

By far, one of the most essential rules to consider is providing ample wait time when questioning ELs; in mathematics, this applies to all students. Cognitive processing demands extra time for the following to occur in the learner's brain:

Step 1	A question is asked in the target language.
Step 2	The brain translates the question into the native language.
Step 3	The brain calculates the answer in the native language (assuming the student comprehends and is capable of doing the math).
Step 4	The brain then has to translate the information back into English.
Step 5	The learner must speak (pronounce) the answer Ariza, 2010).

In U.S. culture, students are uncomfortable with prolonged silence. Ariza et al. (2002) maintains that, by the time the student is ready to speak, the teacher, thinking the student does not have the answer, has moved on to another student, saying, "Can anyone help Tran with that answer?" Or classmates are wildly raising their hands in the air to give the correct answer.

Some teachers tend to ask multiple questions: for example, "How do you think John would have felt if he couldn't find his lost money? Do you think he would have told his father that he had lost it? Would his father have punished him?" The EL does not really know what question to answer. To avoid putting a student in an awkward position, the teacher should ask the student a specific question and say, "Think about this question and I will get back to you for the answer." After questioning other students, which gives the EL time to translate and calculate, the teacher can return to the student for the answer. Of course, you must be certain the student understands the question. This questioning technique can be used on a buddy system so they can work out the problem together (Ariza, 2002; Ariza, 2010).

By being aware of the above factors, the teacher can make a difference in ELs' learning of math by simply focusing on the literary strategies, cultural awareness strategies, and effective teaching strategies. Learning about the best approaches to effectively teach students definitely applies to ELs. As you educate yourself about your students' cultural and academic backgrounds, you will be rewarded with a sensitivity and respect for the diversity that exists within your classroom.

FINAL POINTS

- Math students need lots of visuals to explain concepts.
- Use manipulatives to show abstract concepts.
- Use chunking, small amounts of language, step by step direct instruction to show ELs how to attack math problems.
- Be aware of words with multiple meanings.
- Be sure to use culturally relevant information for reaching students academically.
- Be sure the material makes meaning to the student.

Discussion Questions and Activities

1. Using a teacher's math text, choose a lesson and modify it for beginning, intermediate, and advanced language learners.
2. Find ten examples of word problems and examine them for clarity. Would an English learner have difficulty interpreting the language and solving the problem? Show how you can rewrite the language to make it very clear. Show how you could use manipulatives to make the concepts clearer.
3. Invite people from other countries to demonstrate how they solve addition, multiplication, subtraction, and division problems. How difficult would it be for you to change your way of calculating mathematically to a method that might be the reverse of how you calculate mentally?
4. Discuss how you could teach a student the "American" method of mathematical calculations, which may be very different from how the student was taught in his or her native language. Discuss the issues that may arise.

Resources

Scholastic
http://www.scholastic.com/teachers/article/10-ways-help-ells-succeed-math

NYC DOE, EL Considerations for CCSS Task Alignments in Math
http://schools.nyc.gov/NR/rdonlyres/9E62A2F2-4C5C-4534-968B-5487A7BD3742/0/GeneralMath-StrategiesforELLs_082811.pdf

Strategies for teaching math, PowerPoint
http://www.tsusmell.org/downloads/Conferences/2005/Moore-Harris_2005.pdf

Colorin Colorado: Math strategies
http://www.google.com/url?sa=t&rct=j&q=&esrc=s&frm=1&source=web&cd=4&ved=-0CDoQFjAD&url=http%3A%2F%2Fwww.colorincolorado.org%2Farticle%2F30570%2F&ei=-rKEDU9kbwqaRB-_vgMAH&usg=AFQjCNFHsH1Yqd-QTrNHaasGYEtY9LDbHw

Helping English learners in the math classroom
http://www.colorincolorado.org/article/math-instruction-english-language-learners

Multiple websites for math strategies for ELs
https://www.google.com/#q=math+strategies+for+ells

Teaching Math in a Title One classroom
http://www.youtube.com/watch?v=Kst4KJrk3MU

Krashen's work
http://www.sdkrashen.com/content/books/principles_and_practice.pdf

Basic math vocabulary
http://www.youtube.com/watch?v=osA3KUHtA1s

Math vocabulary
http://www.youtube.com/watch?v=woFb6RxykZE

Common Core Standards in math, for ELs
http://www.youtube.com/watch?v=gUfpnIbq4TA

Supporting English learners in math
http://www.youtube.com/watch?v=VESnRwbtslg

References

Adams, T. L. (2003). Reading mathematics: More than words can say. *The Reading Teacher, 56*(8), 786–795.

Ariza, E. N. (2002). *Fundamentals of teaching English to speakers of other languages in k-12 mainstream classrooms*. Kendall Hunt.

Campbell, A. E., Davis, G. E., & Adams, V. M. (2007). Cognitive demands and second-language learners: A framework for analyzing mathematics instructional contexts. *Mathematical Thinking and Learning, 9,* 3–30.

Edge, D. & Ashlock, R. B. (1982). Using multiple embodiments of place value concepts. *Alberta Journal of Educational Research, 28*(3), 267–276.

Hill, J. D. & Miller, K. B. (2013). *Classroom instruction that works with English language learners*. ASCD.

Hull, T. H., Balka, D. S., & Miles, R. H. (Eds.). (2009). *A guide to mathematics coaching: Processes for increasing student achievement*. Corwin Press.

Loomis, M. (2012). *Vocabulary in math: A professional development project designed to improve students' comprehension with math problems* (Doctoral dissertation, State University of New York at Fredonia).

Schleppegrell, M. J. (2007). The linguistic challenges of mathematics teaching and learning: A research review. *Reading & Writing Quarterly, 23*(2), 139–159.

Skovsmose, O. & Borba, M. (2004). Research methodology and critical mathematics education. In *Researching the socio-political dimensions of mathematics education* (pp. 207–226). Springer, United States.

Tompert, A. (1990). *Grandfather Tang's story*. Knopf Books for Young Readers.

CHAPTER 11

TEACHING SCIENCE TO ENGLISH LEARNERS

Lindsey Laury

KEY POINTS

- Science can improve content knowledge while improving English literacy.
- English learners face barriers in science instruction.
- Improve science content instruction by using literacy strategies
- ELs in the classroom can be a great benefit for students to learn about other cultures.

Andrei, a bright and energetic seventh grader, recently moved with his family from Bulgaria to the United States. Back home, he developed a passion for nature at an early age, and began asking questions about astronomy, biology, and even chemistry; science quickly became his favorite subject. He loved raising his hand in class and listening to the teacher talk about the fascinating world he lives in. On the first day of school in the United States, he gazes around the science classroom at all of the unfamiliar words on the wall. The teacher begins to provide instructions to students, but she is talking too fast in a language that Andrei barely understands. He quickly begins to feel discouraged and overwhelmed. Andrei feels like science will no longer be his favorite subject in school.

There is arguably no other subject that allows the opportunity for visually enriching and interactive instruction more than in the science classroom. Students have the opportunity to participate in numerous hands-on activities and project-based learning tasks. Science allows the opportunity for a student to explore and investigate the world we live in. It is paramount for teachers, both at the elementary and secondary level, to introduce to all students equally the beauty of nature and scientific inquiry. Teachers should take advantage of the dynamic nature of science instruction to not only improve content knowledge, but improve English literacy as well. In this chapter, we will briefly explore the barriers English learners face in science instruction. Additionally, this chapter focuses on methods to improve content instruction for English learners along with strategies to promote English literacy while in the science classroom.

Challenges in the Science Classroom

While students new to the English language will eventually acquire social language proficiency skills through everyday social interactions and communication with their peers, these conversations are vastly different than the language used in the science classroom. This unique range of vocabulary is referred to as the **academic language** of the classroom. Academic language is defined as "the language of the classroom, of academic principles (science, history, literary analysis) of texts and literature, and of extended, reasoned discourse" (Gersten, Baker, Shanahan, Linan-Thompson, Collins, & Scarcella, 2007, p.16). In a typical secondary science classroom, students will be exposed to approximately 500 new words in general science, 1,200 new words in biology, and 1,000 new words in earth science (Dong, 2011). Even for the most proficient English speakers, learning the academic language of science can be a rather cumbersome process. Words like meiosis, polarity, and heterotroph are simply not used in everyday language. As a result, EL students may become discouraged in the science classroom. It is as if science were a complete language in itself! Additionally, the language used in the science classroom is a derivation of multiple languages unrelated to English, usually Latin or Greek, but also Spanish. For example, when introducing plant science to students, photosynthesis is Latin, chlorophyll is French, glucose is a French modification of Greek, and chloroplast is also Greek, translating to "one who forms green" (Carrier, 2011). This is just one example of the extraordinary diversity of language that is found in the science classroom. (For native Spanish speakers, often the scientific vocabulary is a cognate, so it is wise to try to relate the Spanish word in case the student is already familiar with the word. See further discussion in this chapter.)

An additional challenge that English learners face in the science classroom relates to how many Western cultures perceive the methods of scientific inquiry in comparison to other cultures throughout the world (Figure 11.1). In the United States, typically the prevailing attitudes about science are that we need to strive for continuous improvement; progress is a linear pattern, and science advances civilization. An overarching American value appears to believe that over time, science and technology improve the quality of life, and the complexity of our thinking. This is a starkly contrasting viewpoint to many other cultures. For example, in Native American cultures and several other groups, science and society are viewed in a more circular fashion. By looking at science through this "cyclical lens," these cultures believe that society is most benefited when traditions and knowledge of ancestors are preserved and revered, not challenged by new ideas ("Native American," 2017). These conflicting ideologies can be difficult for certain EL students as they may perceive ideas in the classroom as a challenge to their own preserved beliefs. As science teachers with students from many different cultural groups, we must be cognizant of the variation in preserved beliefs and preconceived cultural ideas these students may have (Ariza, 2010).

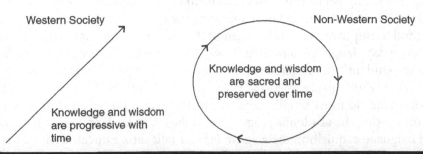

Figure 11.1 Western and Contrasting Non-Western Societal Ideologies

Methods to Improve Content Instruction

Support the Development of the Academic Language of Science

For many students, the science classroom is the very first time in an academic setting that extensive memorization of new key terms and unfamiliar concepts are required for success. For ELs who are still in the preproduction (or entering stage) and early production stages of second language acquisition, this can be especially daunting. In addition to learning traditional English vocabulary, EL students will be exposed to hundreds of new science vocabulary words in a short amount of time. Finding ways to help support the development of the academic language of science is one crucial way to aid EL students with content development and understanding in the classroom. With English learners in the earliest phases of second language acquisition, using translation software (such as Google Translate, or Babylon) can aid teachers with communicating with their students. Teachers can use this software to translate key terms and big ideas for students prior to or accompanying the science lesson. As the EL becomes increasingly proficient with the academic language used in the classroom, fewer supplementary materials will need to be used over time. (Strategies like keeping vocabulary journals will assist greatly in keeping new vocabulary words in one place to be referred to repeatedly.)

As with all class subjects, the use of visually supportive materials is extremely beneficial for all students, especially English learners. A majority of concepts found in the science classroom are abstract in nature and require various approaches to instruction in order to solidify comprehension. Using interactive computer simulations containing animations and graphics are beneficial for contextual support of complex academic content (Ryoo, 2009). By engaging students in inquiry-based science activities, students have the opportunity to "do" science and participate in engaging activities, instead of relying on rote memorization of scientific facts.

Changing the delivery method of unfamiliar vocabulary to English learners can also scaffold their academic language development in the science classroom. Traditionally, new vocabulary is introduced through the process of **frontloading**. Frontloading language simply means introducing important vocabulary terms prior to lesson delivery (Heritage, Silva, & Pierce, 2007). The goal of frontloading vocabulary is to deliver the important content to English learners prior to the lesson, so that during the lesson it will provide the crucial background information to understand content. However, the problem with frontloading terms while working with EL students is that this method of vocabulary acquisition is isolated in nature; it will not necessarily "stick" or seem relevant to students. It is often difficult to teach isolated terms and students successfully comprehend ideas holistically. Instead of frontloading, EL students benefit most through the process of **reloading** complex vocabulary. By reloading the language, "We take advantage of the science experience to situate the meaning of the vocabulary within the lesson" (Weinburgh & Silva, 2012). As new words emerge into the lesson, they are embedded within the experience of learning for the English learner, instead of in an isolated fashion as with frontloading. As a result, vocabulary will not be explicitly taught until *following* the lesson.

Another method to improve the development of the academic language of science is to first teach the concept using "everyday" language, and then slowly integrate the scientific language into the "everyday" language. Once the student has mastered the content using everyday language, the idea can be progressively communicated wholly using scientific vocabulary. This will help the EL student relate unfamiliar and complex vocabulary to more familiar and comfortable terminology. It is important to note that the intensity of incorporating the academic language into the everyday language will vary based upon what stage of second language acquisition the English learner falls into. Educators should closely observe the everyday language used by the student in the classroom and use that particular proficiency level as a baseline for communicating scientific language with students. By using primarily nonacademic language

TABLE 11.1 Spanish–English Science Cognates

English	Spanish	English	Spanish	English	Spanish	English	Spanish
Periodic table	Tabla periódica	Observations	Observaciones	Fruit	Fruta	Structure	Estrucura
Organisms	Organismos	Nitrogen	Nitrógeno	Minerals	Minerales	Function	Función
Animals	Animales	Atmosphere	Atmósfera	Ocean	Océano	Electricity	Electricidad
Carbon cycle	Ciclo del carbono	Hypothesis	Hipótsis	Analyze	Analizar	Thermometers	Termómetro
Kinetic energy	Energía cinética	Experiments	Experimentos	Botany	Botánica	Space	Espacio
Genetic	Genético	Galaxy	Galaxia	Centimeters	Centímeros	Dominant	Dominante
Ecosystem	Ecosistema	Extinction	Extinción	Vitamins	Vitaminas	Potential Energy	Energía potencia
Atoms	Átomos	Volcano	Volcán	Solar System	Sistema solar	Scientist	Científicos

at the beginning, a foundation is created that can be built upon to develop a more complex vocabulary and deeper understanding of crucial science topics (Ariza, 2010).

In addition to using everyday language to supplement science instruction, teachers can take advantage of an EL's proficiency in their first language to supplement their science learning in a second language; this is especially true for Spanish-speaking students. There are thousands of words used in both English and Spanish that have Greek, Latin, or Arabic origin. As a result, these unique words, known as **cognates**, have similar sound, spelling, and meaning in both languages. For example, nucleus is *núcleo* in Spanish and Portuguese and *noyau* in French. There are more than 20,000 English–Spanish cognates and a large percentage of these words are academic in nature (Montelongo, Durán, & Hernández, 2013). Teachers should familiarize themselves with Spanish–English cognates that are present in the science classroom in order to aid EL students whose first acquired language is Spanish. Table 11.1 illustrates common Spanish–English cognates that teachers can use in their classroom to scaffold students with difficult science vocabulary, although there are hundreds more.

Develop Meaningful and Relevant Science Content

It is paramount for science educators to develop academic content that is both meaningful and culturally relevant to English learners. A simple method to create more relevant material for ELs is to first discover the prior knowledge and experiences that students have relating to a particular topic in the classroom. From there, one can then build from the student's foundational knowledge to develop a greater overall understanding. Dong (2013) provides useful recommendations for teachers to effectively tap into an English learner's prior knowledge of topic:

- Provide surveys at the start of the school year or before a lesson asking about background information and prior knowledge the student may have. Some suggestions include:
  o Home country, native language, or cultural background
  o Perceptions of a particular topic (e.g., climate change, evolution, or genetics)

    o Years of experience in a science setting in their previous school years or particular subjects in science they have already received exposure

    o Favorite topics or what the student finds most interesting about science

    o What is most challenging to the student about science

    o Preferred learning styles (memorization, visuals, listening to discussion, drawing pictures, etc.)

- Partner with ESOL and bilingual teachers to learn about EL proficiency levels, their native language, and cultural background.
- Partner with ESOL and bilingual teachers for tips and strategies to teach difficult vocabulary to EL students based on their prior knowledge and individual needs.
- Encourage students to express their familiarity with a topic prior to the lesson. For example, asking a student "What do you know about . . ." or "What comes to mind when you think of . . ." or "How would you translate . . . into your native language?"

Culturally Relevant Teaching

Recent studies argue that science topics facilitate more effective learning when it is relevant to a student, and teachers who are capable of providing science topics in perspectives appealing to students will experience greater success within the classroom; this teaching method constructs a topic that is perceived as **culturally relevant** (Jackson & Jackson, 2011). This strategy advocates that the culture of science and one's own culture should contain overlap. For example, if a high school environmental science teacher wanted to make the lesson about ecosystems culturally relevant, she could ask students to present to the class the ecosystem that most heavily dominates their country of ancestry. The topic becomes more significant to the student because it is now more relatable. Integrating culturally relevant examples and activities into the science classroom will aid in a more meaningful and engaging experience for an English learner. Culturally relevant science teaching helps connect students' experiences to their prior knowledge and lives at home. This connection is in large part a result of learning by doing, and connecting activities to prior experience students already have had outside of the classroom. Patchen and Cox-Peterson (2008) provide an outline of recommendations to create a culturally relevant science classroom:

- Ask authentic questions through inquiry-based instructional methods.
- Allow for students to work in a multitude of settings: individually, in pairs, or in cooperative learning groups.
- Bridge classroom experiences to lives at home and daily experiences.
- Permit student autonomy by shifting authority to promote independence.
- Allow students to participate in decision-making processes in the classroom.
- Encourage active, authentic, and engaging conversations.
- Ensure students feel safe and able to express different perspectives and ideologies.
- Support understanding through building confidence of all students in the classroom.

Literacy Development in Science Classrooms

Imagine if scientists were unable to successfully communicate their observations and research to their colleagues. Without effective reading and writing skills, scientists would be incapable of developing publications, efficiently presenting information at conferences, or sending meaningful emails to individuals from all over the world in their associated field. Effective reading and writing skills are paramount for scientists to successfully correspond their ideas to their peers and promote new questions to be proposed; these ideas are equally important in the science classroom. Literacy skills can be integrated into the classroom to benefit English learners by emphasizing the process of scientific inquiry. Teachers can treat their classroom as a miniature scientific community and promote literacy development through a multitude of ways. Cox-Peterson, Melber, and Patchen (2012) provide excellent examples to promote reading and writing development for English learners in the classroom:

- **Observation Journals**—have students maintain their own journals to record what they see during observations, field trips, or even simply when they look outside their classroom window. Journals also allow students to monitor their progress and allow for reflection at the end of the school year. Students can observe their literacy development over time by keeping information consistently logged in one location.
- **Data Notebooks**—similar to observation journals, data notebooks allow students to systematically collect and interpret data during the school year. Collecting accurate data is arguably one of the most important steps of the scientific method; data notebooks will promote literacy while simultaneously emphasizing a crucial component of scientific processes. These journals can be both quantitative (numerical) and qualitative (descriptive) in nature. Once students have their data sets, other academic skills can be applied. For example, students can translate their data into charts or graphs. This is paramount due to the increasing difficulty students have when interpreting tables and graphs during standardized testing.
- **Read, Read, Read**—increasing exposure to science-related texts will benefit not only English learners, but all students in the classroom. Newspapers, scientific journals, magazines, picture books, or any visually appealing texts are beneficial to promote student literacy; even fictional texts are a great addition to the science classroom. For example, teachers could use an engaging science fiction book and following the reading of the book instruct students to record in their journals between accepted scientific principles and fiction found throughout the literature.
- **Write a Script!**—Most students love the opportunity to get out of their seats and interact with each other in ways different from the traditional teacher-centered instructional approach. Teachers could encourage students to write a script relating to a scientific event or process. Students could then act out the script they have created individually or in cooperative groups. Writing an original piece would foster creativity in the science classroom while also emphasizing the development of important writing skills.

Contribute to all Components of Literacy

There are a multitude of literary components necessary for the success of an English learner in the science classroom. They must be able to not only read and write, but communicate their knowledge coherently and effectively listen to instructional content. English learners must also develop the ability to interpret and design pictorials and graphics used to organize information in academic text. Lee and Buxton (2013) designed five major components of literacy development in the science classroom that they believe is vital to the success of EL students in all major facets of literacy (Table 11.2).

Buxton and Lee particularly emphasize that literacy development is paramount for *all* students, not only English learners. If science teachers habitually incorporate effective language-promoting strategies into their daily instruction, every student in the classroom will benefit. Effective literacy

TABLE 11.2 Strategies to Promote Literacy in Science

Five Literacy Strategy Domains	Examples
(1) Literacy strategies for *all students*	• Use pictorials and graphics • Activate prior knowledge • Write narratives based on science concepts
(2) Language support strategies	• Incorporate hands on, inquiry-based activities into instruction • Emphasize social interactions • Create multiple nodes of content representation • Integrate key terms into relevant context
(3) Discourse strategies	• Reduce language load (e.g. allow for longer wait time, clearly enunciate ideas) • Paraphrase, use synonyms, and reiterate ideas
(4) Home language support	• Encourage bilingual students to assist less proficient students • Introduce key concepts in home language as well as English • Use cognates to support understanding
(5) Home culture connections	• Construct material that is applicable and culturally relevant to the EL's life

Source: Lee and Buxton (2013)

development is not only the ability to read and write; students must also develop the capacity to reason and critically consider what it is they have read. Using a variety of graphic organizers will allow students to more effectively synthesize their ideas and critically examine the material that they have read. For example, if a student were instructed to read and take a practice quiz regarding photosynthesis and cellular respiration, they may not actually be developing a meaningful understanding of such convoluted topics. However, instructing students to synthesize their ideas by using a graphic organizer would provide opportunities to critically reflect on the content they have studied. Students constructing a Venn diagram or double bubble map (Figure 11.1) relating to photosynthesis and cellular respiration would have an advantage over students who simply read the material and take traditional notes. Using a graphic organizer would answer key questions such as "how are photosynthesis and cellular respiration related?" and "how are they different?" Actually seeing the interconnectedness of science topics allows for a deeper and more meaningful understanding for EL students.

FINAL POINTS

- Culturally relevant teaching can have far-reaching effects on the learning.
- Science can improve content knowledge while improving English literacy.
- Use strategies and accommodations to improve content comprehensions.
- Utilize cognates for students to make language connections between L1 and L2.

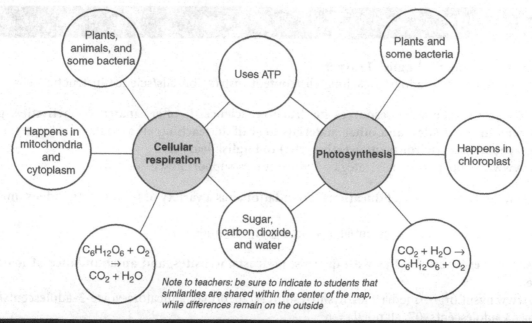

Figure 11.2 Double Bubble Map to Compare and Contrast Ideas

Discussion Questions and Activities

1. Using online resources, list ten additional English–Spanish cognates relevant to the science classroom. Describe a way in which you would use these cognates to benefit ELs during instruction. Try doing this activity with another language according to the cultural groups in your classroom. Perhaps the students can help you make their own cognate list.

2. Current research advocates that designing science lessons that are meaningful to an English learner is paramount for their engagement and success in the classroom. What does this mean to you as an educator? Briefly provide an example of a science lesson that you could modify to integrate relevant content for an English learner.

3. Design a graphic organizer of your choice (Venn diagram, double bubble map, flow chart, etc.) to demonstrate the relationship between two important science concepts.

4. Cultural relevancy is very important to know about because students may find personal meaning in objects, principles, or ideas that have different meaning (or no meaning) to the teacher. For example, the owl signifies good luck in the Colombian culture, but holds negative meaning in the Seminole culture. Choose a culture to research that interests you. Create a science lesson plan that reflects cultural meaning for the student. For example, if the student comes from a culture that cherishes oral storytelling, create a lesson that will include storytelling.

Resources

Science Instruction for English Learners
http://www.colorincolorado.org/teaching-ells/content-instruction-ells/science-instruction-ells

This website is laden with resources for teaching science. It offers materials, activities, graphic organizers, internet sites, and other materials to scaffold teaching all aspects of science (anatomy, biology, chemistry, environment, weather, etc.) to English learners
https://www.edutopia.org/blog/strategies-and-resources-supporting-ell-todd-finley

Edutopia, the George Lucas Educational Foundation, has a variety of topics, with videos, materials, and resources
http://oedb.org/ilibrarian/50_essential_resources_for_esl_students/

50 Essential resources for ELs with quizzes, podcasts, websites, and an abundance of material to utilize
http://www.nysut.org/~/media/files/nysut/resources/2010/may/educators-voice-3-adolescents/educa-torsvoice3_adolescents_07_ell.pdf?la=en

Science for the English learner
http://www.colorincolorado.org/blog/teaching-science-english-language-learners-what-do-ngss-tell-us

The ColorinColorado website contains a wealth of information for every topic imaginable. The page discusses the Next Generation Science Standards (NGSS) and how to use the science standards with English learners
https://www.youtube.com/watch?v=y-ckn42YGCw ELs and Science: What strategies can I use?

This is a short video that shows strategies that can be used in teaching science
https://www.ixl.com/promo?partner=google&campaign=3217&adGroup=Science+Websites&redirect=%2Fscience%2Ftopics&gclid=CIWiqPjKndMCFciFfgodU2wB7g

Interactive science website for ELs with vibrant visuals and fun facts about the sciences
https://www.ciwf.org.uk/education/downloads/science/?gclid=CNyYoLjLndMCFQpofgodsaYFfw

Free resources for science teachers

References

Ariza, E. N. (2010). *Not for ESOL teachers: What every classroom teacher needs to know about the linguistically, culturally, and ethnically diverse student.* Boston: Allyn & Bacon.

Carrier, S. J. (2011). Effective strategies for teaching science vocabulary. *UNC School of Education.*

Cox-Peterson, A., Melber, L. M., & Patchen, T. (2012). Teaching science to culturally and linguistically diverse elementary students. Boston, MA: Pearson Education.

Gersten, R., Baker, S. K., Shanahan, T., Linan-Thompson, S., Collins, P., & Scarcella, R. (2007). Effective literacy and English language instruction for English learners in the elementary grades. (IES Practice Guide NCEE 2007-4011).

Heritage, M., Silva, N., & Pierce, M. (2007). Academic English: A view from the classroom. *The language demands of school: Putting academic English to the test*, 171–210.

Kelly-Jackson, C. & Jackson, T. (2011). Meeting their fullest potential: The beliefs and teaching of a culturally relevant science teacher. *Creative Education*, 2(4), 408–413.

Lee, O. & Buxton, C. (2013). Integrating science and English proficiency for English learners. *Theory Into Practice*, 52(1), 36–42.

Native American. (2017). *Healthandhealingny.org*. Retrieved April 9, 2017, from http://www.healthandhealingny.org/tradition_healing/native.html.

Montelongo, J., Durán, R., & Hernández, A. (2013). English-Spanish cognates in picture books: Toward a vocabulary curriculum for Latino ELs. *Bilingual Research Journal*, 36(2),

Patchen T. & Cox-Petersen A. (2008). Constructing cultural relevance in science: A case study of two elementary teachers, *Science Education*, 92(6), 994–1014.

Ryoo, K. (2009, January 1). Learning science, talking science: The impact of a technology-enhanced curriculum on students' science learning in linguistically diverse mainstream classrooms. *ProQuest LLC*.

Weinburgh, M. H., & Silva, C. (2012). An instructional theory for English learners: The 5R model for enhancing academic language development in inquiry-based science. *Handbook of educational theories*, 291–301.

CHAPTER 12
TEACHING SOCIAL STUDIES TO ENGLISH LEARNERS

Rina Bousalis

KEY POINTS

- To distinguish the meaning and importance of social studies.
- To identify possible challenges teachers face in teaching social studies to English learners.
- To examine the ways English learners can be effectively taught social studies.
- To recognize the ways in which English learners have the ability potential to benefit the social studies classroom.

Reciprocity Between Teachers and English learners in the Social Studies Classroom

"When ELs kept coming in to my 4th grade classroom, I wondered how I was ever going to teach these young newcomers not only English, but also about the history of the United States, a country they knew nothing about or perhaps didn't care about learning since it wasn't their home country. However, I soon realized that regardless of their limited English, not only were my ELs motivated to learn about the U.S., but also had the power to teach the rest of us a thing or two about people, places, and events they experienced—things we never would have learned in a textbook."

—*Fourth-grade teacher*

Many immigrants—individuals who move from one country to another—continue to come from all over the world to live in the United States either voluntarily, involuntarily, legally, or illegally, for a number of different reasons (e.g., education, career opportunities, family reunification, fleeing from ethnic, racial, political, or religious persecution). Although some settle in traditionally uncommon places such as rural or suburban locations, all immigrants continue to help us form a richly diversified nation to impact our elementary and secondary classrooms. Of the over one million immigrants that enter the United States each year, roughly 9 percent are youth between the ages of 5 and 17 who have little or no ability to speak English. In addition to the U.S. born children who grow up in monolingual non-English-speaking households, these English learners are placed in elementary to secondary mainstream classrooms everyday across the nation and become part of a school's English Learning (EL) program as well as a statistic in our nation's English learning population (Zong & Batalova, 2016). As immigration rises, teachers, schools, and school districts may face challenges in teaching ELs in the effort to meet academic and English language state standards requirements. Although it is important that educators teach all students with the same amount of attention, consideration, rigor, and belief that students have the potential to learn, this task can be challenging for mainstream teachers who teach social studies to ELs.

Rather than a hindrance, ELs should be viewed as assets to the social studies classroom. Immigrant students can teach others their stories, the different ways they live, the way they view the world, and how they have experienced life. Immigrant youth, particularly refugees, who have witnessed conflict and violence in their homeland, who may have little or no prior schooling, and who have experienced difficulties in trying to reach the United States from places such as Africa, Central America, and the Middle East, possess first-hand knowledge of the geographic, historical, political, and economic causes of events discussed in social studies classrooms. They can then share these explanations with their fellow students. By offering stories about people, places, and events, these young students are the essence of social studies. As history is based on perspectives, immigrant youth are authentic and primary resources from which other students will learn.

What Is Social Studies?

Although social studies is mainly viewed as a body of knowledge taught through four major disciplines: History, Geography, Government, and Economics, social studies is a canopy for an abundance of inter-related disciplines (e.g., civics, psychology, and sociology) that essentially tell the story of people, their history, the places they live(d), the causes and consequences of events they create(d), and their influence and impact on nature. Social studies highlights the attributes of culture such as language, religion, and traditions, examines how culture shapes identity, and recognizes how culture affects society. Grounded in citizenship education, social studies encourages students to not only become good citizens, but to acquire the knowledge and skills needed to make well-informed decisions (National Council for the Social Studies, 2010). Since social studies is the study of people and immigrants are the foundation of the United States, why is it that teachers face challenges teaching social studies to English language earners?

Problems for ELs and Social Studies Teachers

Social studies, particularly U.S. History, can be disheartening for ELs. In addition to having little or no English skills, ELs' lack of background knowledge about the United States, unfamiliarity with complex vocabulary, and difficulty in pronouncing names of people, places, and events can hinder ELs opportunity to learn social studies. As social studies is generally viewed even by non-EL students as a boring and tedious subject filled with lectures, note-taking, and the memorization of facts and dates, social studies can be more difficult for bilingual students. Explaining the significance of an important U.S.

historical event can be especially challenging for ELs if they have no prior knowledge or recollection of what happened ages ago. In the case of immigrant students who develop culture in their homeland prior to emigrating to the United States (in countries that may be culturally dissimilar to the United States), immigrant EL students may feel historically, geographically, economically, and politically disconnected upon arrival. For example, immigrant EL students would not be familiar with the U.S. democratic system or the meaning of U.S. political terms if they fled from a home country that was run by a dictator or totalitarian government. Students may be from a society that only permits the teaching of the history of that nation, or which educates using censored textbooks. The manner in which students have been raised in their native country plays a role in how they initially approach social studies here in the United States.

As society often assumes ethnicities exhibit certain stereotypical characteristics (e.g., Asians are intelligent), educators' preconceived notions about certain immigrants' ability and speed in understanding social studies concepts predetermines teachers' expectations. However, there could be many reasons as to why ELs do not learn English or social studies concepts as fast or as well as educators believe they should. Educators often fail to take into account that immigrant EL students may be feeling alone in their new home or may not have English-speaking support in or out of school (for example, an EL may be surrounded by schoolmates who speak that student's native language, or family members who do not speak English). Depending on where immigrant EL students originated from and why they migrated to the United States, they may have had their previous schooling interrupted, may have never gone to school, or may have no documentation that provides an accurate record on which grade level they fully completed or should presently be enrolled in. In situations such as these, immigrant EL students have little chance to explain where they academically stand, what they are capable of, and why they are not meeting the demands and expectations of their teachers and schools. Even if they had English instruction in their native country's school system prior to migrating to the United States, without having lived in the United States long enough to build cultural literacy or to meet the academic and linguistic expectations of the United States's educational standards, teachers cannot assume that ELs are less or more capable of mastering English or social studies concepts than American students, simply based on internal, external, and stereotypical factors. As one's ability to learn goes hand in hand with one's prior knowledge and experiences, it could be argued that American students would lack the know-how and the speed in learning a foreign language or explaining a political system that plunges its citizens into a civil war, genocide, and a mass exodus from a country without having experienced the wrath of a totalitarian government.

High-Stakes Testing

With social studies' focus on people and its abundance of disciplines that are related to life, one would expect that social studies would be more valued. However, with the growth of the standards movement, prioritization of Science, Technology, Engineering, and Mathematics (STEM) subjects, and increased teacher preparation for high-stakes testing, over the years social studies has grown into a less important subject. In addition to a lack of instructional time devoted to social studies in elementary grades, secondary educators face an even greater challenge in teaching social studies to newcomers to the United States. Teachers of high school ELs are under pressure to focus on English proficiency and rush to prepare ELs for their high school End-Of-Course (EOC) assessments. Required to follow teaching and pacing curriculum guidelines and show evidence of adequate yearly progress (AYP) for *all* students regardless of English language proficiency, educators often find it difficult to teach meaningful social studies while surrounded by high-stakes testing mandates and submerged in graduation requirements. As high-stakes testing is presently used as a means to determine student progress and teacher performance, educators must face the dreaded practice of comparing ELs' test scores to a "norm" group of students who often perform better than their academically and linguistically disadvantaged EL peers. Although teachers must abide by legal requirements, social studies educators generally understand that these test scores do not show the reality of an EL student's academic capabilities; rather, an EL's performance on high-stakes tests is often a matter of linguistic difficulties. For this reason, high-stakes testing frequently causes ELs to be misdiagnosed, too quickly labeled as "slow" or learning disabled, and often placed in Special Education Services (SES).

In the teaching of social studies, Lev Vygotsky's (1978) "Zone of Proximal Development (ZPD)" theory works well with its belief that *all* students have the potential, or the ability, to learn and that a student's ability to learn should not be underestimated (p. 34). Measures of intellect consist of not only social studies test scores, but also on the development of language. Through well-guided and effective social studies instruction by knowledgeable and experienced adults, preferably teachers, encouragement to learn, and interaction with other students, ELs will have the proximity, or potential, to learn through cultural and social experiences. This approach requires extra time, one-on-one personal assistance, cooperative group activities, and fair treatment in the assessment and evaluation of academic progress. Through social interaction in the social studies classroom, ELs will be able to critically think, discuss, collaborate, and construct new knowledge. As ELs need time to learn because they may have a longer path to travel on their way to master the English language and social studies content, it is important to examine whether ELs' problems derive from a lack of English language skills or from actually having a disability. A student's culture, where he or she is from, what he or she has experienced, how he or she thinks, and how proficient he or she is in his or her first language should be taken into consideration in order to fairly and accurately assess an EL's social studies and linguistic abilities.

Textbooks

As the textbook has too often become the primary source for teaching social studies, particularly in the teaching of U.S. History, it is no wonder that a majority of students find the content to be dry, promoting a one-sided perspective, and covering too much with too little depth. Since the social studies textbook is filled with dense text and monotonous readings that fail to consider student learning syles, background, academic levels, and language proficiency, ELs often find it difficult to read, learn, and understand social studies through this traditional classroom medium. Since social studies authors and publishers have the authority to decide which topics will be featured and which ones will not, textbooks tend to include a more narrow and selective coverage of events, ethnicities, countries, cultures, and perspectives, often missing the ones which students in the classroom represent. To avoid confrontational topics and the chance of offending any ethnic, racial, or religious group, publishers often hesitate to cover controversial issues or include a variety of perspectives; this not only hampers critical thinking and brushes aside important topics that need to be addressed, but also causes students to view social studies as a subject unrelated to their lives and the real world. Since social studies textbooks are written under the assumption that all students have the prior knowledge essential to making sense of unexplained concepts, ELs will not be able to interpret social studies if they cannot comprehend what is written. Therefore, it is vital that social studies educators use the textbook as a secondary source of information for lesson planning and instead integrate literature, primary documents, technology, and other forms of visually engaging and coherently created materials to effectively teach social studies to ELs. Moreover, it is imperative that social studies educators not assign work through textbook readings as this form of teaching and learning will only contribute to the recalling and rote-memorization of content for ELs.

Teacher Discouragement

Elementary educators often feel discouraged to teach social studies not only to ELs, but to all students. Although teachers' feelings toward social studies can be attributed to a lack of content knowledge or personal interest, the justification for not teaching social studies often goes beyond a teacher's power. As school policy tends to make the decisions on what educators can teach, their lack of teaching social studies is often attributed to an educational emphasis on standardized testing and focus on STEM subjects. As elementary teachers are required to spend a majority of their day teaching STEM subjects, the pressure to teach to the test decreases teachers' independence and the ability to choose topics with student interest in mind. Instead of spending time creating teacher-made resources that could be tailored toward individual and differential instruction, a teaching approach that would better serve ELs, teachers often have little choice in having to use the textbook as their main source of instruction. Given the fact that teachers have little incentive to teach social studies, their attitude can also be due to not knowing how to implement EL strategies, and therefore finding themselves unable to support the needs of ELs. Teacher bias against immigrants or non-English speakers may also come into play as teachers might view culture as a racial or ethnic issue. Since teachers are held accountable for their low scores, they may choose to overlook bilingual students altogether and succumb to the sink or swim approach by letting ELs learn English and social studies content entirely on their own. Secondary teachers, as well, may find it discomforting to go beyond the surface when discussing topics such as the Holocaust, Japanese internment camps, terrorism, or current events related to immigration policy when realizing that students from the countries represented in the topics under study or featured in the media are sitting in their class. Learning opportunities that teachers fail to take hold of due to fear of repercussions from administrators or the unwillingness to go above and beyond what the textbook offers will sever the opportunity for both students and teachers to connect and hinder the enhancement of teaching and understanding social studies.

Solution to Problems

For teachers to realize the benefits that ELs bring to the classroom, it is important that teachers first know who their students are and what their students can do. By honing in on their academic, cultural, linguistic, and social background, teachers can use this information to better understand students' needs, and help make curriculum and instructional decisions. By examining all aspects of a student's life, teachers will be able to offer culturally relevant instruction, by identifying an EL's use of home language in and out of the classroom, linking aspects of students' culture to social studies content, and diagnosing students' strengths and weaknesses. Becoming aware of students' family situations (e.g., possible dysfunctional home life or family having a hard time adjusting to the United States), socioeconomic positions (perhaps have little or no text or technology resources available), culture (traditions and customs necessary or helpful to know), and other factors that could have an effect on a students' social, mental, and academic standing will help teachers make sound academic decisions on student learning and provide a smoother path to social studies and linguistic success.

Students also need to get to know each other in order to recognize culture better, share experiences, build relationships, and expand their understanding of people. As there is a connection between feelings of belongingness and academic achievement (Shah, 2011), students need to be around others to learn from and teach one another's history. For example, what immigrant students, both ELs and non-ELs alike, can bring to the classroom is invaluable. Immigrants *are* social studies; they can teach fellow students, as well as the teacher, about people, places, and events about which most have never heard about or do not have any deep understanding. Immigrants can set the record straight about global crises that the general U.S. population only hears about through the media for many of the immigrants were there and experienced the events first-hand. Immigrant youth in our classrooms can share with the class the difficulties in migrating to a new country, what it was like being forced to flee from their place of birth and never being able to return, and the true causes of events that are playing out on the global stage that most American youth may not fathom or ever experience. As U.S. youth today are targeted by social media, which disseminates political rhetoric on controlling immigration, propaganda-like messages about immigration policies, and politicians taunting "English only" bills, immigrant students who have undergone the experience of forced migration can disclose first-hand what a refugee is, the reason one leaves one's homeland, and how the media portrays a distorted view of immigrants and immigration. The nativist mindset inspired by encouragement for U.S. citizens to take on an English-only stance, continued adherence to the melting pot "See us and be like us" theory (Knauer, 1994, p. 162), and the insinuating belief that immigrants are draining U.S. resources and altering American culture, language, and values can negatively impact the classroom.

In response, immigrant ELs or ELs who are the children of immigrants can make American students aware of what immigrants bring to the United States and offer a different perspective of immigration before the media's misconceptions find their way into future history textbooks. As the media tend to define an immigrant as a statistic, it is important that students recognize immigrants as individuals, realize that **culture**, a major characteristic of social studies, **impacts**:

Human action	History
Behavior	Psychology
Ethics	Civics
Pride	Nationalism
Power	Government
Economic status	Economics
Group membership	Sociology
Geography	Religion, that "leaves indelible fingerprints on so many aspects of society" (Park, 1994, p. 31).

Since the study of people makes up the subject of social studies, a greater appreciation of immigrants and ELs should be observed in the social studies curriculum as these individuals not only offer doses of reality in concepts taught, but also shed light on the human experience. As students are largely misinformed about happenings in the world, teachers should allow students the opportunity to connect to the history of past and present people, be aware of those from different backgrounds and their experiences, and be open to communicate and learn from one another. Although opponents of immigration view immigrants as a hindrance to the classroom, proponents believe that **immigrants are pools of knowledge that textbook lectures can rarely duplicate**. The benefits of having immigrant students in the social studies classroom outweigh the challenges in helping ELs learn English or become adjusted to their new environments. As the immigrant Olúfémi Táíwò (2013) points put, "Yes, we have good reason to come here; but don't forget that you have equally good reason to welcome us . . . although we are grateful for the reception accorded and the opportunity afforded us, our hosts should consider that the advantages have not been one-sided" (p. 1). What immigrants contribute should be viewed as enrichments to American society, praised for helping to create a strong nation, and commended for bringing innovative ideas to the United States (Martin, 2012). Immigrant youth in our classroom today will play a role in society tomorrow. Therefore, immigrants should be regarded as **treasures**, assets, and individuals who have the potential to do great things. And what a gift it is to learn a second language, as well as a challenge to go from zero English to proficient. Is it not an accomplishment to master English? As some students originate from a home country that requires them to speak two languages, what a feat it is having to learn two languages and now a third, an achievement that many of us take for granted and give little credit for doing. We should not undervalue ELs or think less of their academic abilities due to their lack of English language skills. Teachers would do well to remember the following: "Don't let lack of English language literacy be a barrier—you may have the next Nobel Laureate in your class" (Hanna & Kucharczyk, 2016, p. 2).

Learning Strategies

Social studies lessons can be designed for ELs in a way that supports their language learning yet does not bring attention to their limited language proficiency or treat them as "handicapped." Lesson planning should begin by focusing on the "big ideas," or overarching concepts vital for students to gain understanding of and meaning in social studies content. Concepts should be related to the topic and students' lives. In addition to state content standards, it is important that language learning objectives be considered, as well as important terms and vocabulary that will assist in developing EL's literacy skills. As an added resource, the National Council for the Social Studies (NCSS, 2010), a social studies organization dedicated to promoting the value of social studies and helping educators teach social studies, created a list of ten interdisciplinary themes (Figure 12.1) that teachers should focus on while teaching social studies. Using this structure, ELs can be guided to master the social studies topics related to the themes with teacher support.

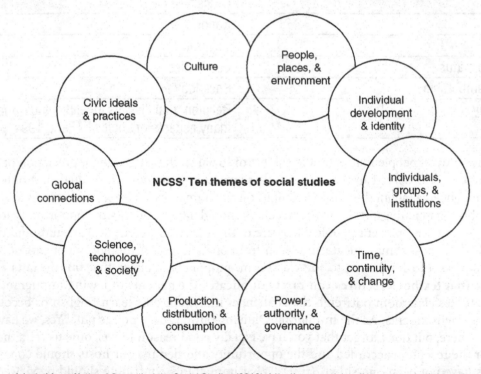

Adapted from National Council of the Social Studies (2010), http://www.socialstudies.org/standards/strands

Figure 12.1 NCCS Ten Themes of Social Studies

With NCSS' themes in mind, it is vital that teachers give ELs opportunities to use both social studies content knowledge and vocabulary terms by engaging students in one-on-one and/ or classroom discussions and in mixed groups. Although activities should be engaging, they should not be superficial endeavors that offer meaningless content knowledge (e.g., multicultural crafts that lack depth, cultural holiday parties, and "busy work" worksheets) regardless of any belief that they will assist ELs in word recognition or offer students a multicultural experience. Depending on grade level, students can be given:

Primary Grades (K–3)	Multicultural Picture Book Read-alouds: Students can examine a person, place, or historical event which they can relate to.
Intermediate Grades (3–5)	Role Play/Reader's Theater: Students can act out a historical event such as the Boston Tea Party, Columbus landing in the New World, or slaves escaping to the North for freedom in the Underground Railroad.
Middle School Grades (6–8)	Socratic Seminars: Students can actively and cooperatively engage in various types of Socratic Seminars such as Four Corners and Inside-Outside Circles that involve student-led questioning and in-depth discussions.
High School Grades (9–12)	Case studies: Students can place themselves in the storyline and consider how they would solve the dilemma in focus (e.g., Supreme Court cases, culture-related stories, or women's rights issues).

In addition to planned discussions, unplanned or spontaneous discussions (teachable moments) should be welcomed and encouraged.

An educator must take into account whether or not the activity is actually helping ELs master the English language or is simply an activity that students would enjoy doing. Hollow activities do little to help ELs increase their language proficiency and understand social studies content.

To solve the common problem of ELs lacking opportunities to practice their English learning skills, the World-Class Instructional Design and Assessment (WIDA) framework was created by a consortium of State Education departments that also designed the K–12 English Language Development (ELD), standards and assessments that help guide and support teachers during language instruction within five subject areas (e.g., Social and Instructional Language Arts, Mathematics, Science, and Social Studies). The standards help teachers recognize students' English proficiency levels and language skills, create realistic, as well as accurate, types of assessment that go beyond pencil and paper tests, and find ways for ELs to practice English, and offers suggestions on how to teach ELs at different stages of language acquisition (WIDA, 2014).

Similar to WIDA's suggested resources, social studies instruction should incorporate the use of resources such as:

Geographic tools such as maps, globes, and atlases	ELs can visualize and understand longitude, latitude, place, regions, absolute and relative location, legends (map keys), and spatial-perception.
Realia, or real objects	Students can observe and touch artifacts or items that express culture during a specific time period.
Archeology finds	Students can observe cultural items such as pieces of art, pottery, or stone carvings.

Graphs and charts	Students can compare and contrast data while integrating math (e.g., population, Gross Domestic Product (GDP), homelessness, unemployment, and inflation).
Graphic organizers, Concept maps, Venn diagrams, and T-Charts	Students can organize events by themes or chronology, display cause and effect, categorize concepts, or compare and contrast figures and events.
Timelines	Since exact dates are not prioritized, timelines could be created per decade, era, or by broad periods of time (e.g., Antebellum era, Civil War, and Reconstruction Period).
Technology	Instructional tools such as videos, documentaries, virtual field trips, online gaming, interactive maps, GPS/Google Earth, and photo images retrieved from the internet can enhance the understanding of social studies.
PowerPoints and ELMOs	Instructional tools such as these should include simplified text and bolded words to highlight and clarify important social studies content and vocabulary.

Assessment

Since ELs require modified social studies lessons to accommodate their academic and linguistic needs, it is best practice to create teacher-made assessments or use informal and simplified assessments.

Informal or simplified assessment	Short quizzes, exit slips, teacher observation, or other forms of simple assessments that will show growth.
Traditional or formal assessment	Standardized, multiple choice, fill-in-the-blank, and true/false tests.
Portfolios	Academic and language accomplishments could be documented through the use of a portfolio, a compilation of work gathered over a semester or year that shows evidence of a student's progress. Portfolios are especially suited for writing samples since text can display students' strengths and weaknesses and development over time.
Other forms of informal assessments	Observation checklists, rating scales, anecdotal records, and interviews can be used to identify students' problem areas.

Interview/Questionnaire

An interview questionnaire that is administered one-on-one (teacher reads questions and writes down answers for EL student) at the beginning of the school year is an example of an informal assessment that helps social studies teachers discover students' background knowledge. The questionnaire allows for teachers to find out what a student's attitude is about school and social studies, and to discover what everyday life experiences are currently influencing the student. The wonder of this type of assessment is that the questions instigate discussion and encourage the formation of a rapport between student and teacher.

Social Studies Questionnaire/Interview

Name _____ Date _____

1. To me, Social Studies is _____
2. I am curious about the topic of _____
3. I often wonder about _____
4. The historical event that I am familiar with and interested in is _____
5. History is _____
6. Geography is _____
7. Government is _____
8. Economics is _____
9. Learning a new language is _____
10. My teacher is _____
11. Meeting new people is _____
12. I wish my parents knew _____
13. School is _____
14. Someday I would like to visit _____
15. To me, art is _____
16. I like to read about _____
17. On weekends, I like to _____
18. Technology is _____
19. To me, writing is _____
20. I hope that I can someday meet _____

The Arts

By integrating the arts (art, music, and dance) into the social studies curriculum:

Educators could reach immigrant students who may have been traumatized during migration or are having trouble adjusting or speaking.	Rather than write, a student may want to draw a picture, act out a scene, or create a song to express a concept, explain how he or she is feeling, or portray what he or she is experiencing.	By using photographs, illustrations, paintings, and other types of visuals, students will be able to engage in historical understanding and transfer concepts from abstract to concrete.

Literature

As literature (e.g., trade books, chapter books, novels, picture books, and comic books) can engage learners in the social studies classroom, teachers should use literature:

As a supplement to the social studies curriculum.
As a foundation to build lessons.
To expose a multitude of perspectives often absent from the textbook.
To help eliminate stereotypes.
That focuses on the development of language.
That displays positive and inspiring portrayals of culture and identity,
That includes authentic accounts of historical experience.
That represents the cultures of students in the classroom.

Writing

As social studies goes hand in hand with writing, students will have a multitude of opportunities to:

Show what they have learned.
Review what they have written.
Illustrate their thoughts.
Express their life experiences.
Document their questions.
Compose narratives.
Elaborate on history.
Gain insight.
Reflect on content learned.
Practice vocabulary.
Improve their English language proficiency.

FINAL POINTS

- Every day across the United States, immigrants become part of a school's English Learning program.

- As immigration rises, mainstream social studies teachers face challenges meeting ELs' academic and linguistic needs.

- With the standards movement, prioritization of Science, Technology, Engineering, and Mathematics (STEM) subjects, and teacher preparation for high-stakes testing, over the years educators have often felt discouraged about teaching social studies to ELs.

- Rather than consider ELs a hindrance, teachers should view ELs as an asset to the social studies classroom and curriculum.

- Based on an immigrants' migration experience and reason for leaving their homeland, immigrant ELs can teach their peers, as well as their teacher, about their first-hand knowledge of geographic, historical, political, and economic events often missing from the social studies textbook.

EL MODIFIED LESSON PLAN	

Grade: 5th
Topic: Causes and Consequences of the Civil War
Time: 40 minutes
Objective: Identify the causes and effects of the Civil War
Materials: Computer, PowerPoint, Paper, Pencil, Pen, Textbook

Unmodified	Modified
Opening: Teacher will ask "What do you know about the causes of the Civil War?"	*Teacher will show students photographs of significant figures and events that led up the Civil War.*
Procedure: Teacher will show a PowerPoint on the various factors and events that caused the Civil War.	*Teacher will explain the meaning behind the words "Civil" and "War." Teacher will unpack the term "Civil War," and begin by looking at the word "civil." Teacher will explain that "civil" is a word that involves people, and will give other examples of civil, like being civil, and civil obedience. Teacher will point to children in the classroom and stress that "civil" is about people. Teacher will then focus on the word "war," and show different pictures of soldiers fighting.* *Throughout the PowerPoint, teacher will focus on the major concepts:* 1. *The Missouri Compromise: How it involved the state of Maine, how Maine was admitted as a free state whereas Missouri was admitted as a slave state. Teacher will go to the classroom map and point to where those two states are located.* 2. *Kansas Nebraska Act: Discuss how it was a law that resulted in mass violence about slavery.* 3. *Slavery: Teacher will show pictures of slavery and explain what slavery is.*

	4. *Anti-slavery Rebellions: Teacher will discuss the Nat Turner Rebellion and John Brown Rebellion that caused bloodshed as well as the enactment of stricter laws. Teacher will show pictures of Nat Turner and John Brown (Nat Turner was African American while John Brown was a white abolitionist). Teacher will take the word "abolitionist" and explain how the root word "abolish" means "to stop."* 5. *Fugitive Slave Law: The Northerners were per this law obligated to send runaway slaves back where they came from. However, since Northerners did not always return runaway slaves, this made Southerners angry. The teacher will return to the map and point out where the South and North was divided.*
Activity: Students will use their textbooks and answer end-of-chapter questions.	*Students will be put in mixed groups so they can help each other. Students will create a graphic organizer and use information from the Power-Point and textbook. Students will label each bubble of the graphic organizer with the event, list information, and draw a picture related to the event if they so choose. Students can draw pictures of significant figures, states, or regions of the United States. ELs can have their dictionary with them and have open the map at the back of the textbook for assistance.*
Assessment: Students will be given a quiz.	*Teachers will assess ELs by observing their participation and effort in the activity.*

Discussion Questions and Activities

1. Create five ways that you as a teacher can help ELs learn social studies.
2. How is the media affecting society's perspective of immigrants? Name and discuss the primary issues that face immigrants and refugees in today's political climate.
3. Create a document that can be used with your EL students so they can be assessed in the social studies classroom.
4. What are some ways teachers can help ELs increase their English language proficiency and master social studies content at the same time?
5. What have you learned from immigrant students in your class who come from a different background than yours?
6. In partners, interview two students who are new to the culture. Compare and contrast your answers to see if there are similar answers.

Resources

http://www.colorincolorado.org/article/preparing-engaging-social-studies-lesson-englis-language-learners

Lessons for ELs
http://www.colorincolorado.org/teaching-ells/content-instruction-ells/social-studies-instruction-ells

Preparation for ELs content instruction
http://www.colorincolorado.org/resource-topic/content-resources-social-studies

Content resources for ELs in social studies
http://steinhardt.nyu.edu/scmsAdmin/uploads/004/740/NYU_PTE_SocialStudies_for_ELLS_Oct2009.pdf

ELs and Social Studies
https://www.socialstudies.org/publications/socialeducation/october2009/social_studies_for_english_language_learners

National Council for Social Studies
http://www.campbell.k12.tn.us/documents/ESL/ELL_SS.pdf

Modifying strategies for ELs in Social Studies
https://www.amazon.com/Teaching-History-Social-Studies-English-Learners/dp/0205627617/ref=pd_lpo_sbs_14_t_2?_encoding=UTF8&psc=1&refRID=PA4GWP239E5KPZKF62NC

Teaching Social Studies through SIOP
http://study.com/academy/lesson/modifications-for-ell-students-in-social-studies.html

Modifications for ELs in Social Studies
http://www.tesl-ej.org/wordpress/issues/volume14/ej56/ej56r7/

Teaching Social Studies to ELs
www.coedu.usf.edu/main/departments/seced/Faculty/documents/NCSS.ppt

Including ELs in Social Studies

References

Hanna, H. & Kucharczyk, S. (2016, November 22). *Five ways to help migrant children settle in your class*. Retrieved from Guardian News and Media Limited: https://www.theguardian.com/teacher-network/2016/nov/22/five-ways-to-help-migrant-children-settle-in-your-class

Knauer, K. (1994). Magic shadows from a melting pot. In *Bridges and Borders*. Readings from TIME magazine 1923–1994 (pp. 162–163). New York, NY: Warner Books for TIME.

Martin, A. (2012, June 25). Immigrants are crucial to innovation, study says. *New York Times*. Retrieved from: http://www.nytimes.com/2012/06/26/business/immigrants-played-role-in-majority-of-us-technical-patents-study-finds.html

National Council for the Social Studies (NCSS) (2010). *National curriculum standards for social studies: A framework for teaching, learning, and assessment*. Retrieved from https://www.socialstudies.org/standard

Olúfémi, T. (2013, June 9). What immigrants bring to America. *The Chronicle of Higher Education*. Retrieved from http://www.chronicle.com/article/What-Immigrants-Bring-to/139649/

Park, C. C. (1994). *Sacred worlds: An introduction to geography and religion*. Routledge: New York, NY.

Shah, N. (2011). Combating anti-Muslim bias. *Teaching Tolerance, 39*, 34–37.

Vygotsky, L., (1978). Interaction between learning and development. *Readings on the Development of Children, 23*(3), 34–41.

World-Class Instructional Design and Assessment (WIDA). (2014). *English language development (ELD) standards*. Retrieved from https://www.wida.us/standards/eld.aspx

Zong, J. & Batalova, J. (2016, April 14). Frequently requested statistics on immigrants and immigration in the United States. *Migration Policy Institute*. Retrieved from http://www.migrationpolicy.org/article/frequently-requested-statistics-immigrants-and-immigration-united-states

CHAPTER 13

TEACHING ELs LITERACY THROUGH THE ARTS

Susannah L. Brown

KEY POINTS

- Teachers will be able to make the connection between arts and literacy concepts.
- Arts integration supports ELs language development.
- Teachers can use creative literacy strategies that are appropriate for ELs.

Jonas, a second-grade English learner (EL) works with his teacher, Mrs. Gomez to activate prior knowledge using a picture book, Journey by Aaron Becker (2013). Mrs. Gomez uses the picture walk strategy to begin the discussion. Jonas points to the girl in a bright red boat on the cover of the book to indicate that she is the main character in the scene. Mrs. Gomez asks, "Jonas, where do you think the girl in the red boat is going?" Jonas points to the castle, while Mrs. Gomez states, "Castle, the girl is going to the castle." Mrs. Gomez writes the word castle on a sticky note and places it on the castle in the illustration. She also writes the word girl on a sticky note and attaches it to the illustration. "Jonas, what do you think this book is about?" Jonas explains that the girl is going to live in the castle. Mrs. Gomez asks Jonas to explain why he thinks the girl will live in the castle and poses a question that maybe the girl is visiting the castle and another character is inside. By asking questions about the illustration and labeling items on the page, Mrs. Gomez is activating prior knowledge, connecting what Jonas already knows with his predictions about the story. As Mrs. Gomez and Jonas discuss the illustrations in the book, Jonas is building vocabulary and strengthening his communication skills.

Questions for classroom application
- How can teachers use vocabulary building strategies that connect to visual art?
- What strategies connect to other art forms (music, dance, drama)?

Chapter Introduction

The benefits of integrating the arts with literacy for ELs are multifaceted. The use of illustrated texts or picture books capture students' imaginations and motivate reading. "Picture books are a marriage of literature and the fine arts in a unique literary form" (Kasten, Kristo & McClure, 2005, p. 147). Using visual imagery to identify characters, settings, and potential plots connects text to meaningful interpretations. The concept of art as communication links learning to meaningful creation that shares ideas in a variety of forms or media (visual art, drama, dance, and music). The integration of art forms allows students to invent and create a variety of interpretations. Arts integration is an effective means to facilitate children's understandings in literacy (Klein & Stuart, 2012; Marshall, 2005). By learning through the arts, ELs are provided opportunities to express their unique comprehension and move beyond language skills to communicate ideas through expressive media (i.e., visual arts of painting, drawing, and sculpting). This concept is illustrated in *Marianthe's Story: Painted Words and Spoken Memories* by Aliki (1998), an illustrated children's book that described a young girl's literacy journey beginning with painting as a form of communication since she does not speak English. Once Marianthe begins to learn English, the second story, *Spoken Memories*, explains her personal immigration story. Students who are engaged cognitively, emotionally, and physically, learn and remember more. Arts integration provides different avenues of thinking, reacting, and reflecting (Gardner, 1999; Gullat, 2008).

As an integral part of language development, the arts provide opportunities for students to engage in active learning. The physicality of the arts appeals to students. For example, the manipulation of paint on a canvas or the motion of playing an instrument provides for physical learning connected with cognition and affective learning. For ELs, this physical learning is particularly motivating as physical movement provides learning experiences that are memorable when connecting to prior knowledge. Students quickly realize the power of the arts to communicate their ideas and enjoy creative process. "The arts are the child's first language" (Koster, 2009, p. 8). "In the 21st century, students need to be prepared for a new information age. Educational interventions in art education that foster creative thinking, imagination, and innovation for all students are important tools for generating solutions to real-life problems both now and in the future" (Zimmerman, 2012, p.4). Since communicating through the arts reflects the natural process of learning, teachers may find an arts-integrated approach easily adapted to language arts when supporting ELs in the classroom.

Arts and Literacy

Developmental readiness for reading and writing involves all the physical and physiological components necessary. For example, when a child can focus his eyes on print, then he is ready to read text. Another example would include the ability to track along words in a sentence when reading aloud or using an index finger to point to words that are spoken. A child is ready to read when she recognizes environmental print (logos, icons, signs, and graphic advertising symbols). Reading readiness is an important factor in determining when to begin instruction. Emergent literacy describes when a child begins to read and write that is supported by a print-rich environment. When working with older students who may or may not have already learned how to read and write in their native language, teachers may need to consider the basic literacy concepts previously described. ELs gain valuable literacy skills when recognizing environmental print. Building upon experiences connects spoken language to text and eventually leads to comprehension of a new language. Language arts includes reading, writing, listening, speaking, viewing, and visually representing. The addition of viewing and visually representing into literacy connects the arts as meaningful expressions of knowledge. Visual thinking and problem-solving support "serious thinking dispositions that are valued both within and beyond the arts" (Hetland, Winner, Veema, & Sheridan, 2007, p.vii). Becoming artistically literate is the process where students learn to use artistic materials and tools along with techniques in order to share a creative perspective of the world. Making marks is the first step to writing. Children draw lines and squiggles at an early age to represent their ideas. As language is developed, young children begin to verbally describe the lines and marks as objects, people, and places, and a symbol system is developed to communicate their thoughts. A graphic symbol system requires students to recognize culturally appropriate symbols and interpret these marks for meaning (Cartwright, 2008). If the graphic symbol system is unrecognizable, the student is at a disadvantage and must learn to visually discern each symbol and attach meaning. This is where the arts support literacy by building a student's experiences through engagement. An excellent illustrated book to share with students to introduce the topic of learning language while immersed in a new culture is *The Arrival* by Shaun Tan (2006). In this graphic text, a father is forced to leave his wife and daughter and travels to a new land filled with strange people, places, and customs. The father used drawing as a form of communication to find lodging, food, and work. Each time the father meets a new person, he learns about their personal immigration story and the hardships that were endured. As the story progresses, the father learns the new language and sends for his family to join him in the new land. The last pages illustrate his daughter assisting a new arrival to the city, which demonstrates the full circle of kindness in the community. Strategies that involve picture books include:

Split Images (students take turns verbally describing illustrations in pairs);
Visual Read Aloud (VRA);
Ten Important Words (students list words on notes and define in groups);
List-Group-Label (students list words and organize into categories in collaborative groups);
Sketch to Stretch (drawing the theme or main idea);
Shape or concrete poetry (words and phrases that form pictures);
Bilingual or multilingual books and vocabulary flash cards.

Although the strategies that integrate the arts with literacy are varied, each strategy has more impact when paired with a text that interests students. Teachers can learn more about their students' interests through reading interests surveys. "All about me" books are another strategy to learn more about students' interests and can be designed and illustrated by students. Connecting nonfiction and fiction texts with effective literacy strategies encourages students to read more, which in turn provides opportunities to engage their language development. There are many illustrated books that feature art that can be used in the classroom (see Table 13. 1).

TABLE 13.1 Suggested Children's Books Featuring Art

Title and Author	Visual Art Topic
The Artist Who Painted a Blue Horse by Eric Carle	The Fauvre artist movement with emphasis on color and painting.
Roy Lichtenstein's ABC By Bob Adelman	Pop Art illustrations by artist focusing on design and color while learning letters.
Ed Emberley's Great Thumbprint Drawing Book by Ed Emberley	How to create fun characters using your thumbprint with emphasis on expression, line, and color.
Frida Kahlo: The Artist Who Painted Herself by Margaret Frith	The artwork and life of Frida Kahlo are featured with an emphasis on perseverance and emotional expression through self-portraits.
Art and Max by David Wiesner	Art history movements are featured during a painting session between two friends and personal expression through the artistic media is emphasized.

Using picture books to help students learn new language is a powerful strategy. Applying literacy strategies with nontext examples first allows students to use multiple modalities when creatively expressing their understandings.

Reading Through the Arts

Since reading comprehension can be challenging for ELs, teaching first through the visual arts allows for practice and application of comprehension skills that can be used when reading text. Learning to read illustrations assists ELs to connect the images with text. Students are motivated by visual art and most have something to say about an artwork. The visual read aloud strategy (VRA) is the process in which a student discovers meaning within the details of an illustration. Another benefit occurs when teaching the art criticism process (describing, analyzing, interpreting, and interpreting images), which strengthens students' language development by scaffolding fiction and nonfiction text with images (Klein & Stuart, 2012; Keene & Zimmermann, 2007). The art criticism process involves talking and writing about images (visual art) and performances (music, drama, and dance). The educational process of art criticism involves four basic steps: description, analysis, interpretation, and evaluation. Students discuss artistic works and performances using questioning and the inquiry process. The discussion begins by asking students to describe what they see in the creative work. Lines, shapes, forms, colors, values, textures, space, and patterns can be identified. The next step of the art criticism process involves analyzing the work through the principles of design. Balance, variety, emphasis, repetition, movement, unity, and contrast are discussed when analyzing expressive work. Contextual information about the work and the artist/musician/dance/actor leads students to explore different interpretations. The desire to better comprehend the work and its meaning evolves into interpretation, which enhances the relationship between the viewer and work. Students need to think through the interpretive process in order to connect their personal experiences with the creative work. The final step in the criticism process is evaluation. Students decide and support their decisions through concepts that were discussed during the process of description, analysis, and interpretation. Students build a rationale of why or why not they think the creative work has value or worthiness. Higher order thinking skills are used throughout the criticism process (Feldman, 1993; Maker, 2005).

In order to make connections between text and images, students need to understand the literacy strategies that are being utilized. Focusing on specific strategies during literacy instruction enhances metacognition. One approach to enhance metacognition used by educators is the explicit teaching model. Using the explicit teaching model to focus on why specific strategies are used and to instruct students to analyze the reasons for their ideas is an important part of literacy learning (Keane & Zimmerman 2007). In this approach, students should first understand the literacy strategy through an introduction by the teacher. Next, the teacher models the use of the strategy and guides practice with the students. Independent application of the strategy allows students to express their understandings. Finally, students should share what they thought about using the strategy with other children and the teacher. This model allows the students to become comfortable using the strategy and leads to independent application when new situations occur. In explicit instruction, the teacher and students preview meanings of unknown words before reading, explain context during reading and review new words after reading. Often teachers will model a Think Aloud strategy that identifies new words during a read aloud session. The teacher will write the new word and add this word to the classroom word wall (a display or bulletin board of words from lessons) or ask students to add the word to their personal dictionaries, which can also be illustrated. Eventually, students will have a toolbox full of strategies that they can choose from depending upon the learning experience. Preparing students for the future through the development of 21st century skills that emphasize creativity and critical thinking is an important part of the learning process.

Voices From the Classroom

"As an elementary educator, I like to cover the classroom walls with lots of visuals that relate to a thematic unit. I use maps, charts, signs, posters, artwork, and photographs to encourage students to explore what they know about the study topic. Often my students will create labels and attach new vocabulary words to objects and images in the room. I believe the visuals stimulate my students' interests."

Questions: How can teachers use classroom visuals to begin small group discussions?

How can student artwork stimulate discussion and increase vocabulary?

Reading Strategies and the Arts

The main goal of reading is comprehension and helping students connect what was read to their lives and the world around them (text to self, text to text, and text to world). Making meaningful connections builds literacy skills (Zimmerman & Keane, 2007). Teachers focus on three types of reading strategies: (1) before reading strategies (i.e., Picture Walk, Visualization, Predictions, and Anticipation Guides), (2) during reading strategies (i.e., Questioning and Think Aloud), and (3) after reading strategies (i.e., Summarization, Comprehension Questions, and Response Writing). Teachers plan specific strategies to meet the needs of students in each reading group. The following description in Table 13. 2 by a classroom teacher is an example of specific reading comprehension strategies that scaffold language learning and integrate the arts. As you read along the narrative, notice that strategies are organized and numbered for lessons that engage students before reading, during reading, and after reading. This is a typical strategy when planning lessons for ELs as using multiple approaches guides students through the reading process.

TABLE 13.2 Reading Strategies and Visually Representing Comprehension

Before Reading	During Reading	After Reading
(Strategy #1) Activating Prior Knowledge through Picture Walk—Each student has a file folder for before reading, during reading, and after reading. Sticky notes and colored markers are provided for the students by the research. Before reading, the teacher and students look at the front cover and predict what the story will be about. Next, selected illustrations throughout the book are discussed orally and students record their responses	(Strategy #3) Words/Text and Images Chart—(Strategy #3a)—Students use a small sticky note arrow to indicate unfamiliar words in text. The group discusses words (some words may have been indicated as unfamiliar by other students) and brainstorms how they can discover the meaning (look in dictionary, ask a friend, associate with words in text that they already know). Meaning is associated with each word.	(Strategy #5) After Reading Folder—The After Reading Folder is divided into three columns: (Strategy #5a) Important Details from Text; (Strategy #5b) Illustration of Detail; and (Strategy #5c) Summary in My Own Words. Children will record their answers for each column and add their sticky notes to their file folders. First, the teacher models and guides the children step by step and then students complete the work independently.

on sticky notes for each column on the file folder. (Strategy #2) The Before Reading folder will be divided into three columns: (Strategy #2a) Illustration (children draw something on the sticky note that catches their eye during the picture walk), (Strategy #2b) Prior knowledge link (What do we know?), and (Strategy #2c) Prediction (What could happen based upon the picture?). Children will record their answers for each column and add their sticky notes to their file folders, which will be photographed by teacher and analyzed after intervention according to the sequence of sessions. First, the teacher models and guides the children step by step and as the sessions move forward it is hoped by the teacher that the students will apply strategies independently and more frequently.

(Strategy #3b) Each student has a Word/Text and Image chart for recording unfamiliar words and illustrating the meaning of these words (student keeps as a word bank or personal picture dictionary). (Strategy #4) During Reading Folder—The During Reading Folder will be divided into three columns: (Strategy #4a) Questions, I wonder why prompts; (Strategy #4b) Illustrations of Events from Book to Provide Evidence; and (Strategy #4c) Inference. Children will record their answers for each column and add their sticky notes to their file folders. First, the teacher models and guides the children step by step.

Teaching literacy integrated with the arts for ELs encourages the use of strategies that support all levels of language learning. Reflection by teachers after using a new strategy is an important part of professional development and provides valuable information for future implementation. The following teacher voices feature explains how one teacher considered the process after utilizing the strategies listed in Table 13. 2.

Teacher Voices

"After implementing the series reading lessons, I decided to no longer use the folder as a drawing and organizational tool. Instead, I designed several different graphic organizers based upon the theme of the book and focused on the main idea, supporting details, problem, and solution. Students were allowed to draw, color and write on the graphic organizers. I used the strategy "Stretch to Sketch" during several reading sessions. Students seemed to like this paper format better to design their own ideas about the story or focus on a specific part of the story that was meaningful to them. While reading, students used sticky notes of various colors with icons drawn on them and attached to specific parts of the story. For example, a sticky note with a red heart can be attached to the sentence describing a student's favorite part of the story. I decided to use the heart (This is my favorite part), two eyes (I see a detail in the picture that I can discuss), "?" (I have questions about something that I don't understand),"!" (This part of the story is exciting or surprising), and "LOL" (This part of the story is funny).

By counting the number of times each student used the specific strategies, I could assess if there were any increases in using specific strategies over time. This was a complicated process and since I was actively involved in the reading aloud process, asking questions, prompting, and modeling reading behaviors. After looking over my assessments, I discovered specific students utilized certain strategies more often and that the use of these strategies carried over to independent classroom assignments. As a teacher, this was a great reflection to realize that the reading strategies impacted learning beyond the focused lesson."

Questions:
How can you design before, during, and after reading strategies that integrate the arts?
Can you adapt the featured reading strategies to include music, drama, and dance components?

Literacy Mini-Lessons
Many teachers use a mini lesson format when teaching literacy lessons. This format includes: a connection (to learning for unit of study or future learning), modeling by teacher, active engagement (students practice the strategy), and a link (connect to daily work or ongoing assignments/units). This format guides teachers to focus on specific strategies during small group work during a literacy block (Calkins, 1986; Teachers College Reading and Writing Project, 2009). In Table 13. 3, an example of a mini lesson that integrates the arts with literacy learning strategies is explained.

TABLE 13.3 Meeting Students' Needs during a Reading/Writing Mini Lesson
Mini Lesson Format Adapted from Teachers College Reading and Writing Project, 2009, and Lucy Calkins, 1986.

	Student(s):	Teacher:	Date:
	Fourth Grade	Susannah	Brown 4/11/17
1.	Lesson Title: "Tar Beach" by Faith Ringgold **Looking for the details in a Story** **Focus Area: Before Reading Strategies of a Visual Read Aloud (VRA)**		
2.	**Lesson Purpose and Skill or Concept:** Students will focus on the artwork of "Tar Beach" by Faith Ringgold and describe the details of the painting to predict what the story is about. Using the VRA strategy, students will describe how the five senses are used in the artwork.		
3.	The WIDA English Language Development (ELD) Standards **The English Language Development Standards**		

English Language Development Standard 1	English learners **communicate** for **Social** and **Instructional** purposes within the school setting
English Language Development Standard 2	English learners **communicate** information, ideas and concepts necessary for academic success in the content area of **Language Arts**

4.   Instructional Materials: *Books, handouts, supplies, anchor charts, etc.

"Tar Beach" by Faith Ringgold, 5 senses worksheet for notes (in Spanish and English)
(**Key**: **veo**-I see; **gusto**-taste, pleasure; **oigo**-I listen; **toco**-I touch)

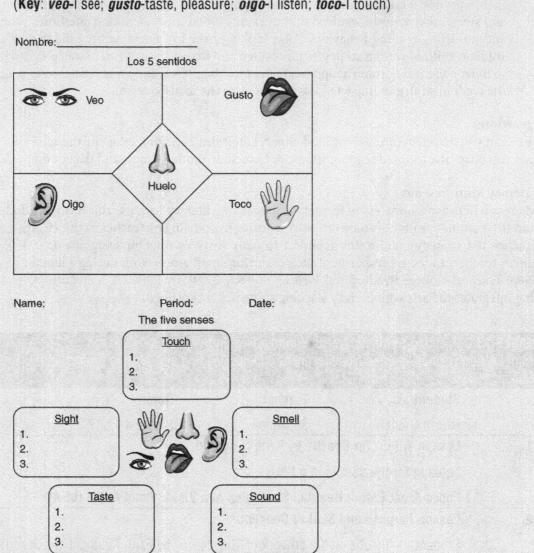

5.   Read-Aloud/Think-Aloud (First 10 minutes) *Book title & author

"Tar Beach" by Faith Ringgold

The students will look at the cover illustration/artwork and discuss with the teacher as whole group. Students will describe the artwork using the five senses. During the discussion, the students will write notes on the 5 senses worksheet. Students will predict what they think the story is about using the VRA strategy.

6.	**Mini Lesson: *Describe each component (focus on 1 strategy)**

Connection (to prior learning): The teacher will read the title of the book and show the artwork by Faith Ringgold to the students. The teacher will ask: "What is a tar beach?" Using the images as their resource they will discuss in groups of 4 (table team) and report to the teacher what they think the title means. This will lead the teacher to use the VRA strategy.

Teach (model strategy or technique): Using the VRA strategy, the teacher points out the top of the roof in the artwork as the "tar beach" and describe how a tar roof feels like on a hot summer evening, smells like after the warm day, looks like, and sounds like when you walk on it. Next, students get the 5 senses worksheet.

Active Engagement (guided practice): Using the 5 senses worksheet, the students work first as a whole class under the teacher's guidance. Students verbalize what they see in the artwork and describe the senses that are associated with the details. The teacher writes a list of descriptive words on the board from the discussion and students are encouraged to use these words to help them describe the artwork.

Link (give student a hook to remember the strategy during independent practice)

The 5 senses worksheet links the student learning in the group to independent learning. The students complete the worksheet independently trying to describe as many details of the artwork as they can. The illustrations on the worksheet will help to remind the students to use all 5 senses when describing the artwork.

7.	**Writing Workshop:** Writing by the student should be related to the reading portion of the lesson.

Students will write the details from the artwork that were discussed on the 5 senses worksheet. This is a note-taking writing assignment. Students will write a brief statement that summarizes their predictions at the end of the lesson.

8.	**Assessment:** Include a formative and summative assessment based on your learning objectives.

Students complete the 5 senses worksheet during the discussion and the teacher will review with them during the lesson (formative).

At the end of the lesson, students will each write a brief statement that summarizes what they predict the story is about (summative).

9.	**Classroom Management:** Explain how you will plan a learning environment that is conducive to learning including modeling, guided, and independent practice.

The classroom rules will be posted on the board for all students. Consequences and Rewards are outlined and explained to students. The teacher will model appropriate behavior during the discussion of the artwork and students are expected to behave respectfully to their peers during the discussion. During independent practice, the class will focus on their work at their desks and the teacher will circulate and assist as needed. A class reward for work well done may include art studio time, where the teacher guides students through an art lesson using a variety of materials.

10. **Use of Technology (Connections or Extensions):** Describe how you will incorporate technology into your mini lesson.

The teacher will link to the website:

http://www.faithringgold.com/ringgold/default.htm

The teacher will discuss information found on the website with the whole class. During Computer Time, students may select to further explore this website.

11. **Two Adaptations or Accommodations for Diversity (EL, ESE, Learning Styles, Gifted):**

A. A list of descriptive words can be brainstormed as a class and listed on a chart or on the board for students to refer to during the discussion. This helps ELs because they can select words that they know and other students can add to the list as the discussion continues in small groups.

B. Gifted students can research Faith Ringgold through technology on the class computers/iPads and present biographical information that they read in the story, "Tar Beach." They can share the information in groups or write a short paper.

12. **References (APA format):** Cite 3 references/resources for strategies to improve instruction.

*Ringgold, F. (2016). *Faith Ringgold.* Retrieved from http://www.faithringgold.com/ringgold/default.htm

*Ringgold, F. (1991). *Tar beach.* New York, NY: Random House Publishing Company.

Smilan, C. & Towell, J. (2006, May 2). *Expanding the definition of literacy for preservice teachers through art-based learning.*

Unpublished lecture delivered at the 2006, International Reading Association, Chicago, Ill.

Towell, J. & Smilan, C. (2009). Teaching literacy through the visual arts in a multicultural world. *Journal of Reading Education, 35*(1).

Sipe, L. R. (2000). The construction of literary understanding by first and second graders in oral response to picture storybook read-alouds. *Reading research quarterly, 35*(2), 252–275.

13. **Teacher Recommendations:** List 3 strategies you recommend for teaching this skill and the rationale for each.

A. VRA—Visual Read Aloud—This strategy allows for students to describe the visual (cover illustration or other artwork) to help ignite the senses before reading. In this lesson, students use this strategy as a prediction tools in anticipation of reading the book.

B. Picture Walk—This strategy allows students to anticipate the story details prior to reading the text by looking at the illustrations. This strategy supports visual learners and ELs by focusing on images to set the stage for what will be read.

C. Split Images—This strategy allows students to describe in words an illustration to another student who is closing their eyes or turned around. This is a good strategy to increase vocabulary use and attention of details in images. Also, this strategy allows students to work in pairs to support collaboration.

14.	**Strategies for ELs:**
	1. Activate Prior Knowledge—KWL charts and Anticipation Guides
	2. Immerse in a print-rich environment
	3. Frequent checks for comprehension
	4. Allow for collaborative group work
	5. Use Sensory Supports—visuals
	6. Use Graphic Supports—anchor charts and graphic organizers
	7. Use Interactive Supports—small group work and partner work

Engaging students and activating prior knowledge strengthens comprehension. Link new information with known information through sensory, graphic, and interactive supports to stimulate reading and writing motivation. Sensory supports include strategies such as real objects, illustrations, photographs, videos, and models. Graphic supports provide a visual organization of concepts (i.e., charts, tables, graphs, and timelines). Interactive supports involve working with others in small collaborative groups or pairs or with mentors and tutors (WIDA, 2012). Connecting the mini lesson format to strategies that are effective with ELs, helps teachers to better plan group and whole class literacy lessons (see Table 13. 4).

TABLE 13.4 Mini Lesson Strategies for ELs

General Strategies	– Use lots of visuals and expressive body movements along with exaggerated facial expressions
	– Demonstrate using the same materials the students will use for the lesson
	– Use clear, concise language and repeat key information
	– Consider pre-teaching prior to your mini lesson with the whole class, i.e., when teaching idioms or metaphors (figurative language that might be confusing for ELs), review the concept with a small of group first.
Connection	– Use gestures (pointing) to indicate materials and information on charts
	– Allow students to verbalize the lesson connection to a partner using key words from the lesson connection
Demonstration (Instruction by Teacher)	– Act out or dramatize the steps
	– Use gestures and point to charts illustrating the steps for using the strategy
	– Use text with illustrations that support comprehension
Active Involvement	– Have children use gestures during work
	– Use a familiar text if appropriate with illustrations
	– Complete one active involvement strategy as a whole class to model, then have independent practice
	– Create mixed ability work groups that include students that can mentor others
Link	– Dramatically act out the link to model behavior and use of strategy
	– Use "Think Aloud" questions to link to learning

If students have limited experiences with the study topic, create experiences through field trips, guest speakers, and the use of technology. Websites that have live action feeds or video recordings make a virtual field trip possible. For example, if students were studying manatees several nature centers in Florida have live cameras that capture daily gatherings of this gentle creature (http://www.savethemanatee.org/savethemanateecam.html). Visiting an art museum from around the world is possible through websites helping students explore artwork and conduct research online (Spaulding, Carolino, & Amen, 2004).

FINAL POINTS

- Art integration within the literacy curriculum can support student learning by allowing for multiple forms of expression (Fowler, 1996).
- In personal practice, selecting children's literature that supports art and language learning is an effective strategy for students.
- Teachers can use the described strategies as starting points to begin integrating art into the literacy curriculum. "The integrative abilities of the visual arts position it at the center of school curricula and play an essential role in linking all subjects, while keeping the arts' integrity as a domain of knowledge that is fundamental in diverse learning environments" (Zimmerman, 2012, p. 2).
- Including teacher read aloud sessions is effective in modeling fluency for students learning a new language. Reading aloud in the classroom is an important part of reading instruction (Trelease, 2013).
- Allowing time for writing and creative expression is equally important in a literacy classroom. Combining artistic expression with the written word is especially effective for ELs. Arts engagement motivates students and allows for freedom of expression and choice, very important aspects of learning valued by teachers and students alike.
- In preparing all students to be effective communicators in the 21st century, the ability to comprehend multimodal literacy is imperative.
- Creativity is an essential skill for children to learn and use in our 21st century. As educators, we develop, nurture, and strengthen students' creative expression (Leong & Bodrova, 2012).
- Multimodal literacy is defined as "the practice of moving from one sign system to another (e.g., transmediation from verbal-visual, visual-verbal, visual-spatial)" (Martinez & Nolte-Yupari, 2015, p.12).
- Integrating art with language is one example of multimodal literacy. Expressing knowledge and understanding through different media supports students' literacy development and is an important goal of education.

Discussion Questions and Activities

1. You can integrate the arts into your classroom using a variety of strategies. Have you ever experienced learning in an arts-integrated classroom as a student? Discuss how you felt and what you learned through arts integration.

2. When planning an arts-integrated literacy lesson what strategies do you think would be most helpful for ELs? Plan five activities that involve the arts and literacy strategies described in this chapter.

3. Look at news headlines, advertising, textbook content, classroom and school displays, etc. Do you see elements of arts integration reflected in schools and communities? Think of five examples to share with your group.

4. How can teachers inspire parents and guardians to include the arts in language learning? What strategies could be adapted from the classroom to make a stronger home connection using the arts as entry points? Discuss two examples with your group.

Resources

For Teachers of English Learners (ELs) when integrating the arts
http://www.getty.edu/education/teachers/classroom_resources/curricula/esl3/

The J. Paul Getty Museum provides in-depth curriculum that focuses on ELs and the arts. Many other resources through this organization are valuable when planning an arts-integrated literacy unit.
https://artsedge.kennedy-center.org/educators/how-to/supporting-individual-needs/supporting-ell-with-the-arts

The Kennedy Center for the Arts provides lessons that teach important concepts in both the arts and literacy, which can be used for classroom teachers
https://www.teachingenglish.org.uk/article/art-classroom

The British Council provides valuable information and a rationale for classroom teachers interested in teaching literacy through the arts
https://www.theartofed.com/2014/12/31/help-your-ell-students-in-art-class-with-these-simple-steps/

This site has many different resources but this particular page explains very clearly simple supports that can be used in any classroom for teachers that integrate the arts in literacy lessons
http://www.colorincolorado.org/article/how-support-ell-students-interrupted-formal-education-sifes
This online article is part of a wonderful website

References

Calkins, L.M. (1986). *The art of teaching writing.* Portsmouth, NH: Heinemann.

Cartwright, K.B. (Ed.). (2008). *Literacy processes: Cognitive flexibility in learning and teaching.* New York, NY: Guilford Press.

Eisner, E. (2002). The Arts and the Creation of Mind, In Chapter 4, What the Arts Teach and How It Shows. (pp. 70–92). Yale University Press.

http://www.arteducators.org/advocacy/10-lessons-the-arts-teach#sthash.voUAs3y1.dpuf

Feldman, E.B. (1993). *Practical art criticism.* Upper Saddle River, NJ: Prentice Hall.

Gardner, H. (1999). *Intelligences reframed: Multiple intelligences for the 21st century.* New York: Basic Books.

Gullatt, D. E. (2008). Enhancing student learning through arts integration: Implications for the profession. *The High School Journal, 91*(4), 12–25.

Hetland, L., Winner, E., Veenema, S., & Sheridan, K. M. (2007). *Studio thinking: The real benefits of visual arts education.* New York, NY: Teachers College Press.

Kasten, W. C., Kristo, J. V., & McClure, A. A. (2005). *Living literature: Using children's literature to support reading and language arts.* Upper Saddle River, NJ: Pearson.

Keene, E. O., & Zimmermann, S. (2007). *Mosaic of thought: The power of comprehension strategy instruction.* Portsmouth, NH: Heinemann.

Klein, J. & Stuart, E. (2012). *Using art to teacher reading comprehension strategies: Lesson plans for teachers.* Lanham, MD: Rowman and Littlefield Education.

Koster, J.B. (2009). *Growing artists: Teaching the arts to young children.* San Francisco, CA: Cengage Learning.

Leong, D.J. & Bodrova, E. (2012). Assessing and scaffolding: Make-believe play. *Young Children, 67*(1), 28–34.

Marshall, J. (2005). Connecting art, learning, and creativity: A case for curriculum integration. *Studies in Art Education. 46*(3), pp. 227–241.

Ringgold, F. (2016). *Faith Ringgold.* Retrieved from http://www.faithringgold.com/ringgold/default.htm

Sipe, L. R. (2000). The construction of literary understanding by first and second graders in oral response to picture storybook read-alouds. *Reading research quarterly, 35*(2), 252–275.

Smilan, C. & Towell, J. (2006, May 2). *Expanding the definition of literacy for preservice teachers through art-based learning.* Unpublished lecture delivered at the 2006, International Reading Association, Chicago, IL.

Spaulding, Carolino, & Kali-Ahset. Immigrant Students and Secondary School Reform: Compendium of Best Practices. Written on behalf of The Council of Chief State School Officers (CCSSO). 2004. Retrieved from http://www.ccsso.org/content/pdfs/BestPractices.pdf

Teachers College Reading and Writing Project. (2009). *High frequency word assessment (Grades 3–8).* Retrieved from http://readingandwritingproject.com/public/resources/assessments/spelling/spelling_word_list_directions.pdf

Towell, J. & Smilan, C. (2009). Teaching literacy through the visual arts in a multicultural world. *Journal of Reading Education, 35*(1).

Trelease, J. (2013). *The read-aloud handbook.*7th edition. New York, NY: Penguin Books.

WIDA. (2012). *The WIDA standards framework and its theoretical foundations.* Retrieved from https://www.wida.us/standards/eld.aspx

Zimmerman, E. (2012). *A case for integrating art into a variety of teaching and learning environments.* Retrieved from http://www.arteducators.org/advocacy/NAEA_WhitePapers_4.pdf

Children's Literature References

Adelman, B. (2013). *Roy Lichtenstein's ABC.* London, England: Thames & Hudson.

Aliki (1998). *Marianthe's story: Painted words and spoken memories.* London: Greenwillow Books

Becker, A. (2013). *Journey.* Sommerville, MA: Candlewick Press.

Carle, E. (2011). *The artist who painted a blue horse.* New York, NY: Philomel Books.

Emberley, E. (2005). *Ed Emberley's great thumbprint drawing book.* New York, NY: LB Kids.

Frith, M. (2003). *Frida Kahlo: The artist who painted herself.* New York, NY: Grosset & Dunlap.

Keene, E. O., & Zimmermann, S. (2013). Years later, comprehension strategies still at work. *The Reading Teacher, 66*(8), 601–606.

Maker, C. J. (2005). *The DISCOVER Project: Improving assessment and curriculum for diverse gifted learners.* National Research Center on the Gifted and Talented, University of Connecticut.

Martinez, U., & Nolte-Yupari, S. (2015). Story Bound, Map Around: Stories, Life, and Learning. *Art Education, 68*(1), 12–18.

Ringgold, F. (1991). *Tar beach.* New York, NY: Random House Publishing Company.

Tan, S. (2006). *The arrival.* New York, NY: Arthur A. Levine Books.

Wiesner, D. (2010). *Art and Max.* New York, NY: Clarion Books.

CHAPTER 14

VOCABULARY DEVELOPMENT IN A LITERACY CURRICULUM (FROM ELEMENTARY TO OLDER ELs): AN ACTION PLAN

Kate Mastruserio Reynolds

KEY POINTS

- Ways to differentiate levels of proficiency while factoring vocabulary knowledge.
- Steps to integrate research on vocabulary learning into instruction.
- Steps to utilize evidence-based, field-tested strategies for vocabulary teaching and learning.
- Use Common Core Standards to introduce more advanced vocabulary and promote higher levels of learning.

In one third-grade general education class at Cedar Riverside Elementary, I met Dayax*, who had grown up in Minneapolis (*pseudonym). Dayax was older than his peers due to interrupted formal learning. He had been in several different schools due to family issues and was at that time in foster care. He had also missed long periods of academic preparation. The school chose to place him into third-grade, so he had more time to catch up with his peers prior to engaging in more complex academic topics.

Dayax's home language was Somali. He had some proficiency in oral, social English, but his literacy was not adequately developed for the grade level. I was asked by Dayax's teacher to work with him on sight word vocabulary, reading and writing, which I did in a one-on-one basis for two hours daily for one academic year.

Informing Instruction With Placement and Needs Assessment Results

The choices in Dayax's individualized instruction were based on extensive research and reading on vocabulary and literacy development, Dayax's WIDA W-APT placement (WIDA-ACCESS Placement Test—see www.wida.us/assessment/W-APT/) results (see Figure 14.1 for a hypothetical example) and needs assessment. Understanding where to begin instruction with Dayax was a challenge, which I undertook by commencing with a *needs assessment* of his reading, writing, and social and academic vocabulary. I engaged Dayax in a series of literacy tasks and games in a low-stress environment in order to diagnose specific needs sets. Based on his W-APT scores and my needs assessments tasks, I developed my action plan (see Figure 14.1, 3rd column).

Language domain	Proficiency level	Areas in which instruction was needed
Speaking	3	• Expanding sentence lengths from simple to compound sentences • Enlarging oral social and academic vocabulary to include more specific and descriptive vocabulary • Interactive oral language practice for fluency
Writing	1	• Writing simple sentences and expanding to compound sentences • Taking notes including new academic vocabulary words; labeling visuals • Recognizing the parts of speech in a simple sentence
Listening	2	• Comprehending simple and compound sentences in oral social and academic language • Developing comprehension check strategies
Reading	1	• Enlarging written general and academic vocabulary through narrow, extensive reading • Expanding sight word recognition to longer words from readings • Practice reading independently and with guidance
Oral Composite Proficiency Level	2.5	
Literacy Composite Proficiency Level	1.0	
Grade Adjusted Composite Proficiency Level	1.7	

(See WIDA Performance Definitions for scale interpretation at **WIDA Performance Definitions**; https://www.wida.us/standards/RG_Performance%20Definitions.pdf)

Figure 14.1 Dayax's Hypothetical W-APT Score Report

Types of Vocabulary Geared to Students' Needs

Generally, teachers know, based on the learners' age(s), interests, and location of instruction, the purpose for students' vocabulary. These areas determine whether learners require personal/social or survival vocabulary, or if their needs and goals are more academic (i.e., core content of math, literature, history, and science) or specific purposes (such as engineering, law, or business). Dayax required academic language and vocabulary, so I sought out more specific knowledge about Dayax's academic vocabulary. Research by Cummins (1979, 2008) on social and academic language influenced me to identify the kinds of vocabulary Dayax needed to build enough background knowledge for comprehending readings and to serve as a foundation for his writing. Cummins' research differentiated the language needed to participate in social communication (e.g., informal conversation to establish and develop relationships) and academic language (e.g., the language terms and phrases used by academics to explain their word, usually in a formal format). Using grade-level Academic Word Lists (see Coxhead, 2000; Gardner & Davies, 2013), I created activities for Dayax to indicate this academic vocabulary familiarity. The word lists came from grade 2–3 from Berkeley Unified School District (http://www.berkeleyschools.net/wp-content/uploads/2013/05/BUSD_Academic_Vocabulary.pdf) (see Figure 14.2) since Dayax had interrupted formal schooling. I needed to know what he was missing.

Grade 3 (p. 30)

although	collect	defend	effect	in general	maximum	question
analyze	comparison	define	event	however	minimum	reason
anticipate	completely	determine	evidence	identify	occur	recall
cause	conclude	disagree	exclude	include	organize	regularly
characterize	constant	discuss		information	place	request
claim	contrast	draw	former	investigate	point out	require
class	create	draw conclusion	frequently	justify	prior	required
classify	critical	draw upon	general	label	process	research
respond	response	review	sequence	support	various	

Grade 2 (p. 31)

above	characteristics	direct	in common	object (n)	rank	reverse
ago	check	enough	interest	plan	rare	several
apply	clear	ever	interesting	portion	ready	solution
argument	compare	explanation	introduce	possible	reduce	solve
arrange	complete	few (adj)	item	prepare	relate to	
behind	conclusion	free	less	probably	relationship	
benefit	decide	important	miss(ing)	prove	restate	
category	deep	impossible	model	purpose	results	

Figure 14.2 Curated Academic Word List Grades 2–3 for Dayax

To determine the student's level, they are given several types of assessments to complete. The kinds of item formats for the vocabulary needs assessment included close-ended exercises, such as matching, fill in the blank with work bank, sentence creation and multiple choice (see Figure 14.3). I did not use drawing or picture matching, as I would in other cases, because the academic words were abstract.

Matching: Choose the definitions that fit the word on the left.

1. _____ contrast
2. _____ defend
3. _____ review
4. _____ classify

a. to put things into groupings
b. to go back over an event or reading
c. to think about what two things have that are alike
d. to stand up for someone or something; to protect

5. _____ wonder
6. _____ reduce
7. _____ plan
8. _____ introduce

a. to make something smaller or less
b. to show someone something for the first time
c. to think about something; to be curious
d. to think and map out your actions

Fill in the Blank with Word Bank

decide   trait   solve   portion   ago   checked   label   general

1. Juanita wanted a book about volcanoes in _____.
2. The banker _____ the account to see if there was enough money.
3. It was clear the son had the _____ of the father since they had the same hair and eyes.
4. The dancer _____ to do a new style of dance.
5. At the grocery, I read the _____ to make sure the food was healthy.

Sentence Completion: Choose a word that will complete the sentence you make up.

above   behind   rare   Less   frequently   place   point   out   event

1. The store was _____.

2. The bird was _____.

3. In math, we _____.

4. She has _____.

Multiple Choice

anticipated   evidence   sequence   maximum   characteristics   explanations   state   object

1. When I clean my room, I like to _____ my activities.
2. The dog had all the _____ of its mother.
3. Sarah _____ going to the park on the weekend.
4. The police officer gathered _____ to find the person who took the car.
5. The teacher gave us an _____ of the homework.

Figure 14.3 Sample Item Formats for **Vocabulary Needs Assessment**

Evidence-Informed Teaching of Vocabulary in Literacy Development

Grade-Level Social and Academic Language

In grades 1–3, learners build academic language of language arts. Language arts in these grades is based heavily on narratives on fictional topics. In other words, the storytelling in fictional narratives would support Dayax's needs in social language development. Since he was stronger in social language, it was logical to build his social language through independent, yet scaffolded, readings. I decided to provide sequenced stem sentences for Dayax to use to retell events from the narratives in written form (see Figure 14.4), which he could do independently; however, I knew I needed to review them with him to make sure that his sentence-level writing was comprehensible and relatively accurate. We discussed sentence structures, grammar, and vocabulary in our reviews.

At third grade, Dayax was also encountering some abstract academic language in nonfiction readings. So, efforts to develop basic academic vocabulary in leveled, nonfiction readings on science (e.g., animals, climates, environments), and American social history (e.g., biographies of Martin Luther King and César Chavez) would build his background knowledge on the topics, but also his academic vocabulary for future use through guided readings on the academic topics. After reading these texts in a guided reading format, Dayax and I would use the Language Experience Approach (see https://k12teacherstaffdevelopment.com/tlb/understanding-the-language-experience-approach-lea/), complex graphic organizers (see Figure 14.5), and simplified summaries of the readings (see Suffragette example below). He also

Tell the story.... Volver a contar la historia.... Name: ____________ Date: ________

- **Directions:** Pick a friend to tell the story and write the events (things that happened) in order.
- Who will you write to? My friend's name is ____________.
- The characters (people in the story) were ____________.
- They lived ____________.
- The first thing that happened was ____________
- ____________.
- Next, ________ (the characters) ____________
- ____________
- ____________.
- Then, ____________
- ____________
- ____________.
- Finally, ____________
- ____________
- ____________.
- I liked this part of the story: ____________, because ____________.
- I did not like this part of the story: ____________, because ____________.

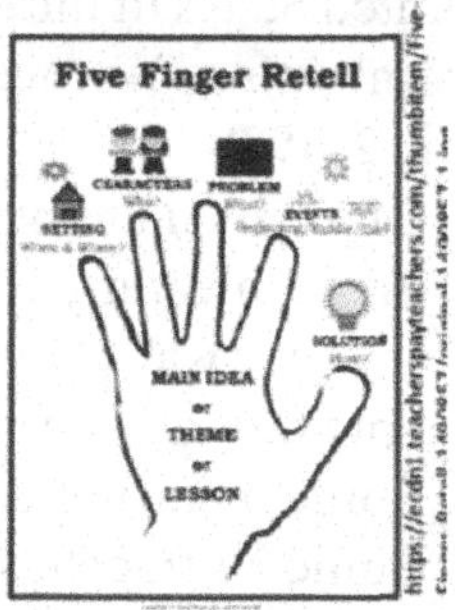

Figure 14.4 Sequenced Stem Sentences

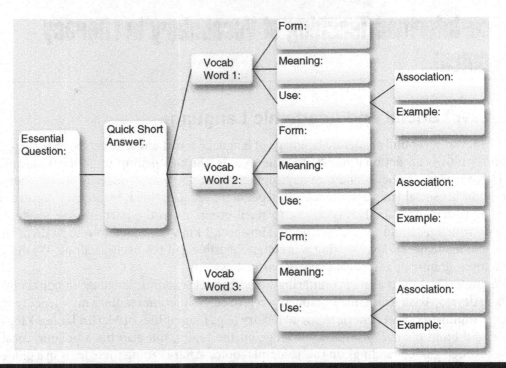

Figure 14.5 Essential Question and Vocabulary Graphic Organizer

identified key vocabulary that he wanted to place in his vocabulary journal and make flashcards for future reference.

An example of a simplified text that I employed for older students was Suffragette history. Below is the version I simplified.

Suffragettes was the term for a women's movement who wanted to win right to vote in the Britain and United States in the early 1900s. There were many laws that prevented men without property and women from voting. Women did not win the right to vote in the United States until 1919 and in Britain until July 2, 1928.

Many men and women did not want women to vote. The people were opposed to (against) universal suffrage, meaning the right for all citizens over 18 years old to vote, said and did many things to stop them. One way people tried to stop the Suffragettes was to say they were unfeminine or unladylike. Some people thought it as unnatural for women to vote.

Some men supported the right for women to vote.

Some Suffragettes protests in marches and rallies (i.e., meetings with public speakers). Other Suffragettes protested by starving themselves and were force fed. Some Suffragettes protested by refusing to complete the 1911 census (i.e., the counting of people in a country).

Many Suffragettes had to hide their names and identities, because they were worried they would be hurt. Some Suffragettes supported the movement, but were not always active. So, it is hard to estimate how many Suffragettes there were.

Adapted from Historyextra's 10 Thing You (Probably) Didn't Know about the Suffragettes, October 12, 2015. (http://www.historyextra.com/article/social-history/10-facts-about-suffragettes).

What Is Knowing a Word?

I considered the research on understanding the meanings of words. In order to understand the meanings of words, individuals may have a *receptive* or *productive* knowledge of the word. When an individual recognizes the meaning of a word in context (listening and reading), it is receptive knowledge; however, then the individual can actively use the word accurately in speaking or writing, it is productive knowledge. Nation (2001) expanded the concept to include the **Form** (i.e., oral, written, and word parts), **Meaning** (i.e., concept expressed, referents, and associations) and **Uses** of the word (i.e., grammar function, collocations and sociocultural uses, contexts, and constraints) (see Figure 14.6).

In order to be competent users of words, according to Nation, learners should know each of these word features. I decided our word study would include discussions and depictions of new words to include these features. Likewise, our sight word index cards would have word feature notes on the back. These word features allowed us to play engaging guessing games with the words based on specific contexts. For example, if I was to go to a science lab, what words would I use? Answer: evidence, analyze, discover, describe, and research. What kinds of words are these? Who uses these words? Where do we find these words in our lives?

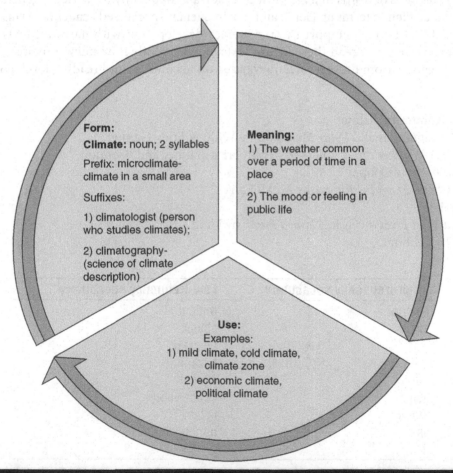

Figure 14.6 Example of Form, Meaning, and Use Graphic Organizer of Climate

How Many Words Do Learners Need to Know?

According to Nation (2014), English learners need the most frequently occurring 6,000–7,000 word families to comprehend oral language, but need 8,000–9,000 word families to comprehend most written texts. This concept is called *high-frequency vocabulary* and describes common words; *low-frequency vocabulary* are highly specialized words that are not commonly used (see Figure 14.7).

At beginner levels of proficiency, English learners have roughly 2,000 high-frequency vocabulary words, whereas intermediate learners have roughly 4,000 words in their lexicon (Nation, 2006). In research, Zahar, Cobb, & Spada found that word frequency is 3–4 times more important for beginners than for intermediate and advanced students (2001). Dayax and I needed to vastly increase his vocabulary and to do so in memorable and engaging ways.

Which Words Do Learners Need?

I sought additional guidance on which words to teach for social and academic purposes, so I referred to the Common Core Standards Tier words (http://www.corestandards.org/assets/Appendix_A.pdf). The Tiers refer to categories of words that are most common and frequently used Tier 1, general introductory cross-curricular academic terms at Tier 2, and low frequency, specialized academic terms at Tier 3.

I determined that I could support Dayax's literacy development with narrative texts that included Tier 1 vocabulary. He could read these fiction texts independently if he knew a majority of the words, so we selected readers from the school library based on his interest and reading level. For example, we read

- Arctic and Antarctica Habitat:
  - *Animal Adaptations* and *Polar Mammals* by Whitt & Fries-Gaither
  - *Antarctica's Weather and Climate* by Whitt, Fries-Gaither and Brannon
  - *Polar Animals* by Cooper
  - *Puffins Climb, Penguins Rhyme* by McMillian
- Desert Habitat:
  - *Way Out West Lives a Coyote Named Frank* by Lund
  - *Deserts* by Gibbons,

High-frequency vocabulary	Low-frequency vocabulary
school	mitigate
child	abyss
car	bespeak
tree	byzantine
of	citadel
what	conceivable
doing	fallacy
is	nonchalantly
I	

Figure 14.7 High- and Low-Frequency Vocabulary Comparison

- ○ *Desert Night, Desert Day* by Fredericks
- ○ *The Seed and the Giant Saguaro* by Ward
- ○ *Why, Oh Why are Deserts Dry* by Rabe
- Rainforest Habitat:
  - ○ *One Small Place in a Tree* by Brenner
  - ○ *One Small Square: Tropical Rain Forest* by Silver
  - ○ *The Magic School Bus in the Rain Forest* by Moore
  - ○ *The Rainforest Grew All Around* by Mitchell
- Grasslands and Plains:
  - ○ *An American Safari: Adventures on the North American Prairie* by Brandenburg
  - ○ *One Small Square: African Savanna* by Silver and Wynne
  - ○ *A Walk in the Prairie* by Johnson
  - ○ *Explore the Grasslands* by Jackson
- Ocean Habitat:
  - ○ *Here is the Coral Reef* by Dunphy
  - ○ *Somewhere in the Ocean* by Ward
  - ○ *The Hidden Forest* by Baker
  - ○ *Down, Down, Down: A Journey to the Bottom of the Sea* by Jenkins
  - ○ *Manatees* by Marisco

According to the WIDA W-APT assessment that the school administered, Dayax's language proficiency was 1.7, which indicated that he needed support from *visual representations* of language in content areas while he developed his general academic vocabulary. Many of the 2nd and 3rd grade level readers have visual supports.

If too many of the vocabulary were unfamiliar, the text was too far above his comprehension to read independently. We previewed texts together, so I could determine his comprehension of vocabulary (i.e., comprehensible input (Krashen, 1989)). If he encountered a new vocabulary term that he could discern using context clues, I did not explicitly teach it; although I would check his comprehension and at times add information to deepen his understanding of the word. If the text was too far above his independent reading level, we identified other texts.

When working on his academic language proficiency in guided reading sessions, the same approach applied to incidental vocabulary learning. However, if it was not possible for him to comprehend the new word incidentally during his academic reading, I would explicitly teach it. According to Hulstijn (2013), incidental learning is "'picking up' an unknown word from listening to someone or from reading a text" (p. 2632). Even though some words may be read and understood incidentally, they may only be remembered receptively, not for recall and productive use; therefore, educators must be informed about key sight words and grade-level word lists in order to highlight a key word for learners.

Evidence-Based Practices to Unpack New Words

If I needed to highlight or explicitly teach an unfamiliar or key word, research supports the instruction of new vocabulary words through word study, which can include teaching word origins, roots and affixes (see Hirsh, 2017), analyzing lexical chunks (see Hellman, 2017), and conducting semantic feature analysis (see Amer, 2017) (see Figure 14.8).

Example: Word Origin, Roots, Affixes

Word	Meaning	Word origin	Root	Prefix(es)	Suffix(es)
require (verb)	Need to do something; necessary	Latin—to seek	require	Prerequirement—pre—meaning before	• requires (3rd person present tense verb) • required (past tense verb; past participle) • requiring (gerund) • requirement (noun)
inform (verb)	To give or make known	Latin—to teach	inform	Misinformation—mis—meaning wrong Noninformational—non—meaning not	• informs (verb) • informed (verb) • information (noun) • informational (adjective) • noninformational (adjective)

Example: Lexical chunks

Word	Common Lexical Chunks		
request	Make a request	Request a favor	Request information
introduction	Make an introduction	Introduce myself/a friend	Excellent introduction
review	Book review	Read and review	Careful(ly) review
investigate	Police/detective investigate	Investigate a crime	Investigate systematically

Example: Semantic feature analysis of manatees and walruses

Questions	Manatees	Walruses
How are they alike?	• Live in water • Have flippers • Have whiskers • Weigh thousands of pounds (1,000+) • Mammals • Cannot breathe underwater	
How are they different?	• Never leave water • Eat on plants • Have teeth, but they are not sharp • Lives in warm places (e.g., Caribbean, Florida)	• Get out of the water some of the time • Eat clams, plants and animals • Have long tusks • Lives in cold places (e.g., Arctic, Antarctic)
How alike are manatees and walruses?		
How different are manatees and walruses?		
What other animals are like manatees and walruses?		

Figure 14.8

Word study is engaging the learner(s) in unpacking (i.e., discussing) the word meaning, associations, collocations, synonyms and antonyms (see Erten & Dikilitas, 2017), and word features. When Dayax encountered an unfamiliar word, we would employ structured word webs to visually unpack the concept. For example, we encountered the concept of a desert when reading about climates (see Figure 14.9). We discussed what he knew of deserts, which happened to be based on several popular movies. I served as the scribe for him to model how to complete the structured word web, which I speedily drew. I asked probing questions to mine the depths of his understandings of the concept while adding in new information, such as arid, Latin origin, and parts of speech.

In order to further understand the collocations (i.e., two words that are used together often), for example, words that collocate with "climate" are "climate change," "climate zones," and "local climate", Dayax and I employed the website ProWriting for its collocation search (http://prowritingaid.com/collocations-examples/287393/401816/Examples-collocations-of-desert-and-through.aspx). We read through the list and discussed which ones we felt were most common and useful and added them to our structured word web. Key words were also added to our vocabulary journal and flashcards, when appropriate. Finally, I unpacked the word features, which were not extensive.

Repetition of Word Recall through Narrow Extensive Reading

In order to aid learners' retention, they need to encounter and recall words frequently in a short time span, roughly 12 times (Nation, 2014) in a two–three day window; therefore, I chose to conduct guided nonfiction readings with Dayax on topics of interest to him using a narrow, extensive reading approach. The approach is to do a lot of reading on a narrow topic in order to have *the frequency of repetition of key vocabulary words.* **Extensive reading**, on the other hand, is *engaging in a great deal of sustained reading, but not on a narrow topic.* It is vital to have the frequency of encounters with the same word/word family in a short time span (based on the work of Folse, 2006), so the narrowed topical focus for two–three days encounters provide enough repetition and recall of key vocabulary. When we read about deserts, we read a couple of short texts that discussed the topic from different angles and points of view during the short time frame.

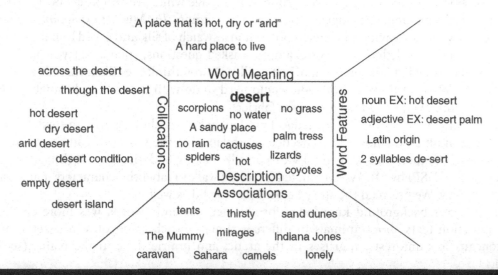

Figure 14.9 Structured Word Web (This Graphic Organizer Can Help Show How to Unpack, or Break Down Word Features.)

Thematic Lists	Structural Lists	Topical Lists	Notional Lists
—are linked to a common theme, but might not have similar word features	—words with similar prefixes, so leaners can retain the meaning of the prefix	—common in academic content, for example, for cell structures: membrane mitochondria organelles	—semantically related words that are linked conceptually, for example, lists of colors, numbers, or size

Figure 14.10 Types of Vocabulary Lists

With Dayax, I chose contextualized, thematic lists of vocabulary generated by the fiction and nonfiction readings. Textbooks present other types of lists, such as *structural, topical,* and *notional.* Thematic lists are linked by a common theme, but might not have similar word features, such as a structural list. A structural list would have words with similar prefixes, so learners can retain the meaning of the prefix. Topical lists are common in academic content, think of the vocabulary list for cell structures (i.e., membrane, mitochondria, organelles, etc.). Finally, notional lists, semantically related words that are linked conceptually, such as lists of colors, numbers, or size. Research supports the instruction of thematic, structural, topical, and semantically-related lists since they build learners' schema (Reynolds, 2017).

Instructional Strategies and Tools

Since Dayax had uneven learning in his past, there were gaps in his knowledge that I needed to fill in to build his background knowledge. I wanted him to keep a vocabulary journal and create flashcards to help in his recall. We started with a hand-written, physical copy, but it became unwieldy. So, we ended up using the online tool, Padlet, which I could organize into short, academic, and social vocabulary lists (see http://www.padlet.com). It served him better.

When necessary, I would build his background knowledge while pre-teaching vocabulary for him to better understand a reading. His language arts class was reading, *The Mysterious Spinners,* a fictionalized tale of the origins of silk weaving in China. I brought in a swatch of silk and asked him questions to probe his experience and knowledge of it. For example, I asked questions, such as: Have you felt this fabric before? Do you know what it is made out of? (It is silk). Do you think the silken threads were long? Were they thin or thick? What do you think you would need to do with them to make a fabric? How many threads do you think you would need to make fabric?

To further build his background knowledge, I pre-taught key vocabulary from the text, such as cocoon, unravel, strand, mulberry, silkworms. I needed to explain that the silken threads came from the silkworms' cocoons. We then watched a brief video on silk making and discussed it (https://www.youtube.com/watch?v=77ktNSPFbwQ). We conducted a picture walk to label the characters' names and link to the key vocabulary. We pre-read the story before his class did as well.

Building Dayax's background knowledge for abstract academic words was more challenging. We co-read nonfiction texts about animals in different climates, such as coyotes in deserts, manatees in oceans, toucans in rainforests, walruses in the arctic, and prairie dogs in the plains (see visuals in Figure 14.11).

These texts lent themselves to visualization and illustration activities to reinforce the academic vocabulary. I employed *instructional conversation* as a strategy to engage Dayax in the academic language of the texts. So, I would ask him questions about the texts and embed the definitions of the academic language,

© Martin Froyda/Shutterstock.com

Manatees in oceans

© Greg Amptman/Shutterstock.com

Toucan in rainforests

© Maciej Czekajewski/Shutterstock.com

Figure 14.11 Coyote in desert (*Continued*)

Walruses in the arctic

© vladsilver/Shutterstock.com

Prairie dogs in the plains

Prairie Dogs and Owls.

Figure 14.11 Coyote in desert (*Continued*)

for example I asked if he could "show me or point to something in the text, or evidence that tells us about" or "tell me what happened in the story, the events."

We would do jigsaw readings along with instructional conversation, for example, "Let's organize the events, or actions, into the order we read them." We would play games with words, such as matching and Total Physical Response (TPR), in which he and I would create actions to represent the words (Figure 14.12). TPR was helpful for words that could be represented visually, such as area, check, collect, deep, point out, reverse, review, and structure, but impossible for others.

For the academic vocabulary that did not lend themselves to TPR, I modeled with instructional conversation and developed visualizations, memory palaces, and mnemonic devices to aid in recall (Figure 14.13).

For example, I placed defend with a character and linked them to a lawyer defending a client. Likewise, I linked evidence with investigate, which mirrored a detective investigating a crime and finding evidence. A mnemonic device Dayax enjoyed was linking seven and several. We also had a missing Miss (Figure 14.14).

Vocabulary Word	Action
Area	We walked around the area of the room.
Check	With one finger, we formed a checkmark in the air.
Collect	With both hands, we "gathered" several invisible items in the air and pull them toward us.
Deep	Holding the left arm horizontally, which served as the surface (of the water or ground), we made diving motions downward with the right hand.
Point out	We pointed with one finger at items.
Reverse	We walked backward.
Review	We retraced our steps.
Structure	We "built" a house structure in the air with our hands.

Figure 14.12 TPR with Content Vocabulary

© Robert Crum/Shutterstock.com

Memory Palace Example

© Robert Crum/Shutterstock.com

Mnemonic Device Example

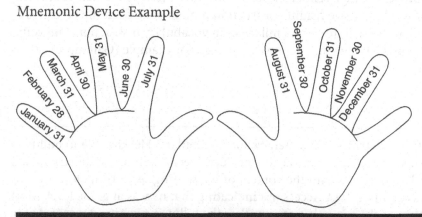

Figure 14.13 Visualization of the Desert Example

Missing Miss Example

© Pressmaster/Shutterstock.com

Figure 14.14 Seven and Several Example (http://www.publicdomainpictures.net/view-Figure.php?-Figure=46976&picture=several-spools-of-yarn)

To aid his recall, I did make some close-ended exercises (see the needs assessment matching, multiple choice, fill in the blank, and sentence completion exercises discussed earlier) on paper and using digital resources following the research of Folse (2006). Some of the digital resources Dayax used for vocabulary practice were Flashcard Stash (http://flashcardstash.com/), Vocabulary Spelling City (https://www.spellingcity.com/), and Quizlet (https://quizlet.com/). I created short academic or social vocabulary lists for him to practice, which he would intensively practice within a two–three day time frame when working on a topic. Whenever possible, I would model the use of the words while embedding the definition in instructional conversation and would link to words we studied in the past. For example, when we were studying walruses in the Antarctic, I mentioned the words subzero and submerge. "In Antarctica, it is very cold. The temperatures are below zero, so they say subzero. Sub means below." "The walruses go under the water, below the surface. They dive under. They are submerged."

While this was a crucial approach for Dayax, these strategies and tools are effective for learners at any age or proficiency level. The key is to make sure that the words are chosen well based on the grade level, needs, and academic word lists. Not all ages of English learners will need the type of literacy-based curriculum that served Dayax well. Middle and high school learners would need fewer fictional readers and more academic texts, but they may need intensive reading instruction nonetheless. Even the demands of a high school English literature class would require some similarities in vocabulary instruction, but would not lend themselves to picture walks and labeling instructional strategies, for example (Gallimore, 2012).

Conclusions

Dayax worked diligently and made great strides in his literacy and vocabulary. He was able to build his social language and fill in some gaps by the end of the academic year. His academic vocabulary took a great deal of attention, but he made progress within the context of his writing. According to his classroom teacher, Dayax made progress on his WIDA Access test indicating that he was at grade level. Most importantly, he was able to integrate into the general education class the following year and received only tier one Response To Intervention (RTI) interventions.

The key instructional strategies, such as instructional conversation, that helped Dayax were **contextualizing intensive vocabulary instruction within independent reading for social language** and **guided reading for academic language**. Dayax's literacy development was two-sided through fiction and non-fiction texts that allowed for narrow, extensive reading focusing on specific vocabulary sets.

FINAL POINTS

- Highlight key vocabulary
- Record vocabulary
- Practice the recordings through engaging and various repetitions using games, flashcards, and vocabulary journals
- Use close-ended exercises to encourage recall and retention
- Integrate vocabulary into instructional conversation

Discussion Questions and Activities

1. Why does narrow, extensive reading allow for adequate repetition of key vocabulary?
2. Why do learners need to know so much about words in order to understand the word's meaning? When do educators need to unpack a word fully versus when should educators give only a synonym?
3. What are the pros and cons of vocabulary journals? How can you organize a vocabulary journal so that it is practical and useful to learners?
4. How is instructional conversation used to help learners build academic vocabulary? How does it change the way educators interact with learners? Can you engage in instructional conversation with a whole class? If so, how? If not, why not?
5. Find a list of academic vocabulary for the grade level you teach or will be teaching. Cluster them into categories. Discuss the patterns that emerged.
6. Choose a reading passage. Identify a list of vocabulary words from the reading. Develop a series of games and exercises to reinforce the vocabulary set.
7. Identify a key academic vocabulary word to unpack using a structured word web such as the one below.

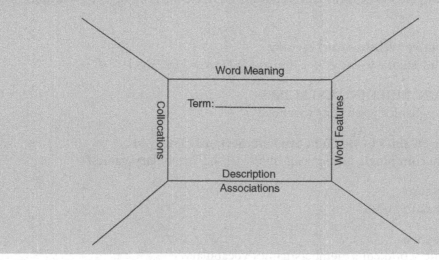

8. Choose one academic vocabulary word and describe its form, meaning, and use as you would to make it comprehensible to an English learner. What online tools can you find to help you with teaching this academic vocabulary word?

9. Choose one prefix (i.e., inter-, pre-, re-, pro-, anti-) to teach the meaning and use. What example words that use the prefix would you include in a short list? What online tools can you find to help you with teaching prefixes?

Resources

Vocabulary development with ELs.
http://www.readingrockets.org/article/vocabulary-development-ells

Keys to Adolescent Literacy
http://www.adlit.org/article/27879/

Early Literacy: Building Vocabulary to Build Literacy
https://www.scholastic.com/teachers/articles/teaching-content/early-literacy-building-vocabulary-build-literacy/

Fostering Literacy Development in ELs
http://www.colorincolorado.org/article/fostering-literacy-development-english-language-learners

Literacy Instruction for ELs
http://www.colorincolorado.org/literacy-instruction-ells

English Learners and the Five Essential Components of Reading Instruction
http://www.readingrockets.org/article/english-language-learners-and-five-essential-components-reading-instruction

Reader's Theater: Oral Language Enrichment and Literacy Development for ELs
http://www.readingrockets.org/article/readers-theater-oral-language-enrichment-and-literacy-development-ells

ELL/ESOL Interactive Websites for Learning
https://researchguides.library.wisc.edu/c.php?g=177873&p=1169756

ESL VOCABULARY BUILDING EXERCISES
http://www.learnenglishfeelgood.com/vocabulary/

10 ESL Vocabulary Games to Get Your Students Seriously Engaged
http://www.fluentu.com/blog/educator-english/esl-tefl-ell-vocabulary-games/

20 Minute ESL lessons
http://www.esl-lab.com/vocab/

ESL Vocabulary games
http://www.eslgamesworld.com/members/games/vocabulary/

References

Amer, A. (2017). Teaching/developing vocabulary using semantic feature analysis. In K.M. Reynolds (Ed.), *The TESOL encyclopedia of English language teaching, teaching vocabulary*. New York: Wiley. DOI: 10.1002/9781118784235.

Coxhead, A. (2000). A new academic word list. *TESOL Quarterly, 34*, 213–238.

Cummins, J. (1979). Cognitive/academic language proficiency, linguistic interdependence, the optimum age question and some other matters. *Working Papers on Bilingualism*, No. 19: 121–129.

Cummins, J. (2008). BICS and CALP: Empirical and theoretical status of the distinction. In B. Street, & N. H. Hornberger (Eds.), *Encyclopedia of Language and Education* (2nd ed., Vol. 2: Literacy, pp. 71–83). New York: Springer Science + Business Media LLC.

Erten, I. H., & Dikilitas, K. (2017). Teaching homographs, homonyms, homophones, synonyms and antonyms. In K.M. Reynolds (Ed.), *The TESOL encyclopedia of English language teaching, teaching vocabulary*. New York: Wiley. DOI: 10.1002/9781118784235.

Folse, K. S. (2006). The effect of type of written exercise on L2 vocabulary retention. *TESOL Quarterly, 40*(2), 273–293.

Gardner, D., & Davies, M. (2013). A new academic vocabulary list. *Applied Linguistics, 35*, 305–327.

Gallimore, J. (2012). *Innovative uses of ASL stories: Teaching literary elements through digital video*. University of California, San Diego.

Hellman, A. (2017). Teaching lexical chunks. In K.M. Reynolds (Ed.), *The TESOL encyclopedia of English language teaching, teaching vocabulary*. New York: Wiley. DOI: 10.1002/9781118784235.

Hirsh, D. (2017). Teaching/developing vocabulary through word origins, root words, prefixes and suffixes. In K. M. Reynolds (Ed.), *The TESOL encyclopedia of English language teaching, teaching vocabulary*. New York: Wiley. DOI: 10.1002/9781118784235.

Hulstijn, J. H. (2013). Incidental learning in second language acquisition. In C. A. Chapelle (Ed.), *The encyclopaedia of applied linguistics*. Malden, MA: Blackwell Publishing Ltd. DOI: 10.1002/9781405198431. wbeal0530

Krashen, S. (1989). We acquire vocabulary and spelling by reading: Additional evidence for the input hypothesis. *The Modern Language Journal, 73*, 440–463.

Nation, I. S. P. (2001). *Learning Vocabulary in Another Language*. Cambridge: Cambridge University Press.

Nation, I. S. P. (2006). How large a vocabulary is needed for reading and listening? *Canadian Modern Language Review, 63*, 59–82.

Nation, I. S. P. (2014). How much input do you need to learn the most frequent 9,000 words? *Reading in a Foreign Language, 26*(2), 1–16.

Reynolds, K.M. (2017). Teaching notional concepts: Time, numbers, distance, size, dimension, shapes, colors and patterns. In K. M. Reynolds (Ed.), *The TESOL encyclopedia of English language teaching, teaching vocabulary*. New York: Wiley. DOI: 10.1002/9781118784235.

Zahar, R., Cobb, T., & Spada, N. (2001). Acquiring Vocabulary through Reading: Effects of Frequency and Contextual Richness. The Canadian Modern Language Review, 57, 541–572. http://dx.doi.org/10.3138/cmlr.57.4.541.

PART 4

ASSESSMENT AND THE

ENGLISH LEARNER

CHAPTER 15

TRADITIONAL ASSESSMENT: WHY IT IS INAPPROPRIATE

Samantha Uribe and Eileen N. Whelan Ariza

KEY POINTS

- Teachers need to provide formative assessment to be sure their students are learning what is being taught.
- ELs might need differentiated instruction if they do not understand instruction.
- If formative assessment shows the students do not comprehend instruction, teachers must rework the lesson and reteach.
- Summative assessment will be the final assessment but it must assess what was actually taught.
- Assessment must measure what it is meant to assess.
- Be sure students are clear about what they are supposed to do.

When I taught fifth grade, I had a student named Alejandra who had moved to the United States from Colombia about halfway through fourth grade, in the previous school year. She had such a strong foundation in her native language and academics that she was one of my top math students, even though she was somewhat of a newcomer to learning English. Her calculations were always perfect, and she would come up to the board and walk everyone through how she got her answers. She was also helpful in supporting some of her less English-proficient Spanish-speaking classmates, as she could explain everything to them in Spanish.

Our math textbook's digital resources included a Spanish version of the textbook and supplementary materials, including all chapter tests. I taught lessons in English but made the Spanish resources available to all of my students to help bridge their language and content learning. I knew that it was also my job to teach English, so as the school year progressed, I switched from Spanish to English tests, and although Alejandra knew the content, she would always score significantly lower. When the school district administered benchmark assessments, this superstar student would always come up in the "red," which indicated that she was not likely to be proficient on the state assessment scheduled for spring.

Students like Alejandra are sitting in every classroom; bright and capable, yet evaluated based on assessments written in complex, academic language that they have not yet fully acquired. Assessments must clearly evaluate what is meant to be assessed. When students are being tested on a particular concept, we have to be sure that we are really measuring what we are trying to measure. For this assessment to be accurate there can be no doubt that the students understand the prompt, the vocabulary, and the problem that needs solving. For example, if a student is given a math word problem, and he or she gets it wrong, how do we know if he or she had problems with the math, or if the problem was with his or her reading?

One year, during the state testing period in South Florida, a question in the exam was challenged because it was culturally biased. The following assignment was presented to fourth-grade students on the writing portion of a standardized state exam:

> Write a three-paragraph essay responding to the following prompt: If you were going out west in a Conestoga wagon, what would your life be like?

While it was clear that the examiners were aiming for a higher order thinking skill, this question is obviously biased because it does not elicit what a true writing assignment is supposed to measure. Instead of evaluating students' ability in written expression, it relies on their knowledge of American history, specifically their familiarity with the pioneers' ways of life. Unless the students know that "out west" implies the unsettled American western terrain that pioneers explored, they will not be able to respond to the prompt with the expected level of detail. Clearly, this assignment gives an advantage to children who have had the exposure to the American perspective of exploration of the West, which is found in popular literature and movies. In other words, this standardized test assesses students' familiarity with the mainstream culture and American history more than it measures writing skills. Although this prompt seems like an isolated example of a culturally biased assessment, the problem is more prominent than one may think.

The purpose of this chapter is to demonstrate how some common tests create obstacles to revealing English learners' understandings and skills, and to offer suggestions on how to create meaningful authentic assessments that work in multilevel classrooms.

High-Stakes Testing and ELs

In an effort to reform the U.S. educational system and to increase the country's overall academic achievement, states administer standardized tests (*high-stakes testing*) to ensure accountability. This idea is congruent with the ubiquitous benchmarks and standards developed to make educators and administrators accountable for the achievement of all learners. According to Herrera, Murry, and Cabral (2007), one of the most significant changes in today's assessment practices is that they have become "increasingly standardized, norm-referenced, and institutionalized" (p. 13). Amid this standardization, English learners (ELs) have been placed at a distinct disadvantage because their achievement is measured against the test scores of native language speakers. The evidence is overwhelming that English learners need more than two years to gain skills in academic language (Cummins, 1982; Snow & Uccelli, 2009) yet in many states, such as Florida, the test results of most ELs are factored in the schools' achievement data and counted toward the overall school grade. In turn, teachers, who are pressured to make linguistically diverse students produce a certain score, spend much of their classroom time on preparing for high-stakes standardized tests in place of teaching more profound content matter. Unfortunately, these test prep activities also take away time from more meaningful performance assessments in which students are evaluated on the knowledge they demonstrate in the process of creating their product.

Standardized Tests Versus Authentic Assessment

When used properly, assessments can guide instruction, evaluate the effectiveness of teaching strategies, place students appropriately, determine whether students should enter or exit programs, and diagnose and monitor student progress. Herrera et al. (2007) define assessment in educational settings as "a range of procedures used to gather information about what students or other individuals know and are able to demonstrate" (p. 3). Assessments can be informal or formal, and they may be used to measure content knowledge or language skills. But they must be *valid* (i.e., measure what they purport to measure) and *reliable* (i.e., consistent among different raters as well as over time). Assessment can be *formative* or *summative*. *Formative assessments* are ongoing, and they are designed to guide the teacher in collecting and analyzing student's work to determine if instruction is on the right track. They are a barometer of how students are doing so far and include and practice tests, unscored reviews of students' knowledge, etc., to see if reteaching needs to be done. A *summative evaluation* is an assessment of the end result of teaching, as in an end-of-the chapter test. No teacher wants to test a student on unlearned material; the idea is to see how much the student knows, not how much the student does not know.

For language minority students, usually a placement test is given to determine what level of English proficiency the student possesses. This is always a rough estimate because it is very difficult to pinpoint exactly what a student knows. Usually, the levels of reading, writing, listening, speaking, pronunciation, and receptive knowledge are unbalanced. Students who have been exposed to English over a long period of time or who may have been born in the United States might have an excellent command or pronunciation and sound native-like but have limited knowledge of reading and writing. I also have had ELs who have excellent knowledge of reading, writing, and grammar, yet have difficulties in communicating orally and understanding American speech. In my opinion, the easier type of students to teach is the latter because they have studied the structure of English and soon will pick up oral skills. Students with English fluency and superb understanding may have ingrained or *fossilized errors* that are almost impossible to correct.

Evaluation Considerations for Testing ELs

In all fairness, to level the playing field, students new to the U.S. school system must be overtly taught about the school's expectations. In addition to learning the culture of the society, a student who is new to the United States will have to become familiar with the culture of the school system as well. This culture will vary from school to school, as private schools differ from public schools, elementary grades differ from secondary, and the postsecondary institutions are different altogether. Students who enter the school system with the same academic behaviors as in their home country schools will be surprised and confused. Students from other countries often tell me that they find U.S. schools to be "easier" than the educational systems in their home countries. Great differences will be apparent in study skills, mechanics of testing, the definition of plagiarism, the morality of doing group work when individual work is expected, and what to expect in order to compete and succeed.

Testing styles will be different in other countries, just as the styles of teaching and learning are different. Often the curriculum in other countries will focus on learning many subjects, and great quantities of detailed information must be learned by rote memorization. U.S. schools have often been blamed for relying on multiple-choice tests instead of more critical-thinking tests. Therefore, schools now try to have students aim toward learning the higher levels of Bloom's taxonomy or Webb's Depth of Knowledge (Webb, 1997); tests may include analysis and synthesis, and students will often be perplexed by the possibility of having more than one answer. Students must be oriented and explicitly taught that thinking for the sake of thinking is an educational value. However, if a student is accustomed to essay tests, the idea of taking a test that has an answer sheet with little bubbles that need to be colored in with a pencil will be foreign, and students must be explicitly taught how to proceed. In China, lately, the multiple-choice test format is favored. However, in many countries, the high stakes tests they give are primarily essay tests. With a variety of testing procedures pertinent to each individual's country, we will see more academic success if we are sure that all of our students know what they are expected to complete at testing time and why.

When students new to the U.S. schools learn that individual work is anticipated and they come from a country where group work is the norm, they might not grasp the idea that "sharing" someone's work is "immoral" and illegal in the United States. In countless countries (Saudi Arabia, Egypt, Poland, Haiti, Japan) being at the top of the class is a survival tactic. Cheating is not just to get a good grade; someone's future position or career might depend on it. The prevailing norms must be explained so that students are fairly evaluated.

> I will never forget the day that I met Arda, a student who had just moved from Turkey to the United States. Though he did not understand or speak English, he was smiling and excited to meet his new third-grade teacher and classmates. That October morning, our desks, which were typically arranged in small groups of four or five desks, were arranged in rows. Students were sitting quietly at their desks, which were cleared except for a No. 2 pencil. Arda had arrived on the first day of our school district's benchmark assessment, which would provide baseline data to help teachers prepare for the annual standardized assessment in the spring. Like all students in our district, Arda was required to complete the test. I did not speak Turkish, so through gestures and modeling, I was able to show Arda how to fill in the bubbles on the test. While students were working silently, I remember looking at Arda and seeing him shrug his shoulders and laugh nervously as he pointed to the test. My heart sank as I saw his smile fade while he spent his first day attempting a test in a language that was completely foreign to him.

When talking about assessment considerations for ELs, it is impossible to ignore standardized testing, which is a reality in today's schools. Standardized tests measure discrete items and the fragmented components of language; questions asked on objective tests neglect the complexities of overall learning and cannot accurately measure the ability of English learners. As succinctly put by Crawford and Krashen (2007), "When tested in a language they don't fully understand, students may do poorly because of their limited English or because they haven't learned the academic material. There is simply no way to tell" (p. 57). In 2002, the No Child Left Behind (NCLB) Act was enacted, and each state became frenzied in an effort to use standardized tests to measure academic gains. We have learned that it takes several years for English learners to make academic gains equal to those of native English speakers (Cummins, 1982; Callahan, 2005), yet we test students who are new English learners. Ironically, teachers are forced to spend more time on teaching to the test instead of offering meaningful opportunities for students to use academic language. With such pressure and economic ramifications placed upon educators all over the country, the demand for elevated test scores must be met to maintain fiscal balance. Although authentic assessment is far more significant as an evaluation tool, schools that have high numbers of language minority students continue to be challenged, just as English-dominant schools are, to demonstrate that they are continuously improving academic achievement of all learners.

In 2015, a revision to NCLB, known as the Every Student Succeeds Act (ESSA), was passed. The legislation offers hope for ELs with regard to assessment practices by using multiple measures to track academic achievement and improvement. States will also have the option to exclude newcomers from testing for a short period of time and continue to report students' achievement for up to four years after they have met criteria and exited from ESOL programs. This will enable school districts to track ELs' progress more accurately.

Using Authentic Assessments

Whenever possible, a range of authentic assessments should be implemented on an ongoing basis as the preferred method of measuring achievement of ELs. According to Herrera et al. (2007), what makes assessments authentic is their ability to directly assess what was learned from classroom instruction, group work, and activities. In other words, alternative assessments measure a student's genuine performance in class. In addition, authentic assessments involve students in the evaluation process, making them more reflective of their own learning. Additionally, authentic assessments are more aligned with real-life situations, emphasizing to students the connection of school activities to the wider world. Types of authentic assessment are many and varied and can include the following:

- Drawings
- Audio or video recordings
- Checklists
- Timelines
- Learning logs
- Reflection journals
- Anecdotal records
- Observation records
- Venn diagrams
- Projects
- Charts
- Informal assessments
- Self-evaluation
- Peer evaluation
- Teacher/student notes on progress
- Portfolios

- Holistic writing rubrics (a rubric that looks at the entire piece of writing as opposed to grading on individual parts of the assessment)
- KWL charts (what you know, what you want to know, and what you have learned, with the emphasis on what has been learned)
- Concept maps depicting what was learned, or any type of performance indicator that demonstrates the level of academic performance the student is doing

Students and teachers can choose artifacts collaboratively, and students can display their work in portfolios to reflect progress. Keep in mind that alternative assessments may show language and content mastery, and that must be accounted for. For example, when grading a writing piece, give two grades—one for the content and one for the mechanical mistakes. The student can be an excellent writer without being perfect and should still be able to get a good grade regardless of mechanical mistakes. You must be sensitive to language acquisition processes and expect mistakes in the language. If students feel comfortable affectively, they will be more inclined to take changes and risk making mistakes.

Considering Students' Language Proficiency

Krashen and Terrell (1983) differentiated first- and second-language acquisition processes by proposing five predictable stages that students experience and advanced through while acquiring a second language:

- ❏ Preproduction
- ❏ Early production
- ❏ Speech emergence
- ❏ Intermediate fluency
- ❏ Advanced fluency.

TABLE 15.1					
	Level 1	**Level 2**	**Level 3**	**Level 4**	**Level 5**
Krashen and Terrell	Preproduction	Early Production	Speech Emergence	Intermediate Fluency	Advanced Fluency
WIDA	Entering	Emerging	Developing	Expanding	Bridging

They suggested that language production evolves from simple to complex in terms of grammatical tense, sentence structure, and word choice and categorized language learners according to stages along this continuum. Krashen and Terrell also "comprehension precedes production" (p. 58), which is an important consideration when planning instruction and assessment for ELs.

The WIDA Consortium (https://www.wida.us) originated in 2003 as a collaboration among Wisconsin, Delaware, and Arkansas and currently includes 39 U.S. states. The goal of WIDA is to promote academic language development and achievement for culturally and linguistically diverse students. WIDA presents an asset-based perspective, which focuses on the benefits of prior knowledge and experience and the potential contributions of second-language learners (WIDA, 2014). The WIDA English language development (ELD) standards expand upon the language proficiency levels proposed by Krashen and Terrell and offer educators a variety of resources to help support ELs as they progress through the stages of language acquisition. Table 15.1 demonstrates how Krashen and Terrell's stages align to WIDA's levels of language proficiency.

Based on these levels of language proficiency, WIDA offers CAN DO Descriptors (https://www.wida.us/standards/CAN_DOs/), which support teachers in differentiating instruction according to what ELs at different proficiency levels can do within each of the language domains (listening, speaking, reading, and writing). You can access the CAN DO Descriptors for your grade level and use them as a guide as you plan lessons that are inclusive of ELs with diverse background knowledge and language proficiency.

The Importance of Questioning

Using comprehension questions during instruction is one way informal assessments manifest themselves in the classrooms. It is important that teachers must leave room for comprehension checks *as* they teach, not *after* they teach. (Armbruster, Lehr, & Osborn, 2017; Wiggins &McTighe, 2005). In a rushed effort to cover material, some teachers may feel tempted to leave off this informal assessment until they have extra time. However, by putting comprehension checks at the very end of the lesson, teachers lose an opportunity to get insights about students' learning of the material. A mastery of questioning techniques will provide teachers with important feedback on what students have or have not grasped. It is important to prepare questions that filter out nonessential matter and bring relevant understandings to the surface. Some basic guidelines for asking questions are summarized below:

- ❏ Ask one question at a time: If multiple questions are asked one after another, the student will not know which one to answer first.
- ❏ Try to keep the wording of the question aligned with the vocabulary of the lesson: Inadvertently substituting vocabulary with synonyms may confuse English learners.
- ❏ Give ample time for response: Second-language learners may require extra time to process the question and formulate the response.
- ❏ If there is no response after ample wait time was provided, rephrase the question: Students may understand you better if you put the question in different terms.

TABLE 15.2 Tiered Questions for ELs					
WIDA Proficiency Levels	**Level 1 Entering**	**Level 2 Beginning**	**Level 3 Developing**	**Level 4 Expanding**	**Level 5 Bridging**
Question #1 (Science)	Provide photos of eggs, hair, scales, newborn baby, etc.; Show me the things that only mammals have/do.	List some things that only mammals have/do.	What makes mammals special?	Which characteristics make mammals special?	Which characteristics are unique to mammals?
Question #2 (Reading)	Point to the most important person in the story.	Tell me the name of the most important person in the story.	Tell me the name of the main character in the story.	Who is the main character in the story?	Who is the main character in the story? How do you know?

Source: Adapted from WIDA Levels of Language Proficiency and Hill and Flynn (2008).

- ❏ When you tell the student to take some time to think about it, be sure to come back to the student and listen to his or her response, recognizing the effort.
- ❏ Be tolerant of mistakes. I always tell language students that they will mangle the language before they dominate it, and as long as they make themselves understood, it is something to celebrate. Instead of publicly "punishing" a student with explicit corrections, model structures and encourage students to repeat when appropriate.

When questioning ELs, it also important to consider their current stage of language acquisition. Although students may be limited in terms of their language production, we cannot assume that they are unable to participate in mainstream instruction or engage in higher order thinking. Based on the learner characteristics outlined by Krashen and Terrell (1983), Hill and Flynn (2008) and Hill and Miller (2013) suggest using tiered questions to engage all ELs, regardless of language proficiency. According to the WIDA Performance Definitions and CAN DO Descriptors, we have a general idea of what to expect from ELs at different levels of language proficiency. Based on these guidelines, we can vary our questions stems to scaffold learning and engage students at the appropriate level of discourse.

Table 15.2 demonstrates how we can modify our questions stems according to students' level of language proficiency. The purpose of the question remains the same; however, the academic language used as well as the desired student's output progresses in linguistic complexity based on how the question is phrased. Level 1 students can respond nonverbally, and with each level, additional language production is expected. The Level 1 and Level 2 questions also include more general terms, whereas more proficient students are expected to know and use key academic terms.

Assessment Accommodations for ELs

Being aware that involving ELs in standardized testing places these students at an unfair disadvantage, NCLB mandated that school personnel provide "reasonable accommodations" to ensure valid and reliable results.

Standardized testing accommodations for ELs may include the following:

❏ Extended wait time for processing questions, or flexible scheduling
❏ Allowance for home-language-to-English dictionaries
❏ The option of taking the test in a quiet environment with a bilingual or ESOL teacher present, or flexible setting
❏ The choice to have the test directions translated into the native language.

Whether or not these accommodations are helpful to ELs in general is debatable. Offering extra time or a separate testing space is not likely to compensate for the fact that academic language acquisition is a complex process that occurs over a long period of time. However, as a guide, these testing accommodations should be used consistently for all classroom assessments, in addition to standardized assessments, to ensure that students can make the most of them. For example, in order for a home-language-to-English dictionary to be helpful, students must be literate in their first language and be accustomed to using the dictionary on a regular basis. In the next section, I will talk more about how you can modify assessments and support your students based on their language proficiency.

Assessment Modifications and Scaffolding for ELs

Although creating assessments that are appropriate is a complex field in its own right, all teachers of linguistically diverse learners should remember this rule: If you adapted the content from the textbook, then you need to adapt available tests. If this rule is not followed, English learners will be at a disadvantage because they will be tested through wording to which they were not exposed. In other words, it is imperative that the language of the academic content and the language of tests remain consistent. Creating assessments that align with the adapted materials may take time, but teachers on the same grade level can collaborate in the process by spreading the objectives among each other and developing modified lessons and assessments that go together. In fact, the proponents of "design backwards" Wiggins and McTighe (2005) explain that teachers can guide students' learning better if they begin to design their curriculum with objectives and essential learning goals, followed by assessments. The actual planning of activities should be the final stage.

One of WIDA's guiding principles promotes the idea that teachers can best support ELs by ensuring that the linguistic complexity and instructional supports match their levels of language proficiency (WIDA, 2010). It is important for teachers to know each student's level of language proficiency to ensure that lesson delivery and assessment are comprehensible. Assessments should be culturally responsive yet match the curricular goals of the classroom or school. For classroom assessments, teachers may also choose to simplify assessment language or incorporate home language use when feasible. Extended wait-time for language processing and opportunities to collaborate with peers are also essential. Table 15.3 provides ideas for how teachers can support ELs according to their current level of language proficiency.

When assessing ELs, regardless of language proficiency, try to ensure that you are focusing on content matter, not necessarily how students can express themselves in English. Always consider Krashen and Terrell's idea that comprehension precedes production; students are often able to understand and make sense of new concepts before they are able to impart that information orally or in writing. Another excellent scaffolding technique promoted by WIDA is use of the native language. This is an effective technique for engaging Level 1 ELs who are still developing even the most basic English language skills but can also support more proficient ELs to produce complex responses or elaborate on what they have provided in English.

TABLE 15.3 Scaffolding Techniques by Proficiency Level (Gottlieb, Cranley, & Cammilleri, 2007)	
WIDA Proficiency Level	**Suggested Scaffolding Techniques**
Level 1 Entering	• Ask questions that require nonverbal responses (point, match, nod, thumbs-up/down) • Provide word and picture banks (English and/or native language) • Encourage native language use • Provide opportunities to draw, label, or manipulate objects
Level 2 Emerging	• Ask WH-questions that require short phrase responses • Provide word banks (English and/or native language • Provide Cloze sentences/frames • Allow students to respond or elaborate orally
Level 3 Developing	• Ask probing questions for students to elaborate • Provide phrase banks • Provide sentence starters/cloze paragraphs • Utilize graphic organizers as alternative products
Level 4 Expanding	• Ask open-ended questions to prompt additional language production • Provide models and exemplars • Offer various assessment formats
Level 5 Bridging	• Ask questions that incorporate key academic terms and concepts

For example, after teaching the scientific method, I showed my students a video clip of a simple experiment being performed and asked them to identify each step of the scientific method within the example presented on the video. One of my fifth-grade ELs, a Level 3 student from Brazil, seemed to understand the concepts while I was teaching but struggled to apply them to what he had seen on the video. When I asked him if he wanted to write the answers in Portuguese, he nodded excitedly and got right to work. I was able to review his work, and using my knowledge of Portuguese, Spanish, and English cognates, it was evident that the student recognized the steps of the scientific method. Because this quick formative assessment focused on his comprehension of science content, and not his English proficiency, allowing him to respond in his native language gave me all the information that I needed.

Assessing ELs' Writing

When English learners' writing skills are being assessed, it is not fair to compare them to native English speakers. One helpful fact to acknowledge is that their cultural background and native language patterns will be reflected in their writing. After correcting thousands of papers throughout the years, it is easy for me to discern what native language a student speaks because I can see it in his or her writing. For example, a Spanish speaker will write run-on sentences and place commas where native English speakers will place periods. A Japanese or Polish writer will omit articles (*a*, *an*, and *the*) because articles do not exist in their languages. An overuse of commas is typical for Russian writers because punctuation rules are more abundant in their language. As for the format and style, it is equally easy to distinguish a paper by students with literacy in another language because the writing may not follow a predictable pattern.

American students are trained to write according to a formula for paragraphs that includes a thesis statement and supporting details. Students are taught that every opinion should have support and that each reference to another author should be properly cited. Even an opinion piece is expected to have a certain structure, which must conclude in a summation of main points. American students are taught to "get to the point," not meander, and create writing that is linear. In other words, directness and clarity are valued both in essays and in writing for academic purposes.

To clarify expectations of students' writing, teachers can develop writing rubrics as a part of their assessment toolbox. A rubric that is truly authentic spells out the outcome(s) that both a teacher and student should be able to see in the end product. In other words, a rubric should reflect the skills that are of particular importance at a given stage of learning. Each requirement in the rubric should correspond to some aspect of students' learning while being quantifiable in case it is necessary to convert it to a percentage or a letter grade. Even though such complex activity as writing will involve skills that may not be mentioned in a given rubric (e.g., using quotes to allow characters to speak for themselves or using compound sentences), this is acceptable because these skills may be targeted in a future rubric. Teachers can seek students' input on creating elements of the rubric based on their self-evaluation of writing strengths and weaknesses. Another important step of using a rubric is demonstrating how a particular product meets or does not meet expectations for each criterion. A model, or high-quality product, should also be provided to set a certain standard for ELs.

Table 15.4 is an example of a rubric that fifth-grade students may use for self-assessment of a persuasive writing prompt based on two passages that present opposing viewpoints on one topic. In the writing sample, they were required to take a side and present an argument by citing text evidence from the readings.

To introduce the rubric, the teacher clarifies the meaning of *very good*, *good*, and *needs improvement*, giving ample examples of each level of quality for the specified criteria. Depending on the objectives of the lesson, this rubric may change its focus, in which case the teacher will rearrange and rename the columns according to the expectations. The teacher might also provide additional support for ELs at varying levels of language proficiency to complete this task. Scaffolding techniques may include a cloze paragraph, bank of text evidence phrases, or simplified texts on the topic.

TABLE 15.4 Rubric for Self-Assessment

	Very Good	Good	Needs Improvement
Conventions	I used capital letters and proper punctuation most of the time.	I used capital letters and proper punctuation some of the time.	I did not use capital letters and proper punctuation.
Focus	I stayed on topic and supported my opinion most of the time.	I stayed on topic and supported my opinion some of the time.	I did not stay on topic or support my opinion.
Content	I wrote three or more paragraphs with many different reasons to support my opinion.	I wrote one to two paragraphs with some different reasons to support my opinion.	I did not give different reasons to support my opinion.
Text Evidence	I used sentence starters to cite text evidence most of the time.	I used sentence starters to cite text evidence some of the time.	I did not use sentence starters or cite text evidence.

As a conclusion, I encourage readers to remember that a lack of English fluency does not indicate a lack of knowledge or intelligence. Assessment should be interdependent, authentic, and designed to be done in conjunction with developmentally appropriate activities that reflect the English learner's true environment (Borsato & Padilla, 2008; Cummins, 1982; DeGeorge, 1988).

FINAL POINTS

- Assessments must measure what they are intended to measure.

- Formative assessments are critical so the teacher will know if students understand instruction or whether the teacher needs to revise and reteach.

- ELs can be helped by appropriate accommodations.

- Standardized tests may not truly assess what the EL knows.

- Nontraditional assessment will probably be the most accurate assessment that the teacher can give to get true determination about the EL's grade level and knowledge.

Discussion Questions and Activities

1. Describe the differences between formative and summative evaluation processes. Think of a learning objective, an activity, and an assessment instrument you can use for the formative evaluation of learning gains. How will you use this instrument to guide your teaching?
2. Design a summative assessment instrument for the learning objective and activities. What determination could you make after giving students your summative evaluation? Discuss whether your summative instrument would be a true assessment of students' learning gains.
3. Considering the assessment you designed in the question above, discuss how you could make it more accessible for ELs at varying levels of language proficiency. How might you modify the product or what type of scaffolding might you, the teacher, provide? Review Table 15.3 or the WIDA CAN DO Descriptors (https://www.wida.us/standards/CAN_DOs/) for ideas.
4. Imagine that you are reading aloud your favorite childhood book to your class and think of an important reading comprehension question that you might ask your students. Considering the tiered questions strategy (Table 15.2), discuss how you could rephrase the question to make it more appropriate for your Levels 1–3 ELs.

Resources

Informal Assessments
http://www.colorincolorado.org/article/using-informal-assessments-english-language-learners

Performance Assessment for ELs
https://scale.stanford.edu/system/files/performance-assessments-english-language-learners.pdf

Time to Reassess Testing for ELs
http://www.hotchalkeducationnetwork.com/assessment-for-ells/

Authentic Assessment
http://www.msdwt.k12.in.us/msd/wp-content/uploads/2011/10/authentic_assessment.pdf

Guidelines for Assessment of ELs
https://www.ets.org/s/about/pdf/ell_guidelines.pdf

Early Learners
https://www.engageny.org/sites/default/files/resource/attachments/nti-july-2012-ells-and-common-core-presentation.pdf

Edutopia
https://www.edutopia.org/resource/checking-understanding-download?gclid=Cj0KEQjwofHHBRD-S0Pnhpef89ucBEiQASEp6LDUJV8Bh99OHOfz-M2vkMxwmQO6q9q0_KxdBFbq4OmUaAtTC8P8HAQ

Reading Rockets
http://www.readingrockets.org/webcasts/1003

West Ed
https://www.wested.org/wp-content/files_mf/1391626953FormativeAssessment_report5.pdf

Assessment for ELs
http://www.colorincolorado.org/school-support/assessment-english-language-learners

Informal Assessments
http://www.colorincolorado.org/article/using-informal-assessments-english-language-learners

References

Armbruster, B. B., Lehr, F., & Osborn, J. (2017). *Put Reading First—K-3*. (2017). *Lincs.ed.gov*. Retrieved 23 April 2017, from https://lincs.ed.gov/publications/html/prfteachers/reading_first1.html

Board of Regents of the University of Wisconsin System (2010).*The cornerstone of the WIDA Standards: Guiding principles of language development*. Retrieved from https://www.wida.us/aboutUs/AcademicLanguage/.

Board of Regents of the University of Wisconsin System (2014). *The WIDA standards framework and its theoretical foundations*. Retrieved from https://www.wida.us/aboutUs/AcademicLanguage/.

Board of Regents of the University of Wisconsin System (n.d.). *Understanding the WIDA English language proficiency standards: A resource guide*. Retrieved from file:///C:/Users/eariza/Downloads/Resource_Guide_web.pdf

Borsato, G. N.,& Padilla, A. M. (2008).Educational assessment of English-language learners. In *Handbook of multicultural assessment* (pp. 471–489). Hoboken, NJ: Wiley.

Callahan, R. M. (2005). Tracking and high school English learners: Limiting opportunity to learn. *American Educational Research Journal, 42*(2), 305–328.

Gottlieb, M., Cranley, M. E., & Cammilleri, A. (2007). Understanding the WIDA English language proficiency standards: A resource guide. *Board of Regents of the University of Wisconsin System.*

Hill, J. D., & Flynn, K. (2008). Asking the right questions. *Journal of Staff Development, 29*(1), 46–52.

Hill, J. D., & Miller, K.B. (2013). Classroom instruction that works with English language learners (2nd ed.). Alexandria, VA: Association for Supervision and Curriculum Development.

Krashen, S. D., & Terrell, T. D. (1983). *The natural approach: Language acquisition in the classroom.* Hayward, CA: Alemany Press

Snow, C. E., & Uccelli, P. (2009). The challenge of academic language. *The Cambridge handbook of literacy,* 112–133. Cambridge: Cambridge University Press

Webb, N. (1997). Research monograph number 8: "Criteria for alignment of expectations and assessments on mathematics and science education. Washington, D. C.: CCSSO.

PART 5
ENGLISH LEARNERS AND THE WIDER COMMUNITY

CHAPTER 16

WORKING WITH PARENTS OF ESOL STUDENTS

Naomi Hagen, Teacher on Special Assignment,

Spokane Public Schools

Erin Meuer, Educator, Spokane Community College

Immigrant and Refugee ESL Program

KEY POINTS

- Teacher–parent relations are different from country to country.
- Parents new to the United States may not realize they are expected to show a presence in the American school setting.
- Parents of ELs are deeply concerned about the education of their children, even though it might not appear that way.
- There are positive steps you can take to teach and encourage parents how to help advocate for their children.

Teacher–parent relations vary widely around the world. Abroad, educators can be seen as deeply respected and venerated members of society whom families invite to homes, meet privately for council, and shower with gifts of food or material worth. In contrast, parent–teacher relationships in the United States are highly functional, with more equality between parent and teacher, with parents sometimes even being higher in the power hierarchy (Hall, 1976; Triandis & Bhawuk, 1997; Hofstede, 2001; Hofstede, Hofstede, & Minkov, 2010). Educators who are not aware of the educational experiences and expectations of a parent can unwittingly disrespect a family and become increasingly distrusted, which will be a hindrance to communication on a day-to-day level and diminish the student's chance for academic and social success over time (Kugler & Price, 2009).

Due to the tremendously competitive nature of the immigration and refugee resettlement processes, families who come to America are often some of the more capable, resilient, and persistent members of their respective societies. We have seen parents who were professors, engineers, medical professionals, or higher-ranking government officials suddenly faced with limited employment options upon arrival in the United States, which are often unskilled positions in food service, hospitality, or general labor. Consider your own source of identity, and how much your sense of self is enveloped in your career or studies, and you can imagine how deeply a loss of career, coupled with a loss of language, culture, and extended family can have a negative impact on a parent's identity. Educators have the unique opportunity to impact a family's health and wellbeing by focusing on the strengths and resiliency of the student, parents, and family. To do this, educators must look past their limited framework of teacher–parent relationships and expectations, and be willing to learn, grow, adapt, and advocate with the families and their cultural communities in the following ways:

1. Recognize the strength of your EL students' parents.
2. Build relationships with the parents and within the communities of your EL students.
3. Empower parents by educating them about how to be active participants in their child's education in the United States academic environment.
4. Advocate for families through collaboration with local agencies and cultural experts.

Recognizing Parent's Strengths

The following transcript is from an interview with a Brazilian-born parent, elementary school educator, and immigrant advocate. Consider her answer to the question, "What do teachers need to know about immigrant and refugee parents?"

"Teachers need to know first that parents care for their kids. Sometimes they are seen as lazy, or that they don't care. That is not the case most of the time. It's that parents have their struggles themselves. They feel afraid to come to school because they don't speak the language, they are trying to find employment, housing, and navigate a new culture. There is a lot going on, and it really takes time for someone to adapt to these new ways of life. And information is not easy to find. That was my struggle as a parent. I didn't know a lot of what was available through the schools. Telling a parent where they can access something is not simply enough. Parents want the best for their children and they want them to succeed. They want handholding to know how to help their children achieve their academic goals, but they don't know who to ask or where to go, or even how to start figuring out where to find the information. Nonetheless, they have made sacrifices for their children to be able to have access to education, have high standards, and goals for their children. They need someone to acknowledge that and help them navigate the complicated process."

Thereza, EL Parent, Teacher, and Advocate (interview transcripts, 2017)

In her analysis, Thereza touches on several key challenges facing immigrant and refugee parents today. The first is their portrayal in local and global media. From the traditional and stereotypical depictions of the confused immigrant with a long unpronounceable name and heavy accent, to more modern images of the lazy yet desperate migrant, or the helpless, victimized refugee, parents of ELs are rarely recognized for the strengths and skills they bring to the host country and the educational environment. In fact, several researchers blame these perceptions for some of the greatest socio-economic and educational barriers facing immigrant and refugee populations during resettlement. In her article *In Pursuit of a new Perspective in the Education of Children of the Refugees: Advocacy for the "Family,"* Dr. Zeynep Isik-Ercan (2012) synthesizes this research in the following statement, ". . . the stereotypical representation of refugees in visual and written media as people who are either helpless, or trying hard to achieve the American dream is intended to produce an emotional effect on the reader," (p. 3029) and goes on to reprimand communities and schools for using "savior rhetoric" in discussing their work with refugee students and families. Likewise, in a recent article following a group of Somali mothers in Canada, Fellin (2015) insists, "These representations not only victimized [the Somali] women, but also essentialized them, replacing their context with the stereotyped identity that sees them as passive victims who need to be helped" (p. 33). Fellin goes on to describe how this kind of victimization illusion creates targets of the refugee mothers by institutions that wish to conform them to the local culture, assuming that they are incapable of raising their own children, and ignoring the fact that these same mothers supply incredible resources for their own children, within the same community, and provide after-school tutoring services, primary language and religion classes, food, lodging, and clothing. She then explains her perspective in the following way, ". . . I am not negating their experiences of adversity. Rather, I seek to consider whether a focus on Somali women's agency may be more effective . . ." (p. 39). Instead of viewing the EL parent as a victim, society in general and educators in particular need to recognize the strengths, experience, resilience, and agency that an EL parent can bring to the community.

Thereza also touches on the topic of EL parent's support of their child's education. While schools often see the parents as uncooperative and unsupportive, this is rarely, if ever the case (Ariza, 2000). For many immigrant and refugee parents, an opportunity for education and a brighter future for their children was a motivating factor behind their resettlement. As Bankston and Zhou state in their 2002 article in the *International Migration Review*, "parents seek to establish themselves in the new land by having their children achieve positions of prestige and respectability through schooling" (p. 395). Parents of ELs are some of the most supportive in American schools; however, they are faced with the challenge of not knowing what is expected of them within the new system. In addition, their traditional cultural perceptions of the roles of teachers and parents may be very different from the same roles in the new host country. In an article on Burmese refugee families in American schools, parent interviews indicated a strong desire both to see their children succeed academically and a desire to support their educational process. On the other hand, they didn't know how to accomplish this. "The parents felt that a barrier between themselves and being actively involved in their children's academic work is their lack of knowledge and experience with curriculum, instructional methods, and the materials. They wished the curriculum and instructional system would be explained to them in the earlier weeks of the school" (Isik-Ercan, 2012, p. 3032). This matter could easily be addressed at the district, school, or even classroom level, if educators are willing to address it.

Not only do these parents support their child's education, many have made unimaginable sacrifices for their children, and education is a top priority. A Syrian mother recently shared the efforts she had to make to ensure her children had access to education during the war, including meeting in secret locations, at unusual times, and taking treacherous and distant routes to get to classes. When her son was awarded a bi-literacy seal validating his fluency in both Arabic and English, she broke down in tears, relieved that someone had acknowledged the seriousness of her efforts to educate her children.

Regardless of where the parents are from: Brazil, Somalia, Burma (Myanmar), Syria, or elsewhere, immigrant and refugee parents are eager to support the education of their children and may be an untapped resource for schools. They are resilient and resourceful, and eager to support the education of their children. For this reason, it is important for schools to consider the following strengths that parents of ELs may bring to the learning environment.

EL Parent's Strengths

- Immigrant and refugee families are strong supporters of education, and many have made sacrifices to ensure their students were educated in the home country and continue to make sacrifices to ensure they are educated in the United States. This support may not look the same as the support that American-born parents exhibit, but is of equal importance and value (Fellin, 2015).
- Immigrant families tend to have a strong sense of family, and the children have a deep sense of respect and responsibility for their families and communities. In this sense, students feel a duty to perform well in school and move toward the academic goals they have set with their families. However, EL parents are not always sure how to get support in the new system, or they may be missing key information that is obvious to American-born parents, educators, and counselors, and therefore not always shared until too late (Isik-Ercan, 2012).
- They love and care deeply for their children. They want the best for them and would do anything for their children. They long for deeper connections with schools and teachers, but are often intimidated or lack the cultural capital to navigate the relationships (Isik-Ercan, 2012).
- Immigrant parents are looking for allies, and are ready to work with those who have shown kindness, empathy, and interest in their families. Taking the time to build a trusting relationship with students' families before getting down to business, making home visits, and ensuring a guided follow through of objectives can have a lasting impact on a child's chance of success (Kugler & Price, 2009).
- Parents of immigrants often push their children academically. They are eager to engage in the student's educational and career counseling, learn and pursue career paths, and enlist qualified tutors for their children (Fellin, 2015; Isik-Ercan, 2012; Kugler & Price, 2009; Bennett-Conroy, 2012).

Key Considerations and Suggestions

Consider implementing the following suggestions as you seek to recognize parent strengths:

- Get to know the systems of education, not only of your students, but also of their parents. Learn the roles of teacher vs. parent from the primary culture and attempt to understand how it might differ from your own perception of teacher and parent rolls. Changing your own perspective can be very helpful in bridging the cultural gap.
- Be explicit about your school's expectations of parents. Host a parent event in the beginning of the school year during which you provide interpreters to explain your school norms and classroom expectations, as well as overview curriculum that may help parents support their children at home.
- Be flexible and creative in finding ways to integrate the educational cultural norms/roles of your student's home countries into your own schools or classrooms.
- Invite EL parents into your classroom, as they are experts on their language and culture, placing them in a new role as the educator themselves. (Be sensitive to cultural norms; this may not always be an acceptable cultural practice.)
- Seek to recognize the ways in which your EL parents are supporting their child's education, even if different from what you are used to, and acknowledge it.

Building Relationships with Parents and Communities

Ms. K is an experienced 5th grade teacher. She has worked with many different types of learners and is experienced in moving struggling students through the ever-increasing rigor of the 5th grade curriculum. She is careful to "try everything" before recommending a student for special education testing, and the few times she has recommended students, they have been successfully referred, tested, and approved for special education support.

This year, Ms. K has continued the documentation of information from last year's 4th grade teacher, who was preparing to recommend one of her new immigrant students, Jacob, for testing. Her school's English Language Development (ELD) specialist has assured Ms. K that the student's struggle is not a result of learning a new language. In fact, there is written documentation from last year's teacher and a district interpreter that the family noticed Jacob had developed much more slowly than his brothers and sisters during the first five years of his life, and the family shared that Jacob had struggled to learn concepts in his primary language as well as in English.

Armed with well-documented paperwork and the full support of her school counselor and the new principal, Ms. K set up a meeting as per her district's protocol to inform the parents of her concerns and obtain permission for testing. Ms. K was very frustrated after meeting Jacob's parents for the first time. What she thought would be a simple informative meeting with the parents went very wrong. The parents, who had been willing to disclose information to last year's teacher regarding the student's irregular childhood development, now denied any such information. While talking to Ms. K. in fact, the parents refused to consent to any testing for the child and informed both Ms. K and the new principal that they might consider enrolling their child in a local private school.

In desperation, Ms. K. went to last year's 4th grade teacher and the ELD specialist to find out if they could shed any light on the situation. While the 4th grade teacher seemed equally perplexed, the ELD teacher shared important information that Ms. K had never before considered. "It's really an issue of culture and trust," she stated. "While you were attempting to gather information to build a solid, knowledge-based case that would be entirely appropriate within American culture, the parents do not know you and have not yet learned to trust you with highly personal, private information about their child."

While the names in this story have been changed to protect the identity of those involved, this situation has occurred in any number of schools and classrooms across the United States. While parents brought up in or intimately familiar with American cultural norms would expect a teacher to have strong documentation and thorough evidence to refer a child for testing, many cultures see the topic of learning differences and special education as a highly sensitive issue, one that they are willing to discuss only with trusted members of their community. Ms. K's mistake was tri-fold. First, she assumed that she could approach this sensitive topic academically rather than relationally, without research into or regard for the previously established cultural perceptions of learning differences in Jacob's culture. Second, in her attempt to take care of the issue efficiently so that she could ensure he receive services as soon as possible, she did not take time to get to know the family and develop a relationship of trust before approaching this topic with the child's parents. Third, she called a meeting in which all of the school representatives were new to the family, in essence, sharing their private family information with strangers. It is no wonder the family felt betrayed by the school and considered sending their child elsewhere. In cases like this, the family can feel threatened or fearful, and may even give false information about the student in order to protect their child.

This scenario is only one of many that occur when educators and other school staff do not understand the importance of learning aspects of the deep culture of their students and failing to focus on establishing relationships of trust in which schools and families can learn from each other (Bennet-Conroy, 2012; Hall, 1976; Kugler & Price, 2009). Immigrant and refugee parents need educators to understand the sacrifices that parents have made for the sake of their children's futures by coming to the United States. This understanding comes from mutual investment in relationship building. If relationships are not built and parent strengths not honored, parents may look at their children's school with tremendous shame or fear. Where parents may have enjoyed higher status in their native country, but are lower status in the United States, the family may suffer an identity crisis and become marginalized. The marginalization will persist if there is not acceptance and valuing of the family's identity and contributions (Agbenyega & Klibthong, 2013).

Fortunately, there are simple efforts that an educator can make that can have a profound impact on the relationship between EL families and schools. As the popular adage from Theodore Roosevelt reminds us, "[Students] don't care how much you know until they know how much you care." In the case of culturally and linguistically diverse students, this extends to their families and communities as well.

Key Considerations and Suggestions

Consider implementing the following suggestions as you seek to build relationships with parents:

- Put obvious and public effort into building relationships with parents, elders, and community leaders. Trust develops over time. Attend community events, find out who the cultural insiders are, and get to know them. Simply inviting the family to school or providing the family with advice does not ensure your efforts are being interpreted as positive attempts at relationship building.
- Establish neutral space outside of the school or the families' homes, such as a community center, where you can interact and build relationships, then develop an environment where you and the parent establish a working community together. In this way, the parent–teacher power paradigm is more neutral. As opposed to meeting only at the school, where the teacher is the expert, the parents have a sense of worth and contribution. This will empower the parents to be the experts on their own culture and develop their cross-cultural identities.
- Host cultural nights where all students, not just the EL families, are invited to inform and learn of a culture's heritage and people. Another way you can do this is by celebrating achievements by the students of a cultural community. Recently, a Spokane high school sought to motivate the Marshallese community by hosting an academic achievement night, where students who were passing their classes received acknowledgement by their families and teachers.
- Home visits can teach you invaluable information about a family. Parents are often eager to have educators visit their homes. In a survey of 25 Burmese families from Myanmar, 24 expressed desire for the teachers to do home visits (Isik-Ercan, 2012). However, under no circumstances should you invite yourself or go into a student's home with the intention of dragging students or parents to schools.
- If you are invited to a student's home, accept. Research the eating habits and gift giving protocol of that family's native culture. Gift giving, receiving, accepting refreshments, etc. follow different protocols in every culture.
- Once a relationship with a family or cultural group is established, arrange visits to the school by culture, language, or family, and provide an interpreter. Invite families often and include them in events, ensuring their language interpretation needs are met.

- When new families move to your region, reach out. Work with the families with whom you have established relationships to secure your identity within that community as an advocate.
- If a family trusts you with the details of their story, respect their privacy. Teachers as advocates can develop a sense of pride, responsibility, and representation as they get to know a family. Applying their own cultural standards, well-intending but culturally unaware educators fall into the trap of using the student's story to access resources and conjure empathy. However, this can be a violation of trust and be perilous to the teacher-parent relationship. Establishing a safe and clear platform for families to share their own stories as they see fit and on their own timeline honors the family's integrity. It seems intuitive and obvious, but avoid putting the student or the family in a spotlight without giving them the necessary sociocultural and linguistic insights and opportunities to practice delivering their story.

Parent Empowerment

Hellena is the mother of an 11th grade student. She does not speak English, and her son has interpreted for her at parent–teacher conferences since he started school in the United States in 6th grade. This year, a district interpreter called her home to ask if she would like interpretation for her son's conference.

"My son usually interprets for me," Hellena replied.

"Our district policy indicates that student's may not interpret for their own conferences," stated the interpreter. "If you need interpretation, we can provide a certified interpreter for you."

Relieved, Hellena responded, "Oh, I didn't know that. My son doesn't really listen to me anymore, and I'm never sure if he is telling me everything. In fact, I don't even know how he is doing in school. I am happy to have an interpreter."

On the day of the parent–teacher conference, a teacher and a counselor were both present for Hellena's meeting as well as the interpreter and her son. As soon as the interpreter walked up to the family to greet them, the son stated in English, "My mom doesn't need an interpreter."

"I have been assigned to this conference at your mother's request," stated the interpreter. "Only your mother can request that I leave."

Sadly, the conference revealed that the son was failing his classes and had not been on target to graduate since the end of his 9th grade year.

The son had been informing his schools that his mother did not need an interpreter for several years. Rather than questioning this, the teachers and office staff had taken his word for it, and when the mother would arrive, they would simply allow the son to interpret. The mother had never been informed, in her primary language, that she could have an interpreter. As a result, she was forced to rely on her son to convey to her what he chose, effectively cutting her off from the educational life of her child and grossly upsetting the parent–child relationship within the home.

After the conference, the district interpretation office assured the mother that a district interpreter would be present for all school–home communication from that point forward.

One of the greatest challenges for parents of immigrant and refugee students is the restructuring of family roles, or role-reversal. Role-reversal is a term used to refer to the exchange of roles within the family in which the child, as a result of greater linguistic and cultural knowledge of the majority culture, act as interpreter, translator, and cultural informant for the parents, shifting the family's power structure, and placing the parents in a role of dependence (Zhou, 1997). These role reversals, often unintentionally supported within the educational system, ". . . create identity confusion and conflict between the generations" (McBrien, 2005, p. 330). As a result, these "Intergenerational conflicts [can] lead to dwindling parental authority and insufficient family communications and have significantly negative effects on children's self-esteem, psychosocial well-being, and academic aspirations" (Zhou, 1997, p. 85).

Anne Makepeace (2006), in a video documentary entitled *Rain in a Dry Land*, records a Somali mother's experience attempting to order a chicken shortly after arrival to the United States. Her son, having learned about the American fast food culture in school, recommends that she go to Taco Bell. Using her young son as an interpreter, the mother asks to see the whole chicken, being puzzled at the small chunks of cooked chicken in a tortilla presented by the clerk. In frustration, the mother and her son head to the local supermarket, only to be frustrated again by the fact that there are only frozen or prepared chickens to be had. Throughout the ordeal, the mother continues to ask her young son for assistance, placing him in the role of cultural informant, and forcing her to play a dependent role while still attempting to act as provider for her family. American schools often encourage and support this role-reversal, albeit unintentionally, by utilizing the children to convey important school information, documents, and reporting to the home rather than using certified interpreters to communicate this information first-hand to the parents. When a seemingly well-intending teacher uses the student as an interpreter, they reinforce this loss of power, and jeopardize the family's status structure. Such actions place undue pressure on the child and usurp familial authority from the parent, as demonstrated in Hellena's narrative above. To empower the parent, it is crucial that schools communicate directly with the parents via translation or interpretation from certified adults outside the family.

The Pitfalls of Using Students as Interpreters for Families and Schools

- Reinforces role-reversal, and changes power structure of the home, which has serious negative consequences between parents and child, child and siblings, as well as parents and teacher.
- Ensures at least partial inaccuracy of message so that the parent is guaranteed to be misinformed.
- Allows student to interpret in their favor, leaving out key details, and revealing only positive aspects of the conversation.

In addition to communicating with parents in their primary language, schools can also empower parents by supporting the language of the home. While many school systems can provide educational support in the primary language through bilingual or dual language programs, others lack the resources or educational policy freedom to do so. This does not mean they cannot support parents in educating their children in the primary language at home. Creating a space to share aspects of the primary language in their child's classroom, offering competency-based credits testing in the primary language, and encouraging and providing space for primary language classes to take place at the school are all ways to empower parents. These practices send a message to parents that the primary language and culture are valued by the school.

Family roles are not the only roles that are challenged when immigrant or refugee parents send their children to school in the United States. Across cultures, certain topics are reserved for the home and family and others are appropriate for the school to address. This line between school topics and home topics is not as strongly defined in the Unites States. Students in America's individualistic society are often encouraged to seek and obtain knowledge as a personal quest so that students may make best decision for themselves. Individualistic societies put a priority on the values of effort, research, and intrinsic motivation as fundamental factors in knowledge acquisition, placing emphasis on the individual's ability to make decisions that will deliver the greatest personal advantage over time. Collectivistic societies, in contrast, view when and how a child receives knowledge as reflected in seasonal change. In this sense, development of knowledge occurs through patience, maturity, and merit and is passed on from one generation to the next through designated elders within the community. Decisions are made to benefit the social group as a whole, requiring significant input from a larger number of elders. Emphasis is placed not only on knowledge itself, but also on who delivers what knowledge to whom, and during what stage of life (Hall, 1976; Hofstede, 2001; Hofstede et al., 2010; Triandis & Bhawuk, 1997).

> To illustrate, Rose is a single mother of four from Sudan who values education immensely. In the refugee camps, she took painstaking efforts to ensure her children made it to school through the perilous and unstable conditions. As such, educators in her native country had deep respect for Rose and would pay her visits to her home occasionally. Rose was excited about the idea of meeting American teachers and invited her daughter's 6th grade teacher to her house on numerous occasions. However, her daughter never passed on the invitation to the teacher because she was embarrassed about the family's small apartment, ethnic food and different food customs, like sitting on the floor to eat. The student reported back to the mother that the teacher was always too busy to come over. Rose felt disappointed and disrespected, and slowly built contempt toward the teacher. Throughout the quarter, Rose told her adult ESL instructor about her frustration with the teacher, and the adult educator attempted to calm Rose by informing her of cultural standards and expectations that the middle school teacher might have been adhering to. Then, one day, Rose's daughter brought home a sexual education assignment. Rose came into her adult ESL classroom waving the assignment and was enraged because the teacher had disrespected her by first rejecting her multiple invitations and later by talking about a private subject with her own daughter.

Teachers seeking to understand these concepts cross-culturally can do so through researching academic literature to the point that it is available, and then must seek out knowledge within the families' cultural communities. Educators will gain a more thorough understanding of parent and student expectations by consulting social experts such as parents, religious leaders, cultural elders, and community insiders as a source of cultural expertise, and in doing so, empower parents both within the community and within the family to support the academic success of their children.

Key Considerations and Suggestions

Consider implementing the following suggestions as you seek to empower parents:

- Use qualified adult interpreters. Under no circumstances should you use the student or siblings to interpret, as it is detrimental to the health and wellbeing of the family structure. Also, understand that using a family member may limit or constrain the type and amount of information you may exchange. You can achieve more tangible communication success if you avoid upsetting the power paradigm of the family.
- Support primary language use. As discussed previously, it is important that students maintain their primary languages to develop literacy skills in English. Taking this further, supporting the primary language empowers the parent in the education of the child and his or her future academic success.
- Do not assume that your students' immigrant parents have access to technology or know how to navigate your school's site. Simply giving them the website or resource location is not enough.

Consider hosting website training nights with interpreters, or having any technological components required accessible at meetings or events, with language appropriate assistance. Also consider the possibility that electricity, technology in general, Internet access, Smart phones, and things we may consider as ubiquitous might not be available to the parents of your students.

- Avoid arranging the environment where the teacher is always the giver of knowledge and power, and the parents as the receivers. Do not wait for the parents to initiate this process. Teach the families how to gain access to the information or resources they need.
- Take time to learn about the parents' former education, work experience, and expectations. Validate their experiences by using parents where they may be experts. Do not assume that a parent is uneducated or impoverished based on their English language level. Many parents may have been high status in their own societies, only to sacrifice that status and career for the sake of their children's futures by coming to the United States.
- Keep in mind that parents may want to assist their children with homework but may be unable to due to language or cultural aspects. One approach may be hosting homework clubs and inviting parents to join, which can be "staffed" by student teachers or volunteers if funding is an issue.
- Make classroom expectations clear. Ideally, this will be a mutual process negotiated by a native culture community leader between the parents and students at a culturally mutual location as mentioned above. However, if the relationship or social structure has not been established enough to do this, this information should come from the cultural leader instead of the teacher or educational leader. Religious centers, community colleges, and community centers make excellent host sites for these events. Topics for consideration include the following:
  - The concept of time, and what it means to meet deadlines.
  - Acquisition of knowledge.
  - The concepts of responsibilities and cooperation, and what the parent, student, teacher, and school need to do to be perceived as cooperative.
  - Parent–teacher communication: How is the parent going to communicate with the schools? Outline the exact process. If the opportunity arises, practice with role play, or prewritten narratives that are typical conversational dialogues. Give them the language that can be used for these types of conversations.
  - Important communication sent to the home: Explain and illustrate what kind of forms, calls and meetings the parents can expect and what the school expects, and what will be perceived if these expectations are not met.
  - Important dates and expectations.
  - Space and sharing: What the student and parents need to know about American behaviors, and what the teachers need to know about these concepts cross-culturally.
- Consult social experts such as parents, religious leaders, cultural elders, and community insiders as a source of cultural expertise.
- Involve parents, elders and/or social leaders in decision making processes around career and educational counseling for the student.
- Include family members and elders in important decision-making regarding topics that may be considered personal. Topics that need to be considered carefully with the family before bringing them into curriculum include the following:
  - Sexual or physical maturity, rites, or rituals
  - Stages of life and corresponding responsibilities
  - Social roles and decision-making
  - Gender roles
  - Age-based roles

Teaching as Advocacy and Collaboration

A Mexican-American student teacher at the high school level was surprised to come to school one day to learn that her cooperating (lead) teacher had decided to do a Dia de Los Muertos (Day of the Dead) celebration with her general education high school class. The lead teacher informed the student teacher that they would be engaging in face painting as a cross-cultural activity. The student teacher was uncomfortable with the activity, as it only explored the surface culture aspects (i.e., what is seen) and not the meaningful deep culture aspects (i.e., what is meant, felt, or represented). However, she felt she did not have the authority to interject. As she half-heartedly participated in the activity about her own native culture, she noticed a group of white male students painting teardrops under their eyes, which is typically associated with gang culture, and not symbolic of Day of Dead face painting. Appalled, the student teacher became increasingly upset and withdrawn. When she returned the next day, she asked the lead teacher if she could do a deep culture presentation on Day of the Dead. She informed the class of the origins, processes, and meanings of the customs. She also educated her students on the meaning of the teardrop tattoos, without implying blame to the participants. Later, in front of the class, the males apologized for being culturally insensitive and inappropriate, stating they had learned a valuable lesson. In addition, the lead teacher acknowledged the dangers of her limited view and the errors of not enlisting the student teacher as the cultural insider.

Whether they realize it or not, teachers are advocates for students and their families. The teacher is often the one who finds out first, even before case workers or family members, if a student is without electricity or food at home, or if a parent is suffering from unemployment or depression. Not only are teachers advocates for their students, but they are also advocates for students' families and cultures. As Linville (2016) writes in *ESOL Teachers as Advocates: An Important Role*, "Advocacy as professional engagement is reflected as well in the concept of *teacher leaders*, teachers who are committed to education both inside and outside the classrooms, who take the time and the responsibility to help school reform efforts, and who are willing to take risks in doing so" (p. 103). Whether or not teachers advocate well for their ESOL students and their families is another story.

An important element of advocacy is collaboration with other institutions that can provide resources for EL families. This collaboration can occur on individual, institutional, and regional levels, but it must be intentional, and information available for families must be accessible. Simply storing information on the internet and telling families how to access it is not enough. Many families do not have access to computers or know how to navigate the webpages in English. It is important that teachers and administrators working with ELs become aware of and build connections with local support agencies.

It is equally important to support parents in the process of advocating for themselves. While parents may need significant support in their initial encounters with their child's school, they will, over time, grow less dependent on this support. As Fenner (2014) describes in her book on advocacy, parent support should follow a model of gradual release. "As EL families feel more comfortable with the school and start to become more involved, educators can begin removing scaffolding supports" (p. 115). As they depend less and less upon supports provided by the schools, it is important to enlist members of EL parent community as leaders, encouraging and creating a space for parents to make their voice heard. As the schools learn to listen to the parent voices, working successfully with and for the EL communities will become apparent.

Key Considerations and Suggestions

Consider implementing the following suggestions as you seek to collaborate and advocate for families:

- Use cultural insiders as experts and liaisons within your own community. If you have a bicultural in-service teacher or student teacher at your institution, identify them as the cultural informant to provide insights on teaching cross-cultural holidays, interpreting political and current events, and various procedures and expectations.
- Keep informed of current events in the family's native countries or with their native cultures. Your students and their families will undoubtedly be impacted by these events. If you have diverse groups of ESOL students, you can make a collaborative effort by dividing cultures/countries among teachers. One teacher takes on the responsibility of staying abreast of the current events for one cultural group. Then, all the teachers get together once a week for a quick exchange about what might be happening in their culturally diverse students' worlds. Your efforts will increase your working knowledge and show your interest in your students' lives.
- Identify and use cross-cultural community leaders as allies. Find out who the individual elder and experts are in the community and access them as cultural and decision-making liaisons. Use these elders to advise and inform parents of school events and processes, and expectations.
- Find out where adults can attend class and keep adult educators abreast of events and opportunities to share with the parents in their own ESOL classes. Likewise, inform your administration and peers of events going on with adult educational centers.
- Seek out the educational and social organizations who serve ESOL. These organizations include public primary and secondary schools, institutions of higher education, social and health service providers, government agencies, and legal institutions such as law firms or advocacy groups. At the minimum, have a working connection with at least one key member of these groups, and if possible, establish a grassroots organization with these institutions. If you can commit to meeting once a month, you will be able to save the time and energy it takes to connect individually. For example, the Spokane Regional ESOL Consortium (SREC) has been able to have a more powerful impact on the immigrant community by working across institutions to host events and allowing families to establish settlement trajectories that go beyond simply meeting the requirements of the classroom.
- Know local resources available for families. Often, our documented immigrant and refugee families have access to many of the same social services as our low-income American born families.
- Keep a comprehensive list of local support agencies such as medical, dental, and vision services, refugee resettlement agencies, mental health programs, immigrant legal support groups, immigrant and refugee advocacy groups, interpretation and translation services, and more that you can readily access.
- Find out the local educational and employment opportunities for adults.
- Stay abreast of career and resource fairs that grant access to agencies that can improve the family's quality of life. Send this information home with the student, translated into native language. Also, share these fliers with educators of adults.
- Introduce yourself to the caseworker or family advocate, and develop a general working relationship, if appropriate.
- Educate yourself and peers on the symptoms of trauma. These symptoms often are viewed as learning or behavioral issues. You may need to advocate for trauma resources for a student who has been misdiagnosed. Consider that trauma may vary from family member to family member, and do not assume that just because a family member has severe trauma, that all members do. Contrarily, it is limiting to assume that because other family members have not shown signs of trauma that your student also will not.

- Actively replace the phrase "illegal immigrant" with "undocumented immigrant." In many states, like Washington, for example, it is against the law to ask about a student or family's immigration status. However, be aware that this status may greatly impact how safe students or their parents view their school. We have seen parents who are worried about being picked up by ICE avoid schools and meetings to minimalize risk. Work closely with your Spanish-speaking churches (and other cultural groups) to establish ways and places to connect with these parents.
- Inform families of their rights and how to uphold them.

FINAL POINTS

- The immigrant family has a rich and valuable set of assets that, if recognized and maximized, can greatly contribute to the social and academic success of your student.
- In addition to identifying what students and their families need, teachers who work with what positive attributes this family brings will ultimately empower the student beyond the classroom.
- Honoring an immigrant's culture, language, and values can lead to powerful growth in not just in the classroom, but in the community as well.
- Teachers have the gift of responsibility to advocate for the immigrant student and family, inside and across institutions.
- An inquisitive, unassuming mind, an open heart and classroom, networking and a clear voice insure immigrant families that you are willing to meet them on this new journey, and that can make all of the difference.
- In addition, the teacher as advocate also works with the community to increase the compassion and understanding around immigrants and their realities.

Discussion Questions and Activities

1. What are some of the strengths that immigrant and refugee parents have? Why is it important to recognize these strengths (*i.e., what they bring*) and not just deficits (*i.e., what they need*)?
2. What are some of the cross-cultural factors that contribute to success for the student and the family? How can these factors be utilized in a positive (or interactive) way?
3. What role does the teacher play as advocate? What five deliberate steps can the teacher do to actively advocate for a student? These plans may be different for each cultural group.

This activity has two parts. It is essential to complete both in order to achieve the objectives of the activity. For part one, students will work in groups of the same scenario (e.g., "Fatima Group"). Part two is a "jigsaw" of the group so that at least one of each of the four scenarios is represented in the entire new group. Part two can be found after the scenarios.

Part One (of two)

Form four groups and assign one of the four scenarios on the following pages to each group. For each group, discuss the following questions:

1. What strengths does the individual possess?
2. What challenges does the individual face?
3. What kind of information would be helpful to know about the individual's family?

Scenario 1: Adult—Fatima

Fatima is from Afghanistan and speaks Pashto and Farsi. She is 45 years old and a pre-literate learner. She cannot read and write in her L1, and is not literate in any language. In Afghanistan, she learned to write her name from right to left in her native script. At her intensive English class, she has developed manual dexterity to print the English alphabet, and she can read and identify numbers up to 100. She can copy a short text from a book although the letters are large. She often does not remember to put spaces between her words. She has learned basic decoding skills and survival sight word reading. She has very little spoken English and has minimal reading comprehension skills.

She has a son and two daughters, and she is very eager for them to do well in their new environment. She makes sure they are ready for school every day, but she cannot help them with their homework at home. She has been invited to attend several meetings at her children's schools, but she prefers not to go. There is no bilingual specialist for the languages she speaks. There is one limited defined interpreter, but he is male and, as a devout Muslim woman, she is uncomfortable initiating conversations with him. In addition, her youngest daughter's 5th grade teacher continually contacts the district's Arabic bilingual specialist to call her at home and to translate for parent conferences. Fatima does not speak Arabic.

Scenario 2: Elementary—Shahada

Shahada is in 5th grade. She is from Afghanistan and arrived in the United States with her mother and two older siblings two years ago. She is the only EL student in her class, and she is the only Farsi speaker in her entire school. Her first language is Farsi, but she only uses it at home to talk to her mother. She is much more comfortable with English now than Farsi, and she uses it to talk to her friends. She is the most comfortable English speaker in the home, and she usually accompanies her mother on outings to the grocery store, bank, etc. to translate.

Shahada did not go to school before coming to the United States. After two years, she has attained proficiency in BICS (social language), but she is still reading at a second grade level. She is struggling to meet grade-level standards in all subject areas, and is embarrassed to read in class. She gets very upset when her teacher tells the class that she is from the Middle East and speaks Arabic, but she does not correct the teacher. She is very social and is often in trouble for talking in class. Her progress reports indicate defiant behavior. Her teacher continues to have a bilingual specialist call home, but there is no response from the mother.

Scenario 3: High School—Rashan

Rashan is a junior in High School. He is from Afghanistan, and his first language is Farsi. He also speaks Thai, having learned it in the refugee camp in order to communicate for his family. He had limited educational experience in Afghanistan but can read and write minimally in his L1. He struggles with handwriting, having learned to write in his L1 from right to left. He has attained proficiency in BICS (social language); however, he has a hearing loss in one ear due to injuries incurred while living in Afghanistan, and he has difficulty hearing many sounds in English. As a result, his pronunciation is progressing slowly. While his ELD teachers can understand him, most of his core content area teachers complain of difficulty understanding him.

He is currently passing Biology with a D after failing last year. He did not pass the EOC (end of course) exam last year and must do so this year in order to meet graduation requirements. He was unable to pass the reading or writing portion of the HSPE (Washington State High School Proficiency Exam) last spring as well. He passed the Algebra 1 EOC last year after taking Algebra 1 for two years, but it is currently the only graduation requirement he has successfully completed. He wants to be a doctor.

Scenario 4: Middle School—Munirah

Munirah is in 8th grade. She is from Afghanistan, where she went to an all girl's school. She is literate in her first language, Farsi, and she took some English while in school in Afghanistan. She has strong reading and writing skills in English and her teacher enjoy working with her, but she does not talk in class. She is mainstreamed in Math, Language Arts, Science, and Social Studies, and she has one period of language instruction with her ELD (English language development) teacher.

Physical Education is the one class she is having trouble passing. She is Muslim and, as an adolescent girl, she wears a hijab (head covering) at all times in public. She cannot show her legs, so she wears leggings under her PE uniform. The other students make fun of her, and she has difficulty making friends. She frequently refuses to "dress out" for PE, and she receives low marks as a result. She eats lunch in the ELD classroom, but there are no other Muslim girls in the ELD program. She often goes home crying.

Part Two (of two)

After each group has finished the discussion, divide or "jigsaw" into several groups of four, with each group containing one member from each of the previous groups so that each of the new groups has a representative for each of the four scenarios. Discuss the following:

1. Have each individual share the strengths and challenges of the individual in their scenario as well as what family information would be helpful for educators.
2. After each of the four individuals has shared, discuss what you learned about the family unit as you listened to the other members of the group.
3. Based on the information in this chapter, what steps can you or your school/community take to support and work with the parent and with the family as a unit?

Resources

http://stories.unhcr.org/refugees

http://culturalorientation.net

https://ethnomed.org/

http://www.colorincolorado.org/

Spokane Regional ESOL Consortium (SREC) http://eslspokane.com

References

Agbenyega, J. & Klibthong, S. (2013). Whole school initiative: Has inclusive education gone astray? *International Journal of Whole Schooling, 9*(1), 3–22.

Ariza, E. N. (2000). Actions speak louder than words—Or do they? Debunking the myth of apathetic immigrant parents in education. *Contemporary Education, 71*(3) 36–38.

Bankston, C. & Zhou, M. (2002). Being well vs. doing well: Self-esteem and school performance among immigrant and nonimmigrant racial and ethnic groups. *The International Migration Review, 36*(2), 389–415.

Bennett-Conroy, W. (2012). Engaging parents of eighth grade students in parent–teacher bidirectional communication. *School Community Journal, 22*(2), 87–110.

Fellin, M. (2015). Raising citizens: Parenting education classes and Somali mothers' experiences of childrearing in Canada. *Journal of Social Science Education, 14*(3), 31–42.

Fenner, D. S. (2014). *Advocating for English learners: A guide for educators.* Thousand Oaks, CA: Corwin.

Hall, E. T. (1976). *Beyond culture.* Gardent City, NY: Doubleday.

Hofstede, G. H. (2001). *Culture's consequences: Comparing values, behaviours, institutions, and organizations across nations.* Thousand Oaks, CA: Sage.

Hofstede, G. H., Hofstede, G. J., & Minkov, M. (2010). *Cultures & organizations: Software of the mind.* New York: McGraw-Hill.

Isik-Ercan, Z. (2012). In pursuit of a new perspective in the education of children of the refugees: advocacy for the "family." *Educational Sciences: Theory & Practice,* Special Issue, Autumn, 3025–3038.

Kugler, E. G. & Price, O. A. (November, 2009). *Helping immigrant and refugee students succeed: It's not just what happens in the classroom.* Washington, DC: Center for Health and Health Care in Schools, School of Public Health and Health Services, The George Washington University. Retrieved Wednesday, April 26, 2017 from http://healthinschools.org/en/Immigrant-and-Refugee-Children/Caring-Across-Communities.aspx.

Linville, H. A. (March 2016). ESOL teachers as advocates: An important role? *TESOL Journal,* 7.1, 98–128.

Makepeace, A. (2006). *Rain in a dry land.*

McBrien, J. L. (2005). Educational needs and barriers for refugee students in the United States: A review of the literature. *Review of Educational Research, 75*(3), 329–364.

Triandis, H. C. & Bhawuk, D. P. S. (1997). Culture theory and the meaning of relatedness. In P. Christopher Earley & M. Erez (Eds.), *New perspectives on international industrial/organizational psychology* (pp. 13–52). San Francisco: The New Lexington Press.

Zhou, M. (1997). Growing up American: The challenge confronting immigrant children and children of immigrants. *Annual Review of Sociology, 23,* 63–95.

CHAPTER 17

BEYOND THE CLASSROOM WALLS: SUGGESTIONS FOR NONINSTRUCTIONAL STAFF

Diana Pett, Renee Zelden, and Eileen N. Whelan Ariza

KEY POINTS

- Noninstructional school personnel often plead for guidance, insight, and professional development in dealing with immigrant/newcomer students more effectively.
- A cafeteria worker may wonder how to handle an anxiety-causing situation for a Russian kindergartener (for example) or other student who is confused about the lunch choices.
- A monolingual school nurse may need to understand whether the tears of a non-English speaker signal an emergency that cannot be handled at school, or just a minor ache.
- Bus drivers, school police officers, custodians, clinic workers, and school volunteers must feel prepared to help newcomer immigrant students make a smoother transition to the realities of U.S. schools.
- Communicative understanding among school personnel, English learners, and their families needs to improve for a smoother transition into the academic realm.

ESOL Teachers and Assistants

One of the first people to make contact with immigrant students and their families may be an ESOL teacher, a bilingual facilitator, or an assistant acting as an ESOL liaison.

Although it is impossible to list all the ways in which an ESOL professional could reach out to newcomers, some salient points and significant activities are highlighted here.

- First and foremost, an ESOL staff member should always be knowledgeable about and maintain a network of ESOL support services and information on county, state, and national levels, especially as they pertain to new EL regulations. Checking in with the district ESOL coordinator (or the counterpart in your logistical area), logging on to a website of the board of education, and signing up for e-mail updates about educational legislation are easy and effective ways of keeping your school informed about issues related to English learners.
- As a word of advice, one proven way to stay abreast of new developments in the field of teaching English as a second language is to become a member of an international, state, or a local association that promotes the interests of ELs.
- TESOL, Inc. is one major source of information, and your own state may have an affiliate organization. It is hard to overestimate the value of professional organizations in offering teachers opportunities to learn from each other.
- In addition to disseminating information, an ESOL professional may also be the "pivot person" who connects all disparate school personnel in their efforts to assist English learners. It is often an ESOL teacher who is contacted by other staff members during their unexpected dealings with English learners. Experienced ESOL teachers have stated that maintaining an updated list of bilingual volunteers (and their schedules) can be of invaluable service for the school.
- Another way an ESOL professional can serve the immigrant population better is by providing office staff with files containing translated school applications, requesting EL students' records from previous schools, and by making inquiries about new students' academic backgrounds. Although school personnel cannot question parents' legal status in the United States, they can and *should* learn as much as possible about students' academic histories to make informed decisions about assigning them to appropriate grade levels and programs. Because an ESOL teacher may be asked for an opinion on grade placement, it is important to learn about various educational systems in different countries and how they compare to schooling in America.

- Excellent resource on this topic: Mazurek, K., & Winzer, M. A. (2006). *Schooling around the world: debates, challenges, and practices.* Pearson Allyn & Bacon; Baker, D., & LeTendre, G. K. (2005). *National differences, global similarities: World culture and the future of schooling.* Stanford University Press.
- In light of tremendous academic diversity within the growing EL population, ESOL professionals need to be knowledgeable about effective instructional materials in order to help mainstream teachers select resources for English learners. They should also be competent in *differentiated instructional strategies* and culturally relevant instruction in content areas, as they may be asked to share pertinent information and classroom management tips with subject area teachers of linguistically and academically diverse groups.
- Arranging and attending parent conferences may be yet another responsibility of ESOL/bilingual professionals. ESL teachers should use this opportunity to obtain emergency information from parents and explain sign-out procedures. Many parents are unaware that in case of an emergency, their children cannot be picked up by a relative whose information is not on file with the school. When ESOL/bilingual teachers assist with interpretation, they should encourage all teachers in attendance to face the parents (not the interpreter) when discussing a student's academic progress. The parents will appreciate this gesture of respect and acknowledgment. Remember to avoid putting the child in the role of interpreter.

Administrators

- Administrative personnel have the potential to benefit English learners in their adjustment to school life. Usually, principals are well informed about the demographics of their communities because certain types of resources and even school funding may be tied to the percentage of the ESOL population. However, it is equally important for administrators to possess the deeper knowledge of students' cultures and use those insights to promote learning and cross-cultural communication in their schools. With this awareness in mind, administrators should plan multicultural sensitivity training and professional development for all staff, including, but not limited to, bus drivers, clinic workers, the school nurse, food service personnel, media specialists, paraprofessional assistants, and custodians. Table 17.1 lists important considerations for conducting sensitivity training and suggests some schoolwide projects that administrators could initiate to benefit their EL population.
- As always, sharing EL-related resources with other schools is essential in light of limited funding for linguistically diverse learners.

TABLE 17.1 Promoting Cultural Awareness: Suggestions for School Administrators

- Help teachers and staff learn more about their students' cultures
- Establish a multicultural committee to identify and resolve EL-related issues
- Consider the needs of ELs when making purchasing decisions
- Plan multicultural events and encourage ELs to participate
- Tailor professional development to the needs of teachers working with linguistically diverse students
- Invest in resources for differentiated instruction to help English learners master content as they acquire English

- **Provide office staff with a file of templates for school announcements in different languages**
- **Organize EL family nights and encourage parents to network with each other**
- **Maintain a bank of bilingual staff and outline their responsibilities in relation to parent communication**
- **Compensate staff for overtime translations, interpretations, or extra duties**
- **Consider investing in translation devices for unexpected dealings with non-English-speaking parents. Use available technology on smart phones, apps, or laptops for translating and interpreting**
- **Schedule book readings in the home languages of ELs and invite parents to participate**

- Keep students and parents informed about the upcoming safety drills and similar school routines
- Watch for signs of asthma attacks, seizures, fainting, or heart trouble in non-English speakers, during fire drills, as they may mistake drills for true emergencies; use a key phrase to let them know it is just a drill
- Go over emergency procedures with English learners (severe weather warning, lockdown, fire evacuation, etc.) before a situation occurs
- Place at least one bilingual staff member on the emergency response team and give him or her an electronic translator
- Brief students on what they must do if they get lost on their way to and from school; such safety information should be clear and unambiguous
- In case of an emergency, students should be reminded to stay with an adult in charge and not to wander off

- Translate information about community resources and make it available in the office and school library (library card application, homework hotline, etc.)
- Seek outside sponsorship from bookstores, electronics stores, and so on to benefit the EL population
- Seek donations of bilingual books, learning CDs, tapes, and games
- Make CDs available for lending
- Train ELs in using the Internet and inform them about all places where Internet can be accessed without charge

Bus Drivers	<ul><li>Because a bus driver is often the first adult to meet and greet a newcomer immigrant student, positive body language is essential in creating an atmosphere of trust (see Roger E. Axtell's *Gestures: The do's and taboos of body language around the world* (1998).</li><li>Drivers should seek help from bilingual personnel to translate bus rules and safety expectations for newcomers.</li><li>During the year, drivers need to inform school personnel about upcoming drills and ensure that such announcements are translated into different languages. If that is not done, they risk confusing or scaring English learners, possibly causing them to run away from perceived danger. In addition to providing translated updates into the home language, bus drivers need to be aware of ways students of other cultures respond to adults.</li><li>For example, Haitian students normally do not make eye contact when reprimanded by an authority figure, which is contrary to what a mainstream U.S. bus driver would expect. In other cultures, an adult raising his or her voice may be perceived as threatening, which may cause a student to shut down or start crying.</li></ul>
Crossing Guards	<ul><li>Crossing guards need to know that traffic and pedestrian laws are not universal; therefore, newcomer immigrant students may not act in a manner that is expected of pedestrians in our society.</li><li>For instance, Russian children may not respond to the directions of crossing guards because they did not have them in their home countries.</li><li>Since in certain cultures traffic lights are perceived as mere "suggestions" for drivers and pedestrians, students from those countries may try to cross the motorway running as long as there are no cars in sight.</li><li>Crossing guards need to be patient and calm as they communicate pedestrian rules with the help of a bilingual teacher.</li></ul>
Food Service Personnel	<ul><li>Cafeteria workers need to understand that immigrant students may have different culinary customs.</li><li>Breakfast items may not be the same for students from other countries. It is important to give those students more wait time as they make their food selections.</li><li>They may not know if an item is sweet or salty just by looking at it, and previous expectations often confuse those who bite into a pastry expecting to taste meat instead of jelly.</li><li>To help students chose items for breakfast and lunch, cafeteria workers should paste pictures and key words by the serving line.</li></ul>

	■ As in other situations, teachers can use the buddy system, pairing newcomers with helpful bilingual students who can explain unfamiliar items on the menu. Rewards, treats, and verbal praise should be used to encourage such interactions. ■ Food service workers should also be aware of cultural and religious dietary restrictions. ■ For example, students from the Middle East, Jewish, or Islamic cultures may not eat pork products or any foods containing gelatin (marshmallows, certain types of pastry, puddings, Jell-O, etc.) or food according other religious rituals and rules. ■ It is therefore important to indicate the use of pork on the menu with, for example, a picture of a pig's face, or the use of gelatin with a picture of a calf's hooves or bones. In addition to pork restrictions, students from Israel may not be allowed to combine dairy and meat during the same meal. ■ It would be culturally insensitive to insist that such students order pepperoni and cheese pizza or get a carton of milk with their beef burger.
Police Officers and Firefighters	■ Police officers and firefighters need to have knowledge of cultural groups living in their communities and learn more about their practices (e.g., rurally based Russian Pentecostal families attempted to smoke fish inside their homes). ■ To assist nonspeakers of English, volunteers who can act as interpreters during emergencies might need to be called on. ■ Police officers assigned to a particular school need to take time to introduce themselves to students. ■ They need to smile and speak softly, keeping in mind that any adult in a uniform may be a menacing sight for ELs who have lived under authoritarian rule. ■ To explain emergency drills and the functions of safety devices in the building, police officers and firefighters should use pictures and demonstrations. ■ Anti-drug information and safety updates should be distributed in multiple languages that are represented in the community.
Psychologists and Social Workers	■ Both psychologists and social workers need to work closely with ESOL professionals to obtain background information about students prior to referring them to special education or counseling services. Immigrants may be victims of trauma and/or PTSD as a result of having to flee their countries. ■ For school psychologists, it is critical to recognize and minimize cultural bias when using diagnostic or intelligence testing.

	■ Careful consideration should be given to the language, format, and setting of any evaluation. It is critical to remember that tests lose their validity once they are translated word for word from English into other languages.
	■ When trying to distinguish between a normal rate of second language acquisition and a learning disability, school psychologists need to use multiple quantitative data as well as anecdotal records. All testing should be done in the native language to be valid.
	■ Social workers should tap into the linguistic resources of the community—seniors, grandparents, older siblings, or neighbors—to reach out to at-risk students.
	■ Schedule home visits with ESOL staff to speak to parents who cannot attend conferences because of lack of transportation.
	■ Both psychologists and social workers should understand that some parents may be working multiple jobs and, therefore, cannot schedule meetings during regular school hours.
Coaches and P.E. Teachers	■ During multicultural training, it is important to inform P.E. teachers and coaches about the barriers that ELs face when they consider participating in school athletics.
	■ Athletics teachers may be surprised to learn that upper-grade curricula in some countries consist solely of academic subjects and exclude physical activity.
	■ Parents of English learners may not recognize the value of P.E. or competitive sports in their children's school careers.
	■ Other barriers to participation include parents' financial constraints and their inability to equip an athlete or send him or her to a training camp. When ELs do participate in school athletics, they may miss preseason or evening practices because they have to work or adhere to religious practices.
	■ To secure participation of immigrant students in sports, coaches and P.E. teachers should seek input of ESOL professionals to ensure better communication between families and schools.
	■ As always, cultural sensitivity and being informed about students' backgrounds are crucial factors.
	■ For instance, opposite sex interactions in games or sports may be restricted in certain cultures, while certain religions (i.e., Islam) prohibit exposure of legs.
	■ Group showers may conflict with some students' cultural values of modesty. Therefore, insisting on specific activities or penalizing students for not participating in a practice that their culture forbids is culturally insensitive.

School Nurses	
	■ In order to provide quality health assessments for all students, school nurses need to ensure the presence of bilingual staff during routine physical exams.
	■ Memos in native languages should be sent home to disseminate information about health concerns, vision screenings, community immunization clinics, and so forth.
	■ Follow up to make certain that parents are aware that information is being sent home. Health professionals should also be informed about the current health challenges in the immigrant communities (immunization gaps, tuberculosis, SARS, AIDS, Zika, Lyme disease, etc.) and become proactive in meeting those challenges.
	■ Since school nurses are mandated to report any suspicion of child abuse and neglect, they must learn how such mistreatment manifests itself in different cultural groups.
	■ Health practices differ among cultural groups, and patients may choose to see a spiritualist (or whomever their particular culture believes) in addition to taking prescribed medicine as an added measure of security.
	■ Be aware and informed about the potential of FGM (female genital mutilation) of girls from cultures where this is a normal practice. Girls may have issues that they will not bring to your attention. It is a very sensitive topic but these traditions still continue, even in the United States. Parents may take the girls to another country to have this procedure performed, but there are pockets of individuals that perform these rituals in the United States.
Technology Specialists	
	■ Technical support personnel must correctly spell ELs' names since they are often entered as passwords for school computers.
	■ Hispanic students usually have two surnames, for example, Lucia Gomez Uribe. The student's last name is Gomez, while Uribe is the mother's last name. Many Asians put their surname first. For example, if a female student identifies herself as Hong Long, Hong will be her last name.
	■ Technology coordinators should communicate with the ESOL department about purchasing and loading English learning software.
	■ They should also familiarize themselves with distance learning professional development programs (especially on cultural sensitivity) because that may encourage participation of teachers who function with crowded schedules.
	■ To help English learners supplement classroom learning, technology specialists need to maintain a pool of learning tools (e.g., science websites and English grammar on CD-ROM), interactive learning websites, and teach students how to utilize those resources.

- If possible, they should post important announcements on the school website in several languages.
- Considering the scope of nonacademic challenges that newcomer ELs encounter in our schools, it is hard to overestimate the crucial role of support personnel in helping those students to better navigate their new academic settings.
- As always, respect for cultural differences and patience are crucial for modeling cross-cultural communication and making our schools more welcoming for English learners and native speakers alike.

FINAL POINTS

- Try to anticipate what newcomers might not understand and prepare information that you can get to parents before problems arise.
- Take the time to research the culture of the students in your schools. Every culture is different and the more you know, the better you will be able to assist your ELs.
- Students may be immigrants who have left their countries deliberately, or they may be refugees who have left behind tragic circumstances.
- Become aware of issues, practices, and beliefs that might arise in your school population. Think of innovative ways you can find answers to problems.

Discussion Questions and Activities

1. Choose five cultures that interest you and research their health practices. Brainstorm what issues might arise if immigrants from those cultures continue to use healing methods that are not acceptable to the mainstream U.S. mindset.
2. Prior negative experiences of students can result in unexpected situations in the new environment. For instance, when uniformed firemen and their German shepherd appeared in the classroom during a career day, Russian students began to cry hysterically, insisting that they did not want to be taken away. An interpreter explained that the children feared the firemen because of their past encounters with border police in their homeland. Russian Pentecostal refugee families had suffered harrowing experiences during Gorbachev's changing government as they tried to cross the Russian borders, patrolled by armed officers and their hostile German shepherds. Research other conflicts that might arise as a result of previous negative experience in the home cultures. As a teacher of these students, how would you deal with these situations in a culturally sensitive, appropriate way?
3. In some Asian cultures, the rubbing of hot coins against the skin is used for curing sickness, releasing the "bad wind," and restoring a balance in the body. Haitians may use Voodoo, Hispanics may use Santeria, and Native Americans may appeal to the Great Spirit to heal ill health or pain, in addition to or instead of prescribed medication. These culture-specific health practices may appear to be mistreatment to the culturally untrained educator who is mandated to report any suspected child abuse or neglect. As a teacher, you might recognize that your students' families rely on practices of which a U.S. physician would not approve. How can you carry out your job responsibilities and ensure that your students are adequately cared for without disrespecting their home cultures?

Resources

EL strategies for paraprofessionals
http://www.colorincolorado.org/article/ell-strategies-paraprofessionals

Best practices for adolescent ELs
http://www.ascd.org/publications/educational-leadership/apr09/vol66/num07/Best-Practices-for-Adolescent-ELLs.aspx

RTI resources
http://www.rtinetwork.org/learn/diversity/englishlanguagelearners

Coordinating support services for ELs with special needs
https://www.michigan.gov/documents/mde/1-7_383715_7.pdf

ELs in the schools
http://www.asha.org/practice/multicultural/ELL/

Blueprint for ELs' success
https://www.esboces.org/site/handlers/filedownload.ashx?moduleinstanceid=2609&dataid=3933&FileName=NYSBlueprintforELLSuccessFINAL5.29.15.pdf

Professional development for general education teachers of ELs
http://www.nea.org/assets/docs/PB32_ELL11.pdf

Guidelines for training and support of paraprofessionals
http://www.sde.ct.gov/sde/lib/sde/pdf/cali/guidelines_paraprofessionals.pdf

Classroom partners: How paraprofessionals can support all students to meet new standards
https://www.nysut.org/~/media/files/nysut/resources/2013/june/educators-voice-6/edvoice06_03_paraprofessionals.pdf?la=en

Hidden teachers, invisible students: Lessons learned from exemplary bilingual paraprofessionals in secondary schools
https://www.jstor.org/stable/23478665?seq=1#page_scan_tab_contents

References

Baker, D., & LeTendre, G. K. (2005). *National differences, global similarities: World culture and the future of schooling.* Stanford University Press.

Wenger, K.J., Lubbes, T., Lazo, M., Azcarraga, I., Sharp, S. & Ernst-Slavit, G. (2004) Sociocultural dimensions in teacher learning. *Teacher Education Quarterly,* 31(2), 89–111. San Francisco:CCTE.

Mazurek, K., & Winzer, M. A. (2006). *Schooling around the world: Debates, challenges, and practices.* Boston: Pearson Allyn & Bacon.

PART 6

SAMPLER OF CULTURAL GROUPS: THE TEACHER AS CULTURAL OBSERVER

CHAPTER 18

HISPANICS, LATINO/AS, AND SPANISH SPEAKERS

Eileen N. Whelan Ariza

KEY POINTS

- Many countries speak Spanish as their primary language

- Countries that share this common language many have overarching similarities (e.g., importance of family, religion, etiquette, and fictive kin, called *compadrazgo* [godparents] but may be very different in other cultural ways.

- Each Hispanic/Latino culture should be considered as unique identities.

- People from these cultures differ in economic, educational, and personal backgrounds.

- One culture is not interchangeable with another.

Understanding Spanish-Speaking Cultures

Ms. Rivera, an ESOL teacher in a community college, asked her new students to introduce themselves to one another as an icebreaker activity in the classroom. One by one, the students talked about where they were from. "I am Denis, from Kazakhstan," said one. "I am Ya-Chien, from Taiwan," said another. "I am Marlen, and I am Spanish," said the pretty young lady. Ms. Marefka said, "Oh, what part of Spain are you from?" Marlen answered that she was from Puerto Rico, not Spain. "Well then," said Ms. Rivera, "wouldn't you say that you were Puerto Rican, but you speak Spanish?" "Yes," Marlen agreed, "but here on the mainland, everybody call [sic] me Spanish because I speak Spanish. I am tired to correct [sic]."

Hispanic culture consists of the traditions and customs of people with Latin American roots and whose primary language is Spanish. Spanish culture encompasses the heritage and traditions of the people of Spain ("Hispanic Culture—Latin American Culture—Spanish Culture", 2017).

According to the U.S. Census, the term Hispanic refers to Spanish speakers while Latino refers to origin (Latin America). Therefore, individuals from Cuba, Mexico, Puerto Rico, the Dominican Republic, Central America, and South America are Latinos and Hispanic, and people from Spain are considered Hispanic.

The majority of Hispanic/Latinos in the US have been born in the United States. Other Latinos, or Hispanics, trace their roots to the Africans who were brought as slaves to the New World and are designated as black Hispanics (Fitz-Gibbon & Garcia, 2003). It is important to note that we should not stereotype all Spanish-speaking cultures, as they are all so different. To the onlooker, it may appear or sound like all Spanish speakers are the same. However, each area of the world is distinct, with individual social status, customs, music, clothing, education, food, terminology, idiosyncratic practices, language, accents, idioms, religious beliefs and practices, legends, arts, music, literature, cuisine, history, and social and family values. Each family within a cultural group has its own diversity in economics, geographic region, social standing, and traditions, just as the individual person might be totally different from his or her culture. All members of these societies speak the Spanish language, but characteristics may differ throughout most Spanish-speaking countries. "Various subgroups reflect great differences in ethnicity, culture, origin and can cover the racial spectrum, from white, African American, Asian, Pacific Islander and Native American. Hispanics are a mix of European, African and Native American people." (Hispanic Culture—Latin American Culture—Spanish Culture, 2017, p. 1).

The United States as a nation has a population of 50.7 million Hispanics (Pew Hispanic Center, 2017). "Overall, the 10 largest Hispanic origin groups—Mexicans, Puerto Ricans, Cubans, Salvadorans, Dominicans, Guatemalans, Colombians, Hondurans, Ecuadorians and Peruvians—make up 92% of the U.S. Hispanic population. Six Hispanic origin groups have populations greater than 1 million." (Motel & Patten, 2017, p. 1). Many Hispanics/Latinos are of mixed races.

Many researchers have determined that most Spanish-speaking cultures share, to a certain degree, common overarching universal values, including the following:

- *importance of family*
- *religion and spirituality;*
- *love and importance of children;*
- *formalities of etiquette;*
- *interdependence of family and fictive kin, called compadrazgo (godparents or coparents);*
- *hope and faith in a better future;*
- *the idea of "respeto," or respect, in conforming to expected roles;*
- *independence is not seen as a positive value;*
- *family obligations and interdependence are prized ideals, and members support one another.*
- *It is common for families to host members of the family, the extended family, friends, or friends of friends for long periods in the home.*

(Hispanic Culture—Latin American Culture—Spanish Culture, 2017; Cauce & Domenach-Rodriguez, 2002; de Paula, Lagana, & Gonzalez-Ramirez, 1996; Kayser, 1998; McDade, 1995; Perez, Pinzon, & Garza, 1997; and Valdez, 1996).

Traditionally, Hispanics/Latinos are conscious of etiquette; and manners are important if one wants to be considered *bieneducado*, or polite. In addressing elders or professionals, the protocol is to use family names and titles such as *Señor* (Mr.) and *Señora* (Mrs.) or *Señorita* (Miss). **Don** and **Doña** are used with first names to show respect. In certain geographic areas (e.g., in Colombia) you might be addressed as "Su merced," instead of "usted." In a loose translation, "Su merced" means "your majesty."

Other critical factors that differentiate Spanish speakers are the varieties of skin color, facial and physical characteristics, connection with families in the homeland versus the United States, length of time in the United States, assimilation, and language proficiency (both Spanish and English). Looking at these factors, we see how impossible it is to compartmentalize or pigeonhole all Spanish speakers in the same categories (Ariza, 2010).

Xiomara Davila, from Honduras

My name is Xiomara and we live in Texas. I came to the United States from Honduras when I was a little girl because my family said life was too dangerous there. I started kindergarten and I learned English very well. I can understand Spanish but I cannot read or write it because they only teach me English in school. My brother and sister were born two years later and are American citizens, which means they can have access to all the things I could not-like doctors, dentists, programs, and scholarships. I am a senior in high school now, and I am an honor student who will be valedictorian at my graduation. I want to study to become a doctor. I was shocked to learn that I cannot go to college because I am illegal and we do not have money for tuition, and I cannot get a student loan. I am devastated and now I am afraid that I will be deported to Honduras. I have never been back to Honduras and I am afraid because I can't even speak Spanish. I don't know what to do!

As we can see, people of Hispanic or Latino descent come from very different cultures, situations, and possess varying degrees of Spanish language proficiency. *(Carol Chursenoff and Wilma Diaz contributed material for this part of the chapter.)*

As teachers of many different Spanish-speaking students, we noticed these traits of the families of our students. Upon meeting someone and when saying goodbye, a handshake, an embrace, a kiss on one cheek or two cheeks is offered, even if the encounter lasts for a few minutes. Physical proximity to one another may make the mainstream American uncomfortable. Spanish speakers maintain physical closeness to one another during conversation (about 18 inches). English speakers stand about 36–48 inches apart. For Hispanics, physical distance is perceived as being cold, uninvolved, and emotionally distant. This is relevant to a classroom teacher's awareness about avoiding the inadvertent nonverbal message "move away," through body language (Cartwright & Shingles, 2011; Pajewski & Enriquez, 1996). Affection is displayed openly, and hands or arms are used for gesturing in a conversation. Unlike the typical North American gesture of wiggling a crooked finger to beckon someone to come towards you, the entire hand slapped downward is a more polite way of asking someone to come. Sneezes oblige another to say, "salud," and a yawn or belch will be stifled, as these are considered impolite. Additionally, the art of *tirandopiropos* (making flattering remarks to women) is not impolite and is an accepted common occurrence.

According to *CultureGrams* (2004, 2001) some of the general overall attitudes of Hispanic societies are the concepts of individualism, personal pride, and attention to a person's appearance. It states that it is important to project an impression of affluence and social position, which may be reflected by the quality of clothing or possessions one owns (especially if they are made in the United States or other affluent countries) and by political power. People often correct each other's mistakes, point out errors or flaws they see in someone else, or comment on someone's physical appearance (e.g., you have gained a lot of weight). This practice is considered rude by most English speakers.

One of the most disconcerting first impressions I had as a native English speaker in a Spanish-speaking country was being called "*gordita*," which I immediately translated to "little fat one." It did not matter to me that it was supposed to be a name of tenderness and affection. To me it meant I was being called fat. I was also surprised to hear people being called *viejito* (little old man), *feita* (little ugly girl), and *flaco* (skinny one, but not necessarily in a complimentary sense).

As mentioned earlier, the concept of time is seen differently in every culture. Problems only occur when individuals do not know the significance of time to the cultural participants. If the entire country knows that parties do not start until several hours after the indicated time, no problem exists. If the host country functions on the premise that a dinner invitation for 7:00 P.M. truly begins at 7:00, a problem occurs only if the individual arrives late. In many cultures, Hispanic included, the individual is more important than the schedule; in fact, the idea that a party invitation may say the function starts at 4:00 P.M. and ends at 6:00 P.M. is unfathomable to an individual who lives in a society that does not place great importance on time. They ask, "How do you know what time it ends if the party hasn't even started yet?" In this society, punctuality is never expected at a social affair, and time is not fixed. Visitors to countries with the idea that time is a valuable commodity are frustrated because they expect *mañana*, to mean "tomorrow morning," not "some tomorrow in the future." The present time is more important than the scheduled appointment (e.g., a doctor may keep you waiting for a very long time for your appointment, but when you are in your consultation, he or she takes all the time necessary and does not rush). The individual at hand is more important than a previously arranged appointment. Teachers may have difficulty with parents or students who have appointments but do not appear at the appointed hour. They must explain that a schedule of appointments is necessary to make sure everyone has ample time with the teacher.

Ramirez and Casteneda (1974) and Padrón, Waxman, and Rivera (2002) mention the following classroom strategies to be congruent with the learning styles of Hispanic students:

- ❑ Cooperative learning
- ❑ Personalized rewards
- ❑ Modeling
- ❑ Informal class discussion
- ❑ Concepts presented globally, rather than in detail oriented way
- ❑ Explicit classroom rules
- ❑ Personal interaction such as hugs and pats
- ❑ Humanizing the curriculum using humor, fantasy, or drama

In recognition of the cooperative structure of their home culture, Hispanic children often are more successful doing group projects. Students are accustomed to being touched frequently and to having a more one-to-one relationship with adults. Therefore, teaching strategies will be more congruent with learning styles of the student if the teacher offers individual recognition, hands papers directly to students instead of passing them from student to student, and affords students more physical interaction, such as a pat on the arm, or a quick hug. For many students, short-term daily projects are more likely to be completed and to enhance interpersonal understanding than are long-term projects.

Hispanics are predominantly Catholic, although other religions are quickly emerging. Santeria is often practiced by African influenced Cubans in Caribbean religions ("BBC—Religion: Santeria", 2017), and spiritualism is practiced alongside traditional Catholicism, Charismatic and Pentecostal faiths, including evangelicalism, Assembly of God, and other forms of Protestantism ("Latino Religion", 2017). In my classes, I have had several Jehovah Witness, Muslim, and Bahai as well, so we cannot assume anyone's religion based on language.

In many Hispanic countries, religion and religious holidays permeate daily life and may interfere with school attendance. In the home country, religious observations may be linked to education, and a religious ceremony usually is an adjunct to political events. Although no political functions are connected with religion in the United States, individual religious ceremonies, practices, or beliefs might also interfere with school attendance.

Typically, in the home country, students might be accustomed to a more authoritative school system, and whether public or private, all students wear uniforms. Although this is changing, issues such as mixed-gender classes might become problematic because students were often segregated by gender in their home schools. The concept of a mixed-sex physical education class might be frowned upon as well, and even in the same-sex locker room, modesty issues might prohibit a student from changing clothes in front of peers. It is best to check the protocol the student is accustomed to in the home country school. The schools they are coming from in their country could be very parochial and segregated or they could be very modern and advanced.

In the classroom setting, students from other countries are often accustomed to a different classroom setup or desk configurations. Many schools in Latin America do not have traditional American-style windows in the classroom. In Spain, the climate was chillier; therefore, the school structure reflected the climatic needs. In Colombia, Costa Rica, Puerto Rico, or the warmer places in Mexico, the classroom might have a solid wall, except for the top few feet, which is open to the air. Perhaps a window opening exists but usually will not contain glass. Screens are not typical window dressings. I always enjoyed the airiness of these classrooms but found it difficult to concentrate as the outside noise entered the class and seemed to reverberate off the walls. However, the students and other teachers were not affected the same way I was. Perhaps they were accustomed to the *polychronic* (multiple sounds at the same time) cacophony of sounds, whereas, being from the *monochronic* (one thing at a time) U.S. culture, I needed total silence to function as a teacher. Additionally, I found that the accepted noise levels differed in each Spanish- speaking country as well.

Student classroom configurations are also different in each country. Students might have worked with partners, studied in groups, or sat with others in a row of attached desks. In the United States, desk configurations and classroom decorations might change weekly to control student interaction. Instruction in the US school often is conducted in a more democratic manner than what the students are accustomed to in their home countries. An egalitarian classroom can be confusing to those who are used to a more authoritarian or rote approach to teaching and learning. Teachers who quickly mete out corporal punishment for transgressions and improper behavior may often be the norm in other countries, although I have recently been in classrooms that appeared to be "out of control." While the teacher was trying to work with a small group doing a presentation at the front of the room, the rest of the students were busy interacting with one another all over the room, texting, putting on makeup, rubbing each other's backs, sitting on each other's laps, and socializing. It totally depends on the school and the teacher. I also realize that I was a guest in the classroom, so perhaps the behavior was not the daily norm.

Additionally, teaching by rote memorization with less emphasis on critical thinking might cause more difficulty for students from foreign countries. In the United States, teachers are encouraged to use a more cooperative method of instruction, with audiovisual aids, manipulatives, and access to well-stocked laboratories and technology. I recently visited four public schools in Costa Rica, and there was one room in the school with Internet, but teachers did not have Internet or technology access for their classes. One of the teachers did tell the students to take out their smart phones, if they had one, and she had students using the recording function to record and play back the words to practice English. The smart phone could also be helpful for the student to speak into using the home language and the phone will translate to English. The teacher can also speak English into the phone and it will translate to Spanish. Many mobile apps are available these days to assist in communication with students whose language the teacher does not know.

Students from other countries often claim U.S. schools are easier academically because of the differences in academics (such as not being made to memorize). Additionally, U.S. teachers push students along, often believing in the adage that if the student fails, it is the teacher's fault. From what I have witnessed, most other countries expect the student to conform to the teacher, good or bad. This is especially evident in public universities; a certain number of slots are available, and the students across the country compete by taking national exams, for which they study for years. Maybe the top 30 percent of the country's student population can score high enough to be accepted to the public university, which are typically more academically competitive and rigorous than the private institutions. Those who do not make the grade will not get the chance to study that year in the public university. If the student comes from a family with financial stability, then he or she may attend a private university with less academic rigor.

Learners who are socialized with this competitive academic attitude may prove to be extraordinary students in U.S. settings. Other students will be appalled by the competitive attitudes in classrooms in the United States. I have heard comments from overseas students about how different the school system is in the United States because teachers often give students a "break," allow them to use calculators instead of being obliged to memorize formulas and rules, and offer many second chances if students fail. Often they are shocked by multiple-choice tests, or surprised by bubble in answer sheets. Students have asked me incredulously if there is really one correct answer in the multiple choice tests because in their countries they have to write out answers to essay type tests.

Trying to help students succeed in the classroom is the primary goal of U.S. school systems; millions of dollars are spent on compensatory or remedial programs as well as accommodations for exceptional students, gifted students, and financially disadvantaged students. Families from other countries might look upon special education or ESOL programs negatively because "afflictions" or inability to keep up with the class are often thought of as weaknesses due to the person not trying hard enough to overcome the "disability." Participation in these programs might be seen as an insult or retribution for wrong behavior.

Teachers and students might miscommunicate due to misunderstanding nonverbal communication. Appropriate body language and use of personal space differ among cultural groups. Hispanic students might be expected to lower their eyes when communicating with elders, especially when being reprimanded. I noticed this while interacting with students from Puerto Rico and the Dominican Republic. Aside from my recent visits to Latin American schools, throughout my travels in the past, the typical prevailing attitudes I found in the poorer schools were that the teacher is the ultimate authority, is given total respect, is the main contact for the student, and is expected to provide for the needs of the student in all educational capacities. However, student behavior in the classroom appears to be changing due to numerous reasons. I have seen a difference in behavior in the schools with wealthier families. More parents are both working, and students may be supervised by a paid household employee. It is not uncommon for the students to disregard the employee's authority, and act defiantly because of the hierarchic structure of the higher status of the child in relation to the paid help. (In other words, due to the hierarchical societal structure of the student's position, he or she will not behave when the "maid" tries to assert discipline.)

As a language coordinator in a private school in Colombia with very wealthy students, I was only allowed to hire teachers who were attractive, well dressed, with perfect makeup and well-coiffed hair, regardless of English proficiency. The owner of the school informed me that the students, who were from higher socioeconomic backgrounds than the teachers, would not respect a teacher who was not attractive and well dressed. This attitude was quite different from other public school interactions that I had seen. This only exemplifies the fact that everyone comes from a different background and it is up to the U.S. teacher to discover the history of the student, and then set the standards for the classroom expectations.

Another possible difference in the school culture in the United States is when parents are expected to volunteer in the classroom and attend meetings You might find that parents from many other cultures are not involved in the school operation. The school the student came from in the home country probably will not have had guidance counselors, special education teachers, or the PTA. When parents do not interact with schools, they should not be judged as uncaring simply because they do not adhere to U.S. cultural values (Ariza, 2002). They may not know or feel comfortable with these expectations but often will be happy to learn that they are welcome to participate in their child's education.

On the other hand, I have seen communities in other countries (e.g., Costa Rica and Nicaragua) that are extremely poor, yet the school becomes the meeting place for families of the students. In addition to receiving education, the school becomes a refuge, a gathering place, and a community center where the teacher and the families support one another.

The United States has seen an influx of Hispanic/Latino children that arrive alone from countries where there is danger and violence. From October 1, 2013 to August 31, 2015, more than 77,000 unaccompanied children (UACs) from Central America made it to the United States and were dispersed into communities throughout the United States. Under US law, Mexican children will be deported back to their country but UACs (Unaccompanied Alien Children) from countries that do not border the U.S. (e.g., Guatemala, Honduras, and El Salvador) are transferred to the Office of Refugee Resettlement (ORR) within the U.S. Department of Health and Human Services to be processed. The majority of these children are released to a parent, relative, or safe friend in the US and end up absorbed in the community while their court proceedings are moving forward. They may never make it back to a hearing and thus stay in the United States ("Unaccompanied Child Migrants in U.S. Communities, Immigration Court, and Schools", 2017).

When students who are newly arrived in the United States and come from a country where they have limited or interrupted formal education, they are called SIFE or SLIFE students (students with interrupted formal education, or students with limited or interrupted formal education). They have limited reading and writing ability in their native language, and are below grade level academically (Freeman & Freeman, 2002). These students may be escaping from their home countries but the reasons for their limited education are varied: danger, war, gang activity, poverty, or inability to go to school.

> Dr. Margarita Perez, from Worcester State University suggests that we discuss students like Enrique Corona, who walked to the United States from Guatemala because of the social instability of his country. He had about 5 years of schooling in his country, but now he is living in the United States in a group home. His needs are academic as well as emotional and his extensive life experiences are not consistent with traditional American style educational settings. He is an example of a SLIFE (student with limited or interrupted formal education) student who enters middle or secondary classrooms with significant academic gaps, while possessing values and ways of knowing that are not consistent with, and are often undervalued by our schools. While teachers of ELs are asked to develop approaches to promote content knowledge and English language development, teachers of SLIFE students have additional challenges. He has both schooling and emotional needs that require a respectful and safe classroom setting environment. DeCapua, 2016).
>
> You will need to find ways to highlight their strengths and experiences—including interests in finding immediate applications to their learning. These student needs to have foundational skills built to develop their English; background experiences must be connected to the academic content they will be expected to learn. Teachers will need to facilitate existing skills and knowledge so it can be applied to the new material they will need to learn. The academic program must be culturally relevant, equitable, and strategic. Programs must provide alternative instruction such as project and thematic based learning. Teachers need to ensure the school student success team is aware of and supportive of socio-academic and socio-cultural backing that these students will need (DeCapua & Marshall, 2011).

Following are narratives from other types of Spanish speaking students in the United States: Rebecca Gonzalez, whose parents are from Cuba, shares her experience as a first generation Cuban American. She was not brought up in Miami, where many Cubans reside, yet being from a Cuban family, her parents raised her with many of the traditions that come from Cuba.

Growing up in a traditional Cuban household was very different compared to my American friends. For instance, my parents were very strict and always had a close eye on me. My family was reluctant to let me go on playdates with the other kids from school, so instead I was really only allowed to go to my aunt's house and to visit close family friends. In addition to this, my family was very strict. My mother insisted on teaching my sister and me how to clean, so from an early age, I was vacuuming and mopping the floors. However, in an effort to expose my sister and me to more opportunities in the United States, my parents joined a Country Club. Here my parents were comfortable dropping us off at summer camp so we could make friends.

To start my learning, my mom insisted on sending my sister and me to a private Montessori pre-school. The only catch was that my mother became the school president in order to keep a watchful eye on us. What was different between my upbringing and those of my other Latino friends was that my parents, although strict, did not raise us only speaking Spanish. They spoke English with us as much as possible. They were afraid that if we spoke only Spanish, we would have trouble in school. I do not think this helped us, because my parents were native Spanish speakers and not really fluent in English.

From the Montessori Preschool, I went on to public elementary school. I assimilated to it quite nicely. However, I was picked on as a child for my olive colored skin. I would always get questions and comments made to me about why I looked different. The town I grew up in was predominantly White European so most of the kids were white and only a few of us who were not. So due to being picked on, I had some trouble making friends at first.

After my eighth grade year, I transferred to a private high school and I noticed one major difference between the two schools. In public school, my teachers never really took the time to get to know me as me for the most part. I was rather short changed as well. Whether it was due to my heritage or just natural selection, I do not know. Nevertheless, I always felt like the other kids received more of the teacher's attention than I was and I felt as though teachers would purposely not call on me when I would have questions on the lesson. A lot of the time, I felt lost in assignments because of that.

Speaking English at home slightly affected me in my schooling. I had to re-learn Spanish because it was not spoken enough for me to retain it. Nevertheless, once I actually studied it in school, it all came flooding back to me and I now can read fluently and speak semi fluently.

I would like to tell future educators not to overlook students just because of a stigma that may surround their ethnic identity. Everyone is different and if students have the drive to learn, they will strive for good grades. Still, if they are overlooked, or ignored (purposefully or not) they may lose that passion for knowledge and fall through the cracks. Please make an effort to get to know your students so they feel they belong.

Stefani and Nico Castillo, Colombian/American

My name is Stefani, and I am 25 years old. My brother, Nico, is 23. My father is Colombian and my mother is American. My Colombian tia (aunt) and abuelos (grandparents) lived with us from the moment I was born (in Massachusetts) and took care of us while my mother and father worked. They only spoke Spanish with us, so our first language was primarily Spanish. We spoke English with my mother, but my mother spoke only Spanish with my father and his family. As a child, if my mother tried to speak Spanish with us, we told her no—"That's how daddy talks." My mother told me that when we were strolling in the baby carriage, if I (Stefani) saw someone with dark skin, I would say "Hola," but if the person had white skin, I would say, "Hello." My father was very indigenous looking (being of Chibcha, Arawak, and Spanish heritage) and my mother was blonde so I was born with green eyes and light golden skin, but with strong facial characteristics (high cheekbones, straight across eyebrows, and square jaw), like my father's family. My brother was born with green eyes, and very dark hair, but it turned light brown. He looks more like my mother, but definitely has the Colombian nose and cheekbones. Over the years we would frequently return to spend a lot of time in Colombia, only speaking Spanish, but as the years went on, we knew less and less Spanish, because my father spoke more and more English with us. It got to the point where it was uncomfortable in Colombia because we could not communicate in Spanish very well. We were frustrated and sometimes frightened because we did not know what our family and cousins were laughing at. Sometimes in English, we would use Spanish words—some of the errors are fossilized. (e.g., [Stefani] I still call a sweatshirt a sweater, because my dad did that.)

When I was 12 and my brother was 10, my parents got divorced. Sadly, our Colombian family connection was broken and our daily Spanish stopped, but we still spoke with native-like Colombian-Spanish and American English accents. Every year we would go to Spanish immersion schools, where we would confuse people because we sounded like native Spanish speakers but were no longer fluent. We were always placed in the wrong Spanish classes in high school. They would put us in the native Spanish speaker classes because we knew too much, and sounded like native speakers, but we were English dominant and floundered in the native Spanish classes. We wanted to be there because our friends were in those classes, but we did not know Spanish and did not do well and our grade point averages suffered as a result.

We are now adults, but culturally we still identify as Colombian. We feel very comfortable with other Spanish speakers because they are our "gente" (people). One very sad fact is that we feel we have to keep trying to prove we are Hispanic. Even though our name is distinctly Colombian, unless we have tans, our skin is too white, and we are denied being what we are. People ask us to "prove it." I (Stefani) feel such a loss because I lost my Colombian family, my roots, and I can't even claim what I am. "I feel incomplete". Whereas Nico identifies highly with being Hispanic/Latino (definitely Colombian), and associates daily with his bandmates, who are all native Spanish speakers and he feels like they are family. (He calls it "tribal.") He speaks Spanish with them, and is very proud about his constantly improving fluency. He is very comfortable whenever he is in Spanish speaking countries. But no matter the case, both kids feel and self-identify as being Colombian/American.

The more typical everyday cases that teachers will see in their classrooms are the students who arrive speaking only Spanish, and the English will be in different levels of proficiency, if any. In my classes (as an elementary bilingual/ESOL teacher) I had students who knew no English, some had a good grasp of English, or others had a variety of different levels. Some students will have excellent home language academic skills, while others will have interrupted education or perhaps no educational background at all, for one reason or another. One student had a Hispanic surname, but spoke no Spanish. The trick is to determine by assessment where your student is from, the background of the student, the academic and literacy level of L1 (the native language), and the literacy level of English. From that point, you will be able to adjust your instruction. Families will be from any number of Spanish speaking countries, for any specific length of time. Parents will be poor, middle class, or well off. You will hear all kinds of stories, backgrounds, and cases. Try not to assume, but try to inquire as deeply as you can where your students are coming from, geographically, emotionally, as well as academically. Assess your student in the home language. If possible, ask the student to write or tell a story in the L1 (you may need an interpreter.) Language experience approach will work for any age level of your students as long as it is reported via the home or native language.

Ms. Carol's Class

Fifth-grade teacher Ms. Carol moves in two different worlds in her classroom as she works with students on a reading and writing assignment. In one world are her students whose native language is English, and in the other are the Hispanic immigrant children who are in various stages of acquiring language proficiency. Although Ms. Carol has a very limited knowledge of Spanish, she is expected to meet the grade-level needs of her students, including content area academics for the immigrant children who struggle just to understand the enormous complexities of a second language. The students themselves have a great disparity in their educational backgrounds and academic ability, including one girl who has just arrived from El Salvador and does not know letter sounds or words in either English or Spanish. Another Hispanic student has just been tested as "gifted." Not surprisingly, his academic work is on grade level as well, yet the school records still have him designated as limited English proficient. He may remain inappropriately tagged by an educational system that does not have the time or resources to update his status as he moves further along in his academic career.

The Hispanic children in this class are quiet, attentive, and very well-mannered while listening to their teacher give directions. They begin the assignment, many working in pairs. A student's hand goes up as an indication that he needs help with a concept, and Ms. Carol is at his side discussing the student's work in English. A quizzical look tells her that the student still doesn't fully understand. Another Spanish-speaking student sitting nearby explains the concept again, this time in Spanish, and a smile spreads across the face of the boy who had not understood his teacher's first effort. Other Hispanic children try to help the preliterate girl from El Salvador with letter sounds and picture cards she is making, but they have their own assignments to complete. The teacher has no classroom aide or adequate school assistance to help work with this new girl.

Ms. Carol is not alone in her frustration in meeting the complex needs of her students, both academically and culturally, in this diverse classroom. This same scenario plays out in schools throughout the United States. Teachers find themselves under increasing pressure to address the near-impossible task of teaching English learners, while also attempting to meet the unrealistic demands of high-stakes accountability and misguided legislative agendas generated in the present U.S. political climate. Often classrooms are comprised of students from a number of different countries and cultural backgrounds. The teacher struggles not only to understand these children but also to address their very diverse academic and emotional issues.

FINAL POINTS

- Know your students. Do everything you can to find out about their backgrounds, and what they know in both English and the home language.

- Make sure your student is a Spanish speaker before assuming that is the home language. They could speak Portuguese, or one of the indigenous languages from South or Central America.

- Give your student an assessment in the home language to see what they know. It must not be done in English, unless you are trying to assess English proficiency.

- Find another person who can help you assess your learner in the native language.

- Just because the student sounds fluent in either language, don't assume the student has the same abilities in both languages. Sometimes the student will surprise you with how proficient he or she sounds in one domain, but may not be able to read or write.

- Do what you can to provide differentiated learning that suits the individual.

Discussion Questions and Activities

1. Students from Spanish-speaking cultures are called a variety of names such as Hispanic, Latino/Latina, Chicano/Chicana, and so on. If someone is from Guatemala, he or she might be called Guatemalan and may not even speak Spanish. If you were to ask the individuals what ethnic group they are from, they might answer "Mayan." If a student is from Paraguay, he or she might be Guaraní. What are some ways to determine what your students prefer to be called? If you were from the United States, what would you call yourself?

2. You are planning to have a conference with some of the parents of your Spanish-speaking students. Describe some strategies you would use to make the family feel comfortable. How would you greet them? If they didn't speak English well, how would you make your points clear? If you have an interpreter, what protocol would you follow to make the family feel at ease?

3. Discuss multicultural strategies you could implement to show your Spanish-speaking students that you value their heritage. How could you get involved or show interest in their community functions and activities?

4. Make a plan to invite community members from the cultures that your students are from into your classroom. Create five steps you could take to create a plan that would work for your classroom needs. (Example: Create questions for the visitors that the students would like to know about; make sure the speaker is bilingual; find out what the students want to know; have students draw pictures or cut out magazine pictures, or find pictures on the Internet that show what the students would like to be when they grow up; invite those people to speak (firefighter, police, teacher, doctor, etc.))

5. Think about what you will do for the SLIFE student who is in your class. His age is the same as the other students, but he has only had a few years of official schooling. What is the first thing you will do to assess his knowledge? After finding out what he knows, what steps will you take to create a culturally relevant plan for him to succeed in your class?

Resources

- **Educating Hispanic Students**
  http://crede.berkeley.edu/pdf/epr8.pdf

- **Helping Hispanic Students in Your Classroom**
  http://www.unc.edu/world/2011Seminars/LANC_Article_4.pdf

- **Hispanic Heritage Teaching Resources**
  http://www.smithsonianeducation.org/educators/resource_library/hispanic_resources.html

- **PBS Learning Media**
  https://www.pbslearningmedia.org/collection/latino-americans/

- **Hispanic Learning Styles**
  https://www.ericdigests.org/1996-4/hispanic.htm

- **Culture/Learning Styles**
  http://www.ascd.org/publications/educational-leadership/may94/vol51/num08/The-Culture~Learning-Style-Connection.aspx

- **Music and Learning Styles**
  http://www.colorincolorado.org/article/music-and-language-learning

- **Santeria**
  https://video.nationalgeographic.com/video/cuba-santeria-pp

- **Early Learning Literacy in Spanish**
  http://www.colorincolorado.org/article/early-literacy-instruction-spanish-teaching-beginning-reader

- **EL Language Learning and Special Needs**
  http://www.colorincolorado.org/article/addressing-ells%E2%80%99-language-learning-and-special-education-needs-questions-and-considerations

- **Culturally Responsive Instruction**
  http://www.colorincolorado.org/teaching-ells/creating-welcoming-classroom/culturally-responsive-instruction

- **Jigsaw Reading Rockets**
  http://www.readingrockets.org/strategies/jigsaw

- **Learn English**
  http://www.internet4classrooms.com/learn_eng.htm

References

Ariza, E. (2002). Cultural considerations: Immigrant parent involvement. *Kappa Delta Pi Record 38*(3), 134–137.

BBC—Religion: Santeria. (2017). *Bbc.co.uk*. Retrieved April 19, 2017, from http://www.bbc.co.uk/religion/religions/santeria/

Brigham Young University, ProQuest information, learning, ProQuest Information, & Learning Company. (2004). *Culture Grams* (Vol. 1). ProQuest Information and Learning Co.

Cartwright, L., & Shingles, R. R. (2011). *Cultural competence in sports medicine.* Human Kinetics Publishers.

Cauce, A. M., & Domenech-Rodríguez, M. (2002). Latino families: Myths and realities. . . . Latino childrenand families in the United States: Current research and future directions (pp. 3–25). Westport, CT: Praeger/Greenwood. http://dx.doi.org/

DeCapua, A. (2016). Reaching students with limited or interrupted formal education through culturally responsive teaching. *Language And Linguistics Compass 10*(5), 225–237. http://dx.doi.org/10.1111/lnc3.12183

Freeman, Y., & Freeman, D. (2002). Closing the achievement gap: How to reach limited-formal-schooling and long-term English learners. Portsmouth, NH: Heinemann.

Hispanic Culture—Latin American Culture—Spanish Culture (2017). *Explore-hispanic-culture.com.* Retrieved April 14, 2017, from http://www.explore-hispanic-culture.com/hispanic-culture.html

Latino Religion. (2017). *Huffingtonpost.com.* Retrieved April 19, 2017, from http://www.huffingtonpost.com/news/latino-religion/

Motel, S., & Patten, E. (2017). *VII. Changes in the characteristics of the Hispanic population, 2000 to 2010. Pew Research Center's Hispanic Trends Project.* Retrieved April 14, 2017, from Pew Hispanic Center, 2012 http://www.pewhispanic.org/2012/06/27/vii-changes-in-the-characteristics-of-the-hispanic-population-2000-to-2010/

Unaccompanied Child Migrants in U.S. Communities, Immigration Court, and Schools. (2017). *migrationpolicy.org.* Retrieved November 16, 2017. https://www.gcir.org/childrefugeesmigrants

CHAPTER 19

JAMAICANS IN THE AMERICAN SCHOOL SYSTEM: A NEW UNDERSTANDING OF LANGUAGE AND CULTURE

Angela Rhone

KEY POINTS

- Students of color in your classroom might not be African American
- Students from Jamaica and other cultures have concerns and difficulties with American culture, Standard English, and discerning appropriate cultural behavior.
- Even though students of color may speak English as a first language, teachers may think these students need to study English as an additional language.
- Students might be referred to remedial intervention if they don't speak Standard English, and are from a culture where English is a main language.
- Jamaican and Caribbean students from other cultures have an extended family that will help one another.

As a Caribbean teacher who teaches predominantly American preservice teachers in a university in South Florida, my issues in teacher education are centered, around the areas of race, class, gender, and immigration in American society. My purpose in this chapter is to look at the concept of being black in the American classroom. Being in the United States and working with predominantly mainstream teachers, I have noticed that when they see a "student of color" in their classroom, they typically assume that these students are native (U.S.) blacks and that they are from an African-American heritage. However, this assumption is not always true. A "student of color" could be African American, Caribbean, from the continents of Africa, Europe, and also from South or Central America (Glennie & Chappell, 2010; Morse, 2005; Waters & Ueda, 2007).

As a Jamaican professor who has taught undergraduate- and graduate-level courses such as the foundations and history of Multicultural Education, Race, Class and Gender, and Educating the African American, I am now attempting to look at the various experiences of Blacks of the diaspora, as they travel and settle in the United States. My first group of individuals to look at would be my own people and I was determined to write about how I can inform teachers about this complex group of students and their parents whom they will see in their classroom.

These factors are important due to the huge population of Jamaican students in the United States, and the massive immigration myths and basic (possibly incorrect) assumptions that many teachers carry with them as they look at students from the island of Jamaica (and others) as they enter the school system in the United States. Acculturation to the United States is a long process that is subject to the individual's personal experience (Hines, 1997; Kirkwood, 2002).

Teachers who have first generation Jamaican students in their classrooms will encounter tales and stories about the Jamaican language and the culture. I offer suggestions to teachers about culturally relevant pedagogy, especially about the Jamaican students in the U.S. classroom today. According to the 2010 U.S. census, there were 965,355 Jamaican Americans in the United States(http://factfinder2.census.gov/faces/tableservices/jsf/pages/productview.xhtml?pid=ACS_10_1YR_B04003&prodType=table). We have Jamaican students all over the country, so this population deserves attention. It behooves us to understand these students, who grow up here with us.

Basic Assumptions

The first assumption for many who have black students is that all black students are alike. Yes, they are alike in many ways. They come in an array of different skin colors that give no clue as to where someone originates. However, for many Jamaican students, the fact is that although their skin color may be any shades of color or "black"(or even white) their "psyche" has never experienced entrenched ethic conflict or racism among blacks, whites, and other ethnic groups on the island they came from. Many consider themselves only as Jamaicans, but it is only when they reached the shores of America that they began to see or hear or feel or experience the negative remarks about their color, and they really understand stereotypes and their implications, socially and politically, in this country.

In this case, mainstream teachers need to understand that although there are distinct social class differences in Jamaica that are reflected in the schools, the churches, the geographical locations, and the schools they attended when they were in Jamaica, the idea of color was not so much a part of the structural conditions under which individuals lived (Vickerman, 1999). Growing up in a society where political parties and leaders are black, their ideas of blackness do not tie-in or relate with their expectations of who they can be. The question then is: How should the mainstream teacher in the United States, without prior knowledge of Jamaican society, have the ability to accommodate these new students to eventually become model citizens of their new country? I hope this question will be answered by the end of this chapter.

Experiences in the Classroom

Vignettes that exemplify the experiences of black Caribbean students in the pre-k-12 educational system in the United States can be enlightening as well as hurtful. These stories will clarify some of the perplexities that people of color face on a daily basis in the United States.

Vignette 1:

A teacher in a K-12 class was teaching about "stereotypes" common to different ethnic groups in the United States. She listed the stereotypes on the board as the students gave them to her. Finally, she asked the students to tell her what stereotypes are common with regard to Blacks/African Americans in this country. She received many responses from the class and listed them on the board. However, she noticed that there were two black students in the class who were not responding to her question. Therefore, she asked them individually to tell her what stereotypes go with being black in this country. They both answered that they knew nothing about that subject. She later told me that the students were not able to answer the question because they were both from Cape Verde Islands and had only been in the country for a few months.

REFLECTION QUESTIONS

- Why could the students not answer her question? Are all black students supposed to know the answer to this question?
- Do all black students know the stereotypes that are given to ethnic groups and, most importantly, to what extent do pre-K through 12 teachers acknowledge the differences, country of origin, culture, language, and lifestyle between black students in their classroom?
- She is a black woman in my class. She is automatically assumed to be of African/American heritage. Should this knowledge be of interest to teachers?

Vignette 2:

This scenario of basic assumptions about students of color in the American school system cannot be attributed only to white or black American teachers, because foreign blacks who teach in some of these schools also assume that all blacks are of African-American heritage. For the first generation of black students born in this country, the situation can be more of a learning experience for both the professor (the K-12 teacher) and the black students in the class. For example, this scenario has happened to me several times. Many black students in my class have no detectable island accent, thus I assume that they are all of African-American heritage. Much to my surprise, as the semester goes by, many of my black students would state to me that they are of Caribbean descent and although they were born in this country of Caribbean parents, they consider themselves as Caribbean students and not as African-American students. I have noticed that their knowledge and their assimilation and acculturation to the African-American culture and history are nonexistent. In the effort to maintain their Caribbean roots and identity, their parents have created this strained relationship between African Americans and Caribbeans. Thus, many of them have grown up in a culture where their friends and their extended families are very much Caribbean despite the fact that they are black and were born in this country. Are these black-American or Caribbean students in the eyes of their teacher? The two following vignettes are from the experiences of two first generation Jamaican students in a college class at a university where I presently teach.

Vignette 3:

I recently came up from Jamaica. This was not an easy transition but my mom assured me that I would have fun here, but she was wrong. I left behind my home, friends, and way of life. Your school system is different from mine in many ways. While in math class I felt ridiculed by the teacher and my classmates, I had solved the math problem the "wrong way" even though I got the right answer. Why is it the wrong way? Because it isn't your way? I would have preferred if the teacher examined my work and then talked to me. I already feel like an outsider in this predominately white school; I do not need to feel chastised in class too. Maybe I could show you my method. Who knows, you might prefer it.

Another uncomfortable instance was a time in my English class. Apparently, the word here is spelled "color" and not "colour," which the teacher explained. However, she explained it to me like I was an idiot. In Jamaica, I was a straight "A" student but here I am considered inadequate. I want to learn in this country but I want to be treated with respect like an American student. I am not stupid or shy. I do not talk during class because many of the students and teachers see my accent as a sign of lack of intelligence. Jamaica is a beautiful place full of such a rich and kind culture. I have heard the same about America, but show me. . . let me see that. Educate, encourage, and enlighten me to see differently, learn about me, and I will learn from you.

Vignette 4:

Upon arriving from Jamaica at the age of 17, I was placed in an ESOL program for students that cannot speak English very well. At home, I was forced to speak proper English. The hardest challenge for me was to adapt to a new schooling system that I was not accustomed to. I know how to speak English. It is my native language. I also know how to speak Patois. But my accent and the stress I put on words is different than the way American say things.

Language Differences

A major language difference might occur among Jamaican students in the classroom and more importantly between teachers and Jamaican students in your classroom. For example, according to Madden (2009):

> The official language of Jamaica is Jamaican Standard English. The true Jamaican language that was developed on the island does not have an official name. It is sometimes called Patois, Creole, Black English Vernacular or ungrammatical English (Barrett, 143–145) Children speak Patois until they enter school and then they learn Jamaican Standard English.

The implication here is that many Jamaicans students who come to the United States and enter the k-12 school system are placed in ESOL or remedial classes, not because they do not understand the English language spoken, but because the teacher does not understand the vernacular that they bring to the classroom. Many will understand the teacher as he or she speaks English, but understanding Jamaican Patois is much more challenging for the teacher. Just because the child does not speak in a way the teacher can understand does not imply that the student should be placed in a remedial class, laughed at, or made to feel inferior. There should not be a deafening silence in the classroom when he speaks. For many Jamaican students and their parents, a basic assumption that comes with the move to the United States is that the student should be placed in an ESOL or remedial classroom. These words imply shame and worthlessness for the new immigrant student and the parents. Jamaican children struggle with new expectations of the school system in the United States compared to their expectations in the schools in Jamaica. He explains that children not proficient in English find the U.S. school system more challenging and often end up in remedial classes.

Added to the misunderstanding of the language differences that many Jamaican students experience in the classroom is that of cultural differences between their home country and the U.S. school system. Brown (2009) refers to Jamaican students who do not look teachers in the eye. This act is considered disrespectful in the United States. He explains that in the Jamaican culture, staring down a teacher might be misconstrued as disrespectful (Kirkwood, 2002).

The concept of family, and whom the teacher should call if a Jamaican student needs to be reprimanded, becomes another issue. For the Jamaican student, family is not limited to household members, as the children of many Jamaican families are often shifted from household to household for support. In many cases, teachers must not look at this as a deficit in the family, but rather as a different family dynamic where even nonblood relatives remain active for the Jamaican child.

Many parents come to this country to give their children a better life. This better life entails the teacher taking a primary role and responsibility in the raising of this child who is placed in his/her care. Until the parents get into the educational system and understand it, many parents do not show up when they are called by the teacher. This is not because they do not care; this is how the Jamaican culture is entrenched in the idea the teacher "knows best."

Because many Jamaican parents still believe that corporal punishment is the "be-all" of everything, and many work hard to be here, the teachers sometimes are very scared to call Jamaican parents to reprimand their children. Many Jamaican parents reprimand their kids physically and they end up in front of the guidance counselor who is against corporal punishment. The question is then, how should a teacher handle such situation?

On the other hand, because of the existence of social class in Jamaica, sometimes many of the students who come to the K-12 system in the United States are from middle and upper class backgrounds. Those students attended schools in Jamaica that prepared them socially, mentally, and academically to do well in this country. Having a child like this in your classroom will not demand much of your time because this child will adapt easier to the demands of the school system. However, it is incumbent on the teacher to be aware that moving from one culture to the other might cause discomfort to the student. It may take weeks or months for the signs of discomfort by the student to manifest obvious symptoms. At that time, it is important for the teacher to speak to a guidance counselor at the school.

Suggested Pedagogy for Teachers

Realize that the Jamaican child comes with a unique worldview (e.g., from Africa, Europe, Asia, or England) in a sense that many countries have shaped his or her country's economic, social, and political educational systems. When a Jamaican student arrives in this country, he or she is faced with socializing with students who have a much "narrower" point of view of worldwide history and culture than those who are from Jamaica. While teachers must acknowledge the vast diversity Jamaican students have, teachers can incorporate some of this knowledge into the classroom discussion, especially things like Jamaican music, sports, culture, history, and Jamaica's impact on the United States and the world.

One way teachers can be relevant to the student is to constantly involve parents in educational and social activities and try to find another Jamaican student in the school or the community to act as a mentor for the student. This is very important, as teachers will realize that many students arrive in this country un-accompanied by parents and thus having other Jamaican students or parents is essential for their assimilation in the American culture.

Another way for teachers to associate better with foreign students is to attend workshops or seminars on the issues that foreign students will face in the United States. These seminars will provide insight and knowledge on how foreign students think, act, and behave, especially when they are away from their countries and, on many occasions, away from their families and parents. This will help teachers to better understand how foreigners think and the best way to approach teaching them in a more culturally relative way that they can relate to. Teachers can act as role models for the students and as a guide to acclimating them to their new culture and environment.

Teachers must understand that Patois is not rough speech and usually carries a negative connotation. The official language is English, which reflect the British colonial rule. If you listen carefully, you will hear the English that the student speaks. It is perhaps the rhythm of the spoken words or the accent that is unusual. There is not much written language for Patois. Where it can be spoken, it is not easily written.

Many of these new students will not write in Patois, but in Standard English. The implication here is that as the child remains in the class and plays and talks with his friends, his language, and his accent begin to change as he becomes immersed in the culture.

It is hoped that this information will be of interest to many. As an island, we are far more complicated and complex than just Reggae music. We are immigrants here trying to do well and we can become well-rounded citizens with the help of teachers, community leaders and informed parents.

FINAL POINTS

- Teachers are expected to take a more parental role.
- Parents may not know they are expected to be more involved with the class.
- Teachers can be cautious about explaining the laws of corporal punishment to parents.
- Teachers should make an active effort to understand Patois.

Discussion Questions and Activities

1. In a group, create a visual of the diaspora of students of color. What countries and language will they be from and relate to?
2. Choose a cultural group from a country that interests you. Within this country, there will be a group or areas where most of the people are of color. Research the country and group, and come up with a list of cultural characteristics that are different from the mainstream culture (e.g., Limon, in Costa Rica, has a primarily black population that are distinct from Ticos, the white Costa Rican. Or, on the coast of Colombia, you will find more Afro-Hispanic people who are very different from the traditional Hispanic Colombian.).
3. Cultural identity study: Research the cultural differences that you might see in your classroom regarding students of color from other countries. Try to make a comparison with the cultural characteristics, you will find with African-American blacks. It will be very interesting to have participants from these groups work with you on this project because when people begin to reflect upon themselves and their cultures, great insight is often exposed.

Resources

Language-English or Patois
http://jamaica-gleaner.com/gleaner/20130602/focus/focus4.html

How to speak Jamaican Patois
http://jamaicanpatwah.com/b/how-to-speak-jamaican-patois#.WQQ7i9ryu00

Understanding Jamaican Culture
http://education.fiu.edu/jamaica/docs/understanding_the_jamaican_culture.pdf

Understanding and Speaking
http://education.fiu.edu/jamaica/docs/understanding_the_jamaican_culture.pdf

Writing Jamaican
http://www.omniglot.com/writing/jamaican.php

Jamaica Guide

Jamaican Language, Culture, Customs, and Etiquette

http://www.commisceo-global.com/country-guides/jamaica-guide

Helping Jamaican Students
http://www.helpinghandsjamaica.com/

Jamaica tag along
http://www.colorincolorado.org/book/jamaica-tag-along

Jamaica and the substitute teacher
http://www.colorincolorado.org/author/juanita-havill

Culture of Jamaica
http://www.everyculture.com/Ja-Ma/Jamaica.html

References

Glennie, A., & Chappell, L. (2010, June). Jamaica: From diverse beginning to Diaspora in the developed world. *Migration Information Source.* Retrieved from http://www.migrationinformation.org/Profiles/display.cfm?ID=787

Hines, D. (1997). The acculturation of Jamaican children in the American educational system. EDRS.

Kirkwood, T. F. (2002). Jamaican students of color in the American classroom: Problems and possibilities in education. *Intercultural Education13*(3), 305–313.

Madden, R. (December, 2009) Madden, R. The historical and culture aspects of Jamaican Patois. Retrieved from: https://debate.uvm.edu/dreadlibrary/Madden.html.

Morse, A. (2005, March). *A look at immigrant youth: Prospects and promising practices.* Retrieved from National Conferences of State Legislatures website: http://ncsl.org/research/immigration/a-look-at-immigrant-youth-prospects-and-promisin.aspx

Vickerman, M. (1999). *Crosscurrents: West Indian immigrants and race.* Oxford University Press on Demand.

Waters, M., & Ueda, R. (with Marrow, H. B.) (Eds.). (2007). *The New Americans: A guide to immigration since 1965.* Cambridge, MA: Harvard University Press.

CHAPTER 20

MUSLIMS, FOLLOWERS OF ISLAM AND SPEAKERS OF ARABIC

Rachida Faid-Douglas

Afsana Chowdhury and Essam Abdelrasul Bubaker Elkorghli (Personal Communication)

KEY POINTS

- Culture and religion: Facts to better understand Muslim students in the American classroom.
- Clarification: Realities to know about Muslim students in the United States.
- Addressing the religious needs of Muslim students in the classroom.
- Understanding differences about food, dress codes, religion, culture, and language.

As I (Eileen Ariza) sat on the plane on the way to the conference, three lovely young women were approaching their seats. They were speaking animatedly in a language I did not readily recognize. One of the women who sat down next to me struck up a conversation. "Unbelievable that this flight was delayed 4 hours." "I know," I answered. "I am exhausted already." We chatted about where we were heading (Las Vegas) and where we both lived (Fort Lauderdale). As a language teacher, I was interested in the language they were speaking and I asked her what it was. She replied, "Arabic." I said, "I thought so, but I wasn't sure. Those sounds from the throat are really difficult to make." She said, "Yes. Even though I was born and brought up in the United States, I have been speaking it since I was a child. But you know, if I were traveling with my husband, I would be afraid to speak Arabic. We would stick with English. Since I am with just my girlfriends, we are not afraid. People don't seem to pay attention." "I am so sorry," I said, and I felt shame.

This chapter appears in a very special format. It is personalized, narrated by Dr. Rachida Faid-Douglas, a mother of elementary school children in American schools, and an educator herself. I also invited one of my preservice teaching students, Afsana Chowdhury, to respond to the question: What do mainstream teachers need to know about Muslim students? Additionally, another student in the United States, from Libya, writes his thoughts.

Following are their candid, sensitive, and at times, almost painful responses.

Dr. Rachida Faid-Douglas: I want to address the needs of a Muslim student as a teacher in a mainstream classroom, both from the perspective of an individual from a Muslim and Arabic background and as a mother of four children attending public schools. As a teacher, I feel I am in a position of power, but as a parent, even with all the laws on my side, I feel powerless and at the mercy of teachers to help my kids grow and blossom in public schools. I also would like to share with you the experiences of those many Muslim peoples from around the world to whom I am connected through mosques (church in Arabic) or as neighbors.

As a teacher in a K-12 setting, and even as graduate student, I was looked at as a strange creature. I always had to justify myself and felt compelled to show that I was smart, educated, and qualified to teach English to Speakers of Other Languages (ESOLs). I do not know how other minority teachers feel, but I always feel as if I am filling a quota for the affirmative action law, although I am respected by many Caucasian colleagues.

As a parent, I feel the alienation and shame that my kids share with me on a daily basis. I have to constantly clarify, assure, and teach my kids that their heritage and culture count too. They have to learn to express themselves and invite their teachers to include their ways and respect their celebrations. For example, every academic unit could include cultural objectives that infuse beliefs from students' cultures and concepts to make them feel included and cherished. It angers me when I see teachers look at me as an ignorant parent because I come in a veil (Hijab—a headscarf) and sometimes it seems that I am dressed in too many clothes. The first impression I feel they get is that my child is not good enough and that I am not good enough. I am a professional teacher and educator who has been teaching since 1986, both abroad, and in the Unites States, since 1995. I have taught everything from kindergarten to college and have trained many teachers in the United States since 1998. I try to speak to them about meeting the needs of diverse students and they look at me as if they do not understand my accent, or what I am trying to convey. It used to anger me, but I learned to hand them my business card and state my professional credentials, so that maybe I would be respected by my children's teachers.

My daughter wears the Hijab, and in an honors class, she was the only one who looked and dressed differently among all the other students. She was the only one who was asked, "Are you sure you belong here?" My daughter said she empathizes with her African American friend, who shared a similar incident of feeling singled out. My daughter understands that most students who dress like her are ESOL learners.

Another incident made my second-grade daughter, Huda, worried about wearing the veil when she turns nine. She said that at her school, there was an article about the Muslim dress code. The teachers asked the kids how it would feel being a Muslim. Students responded that they would feel weird and nervous. Huda said that she only had to wear the veil to the mosque and she wished her teacher would have said something to clarify the misunderstanding.

HIJAB as a Dress Code

Hijab is headdress that women wear to express modesty, one of the most important objectives of Islam. Muslim women wear Hijab so that society can value them for their intellectual abilities and not as sexual objects. This is the stark opposite of the incorrect assumption that Americans make, which leads people to think Muslim women are oppressed, but the Hijab is a choice a woman makes to express her individuality and freedom in an intellectual, rather than sexual way. Hijab is not only for women, but also applies to men.

Most women in America take off the Hijab because they want to fit in or they feel rejected by others and society. People always ask me if I wear this Hijab in the shower or if I sleep in it. I have been asked if I am bald. One Muslim girl told me that her teacher always takes off students' hoodies and hats as they walk in, and the teacher was going to pull her Hijab off, but exclaimed, "Oh my goodness! That's not a hoodie! You can keep that on!" The young girl shared that her sister suffered bullying from peers because of her Hijab and she asked the teacher for help, but was ignored.

Teachers need to explain to the class about Hijab; most girls who wear it do not participate in class. In addition, sometimes teachers ask students to wear shorts to field trips, which puts great pressure on the parents to go along with the school, even if is against their religion. Otherwise, they have to exclude their kids from these educational experiences.

Another incident that shows how much fear there is from women who wear the Hijab is when a 9/11 memorial event took place at a high school and there was a moment of silence for all the victims. Suddenly, they fired blank cannon. To my daughter's surprise, most students looked at me in fear. I just laughed. Even a Caucasian Muslim student cannot escape stereotyping. For example, my daughter's friend, Nora, explained that she does not feel like she fits in and she is being stared at because some kids tell racist and terrorist jokes about Muslims.

My five-year-old son, Mohammed, is always frustrated with having to correct mispronunciations of his name by his teachers. He emphasizes that the "h" sound in his name is pronounced softly. Mohammed means "the praised one" and we gave him the name of the most compassionate, merciful, enlightened man, just like Buddha. Mohammad was named one of the100 famous people of the last century. He is the prophet of Islam who existed 1400 years ago and is still alive in many people's hearts in the Middle East, China, Africa, Europe, and the Americas. He was gentle and a liberator of many slaves. Unfortunately, this name has been associated with terrorism. Mohammed was a great and sweet man who loved unconditionally. He liberated slaves and women from the darkness and tyranny that existed in the Arab peninsula and around the world at that time. Mohammed was peaceful but had to defend himself and his followers from oppression and ignorance.

Teachers need to be conscious of unwittingly harming children whose names happen to be on the most wanted list. Please do not Americanize their names from Mohammed to Mike or Matt, for example, because of fear. Make the effort to pronounce all students' names as accurately as possible because it is crucial to the development of the student–teacher relationship and the student's very identity.

Diversity in the Muslim World

Many of my daughter's classmates are Muslim from India, Pakistan, or even China or a country in Africa with a Muslim population, but because they do not wear the veil, it is difficult to identify them as Muslims. As you may imagine, many of those students are afraid to wear the veil, or even admit that they are Muslim. These are very bright young people who just do not speak up about their cultures and Islam. They may get angry, or depressed, and go home and express that hatred or misunderstanding from schools. Teachers may appear naïve or ignorant, and may not realize that their knowledge about Islam and the Muslim peoples' diversity is very little or wrong. Muslim peoples are diverse and they make up 2.2 billion of the world's population ranging from China to the Ivory Coast, from Kazakhstan to remote areas in Africa. Muslims live in many parts of the world in Europe, Canada, the Americas, Australia, and Indonesia. They may look very different racially, culturally, and in the ways they carry themselves; they can be Caucasians, Africans, Asians, Arabs, and in between. Unless they are identified by a dress code, there is no way one can associate them as Muslims. My advice to teachers is to ask about their students' cultural and religious backgrounds and use them as spokespeople to enrich their classes, so painful situations can be avoided. For example, one day, a Caucasian Muslim student from Bosnia told me that his teacher made insensitive remarks about Islam. The teacher didn't realize the student was Muslim, and he was offended, but he couldn't say anything because he wanted to fit in.

My son, Adam, looks Hispanic, and teachers don't realize he's Muslim. It hurts him when his culture is insulted in text books and in class in front of students. When he is identified as Muslim, people look at him when someone mentions Osama Bin Laden. Kids say Osama Bin Laden was Muslim and was bad, so they conclude all Muslims are like him. This is an incorrect assumption, so the teacher must clarify that Bin Laden was not a true Muslim and he does not represent Islam and Muslims.

Culturally savvy teachers take the time to inquire about students backgrounds. One such teacher was considerate of religion and asked the Muslims in his class if it was okay to play Christmas music. Of course the students agreed because Islam has no problem with other religions. On the contrary: true Muslims embrace other religions.

Teacher's Advocacy and Positive Role Models

Often, teachers misguidedly state falsehoods about Muslim religion or Arabic background. When this happens, students may feel the need to defend their faith. It may provoke feelings or anger or students may tune out. Not surprisingly, they may speak up and argue a different view to raise awareness in class.

As I mentioned, students often are afraid to identify themselves as Muslims. For example, my son told me that there were two Muslim girls in his class from an Asian country who removed their religious head covering because of peer pressure. Sometimes, teachers' egos interfere when students express themselves and clarify their backgrounds or religion, which may result in teachers ignoring or subtly shutting the students down. Instead of taking this attitude, teachers should encourage students to express themselves in class and sponsor interfaith or multicultural clubs. Averse from the Quran stresses this fact, "Oh human being, we created you as many different nations, man and woman, to connect." It is highly recommended in Islam to learn about others. Imam Hussein, grandchild of Prophet Mohammed, stated that there is no poverty like ignorance.

My daughter Nora's experiences are positive because she is very strong and knows who she is. Her sense of identity is well developed as she was educated for 5 years in Muslim countries where she was respected, which is the norm in the main culture. For her, being a Muslim student is great because she gets to meet many diverse students who embrace Islam. Part of her positive experience is due to her self-confidence in her identity and religion. As a result, she expresses herself in front of teachers and students, and defends or brings the Muslim contribution to the table. She finds that most students are more receptive and curious than teachers. She wishes that teachers were more open and willing to learn about all cultures. Her world history textbook quotes "facts" about Muslims that are biased, especially when it comes to women's issues. For example, it quoted a verse in Quran, but it was not complete and it gave the impression that God said that men are superior and better than women, but left out a crucial verse that showed they are equal but they have different roles. Nora added the other part of the verse to shed light on the bias. Students who have qualities like this need to be encouraged to be leaders and, as teachers, we should empower others to share information about their culture to feel accepted and valued.

Textbook and Classroom Interactions

In the school textbook, there is little information about Muslim cultures and practices, which in most cases, spread ignorance. In language arts classes, stories about all other cultures appear, but usually exclude Islam or Arab cultures. If something appears, it usually distorts reality and shames the kids. For example, one middle school teacher presented a lesson about slavery and showed a graphic clip of Arab rulers with women, supposedly the slaves. That image was pointless and offensive, and gave the wrong idea of Islam, even though that ruler wasn't Muslim. People assume that since he is an Arab, therefore he is Muslim. Arabs are Christians, Jews, and Muslims.

Teachers need to scan textbooks to see if there is anything about Muslims from around the globe. Any topic can be connected to Muslims and their contributions to human civilization range from Algebra, to Alchemy, and other sciences. Certain textbooks touch on Muslim cultures, but they don't spend enough time discussing the ideas. Students may feel different because when Christians talk about their religion, and Muslims comment about theirs, students make comments like, "that's weird." Teachers can be vigilant about inappropriate comments that students may make, and use the opportunity as a springboard for conversation and enlightenment. I was once told by my daughter's friend that her social studies teacher showed a picture of the prophet Muhammad in class. She told him that it was against her religion to show the face of the holy prophet, and the teacher just ignored her.

Many times major holidays are discussed and celebrated in class but others are ignored. My daughter was in her second-grade class and said, "I was so sad today when my teacher showed Hanukkah, Christmas, and Kwanzaa, but did not mention Eid at all. It made me feel mad. My mom got me books about Hanukkah and other celebrations." I would like to see more celebrations of our rich cultures.

When teachers make comments that show their lack of knowledge about Muslims, it puts the Muslim kids in uncomfortable situations where they feel that they have to defend their culture and struggle to fit in class without prejudice. My daughter stated it succinctly: "We do not want people to pity us, but we need to raise awareness about this issue of stereotyping and scapegoating the Muslims. We want to change the perspective on Muslims being viewed as merciless and ignorant. Sadly, this perspective is propagated by the media, which broadcasts extremists who claim the right to do terrible things in the name of Islam. In every religion there are extremists, but the targeted religion for criticism is Islam and that is simply not acceptable because we are all humans and go through the same emotions like others, and that's what unites us."

Food

As a parent, I would love to see teachers and administrators make sure to help kids get food that is *Halal*. A Halal meal means that the meat is slaughtered in a kind and respectful way to the animal. It is very similar to Kosher. A Moroccan first grader said that he has hard time eating a decent lunch and always has to make sure that food does not have meat, pork, or any derivatives like gelatin. He was so compulsive about it that the kids insulted him, calling him "pork kid." Many students complain that they always end up eating cheese or peanut butter and jelly sandwiches or sometimes a vegetarian meal. At my daughter's school, she tells me she is tired of eating lasagna for the whole school year. Sometimes she feels like eating meat sauce. Parents always appreciate teachers who watch out for their student's food.

I am from Morocco, and taught there and in France. I started teaching high school students in the neighborhood of East Flatbush Brooklyn in 1995. I was so nervous to be in front of a class of 30 Hispanic students with whom I had no clue how to relate. I remember feeling terrified and awkward. I had worked with Arab and Muslim students for years before that, and I had no problem relating to them as I knew my role and their role as students. I felt threatened and scared, so I had two choices. I could impose my style and my values on my Hispanic student, or I could figure out the ways to reach out to them and learn humbly how to best serve them. One principle that guided my life as a teacher was to treat others the way I want to be treated. I want to be loved and respected, so I did that with my new students. I believed that kids are kids and they all want to be treated with dignity, respect, and love.

I started to relax and accept the fact that I was ignorant about this population and that I would learn about them, and ask them to teach me. One of my spiritual guides, AL Hassan bin Ali said; "Teach others your knowledge and learn theirs, so you will bring your knowledge to perfection and learn something you do not know." I began to formally learn Spanish with them. I introduced new vocabulary in English and asked them to teach me the same words in Spanish. I carefully wrote the words down and had them to help me pronounce them correctly. I helped them the same way with English. Students felt proud and empowered. With time, I was invited to their social events and churches and I made sure to go with them and I used those as teaching and writing activities. We compared and contrasted American and Hispanic celebrations. As a result of working with them, I became enriched and felt fulfilled as I reached my teaching objectives.

Muslims are educated by sitting in a circle facing each other so the teacher can become a student. We always try to bring what we learn about the universe to our hearts and try to feel the truth and think about the knowledge presented to us about the universe, geography, cultures, peoples of the world, and their languages. We believe that we are all brothers and sisters in Allah (The Divine in Arabic language), so we think and try to feel their pains and their triumphs, their wars, peace, and accomplishments. In the Muslim philosophy, we are invited to understand and relate to what is said about others' civilizations, literatures, and sciences.

Muslim education places the needs of the child first to reach useful knowledge, to help students become better people. Musa Al Kadhim, a grandchild of prophet Mohammed, stated that the faithful try to achieve wisdom and it is one's duty to seek knowledge. Mohammed himself stated that Muslims should learn from the cradle to death and to make meanings of the knowledge that will bring them closer to the divine. As a result they are civilized and at the service of humanity, as we are all brothers and sisters in Allah (the Divine).

As a teacher, I know it is not easy to create a rapport with diverse students because of our own limitations and fears, which lead us sometimes to become closed and rigid. We think about imposing what we know on others; therefore, we force our students to become like us, or assimilate to our values, which we assume are superior or effective. I always remind myself and am aware that I am in a position of power and that I can impose my ways on my students who are different from me. Sometimes, we may inadvertently hurt them. I know that they need to have the opportunity to become successful citizens. I know that we have to be careful to avoid making our kids hate their background, to feel ashamed about where they come from, and to disconnect from their heritage as it may not be helpful to them in America. They have to learn the skills and knowledge in Standard English, and they have to be able to compete in the mainstream society. We are responsible for providing enrichment for all students in our educational system.

Afsana Chowdhury

I'm Bengali. My parents were born and raised in Bangladesh, but I was born and raised here in Florida. I can't really provide my own perspective about Arabs because I'm South Asian and don't personally know many Arabs. Although, as side note, I believe that we do have many similarities in our cultures, regarding family relationships, respect for others, and so on.

Thank you so much for taking the time to make sure that Islam is represented fairly in your book, along with other groups. I really do appreciate it!

I just finished reading this chapter and I honestly love it! I really like that it includes information about permissible food, appropriate clothing, daily prayers, and opposite gender interactions. These things are such an important part of Muslims' daily lives, but it often does not align with the school environment and mainstream U.S. culture and society, which can create difficulties for Muslim students. From my experience, most—if not all—of my teachers never really knew about these things (and I was too shy and quiet to bring them up). Many of us are too shy to ask for accommodations (or afraid that the answer will be "No"); therefore, it is great that the information is included in this chapter so that teachers/future teachers can know about them (and hopefully initiate conversations about them so that accommodations can be made).

When I read the part about a student saying "Why do I have to be afraid to go do my student teaching because I have Arab features?" it really was relatable to me. When I have to deal with people whom I have never interacted with before (whether in stores, offices, school), I worry that I will be treated differently, or dealt with harshly, because I'm clearly Muslim.

One thing that I think people should know is that even the smallest actions or words really help A LOT, even just a smile from a stranger. Anything that shows us that we are not hated, and that we're accepted.

Many Muslims feel anxious when they step outside of their homes, especially nowadays, fearing backlash—whether verbal or physical. Often, these worries really do come into fruition, with mean looks, mean words, and sometimes even physical attacks against Muslims. Sometimes, it can seem as though almost everyone is against us, even though we know that that is not the case. Therefore, really, any small act of kindness that shows otherwise can be a breath of relief.

What also helps is when people seem to care genuinely about our beliefs and practices. Many of us do not bring up the topic because we think people just do not care. Therefore, when they ask about such things out of their own curiosity and out of their will to really understand us, it really is a great feeling. For example, most people just look at us as if we are crazy when they see that we are covered from head to toe, especially when it is hot outside, or they will ask, "Aren't you hot in that?" Few actually take the time to understand us by asking (in a positive tone) why it is that we cover up.

Concerning the student being too shy to ask for what he or she needs, I think it's really important for teachers to reach out to the student and the family, asking if they need any accommodations. However, sometimes the teacher may not be aware that a student is Muslim (some students you can tell are Muslims because of how they dress, but many are not easily identifiable as Muslim by their appearance). In such cases, I guess it would be hard for the teacher to know if they are Muslim or not, unless the student or family brings it up. However, maybe if teachers could include in their "welcome" flyers/emails something like "If your child needs any religious accommodations. . . please let me know!" I think that would be helpful, as many families are not sure what the teacher's attitude is toward Islam/Muslims or even toward religion in general.

In addition, it would help if more books or stories about Muslims were included in classrooms. Schools also often teach about holidays such as Christmas, Easter, and Hanukkah, but never Ramadan or Eid. Including these holidays in the discussion about holidays would really make Muslim students feel included, especially since we don't get days off from school for our holidays like others do for theirs. Students would be proud to share their customs, religions, foods.

Other than that, when it comes to what mainstream teachers need to know about their Muslim students, I think that you've covered pretty much everything in the chapter. The most important thing that they need to know is that to Muslims, Islam is not just a set of beliefs, but rather a way of life—everything we do is based on it.

Essam Abdelrasul Bubaker Elkorghli

Essam Abdelrasul Bubaker Elkorghli is a St. Olaf College international student from Libya. He was born on the last day of 1994 in Cairo, Egypt, being the youngest of three other siblings—two brothers and an oldest sister. He has resided in Libya for the majority of his first 17 years, except for some time spent in Egypt and The Netherlands. He finished high school in Libya in 2012 and was offered the opportunity to repeat the last two years of high school again, but at an International Baccalaureate (IB) boarding school in Norway called United World Colleges Red Cross Nordic in Flekke, Norway. In Norway, he learned Spanish and beginning Nynorsk, while taking other IB classes. His passion to learn further about Norway's history, language, and culture led him to apply to a sister program at St. Olaf College, Minnesota, where he is currently spending his third year, majoring in Economics, Norwegian, and Social Studies Education, with a concentration in Race and Ethnic Studies.

Essam is a devoted Muslim who dedicates time to worship five times a day. Besides his studies and spiritual dedication, he enjoys playing soccer, skiing, rock climbing, and writing music. He plays guitar and bass, the former being his main role in his psychedelic/hard rock band at St. Olaf College. Alongside that, he is employed on-campus as a sound and light engineer for the entertainment venue at St. Olaf College.

I asked Essam what he would add to this chapter if he had the opportunity to talk to educators about what they should know about their students, and he added the following thoughts.

People's first social interaction that occurs on a regular basis outside of home is school with the goal of making the world and the future a better place via educational reforms. Education can advocate for the equal and just rights of every individual in society, especially in more ethnically and culturally diverse societies such as the ones found in the United States; a nation cannot function without the inclusion of all its members. That is why multicultural education is a key to understanding that racism can be stopped solely through education.

Teachers of multicultural students have a big role in changing the perception of the minority culture(s) present in the classroom/school. As an example, a Muslim student who is transferring from another predominantly Muslim nation to a U.S. public school will definitely feel threatened by the looks, statements, questions, and hate acts that we all hear about in our social media feeds. Teachers should always know more about their students, their interests, backgrounds, and belief systems that they affiliate with, which in turn will allow the student to feel cared for by their teachers. That extra percentage of diversity in the classroom adds to the benefit of ideological integration by creating a culturally pluralist classroom, where the presence of minorities is celebrated and by conveying diverse perspectives on different issues through the lens of varying belief systems. This opportunity would allow the students to learn about one another, and potentially understand the differences that exist are not detrimental simply by their very existence. If Muslim students have the confidence to converse freely about their beliefs, they will feel safe within their own identities without feeling that they are being judged negatively, and they will enjoy being a welcomed part of the discussion. As a result, the classroom will feel like a safe haven for the Muslim students because their identities are not distorted, misaligned, or underrepresented.

Teachers have a remarkable privilege—they possess the potential to change student behavior for the better through various pedagogical practices. However, with that privilege, comes an awesome responsibility also, where teachers must educate themselves about the histories and experiences of target groups within the context of the society that they inhabit. In addition to their teaching responsibilities, they need to educate themselves about the cultures of the students in their classrooms, and become familiar about the norms and beliefs about how law and public policy may adversely or beneficially affect these groups. The teacher must be an ally of the students.

Teachers can be allies and show that their classrooms are no place for hatred and prejudices by interrupting negative or hurtful behavior, and obstructing prejudiced remarks or actions by communicating their expectations to the class. With this opportunity, they can then initiate awareness-raising activities and provide knowledge and communication that will build positive opportunities in the classroom, like inviting people from the community to share their lives, talk about being Muslim, and what practicing Islam means. This could go along with other community members who want to share their beliefs and customs as well. Students are usually fascinated by learning new things about people and will be the greatest ambassadors of goodwill once they know personally what the subject is about.

Something many teachers face is the need to be cautious when speaking about religion or politics in a way that sounds like they are proselytizing a belief. When teachers want to be allies to a group that is vulnerable and stand against negative representation of these groups, often times someone might present an argument that is dubious, but the teacher cannot refute it because it goes against the student's religious belief. For example, a student stated in a government class that legislators should criminalize homosexuality, and when asked by the teacher why he believed that, the student stated that it is against God's words in Christianity.

Trying to refute that statement might lead to great argument. Therefore, it might be best if the teacher confirmed that everyone has the right to his or her own beliefs, but a student must have a right to exist and worship according to his and her own doctrine, without penalty, and we cannot assume that all students are thinking the same way. We may not diminish ideological pluralism. Students have the right to believe as they do, but they must be guaranteed freedom and safety to do so, especially on an educational campus.

For the past decade and a half, one could easily argue that the biggest group who has experienced the most scrutiny is Muslims. More than one billion people follow Islam, whether they grew up as Muslims or have joined the religion by themselves (e.g., Mohammed Ali, Michael Jackson, Cat Stevens, John Coltrane, Mike Tyson, Kareem Abdul-Jabbar, and Malcolm X (Adams, 2000). Obviously, this includes Americans. The most impactful representation of Muslims is done through media that always has an agenda, which is typically to create an enemy that has delayed the nation state from achieving its prosperous goals. Nowadays and in recent years, Islam is being blamed for any act of aggression, such that when we hear a shooting happening, the first question we ask is what was the perpetrator and what is his religion. Every time I am with my Muslim friends and we hear another report of a crime, I hear it silently pray, "Please don't be a Muslim; please don't be a Muslim. . . please don't be a Muslim. . ." Then we hear the reporter say the name and hope the religion is not Islam. The media does not help with reducing prejudice against Muslims, as the only time they bring an image of an Arab onto the screen, they are terrorists, or loud, and aggressive. (I remember them doing this with Colombians, when they were the targets for all things bad in the criminal world.)

Classroom Tips

Teachers who happen to have Muslim students in their classroom with Arab names (or other types of names they are not familiar with) should learn their pronunciation correctly. I have heard teachers and professors who have said, "Oh my god, I will never be able to pronounce this name," or "What would you like to be called, because this will be impossible for me to pronounce." This is an understandable challenge that teachers face when they meet students with non-western names that use non-Latin letters (similar to Asian name pronunciations) However, if teachers do not take the initiative to speak to their students after the class and learn their name and how it should be pronounced, the targeted students will always feel that they have been marginalized because of something they cannot control—their name and its sociocultural connotation.

Devoted followers of Islam are required to pray five times a day at certain periods of time during the day. A student typically cannot ask the teacher if they can go out and pray, even though that it is a necessity for them. However, an alternative idea could be implemented. Since it has been proven that meditation as a classroom intervention can reduce rowdiness and negative behavior, then schools can dedicate a large room where students can go freely and meditate, while the religious ones can go and practice their religion in peace. In this way, it allows students to pray during recess or in between class breaks if time permits. The place should not be referred to as a prayer room, per se, since that has religious undertone. If I may share an interesting anecdote to show how the scrutiny of Muslims is persistent, whenever I tell people that I am going to pray, they react in a way that makes me feel that I am too religious or too weak to handle things on my own, without the reliance on a higher power. On the other hand, whenever I say, "I am going to meditate" instead of pray, people state their interest in how I do it, and how I find the time for such commitment, even though the spiritual benefit of actual meditation and prayer are nearly the same.

Teachers of students who come from Arab countries should develop an understanding that each culture has its own modes of social interactions. For example, when Libyans greet one another, they kiss each other on the cheek twice, and sometimes more, depending on the acquaintance. In certain countries in the Gulf (UAE, Yemen, ,people (Arab men) rub each other's noses in a tribal sign of respect. Men and women do not usually touch (no shaking hands nor kissing on the cheek). By the same token, when a teacher is meeting with a student of such culture in a one-on-one setting, the student might not be looking at the teacher directly in the eyes, and instead would be looking down, humbly. That is not because the student does not care about what the teacher is conversing about, rather it is a modest way to show respect for a prestigious figure, such as a teacher. This is not applicable to only Arabs; Somalis and many other countries in the Horn of Africa have the same approach to communicating with the teacher. The teacher should be aware of such types of social interactions, because it guarantees equal treatment and comprehension of all students.

The Language Learner

The role of teaching English as a second or new language can be quite inter sectional and complex, more than what the teachers would expect it to be. Now I will be using myself as a hypothetical example to show how convoluted it is to teach me a language. I am a native Arabic speaker; I started learning English in seventh grade. This means that when I was learning something in English, I would translate it to Arabic and see the English language through the lens of a Semitic language structure. Five years later, I started learning Spanish in Norway through the IB program, I initially saw Spanish through the lens of English—translating sentence structure and syntax from English to Spanish—which was not the best decision, Germanic and Romance languages have different syntax in their writings. However, Spanish and Arabic have more similarities in grammar, vocabulary, and sentence structure than Spanish and English do. Therefore, writing in Spanish became easier once I started thinking in Arabic instead of English (my thinking in Spanish was not developed yet). Lastly, came the part where I started learning Norwegian, and as you might guess, I see the language of Scandinavia through the lens of English because they are similar in many instances and they came from the same language group—Germanic. Overall, it is important for a teacher to understand the syntax of the ESL student's language and see if there are major differences between English and the mother language, while paying a close attention to formal mother language and "street" mother language. Because when I saw Spanish through the Libyan Arabic, it did not make sense, but when I saw it through the formal Arabic, Spanish made much more sense and was easier to learn Spanish. Therefore, what language should I see through if I were to learn Russian?

I thank teachers who try to understand students like me. They are the lifeline that leads us to the future.

TABLE 20.1 Middle Eastern Students Reference Chart—Chart by Lindsey Laury	
Characteristics	**Practices**
Values/Customs	• Families primarily paternalistic • Opposite sex relationships usually not permitted • Strong familial bonds • Elders play a vital role in family dynamics
Schooling/Classroom Environment	• Traditionally authoritative and teacher centered • Complex alphabet system • Calligraphy style writing • Family and students are often very private and humble • U.S. customs such as the Pledge of Allegiances and holiday activities may conflict with cultural obligations
Culture	• **Semitics**—describes Middle Eastern culture and languages • May be from any racial or ethnic background • Israeli students typically adhere to European traditions
Religion	• Can be Arab, non-Arab, Muslim, Christian, or Jewish • Koran (Qur'an) is used (written in Arabic) • Contains Five Pillars as principal tenets of Islam • Participate in fasting and frequent prayer (five times per day)
Clothing	• Women regularly wear a *Hijab* or *chador* (scarf) to reflect modesty • Robes often worn to cover the entire body excluding head and feet • Men frequently wear a *keffiyeh* to promote cultural pride
Touch/Socialization	• Islamic law typically dictates gender segregation in schools • Can be offensive to immediately offer hand during greeting • Cross gender touching is inappropriate • Premarital intimacy is forbidden
Diet	• *Halal* is used to describe food permitted for consumption • Pork or pork derivatives banned from consumption • Foods with animal shortening or using trace alcohol are banned (e.g., vanilla, Dijon mustard, marshmallows, or certain candies)

FINAL POINTS

- Arabs, Muslims, and followers of Islam all widely different and should not be lumped into one group.
- People who are Muslims might not speak Arabic.
- People who engage in questionable acts might be reacting in accordance with their culture, and not their religion (Muslim).
- Islam is a nonviolent religion. Terrorists who commit violence are not practicing Islam.
- Teachers should take every opportunity to learn about their students, and use teachable moments to spread understanding of a gravely misunderstood religion.

Discussion Questions and Activities

1. Every day at the same time, Maha takes a small rug to the restroom and stays there for about 20 minutes. She washes her face, hands, arms, and feet. What do you think she is doing and why? How can you work around this daily routine so that Maha does not miss instructional time?
2. What elements of Arab/Islamic beliefs will probably clash with American cultural beliefs? Can you see similarities or differences among Semitic/Middle Eastern groups? How might they be different from American philosophies or values?
3. Explain what miscommunications might occur as a result of our misunderstanding one another? How could you address these issues in your classroom? Can you think of ways to use these instances as teachable moments in your class?
4. Because the Arab/Muslim/Islamic world is so broad, choose four cultures and create a table that compares and contrasts customs, rituals, clothing, and religious practices. Write a summary of your findings and come to some conclusions. Present your finding to the class.

Resources

Muslim students struggle to practice faith in the schools
http://www.deseretnews.com/article/765554027/Muslim-students-struggle-to-practice-faith-in-US-schools-seek-accommodation-for-religion.html?pg=all

Islamic resources
http://www.ohio.edu/orgs/muslimst/resources.html

The Muslims in the classroom
http://www.bestteacherusa.net/muslim.htm

Connecting with EL families
http://www.colorincolorado.org/principals/family/connecting/

Classroom diversity
http://www.colorincolorado.org/fromtheheart/31184/

Looking into harassment
http://www.colorincolorado.org/ellnews/36389/

Engaging strategies
http://www.colorincolorado.org/pdfs/guides/Engaging-EL-Families.pdf

Lessons learned from immigrant families
http://www.google.com/url?sa=t&rct=j&q=&esrc=s&frm=1&source=web&cd=6&ved=-0CDwQFjAF&url=http%3A%2F%2Fwww.colorincolorado.org%2Farticle%2F38575%2F&ei=asADU-5ajFIWFkQeQhIHQDw&usg=AFQjCNFx_Sw6jkRxpmDp5B7TOfgcEwdxHA

Islam in the classroom
http://www.slj.com/2013/05/resources/islam-in-the-classroom/

Why some Muslims wear the Hijab
http://blogs.edweek.org/edweek/learning-the-language/?page=82

Muslims struggle for acceptance
http://www.usatodayeducate.com/staging/index.php/pulse/despite-gains-many-muslim-students-still-struggle-for-acceptance

References

Adams, M. (2000). *Readings for diversity and social justice: An anthology on racism, antisemitism, sexism, heterosexism, ableism, and classism* (pp. 312–318). New York: Routledge.

CHAPTER 21

CHINESE, JAPANESE, SOUTH KOREAN, AND INDIANS

Linglan Cao, Ke Xu, and Eileen N. Whelan Ariza

This chapter discusses Asians as a cluster, but every Asian culture is different. As with every chapter, they are written for the mainstream teacher to better understand students from Asian cultures. We write about Chinese, Japanese, Korean, and Indian students because of the large number of students in the United States.

KEY POINTS

- Mainstream classroom teachers can develop knowledge and awareness of certain Asian countries' history, language, culture, and educational systems.
- Teachers can learn pedagogical approaches and skills that respond to cultural conflicts of Asian students in mainstream classrooms.
- Mainstream classroom teachers can develop intercultural awareness and competence to interact and teach people of different Asian cultural backgrounds.
- Understanding the background of Asian languages can help teachers predict and treat errors that will be produced by speakers of these languages.
- Cultural mismatches (different cultural connotations) can cause much discord and misunderstanding between cultures in the classroom.

Definition of Asians

We need to clarify what we mean when we use the term "Asian" or "Asian American" in this book. According to the *Asian American Almanac* (1995) and Lai and Arguelles (2003), Asia and the Pacific Islands have at least 30 different ethnic groups with their own religions, cultures, and national heritages. Four major groups of Asian Americans are East Asian (Chinese, Japanese, and Korean), Pacific Islander (such as Hawaiian, Samoan, Tongan, Tahitian, and Guamanian), Southeast Asian (Thai, Vietnamese, Cambodian, Laotian, Burmese, Filipino, Indonesian, Malaysian, and Singaporean), and South Asian (Indian and Pakistani). Groups of immigrants will often settle in ethnic clusters, such as the Samoans in California, Chinese in San Francisco area, or the Hmong in Massachusetts. In this chapter, however, we will only focus on East Asian Americans and Indians but we strongly suggest that teachers make an effort to get to know the cultures of the students in their own classrooms.

East Asian groups that include Chinese (from mainland China, Taiwan, Hong Kong, Macau, and Singapore), Japanese, Korean, and Vietnamese have settled throughout the entire United States, and teachers will quite likely find representatives of these groups of students in their classrooms. Additionally, numerous South Asian students from India and Pakistan are studying and living in the United States. They are usually multilingual and may even speak English as a native language, or one of their native languages. English is a global language, however, and speakers from different cultures converse through diverse dialects, with distinct stress, pitch, and intonation patterns in their spoken language. These deviations from standard American dialects can interfere with the American English speaker's understanding and can cause miscommunication. Later in this chapter, we will discuss factors that will help mainstream teachers understand these cultural groups.

The United States has always been a place that receives many immigrants each year. According to the 2010 U.S. Census data, the foreign-born population in the United States was 38,517,234, which included 10,652,379 Asians. The ACS (American Community Survey) data revealed that the U.S. population in 2010 included 39.9 million foreign-born residents including 4 million Chinese (including Taiwanese), 1.7 million Koreans, and 767,000 Japanese. Asian immigrants come to the United States for a variety of reasons. They come to reunite with family, to work, to learn English, and to seek higher education. One of the biggest motives for coming to the United States is for education. Since Asian countries such as China and South Korea began allowing their students to study abroad, there has been a rapid growth of the number of students coming to the United States to study.

Some Asian students come to America from stable countries, with excellent educational backgrounds and monetary resources, but others come as refugees from war-torn countries with interrupted studies (Brand, 1987; Tillman & Scheurich, 2013). Many U.S. born Asians have lived in this country for generations. Because of these differences, we will see much disparity between Asians new to the country and those who are born in the United States. Additionally, some newcomers come from literate societies (such as the Japanese Chinese, Korean, Taiwanese, Indians, and those from Hong Kong) who are highly skilled with abilities that aid in adaptation to the American work force. Yet others, such as the Hmong, rural Laotians, or Montagnards from Vietnam and some Cambodians, who originally had no access to written language, are not likely to bring skills that are easily transferable to the American labor market (Lee, 2015; Trueba & Cheng, 1993; Trueba, Jacobs & Kirton, 2014).

Shared Cultural Traditions and Values in Asia

East Asia has a historical and cultural coherence as a civilization that came to extensively use the Chinese writing system through which many of the ideas and values of Confucianism were absorbed, and associated legal and political structures of government were established. Buddhism was imported and spread widely (Holcombe, 2011).

Confucianism

Overview:
An ethical and philosophical system developed from the teachings of the Chinese philosopher Confucius, after developed into a set of beliefs to educate common people. Confucius' central message was one of leadership by moral example. He also believed that the key to a good society was individual self-cultivation of moral principles and internalization of virtue (Holcombe, 2011). The core of Confucianism is humanism. The Confucian tradition was instrumental in shaping Chinese social relationships and moral thought.

Influence on Asian Society:
Confucianism influences Asian society profoundly. The values taught by Confucianism include harmony with the family and community, hard work, and a strong emphasis on education (Kim-Rupnow, 2001). Additionally, it promotes respect for elders and those in authority.

Asians are taught to respect the hierarchy in their families, in school or work, and among the people with whom they interact (Bond, 2010; Lee, 1996). In general, Asians expect children or anyone relatively younger to act modestly in front of their elders. For example, when seated at the dinner table, the younger ones may not eat until the oldest person at the table begins, and cannot leave the table before the elders. It is always part of Chinese manners or etiquette to let elders enter a door, and take a seat first. When handing something to an older person, two hands are always used. Older people, or those in power, are never called by name; instead, they are addressed by a title. Teachers in Korea are called *Sonsaengnim*, in Japan *Sensei*, and in China *Laoshi* (old master). All the three versions, however, derive from the same two Chinese characters: 先生, which literally mean "born earlier."

Students rarely address their teachers by their first name, but rather by their last name, which is followed by honorifics such as *Sonsaengnim, Sensei, and Laoshi*. An older brother, or any older male, is called *oppa* (for girls) or *hyeong* (for boys) in Korea and *dage* in China, which simply means older brother. Asian languages, especially Korean, demonstrate this hierarchy. Different forms of a word are used, depending on whether the speaker is talking to well-known peer or an older person.

Everyone in the family has his or her own roles. After the parents, the person with the most responsibility and power is the oldest brother. He is the one who is responsible for taking care of his parents as they grow older. He also becomes the head of the family, should anything happen to his father.

Buddhism	**Overview:** Buddhism is an ancient religion that originally came from India but later spread into China, Korea, and Japan (Holcombe, 2011). It is based upon the teachings of Sakyamuni, or Buddha. Buddhists believe that people are born over and over again, and that all their actions have an effect on their next lives (Kalman, 2009). **Influence on Asian Society:** Buddhism is the world's 4th largest religion with around 350 million adherents all over the world, with a strong influence in Asian countries such as China, Japan, Korea, Vietnam, Thailand, Burma, Malaysia, and Singapore. Many of the holidays and customs in these countries come from Buddhism. Although Christianity is widely practiced, many families in these countries still follow the Buddhist rituals on holidays. Jacobs and Kirton (2014), and Yao and Trueba (2000) explain that Chinese Confucianism and tradition, coupled with Indian Buddhism, have greatly influenced East Asians. Confucian principles focus on ideals such as respect for elders, deferred gratification, respect for authority, the value of discipline and educational achievement, self-control, and familial responsibility. When a student does poorly in school, it is more likely to be seen as a lack of will or motivation than of educational ability. In response, parents may react punitively and increase restrictions on the child. Disorders such as learning disabilities or depression are interpreted as a lack of motivation or as being sick and are seen as shameful. Therefore, great care must be taken to explain these problems to Asian parents so they will realize that professionals can help solve the problem, along with parents' cooperation (Kleinman & Good, 1985; Scior, Kan, McLoughlin, & Sheridan, 2010).
Collectivism	**Overview:** The value of harmony within community and family is practiced in everyday life. Decisions are not made alone. Family welfare is considered more important than individual welfare. **Influence on Asian Society:** Formal education is valued, and academic success is related to family integrity. Success brings honor and prestige, whereas failure incurs shame (Lee, 1989; Shen & Mo, 1990). In the workplace people are not addressed by name but by their title, which denotes their standing within the bigger system. Grown children often live at home, even when they finish university. Sometimes after marriage the wife goes to live with her husband's parents. Parents are consulted even if the children are not living at home. To make a decision alone, without consulting others in the family, would be considered selfish (Kim-Rupnow, 2001).

Conformity to Authority

Asian-American students tend to conform to the ideals of the authority figure, and they are usually more dependent on each other than American students. Asians will be more responsive to reinforcement from teachers and will expect a well-organized, quiet, and well-structured educational environment (Baruth & Manning, 1992; Klein, 2012). Schools are seen as an institution where educators are highly respected and where parents should not interfere. For this reason, Asian parents might believe that educators who expect parental involvement in their children's education are incompetent (Lee, Mock, McGoldrick, Giordano, & Garcia-Preto, 2005; National School Public Relations Association, 1993).

Formality between Teachers and Students

In the United States, we appear to be informal; this misconception can be confusing to others who understand clear lines of formality between teacher and student. Some teachers expect the students to interact with the class, and students are graded according to their class participation. Asian students are not usually comfortable with speaking out or drawing attention to themselves, and they may be hesitant and shy about speaking in class. Standing out or being chastised can be particularly distressing to the Asian child. Listening rather than speaking, speaking softly, and behaving modestly are valued by Asian societies. A teacher cannot accurately judge the student's knowledge by how often the student raises his or her hand to participate in class (Baruth & Manning, 1992; Yuan, 2011).

American school values reflect the culture at large, which espouse traits such as independence, individuality, competition, and self-actualization. Trueba and Cheng (1993) and Castells (2011) explain that Asians often see their self-identity in relation to the group, family, or society, which is a direct contradiction to American values. Self-esteem and confidence are undermined when cultural values clash. As with students from every culture, the disparity between home beliefs and school beliefs may be great (Lee, & Bowen, 2006). For example, unlike the Asian student, it is not unusual for an American student to challenge authority and question teachers. Teachers can mitigate these types of conflicts by creating classroom activities that do not force the students to behave in ways contrary to their upbringing. Peer tutoring and group work will promote natural conversational interaction with native English speakers. Involve the students' family and community support system in the educational experience to provide assistance in language and cultural learning. Finally, teachers must not assume that all students have the same background knowledge that American students have. Not everyone has experienced birthday parties, dressing up for Halloween, Easter bunnies, or even fire drills.

Other Shared Cultural Traditions and Values

Frequently, Asians are stereotyped as the "model minority" or as "whiz kids" and are seen as having special family and educational values, based on Confucian ideas, that lend to their success. However, Lee (2015) and Siu (1992) maintain that the high level of educational achievement of Asian Americans is more likely due to the interaction of cultural and family values with social factors than to natural superiority or being a "whiz kid." The problem with being labeled a "whiz kid" or "model minority" is that real problems are masked and individual problems may be overlooked. If we assume these students are automatically going to be high achievers, we may unintentionally neglect them and later encounter delinquent behavior and inadequate academic preparation. Learning disabilities that are overlooked, language barriers, and misunderstandings of the U.S. school system may impede success (Li & Wang; 2008, and Shen & Mo, 1990).

To help the teacher understand Asian Americans, Baruth and Manning (1992) and Trueba, Jacobs, and Kirton, (2014) suggest that the best way is to become familiar with the Asian cultural values, traditions, customs, home life, and support system of their students. Showing interest in their native languages and encouraging parents to maintain the use of the native language in the home will help the students in several ways. Students will realize that the teacher values their native heritage; at the same time, using the native language at home will give English learners a rich foundation of language that they can later translate into English. Classroom teachers can collaborate with ESOL teachers and use interpreters with limited English speaking parents.

Cultural Features of China, South Korean, and Japan

Many societies in East Asia have historically been part of the Chinese cultural sphere. The languages of East Asia break into separate national traditions, Chinese, Japanese, and Korean, which belong to at least two wholly different language families. It is the shared use of a common written language, rather than the spoken one, that gives East Asia much of its cultural coherence and distinctiveness as a region (Holcombe, 2011).

Major religions in this region include Buddhism (mostly Mahayana), Confucianism or Neo-Confucianism, Taoism, Chinese folk religion in China, Shinto in Japan, Shamanism in Korea, and recently Christianity in South Korea, Japan and China. The Chinese calendar is the root from which Japanese and Korean calendars are derived.

China	
Cultural Tradition and Values	Traditional Chinese culture consists of a wide range of social values and principles, primarily based in Confucianism, Buddhism, and Taoism.
	Chinese traditions play an integral role in everyday life for every person. It is at the very core of Chinese culture and revolves around values and how people interact with each other. It gives a sense of personal identity and sense of self-worth. In China, the social structure is formal and hierarchical. They know where they fit in the structure, abide by the rules there, and play the roles they are expected to play. There is no crossing into other areas. One's individual reputation is very important for the Chinese and they will avoid doing anything that may damage it. They also look more at the group collective than at individualism. They are more prone to look at how their acts affect the whole instead of how it affects them personally. They are more willing to give up and sacrifice for the greater good of the family, the organization or the society. These traditional values help them solve common human problems for survival and become the roots of tradition that Chinese people find important in their day-to-day lives.

Qian (2011) lists five elements featuring the core value of Chinese traditional culture:

1. high value placed on spiritual over material aspect of life; on education and family;
2. emphasis on the role that each individual plays in relation to a family and the society; the sense of responsibility and honor, justice, honesty, and righteousness;
3. emphasis on courtesy, decorum, and the sense of propriety;
4. maintenance of ethics, virtues, integrity, benevolence; filial loyalty to parents and personal loyalty to the employer and friends;
5. pursuit of harmony, which is a complete ideological system consisting of principles such as the Tai Chi philosophy and the yin-yang dialectics that advocate modesty and moderation in handling things and relationships, and avoid going to extremes and using excessive force

According to Confucianism, in order to maintain social order, one needs to follow the Three Cardinal Guides (ruler guides subject, father guides son, and husband guides wife) and the Five Constant Virtues (benevolence, righteousness, propriety, knowledge, and sincerity). More specifically, the family is the cornerstone of any society. As such, harmony between the ruler and subject, father and son, husband and wife is critical to achieving social stability.

Based on these principles, ancient Chinese sages and philosophers established an ideological system that sought to maintain social order and attain a harmonious equilibrium in the world.

Language

Chinese is a family of closely related but mutually unintelligible languages. These languages are known regional languages, dialects of Chinese, or varieties of Chinese. China is a nation bound by one official written language, Mandarin. However, 56 ethnic groups speak 129 languages (excluding thousands of vernaculars and dialects that come from these 129 languages) and use 17 written languages (Xu, 2012). Thirty percent of the population cannot speak Mandarin. Mandarin is shaped and based on the Beijing dialect and some other northern dialects in China. It is not spoken as the first language in many parts of China, but rather has to be learned in schools or from the media. This is important for mainstream teachers to know. We cannot assume all Chinese students speak the same language.

All varieties of Chinese belong to the Sino-Tibetan family of languages, and each one has its own dialects and sub-dialects, which are more or less mutually intelligible.

	S. Korea
Cultural Tradition and Values	Korean culture is greatly influenced by Chinese Confucian tradition, and characterized by extraordinary homogeneity (Lee, 2008). All Koreans speak one language, use a unique and indigenously developed alphabet "hangul," and belong to the same racial stock—part of the Altaic family of races. Due to the family-centered Confucian social ethics, in addition to other traditional cultural legacy such as folkloristic Shamanism, which stresses emotion and affections in interpersonal relations, Koreans usually place much value on family and family-related matters in their lives. They place great emphasis on • education, • personal and familial relations, • personal cultivation, • self-improvement, spiritual and psychological discipline of the self, and • a harmonious personal relationship among individuals. They place great importance on harmony, cooperation, consensus, and social solidarity among members of an organization. This contrasts with the Western emphasis on competition among the members of an organization and may be the chief factor determining the distinctive characteristics of organizational dynamics in Korea and other East Asian countries (TSI, 2013c).
Language	The Koreans are one ethnic family speaking one language. They share certain distinct physical characteristics, which differentiate them from other Asian people including the Chinese and the Japanese, and have a strong cultural identity as one ethnic family. The Korean language is spoken by more than 65 million people living on the peninsula and its outlying islands as well as 5.5 million Koreans living in other parts of the world. The fact that all Koreans speak and write the same language has been a crucial factor in their strong national identity. Modern Korea has several different dialects including the standard one used in Seoul and central areas, but they are similar enough that speakers/listeners do not have trouble understanding each other (Kwintessential, 2004).

	Japan
Cultural Tradition and Values	Much of the culture of Japan has been adapted from that of China, although it has also been greatly influenced by Western countries over the past century. Japanese society is extremely homogeneous with non-Japanese people (mainly Chinese and Koreans) accounting for only around one percent of the population. The family is the basic unit of society and respect for the elders is of great importance. The group is regarded as more important than the individual and social hierarchy is strictly observed, with respect and deference shown to older and more senior people (Somervill, 2012).
	Education is highly valued in Japanese society, and academic achievement is held in great esteem. The importance of hard work and perseverance is instilled into Japanese children from an early age and this remains a fundamental belief throughout adulthood.
	The concept of "face" plays a part in relationships (being embarrassed or ashamed). Much of the behavior adopted by the Japanese is based on making sure that no one loses face. The Japanese tend to be more formal and polite and less physical and personal in their everyday dealing than "westerners." To avoid losing face, the Japanese rarely say "no" directly, nor ask a direct question or give a direct order. Equally, "yes" may not always mean they agree.
	The two main religions that are practiced in Japan are Shintoism and Buddhism, or a mixture of the two.
	Japanese youth are increasingly westernized. The older generation, however, still adhere to cultural traditions. Here are some general cultural norms:
	• The traditional form of greeting is the bow, although foreigners are expected to shake hands. • It can be seen as impolite to introduce yourself. If possible, wait to be introduced. • It is considered respectful to add the suffix "san" to someone's name, and especially respectful to add "sama." • Nonverbal communication is very important and complex. Be aware of your facial expression, tone of voice, and posture when talking. • The oldest person in a group is always revered and honored. In a social situation, they are served first and their drinks are poured for them.
Language	Japanese is spoken almost exclusively within Japan, although it is rarely spoken in any other countries. There are many regional dialects spoken, but there is a standard version of the language called hyōjungo. The Japanese language has few sounds compared to many other languages.
	Written Japanese combines three scripts—*hiragana* (similar to the Chinese cursive script), *katakana* (derived from Chinese characters) and *kanji* (also imported from China). Both Japanese style (vertical columns from right to left) and Western style (horizontal rows from left to right) methods of writing are used (Angloinfo, 2013).

Linguistic Issues of English Learners from East Asian Countries

CHINESE	
Overview	– Chinese belongs to the Sino-Tibetan language family. – Chinese word order is similar to English. The verb comes before the object. It is also completely uninflected, having no tense or plurals or any grammatical modification of word endings. – Chinese is not as much a respect language as Japanese or Korean, since it does not have extensive use of honorifics. It is also monosyllabic. Every Chinese character (written symbol) is pronounced as a single syllable and is a discrete unit of meaning (Holcombe, 2011).
Grammar	– Chinese students often fail to choose the appropriate sentence pattern in English based upon the type of verb to use in speaking and writing. This is especially true with negative statements and questions. They are not used to having to add an auxiliary verb besides using the word "not" to turn a positive statement into a negative one if the verb of the sentence is an action verb. This is because in Chinese they only need to add the word "bu" (not) before the verb to turn it into a negative statement. – They often hesitate about whether they should use "Do you. . .?," "Are you. . .?," "Does she. . .?," or "Is she. . .?." In Chinese, the only thing they need to do to convert a positive statement into a yes/no question is to add one word "ma" and a question mark to the end of the sentence, no matter who or what the subject is, whether it is one or more than one person, or what tense it is. There is no need to use an auxiliary verb or invert the Subject–Verb order. – They may have problems forming "Wh-" questions in English, because in Chinese it is very easy to convert a positive statement into a "Wh-"question. They only need to take out the part they are asking about and fill the gap with the question word.
Missing Copula	– In Chinese, there is no need to use the verb *to be*. – Chinese learners may produce a sentence like "I hungry," "She tired," or "The book in the bag."
	(The following paragraphs are based upon Guo's article published in 2008)
Gender Confusion	– In spoken Chinese, there aren't separate gender pronouns (e.g., he, she, and it, all sound the same, "ta"; his, her, and its, "ta de"). – When Chinese speakers speak or write in English, they often forget to use the appropriate gender pronouns. They mostly default to the masculine versions "he" and "his," which can lead to awkwardness when they refer to woman using "he" or "his." Example: **"He is one of the most talented women I have ever known."**

Singular/Plural Noun Confusion	– In Chinese, there are not separate singular and plural forms for nouns. The context is used to distinguish between singular and plural. – For instance, if someone said "one cat" in Chinese, cat is singular, but if someone said "many cat," cat is plural. There is no separate plural form for cats in Chinese. – When Chinese people speak or write English, they tend to forget to make nouns plural, resulting in awkward-sounding phrases like "we have three dog." They need to be told clearly that in English, if we are to use a noun that is countable, we must choose either singular or plural form of the noun so that they will not produce a sentence like "I am teacher" or "She has book."
Subject–Verb Agreement Confusion	– In Chinese, there is no such thing as verb conjugation to match with the corresponding subject. In English, however, they are all necessary. We say "I like Chinese food," "he likes Chinese food," and "they like Chinese food." – In Chinese, there are not separate forms for "like" and "likes", so one would simply say "He like Chinese food."
Verb Tense Confusion	– In Chinese, there is no such thing as verb conjugation to denote tenses. The context is used to distinguish between past, present, future, and all the other various tenses. – For example, there is a single word in Chinese that means "to run." If you want to use the present tense, you simply say "I run." If you want the past tense, you have to say something like "yesterday I run," where yesterday provides the requisite context. Moreover, if you want the future tense, you have to say something like "tomorrow I run." Therefore, when you are grading your students' writing in English, you will understand the errors your Chinese students will make. Common Verb/Tense Mistakes: • What does she do now? (i.e., What is she doing?) (wrong tense) • We will cancel the meeting if it will rain tomorrow. (wrong tense) • He has read the book last Saturday. (wrong tense) • She good listener. (missing copula, the verb "to be") • Where you find your car? (missing auxiliary, missing "did") • I wish I have wings. (indicative instead of subjunctive)
Omitting or Inserting Articles	– Chinese learners have difficulty using articles, such as "a," "an," and "the" because in their mother tongue there is no need for articles in front of nouns. – They often forget to place the appropriate article when speaking or writing English. You may often hear them say "I went to post office" or "She likes movie." – Sometimes, they insert articles where they are more than unnecessary simply because they are not sure whether those are needed. Thus, we get bloopers like "the God blessed America" or "you gained the weight last month."

Confusing Prepositions	– It is always a great challenge for the nonnative English speakers to master the correct use of prepositions such as "at," "in," "on," "to," "into," "onto," and so on.
	– This part of speech is especially problematic for Chinese because there isn't such a strong distinction among different prepositions in the Chinese language.
	– To English speakers, "he got a job in Microsoft" sounds a bit off, but "he got a job at Microsoft" seems more natural-sounding. However, in Chinese, there is one word (technically, character) that sometimes means in and other times means at, depending on the context.
Mixing Up First and Last Names	– In Chinese, people's last (family) names are spoken and written before their first names, the exact reverse of English conventions. Thus, when Chinese speakers mention English names, they sometimes say them backwards (e.g., "Smith Will").
Vocabulary	– Chinese students also have problems with the list of animal sounds in English. In Chinese, only one word "*jiao*" (meaning "making noise") is needed for all the sounds—all animals make. In English, cows *moo*, dogs *bark*, cats *miaow*, birds *chirp*, ducks *quack*. In Chinese, they all *jiao*.
	– Spoken Chinese is also notably different from Japanese, Korean, and English in being a tonal language. In speech (not in writing), the pitch or tone with which a particular syllable is pronounced determines the meaning of the word (Holcombe, 2011).

JAPANESE AND KOREAN	
Overview	– Japanese and Korean belong to the Altaic language family.
	– Japanese is polysyllabic, with words compounded out of simple basic syllables piled up in an agglutinative manner to make sophisticated grammatical distinctions, such as tense differences.
	– Japanese is a respect language (**keigo**), which uses specific word endings and honorific particles to indicate the relative status of speaker and listener, and also the degree of formality.
Word Order	– The word order of Japanese is also very different from English and Chinese: Subject–Object–Verb. Grammatical particles are also used to mark the different parts of a sentence (Holcombe, 2011).
Common Mistakes Made by Japanese and Korean Learners of English May Include:	Missing articles Subject–Verb Agreement Confusion Verb Tense Confusion. Using simple present tense for a future activity: *We see you next Saturday morning. Absence of copula (to be; I am, you are, etc.) "False negative" in answering tag questions Omission of subject of the sentence Missing Possessive adjectives *My sister is washing face and brushing teeth.* Misuse of comparative and superlative adjectives and adverbs. Inflections for comparative and superlative adjectives and adverbs do not exist in Japanese. This fact can lead to errors in English: ***I promise to work hard more in the future.**

Korean Hangul and English	A noticeable contrast exists between the grammatical structure of Hangul and that of English. Verbs almost always come at the end of a sentence in Korean (Goodman, 1997). For example, in English I say, "**I am Susan**." In Korean I would say, "**Nanun Susan Imnida**" or "**I Susan am**." This can be difficult for the English learner in terms of sentence structure. Articles and prepositions are used in a totally different way in Korean. Using them correctly can be a challenge. Even very good Korean speakers of English tend to drop their articles every now and then.

The English Learner

It is hard to imagine that any EL would not have problems with English grammar. English has rules, exceptions to rules, and irregular verbs. English speakers add an "s" to the third person singular in the simple present verb tense. I have often been at a loss to explain to a student why English speakers say, "in the morning," "in the evening," but "at night." Park (1995) reports a study that found most Korean American students happy about their life in America, but many of them have trouble when trying to learn English.

Cultural and Other Issues of East Asian English Learners

Apart from the linguistic issues mentioned above, cultural issues and some other issues also warrant mainstream classroom teachers' attention.

Sun and Chen (1999) and Wenli (2011) identified three major difficulties experienced by Mainland Chinese students in the United States that still apply today: language ability, cultural awareness, and academic achievements. The major obstacles in the academic and social life of Chinese students included lack of English proficiency, cultural differences, and unfamiliarity with the American classroom environment and university facilities. Among the three obstacles, cultural difference is perhaps the hardest for the Chinese students to overcome. Yuan, (2011) and Zimmermann (1995) state that Chinese students studying in the United States must not only take classes, they must also "adapt or adjust to a sociocultural system which is different from their own" (p. 322).

Chinese students often have a higher level of respect for their teachers based upon their long tradition of respecting learning and teachers, which translates to this idea: Even if someone is your teacher for only a day, you should regard him like your father for the rest of your life (Xu, 2012). This tradition has such as powerful impact on Chinese students that it may trigger a series of negative responses to some of the fundamental beliefs in U.S. classrooms (Xu, 2012). Compared with their peers, Chinese students may be less active in answering the teacher's questions, fearing that they may "lose face," that is, make mistakes and make themselves look like a fool. They may even be less active in asking teachers questions, since they do not want to be seen as trying to question or even challenge the teacher's authority. They may dislike other students who disagree with the teacher.

Having been accustomed to teacher-centered classrooms in China, since the first day they entered school, some Chinese students are in so much awe of their teacher that they may feel too nervous to express themselves freely in their teacher's presence. It is important to note that students may believe that they come to school only to learn from their teacher, not from their peers, and therefore may be reluctant to participate in group discussions, pair work or other forms of collaboration with their classmates, thinking group discussion or pair work is merely waste of time.

China also has a long tradition of respecting seniors. Do not be surprised if students call you auntie, Mom, or even grandma, especially if it has never happened to you before. This is just their way of showing you their utmost respect. Another fact mainstream classroom teachers need to know is that due to the Chinese government's one-child-only policy (e.g., birth control, the family was allowed to have only one child) since the 1980s, most of the Chinese children, including those who are in the States now, are the only child of the family. Without any brothers or sisters, they have been used to being the center of the family and are therefore less willing to share or collaborate with others (Xu, 2012).

Some issues may also stem from the cultural differences, which may cause misunderstanding or miscommunication. There are certain things Americans do all the time but the Chinese avoid doing, such as opening a gift right after they receive it. The Chinese believe that this practice makes the recipient look greedy. In addition, you would never give someone a clock as a birthday gift, which since the word "clock" sounds the same as the word "to terminate" in Chinese. Other cultural superstitions may take you by surprise. Note the following miscommunication:

> Our next-door neighbor Jane (pseudonym), a retired elementary school English teacher, once told us a true story that happened in her class that made us laugh. It was shortly before St. Patrick's Day, so Jane told the class to wear something green to class. The next day, the class broke into groups of 4 or 5 for charades-playing. Seeing Minghai, a Chinese boy, who was the only one in his group not wearing anything green, Jane gave him a green hat which another student passed to her. Minghai hesitated a little, but took it and put it on his head. Soon after the activity started, however, two other Chinese boys in the class began to laugh. Minghai's face quickly turned red as if from embarrassment and humiliation. Then Minghai took off his hat, threw it onto the floor, and ran out of the classroom. In her puzzlement, Jane asked the other two Chinese boys what had happened to Minghai. The two boys then told her that in Chinese culture, a married woman having an affair with another man is said to be putting a green hat on her husband!

Chinese (like the Japanese) has a long tradition of modesty, humility, and self-effacement, which hides their true emotions.

> Those who have watched the movie "Joy Luck Club" may still remember the scene when the Chinese girl, Waverly, brought her American boyfriend, Rich, to meet her mother and the rest of the family as they were invited to the big family dinner. Waverley's mother served the steamed pork, which she always served with special pride, and said, "Ai! This dish not salty enough, no flavor. It is too bad to eat." This was actually the cue for the family to taste it and then proclaim it the best she had ever cooked. Having no idea about all this, however, Rich took what she said literally, and, without much thinking, he grabbed the salt bottle, which was next to him, and began to pour a riverful of salt on the platter, right in front of his girlfriend's mother's horrified eyes. You can imagine what happened afterwards.

Apart from the cultural differences, other more recent serious issues (due to the United States' current presidential administration) also concern mainstream classroom teachers of younger and older students all over the country.

> During a recent TESOL (Teachers of English to Speakers of Other Languages) Convention in Seattle, Ke met some ESOL teachers from California, Arizona, Florida, North Carolina and New York. They all expressed their concerns about their EL students, especially those

undocumented ones. As the new Trump administration is speeding up immigration reform and toughening up on a crackdown on illegal immigration, undocumented students are very much concerned about their future. Students of all ages live in constant fear of being found, detained by ICE, and deported back to their home country. They are also terrified that their parents or other family members will be torn away from them, so they do not want to go to school. "Attendance is declining these days. My EL students have missed quite a few classes since we heard about the ICE crackdown on undocumented immigrants," a teacher from North Carolina said. "We have become more cautious in asking our EL students to complete forms or taking pictures in the classroom," said another teacher from California. "We have gotten oral consent from my principal to give those undocumented EL students a break for a few more absences each semester," two teachers from New York told me. "We email them assignments that they can finish at home, and ask them to email back the finished work for us to check," one of them added. "I have a Fukianese (from Fukien province in southeastern China and Taiwan) girl in my class who is hardworking and intelligent. She helps out in her father's restaurant after school, baby-sits her little sister, and does all her homework on the counter of the restaurant," she said. But she is afraid to go to school.

There are an estimated half a million undocumented immigrants in New York City alone. Public schools are under tremendous pressure in meeting the challenges of educating these children ("State Demographics Data—NY", 2017)

Additional Issues with Asian Students

The Korean student may have a number of problems in a mainstream English situation. If Korean students live in a city with many other Koreans, such as Los Angeles or New York, they may speak English only in the classroom. In talking to a Korean student who lived in the United States, she said that even at school between classes she spoke Korean with the other Korean students. She said that made it harder to progress quickly in learning English (C. Shim, personal communication, November 4, 2003).

Korean students, as well as other newcomers to American classrooms, can expect to face many new hurdles, from cultural differences to language, even to the difference in the way the class is taught. Many teachers in the United States have very little knowledge about Korean culture (Ariza, 2015; Lee, 2003). As a result, miscommunication between the teacher and the Korean student is prevalent. As previously mentioned, the teacher may get irritated when the student does not make eye contact. A teacher may get frustrated when a child who is being scolded smiles and appears to be unconcerned (Han & Thomas, 2010). Sometimes for the purpose of teaching a concept, American teachers may encourage students to debate or discuss issues with them. As in most other countries in the world, this is not the style of teaching that is used in Korea. Additionally, this apparent disregard for boundaries between teacher and student can confuse the child who has been taught not to argue with those in authority. The American educational system often encourages students to share their thoughts and ideas and will grade students on active participation in class. The Korean student may feel uncomfortable with this approach because at home the teacher is always right and is not questioned.

Koreans may experience high levels of stress in the classroom. They are learning in a different way and in a language that is very different from their own. Their parents have high expectations for them, and the children may even feel that acceptance is contingent on their school success (Ariza, 2015; Lee, 2003; Yuan, 2011). Students also feel the pressure to become "American" while still maintaining their cultural identity. One research study showed that, although becoming acculturated to American culture may decrease stress, the participant may feel as if he or she has abandoned Korean traditions and culture, which can cause depression (Oh, Koeske, & Sales, 2002; Yuan, 2011). The pressure to conform to the classroom culture can cause the student to feel torn. Other class members, who may not understand or may not be sensitive to cultural differences, may cause the Korean student to feel ashamed or to feel like an outcast.

Although Korean students tend to do very well in math algorithms, they may have some challenges when dealing with numbers verbally. The unit of numbers in China, Japan, and Korea is based on four digits (万 *wan* meaning 10 thousand) instead of three, as it is in the United States (Furner & Robison, 2004; Wong & Teuben-Rowe, 1997). For example, 235,000 is said "two hundred thirty-five thousand," in English. In Chinese, it is 23 *wan* and 5 *qian* (thousand). In Korean, it is "i-ship sam man o chun" or twenty-three ten thousands five thousand (23,5000).

An American teacher may notice that Korean students have difficulty interacting with their classmates because in Korea a peer is only someone who was born in the same year. Anyone else is either his or her senior or junior (Ariza et al., 2015; Lee, 1996). Koreans will only use a person's name if that person is the same age or younger. The oldest person in the group is the one who "calls the shots" and can tell others what to do. In America, although age has some importance, the "leader" tends to be the one with the most outgoing and assertive personality. Korean students may be offended by a younger student treating them like equals or may be frustrated when a younger student does not follow their direction. In a group project, the Korean student may assume that the oldest child will be taking the lead in the project, where in actuality that may not be the case. Obviously, this trend may cause a problem in the U.S. school where a more egalitarian outlook is observed. The older Korean students may have the younger students carry their books or do their homework, which is contrary to American expectations. Thus, these students are wedged between the old culture and the new culture's value system.

A student may not want a parent to attend a school function or a teacher conference. This may be because of embarrassment about the differences in culture. It is more likely that the student is worried about the limited English proficiency of his or her parents (Park, 1995). In Park's study, 80 percent of the students participating wished that their parents could speak English well.

Students who are in a mainstream class and are pulled out for an ESOL class may experience some shame. If a student is in a class for exceptional students with learning disabilities, the shame is even greater. Many Koreans do not understand or recognize disabilities of any kinds. Although being in an ESOL (or ENL, English as a New Language) class is certainly not a disability, the child may perceive it as such. Parents may just ask that the child remain in the mainstream class, and they will get a tutor at home. Koreans tend to see a disability as a failure or a curse upon the family (Kim-Rupnow, 2001). Parents may deal with the disability without help and hope that the child will grow out of it. Children frequently use the Korean word for handicapped as an insult to tease others. After viewing the movie, *I Am Sam,* about a mentally handicapped father, a Korean friend said, "When I was watching the movie, I was so frustrated." When asked why, he said it was because Sam did not try to get better. This is an educated, well-spoken man who did not understand disabilities at all.

A student may not volunteer to speak in the classroom due to the influence of Confucianism's concept of *formalism* (Lee, 1996; Xu, 2012). Formalism emphasizes accuracy, rather than fluency. English classes in most Asian cultures are much more formal than that in the States. Unless students can say the sentence correctly and know beyond a doubt that the answer is correct, they may hesitate, or even refuse to say anything due to the fear of making any mistakes and the consequent embarrassment in front of the whole class, especially when surrounded by native speakers. We have seen this firsthand in the classroom. Or, if the student does not understand, he or she may not admit it, but will go home and try to learn it alone. Very bright students may not answer a question unless they are positive they can say the answer perfectly.

Therefore, when an Asian student, or any EL for that matter, volunteers to answer a question and forgets the English word or answers in the native language, the teacher should complement the child for participating, rather than reject the answer (Lee, 2003; Ariza, 2015).

Similarly, in a multicultural class, the teacher may also notice the obedience and politeness of Japanese students. They always do their homework and never disturb the class. This ethic comes from their society. From a very young age, they are taught to do all of the assignments they are given. They are also taught to respect the teacher and do whatever she tells them to do (Ikeda, 2010; Xu, 2012).

However, this ethic is not always good, Ikeda argues. Since they do not want to disturb the class, Japanese students often do not ask the questions that they have. Instead, they ask their peers questions or check in the books after class. Since they are very reserved, they do not participate in an outgoing manner like Europeans and Latin Americans. They believe that saying their opinions in front of the class is a form of "showing off." They believe that their job is to memorize the information the teacher presents. Since they are so quiet in the class in this manner, the teacher might wonder whether they understood or not. The teacher needs to pay special attention with regard to this point and assist the students by calling on them by name, encouraging them to participate more freely, and giving some kind of leadership responsibility in class.

Aside from being reserved, there are other factors to be aware of due to cultural differences. It is better to avoid putting the Japanese student on the spot. It is okay if the student successfully accomplishes the task, but if he does not, especially if he is older or is socially at a higher position than the rest of his classmates, he will be very embarrassed. It is better to avoid physical contact and winking. Since the Japanese are not accustomed to these situations, they feel uncomfortable, or in the worst case, they get the wrong idea. The Japanese usually do not use eye contact while they are talking with others. This does not mean that they are insincere or guilty of wrongdoing. In addition, they do not accept compliments because accepting compliments means that they admit that they are good, which they believe to be conceited.

Cultural characteristics, such as status, social class and social distance, exclude certain discussion topics from the classroom and do not promote spoken English. The typical instructional style for Japanese education is the teacher centered learning model with a direct approach. Japanese students prefer explicit instruction above interaction and classroom discussions.

Formality, social class, and status determine life in Japan. In the heterogeneous EFL (English as a foreign language) classroom, students are very sensitive to discussions and questions that might reveal their descent and preferences. The ESOL teacher should avoid talking and asking about the following (van de Kreeke, 2010):

- Bukamin (lower class)
- area student lives in
- university/school of student
- hometown of student
- parents' jobs
- dialect
- political beliefs

In general, younger people are more familiar with and open toward Western discussion topics than the older generation.

Various cultural characteristics of Japan make it harder for teachers to promote interactive English conversation. Japanese students' participation in the classroom is greatly affected by the following factors:

Status and power—In the Japanese classroom, power struggles result in situations where students do not get involved into discussions because they have to respect higher ranked students. These power issues can be extended to age and gender. In addition, students might be afraid to be ranked as lower class when asking questions or giving the wrong answer.

Social distance—Students refrain from asking the teacher questions and pretend to understand something they do not rather than asking for clarification.

Group harmony—In Japan, everything is done within the function of the group. Individuals are conscious of maintaining harmony and therefore will not quickly express their own opinion.

Silence—During conversations and when thinking, silence is quite normal in Japan.

This list of Japanese cultural differences is by no means conclusive. By showing respect for and understanding of the Japanese way of living, it will be much easier for the teacher to be accepted.

Although most Asian cultures emphasize studying and being disciplined in schoolwork, which does not imply that school comes easy to every Asian student. The American stereotype of the "Asian whiz kid" can put an added burden on the child, which can cause emotional distress and school failure (Huang, 1993; Li, & Wang; 2008). Teachers and other students may just assume that this child will do very well with little struggle, when in fact that may not be the case. Many teachers who are accustomed to the overachieving Asian student suffer from this illusion.

Although Korean students are taught to respect their elders and those in authority by age or position, they still have a strong sense of right and wrong. Korean culture emphasizes the deference to authority and the priority of the group over the individual (Kim, 1981; Xu, 2012). In Kim's study, Korean students gave priority to the authority figures who gave directions based on correct moral judgments. Therefore, Korean students probably have a strong enough foundation to resist orders from older children who encourage them to do the wrong thing. This can cause conflict as they struggle with wanting to do the right thing yet violating their own sense of respecting authority.

> In one of my ENL adult classes at Harvard University, an older Korean diplomat (who was trying to improve his English for a program at MIT) had the younger students waiting on him, carrying his books, and doing his assignments. The older man was a high-ranking politician in Korea and it was very difficult for me to stop the behavior. That was an excellent example of how strong cultural influences are.

Rather than hinder the progress of the mainstream class, I believe that having an Asian student, or any other foreign-born student, can be a benefit to the class. Other students get a chance to learn firsthand about another country and culture. Asian students are taught to be diligent, and this could inspire others in the classroom to invoke the same study habits. Although the Asian student may need to become accustomed to the lack of hierarchy when working on a group project, he or she is already familiar with the idea of community and may work well with others and encourage others to do the same.

Using examples of the student's culture and language in the classroom can be beneficial to the entire class and can put the immigrant students at ease. "When home languages and cultures are included in the classroom, students feel they do not have to 'give up' their identity and background to learn English" (Edelsky, 1996, as cited in Wong & Teuben-Rowe, 1997, p. 1; Delpit & Dowdy, 2008). As teachers, we can help students feel included rather than excluded from the class. It is the responsibility of the teacher to help the students develop language and social skills, without making the students feel they have to give up their own cultural and personal identification with their native culture (Delpit & Dowdy, 2008; Oh et al., 2002).

One way to encourage understanding of the intricacies of language and writing would be to showcase different writing systems in the classroom (Ariza & Lapp, 2012; Wong & Teuben-Rowe, 1997). Students can become aware of the various writing systems that exist and compare them to English. Native English speakers might feel the thrill of having the Korean student write their English names in Hangul. The teacher can spend some time discussing the different systems and how they are read (right to left, left to right).

A classroom could have some decorations from the students' native countries, material published in the students' home language, and some resources or activities about their home country. This can help the newcomer to feel more at ease and respected (Ariza et al., 2015; Lee, 2003) while inspiring the English speakers to find interest in other cultures. in addition, a teacher can occasionally mention the other countries' events and compare them with American holidays and so forth. For example, U.S. Thanksgiving and Chusok could be discussed, or students could compare the Korean representative system and the U.S. Congress. Common Asian customs can be demonstrated, such as bowing to greet one another, as the students explain the different types of bowing. Students from other cultures are fascinated as they watch the different Asians demonstrate how they bow to their parents as a measure of their degree of respect (e.g., the bow may find the person prostrate on the floor). Let the student share about a Korean game such as Yut Nori, a game involving four sticks. Teachers need to understand that when the home and school behaviors share congruity, children maintain respect for their home heritage (Ariza, 2009; Lee, 2003).

Students from other countries often bring their native foods to eat in school. For example, even those students who have been in America for quite a while eat their native food for lunch. Different smells and tastes will be evident in the lunchroom. Instead of having a situation where other students ridicule the student for eating something different, the teacher can set the mood by showing curiosity about the food (Ariza, 2009; Lee, 2003). It can become a learning experience where students can compare their native Asian with American diets. The teacher can exploit this great opportunity to share multicultural customs by highlighting different foods people eat, as well as expectations we have about what constitutes certain meals. For example, Americans eat bacon and eggs, cereal, pancakes, and waffles for breakfast, whereas many other people eat rice, fish heads, and soup.

Asian names may seem like unusual tongue twisters to the native English speaker. As in Chinese and Vietnamese cultures, the family name is usually first, so a child may tell a teacher he is Kim, Chang Soo, Kim being the family name. The given name of a Korean has two parts. One part of the name is generational. It was determined many generations ago and is now a part of their family history. All the children born in the same generation have the same name (Choi, 1991; Xu, 2012). The other part of the name is usually given by the paternal grandfather or the oldest male relative on the father's side. Many Korean and other Asian children take on Western names for their English classes. They may choose a name from a TV show or just pick a name that they like. As an interesting interchange, the class could let the Korean student give Korean names to the others to help the children become more at ease with the difference in names. To correctly pronounce a student's name, no matter how foreign sounding it is to the teacher, is a great gift of acknowledgment that builds a student's self-esteem (Ariza, 2009).

Teachers should also keep in mind that it is important not to inadvertently embarrass or humiliate any child but to pay careful attention to the student's struggle. Words or actions that may not be a problem for a native-English-speaking student could cause problems for the Asian student. It is necessary to remember the Korean concept of *chaemyon*, or self-respect. Teachers should use appropriate words and indirect expressions when correcting or admonishing the student (Lee, 1996). The teacher should also not insist that the Korean child look him or her in the eye (Ariza, 2009).

Of crucial importance in working with English learners is the concept of "wait time" when asking questions. Language learners may not respond right away, as they need time to put together the answer in English and to reflect on what is said. For this reason, feel comfortable in allowing an extended period of time for the EL to think; don't expect an answer right away. Consider periods of silence an opportunity for reflection (Ariza, 2009; Ariza & Lapp, 2012; Huang, 1993). Ask one question at a time, provide clear information as to exactly what is being asked, and give clear guidelines as to what is expected. Try to encourage Asian students to voluntarily participate in discussion, and then be sure to acknowledge their efforts and willingness to share.

The behavior of some Asian parents might frustrate the teacher in the United States. It is not uncommon for a parent to be late or not show up for a meeting. For example, Korean time is polychronic (i.e., they perform multiple tasks simultaneously). Whereas Americans will attend to one person at a time, Koreans do not. Koreans perceive time and events as an "unfolding process" (Lee, 2003), as compared to the Western way of looking at events independently and scheduling them that way. In other words, events happen as they happen, instead of at an appointed time. Teachers need to be patient when a parent is late or misses a meeting, as no offense is intended toward the teacher. Do not confront them (again, the concept of *chaemyon*), as they must save face. When scheduling meetings, indicate the importance of appointment times and explain that there are other appointments scheduled after theirs. When a parent misses a meeting, it may be because of work. Working long hours is typical of Asian workers.

As with all parents, when meeting to discuss their child, a teacher needs to be careful not to criticize the child (Ariza & Lapp, 2012; Lee, 2003). Discuss the child's strengths before looking at problems. Give specific guidelines for improvement, and ask for help from the parent. Make it very clear that any academic problems are not a source of shame. Rather than having the parent feel that an ENL class or extra tutoring means the child is slow, the teacher can help the parent to see that it is an opportunity for the student to progress. It is also a great time for the teacher to ask about the student's cultural and family background. This will help the parent feel that the teacher is open and interested in the child. Additionally, assure the parent that speaking the native language at home is important and that it won't interfere with learning English (Ariza, 2009, 2012; Lee, 2003). It is now commonly believed that the richer the language and literacy foundation the child has in the native language, the easier it is to transfer knowledge to the second language (Cummins, 2000; Freeman & Freeman, 2004).

Parents may have trouble speaking English, but don't automatically assume that they are not proficient in English (Lee, 2003). Many people in Asia are learning English independently. Most Asians tend to be well educated in their home countries, so a parent may very well have high English language skills. Chances are they have some English foundation, as English is so prevalent in many Asian countries and students may know more written English than verbal, as they all learn it in middle school and high school. When communicating with parents, it is a good idea to use written communication rather than the telephone as it will be easier to get your point across (Ariza, 2009). If you should visit an Asian home, be prepared to take off your shoes at the door, as this is part of their cultures.

Asian parents are very serious about wanting their children to succeed academically. Don't be surprised if you receive gifts from some Asian students because sometimes students give teachers extravagant gifts in hopes of getting a more favorable grade. It is very common for teachers to receive small gifts from parents in China, Japan, and Korea. Parents want to show their appreciation of the teacher's hard work, patience, and sometimes extra time and help their children receive. In some Asian cultures, such as that of China, parents may feel hurt if their gifts are not accepted.

As the Asian populations in the United States grow, it becomes increasingly necessary that educators learn about the cultures, which can be very distinct. No longer can we assume that all students fit under the title of "American" or "Asian" and can just learn things in the same way. Students need to learn academics, but they also need to learn about new ways of adjusting without losing their own cultural identity. We as teachers play a significant role in helping the students to develop biculturally. We need to relate to Asian students, as they come to us: following a hierarchical structure, needing silence at times, and going home to an environment, which may be traditional in practice. We need to reach out to the parents and invite them to be a part of their child's educational life. We need to educate other students in the ways of Asian groups, so they in turn can reach out to the Asian student as an individual. If we are going to help these students succeed, we must be proactive in ensuring that success will take place.

Cross-Cultural Communication Problems

Miscommunication between Asians and Americans can easily occur, regardless of how much each culture has in common. All cultures have hidden dimensions that are not evident until they clash with one another. It is difficult for educators to know every culture, but it is important to make an effort to at least try to get to know the beliefs of your students. For example, conceptions of time may differ. Although Americans typically operate in a linear schedule, other cultural groups may not. This disparity may be manifested in broken appointments, tardiness, or an apparent disregard for the teacher's time. Additionally, Asians are often polite, or even seemingly submissive, so it may come as a shock when a dispute results in sudden hostility. This may happen as a result of misunderstanding body language or nonverbal clues. Asians often try to avoid appearing offensive and will not make critical remarks. They often favor ambiguity and will repeatedly nod their heads during conversation (but this does not indicate agreement) and may refrain from making eye contact (Ariza, 2009; Kim, 1985; Matsuda, 1989). The conversation partner might believe that the head nodding indicates agreement, when the listener is only indicating that he or she is listening. A smile might only be confusion or embarrassment, instead of pleasure (Coker, 1988; Ariza, 2009). To determine what the enigmatic smile really means, the teacher can observe the student in different situations and note the behaviors that indicate consent and disagreement.

Spiritual practices may be a factor in misunderstanding certain behaviors or practices foreign to the American culture. Blessing the grounds in certain areas, unfamiliar religious practices (e.g., performing a ritual cleansing where crimes took place before students return to school), and respecting rites that are important to each cultural group are ways to validate the importance of the individual's beliefs and to mitigate potential friction. Many Asian cultures believe in the idea of "ghosts," and want to please or appease the ghosts. For example, after a school shooting, a Cambodian family did not want to return to the school, but it was not because they were afraid of the guns. They would not return to the school grounds until the "ghosts" were appeased (Langford, 2013).

An important issue that teachers are often unaware of is that of the hierarchical imbalance the immigrant family suffers in the United States. Most families recognize the traditional role of the father or the parents as being the head of the household. In America, however, immigrant parents often find their children quickly "Americanized," embracing American culture and moving away from their own culture. It is not uncommon for us to hear about how an immigrant family is divided into two sides while watching Olympic Games, with parents cheering for their home country and children for the United States. In addition, the fact that children pick up English much faster than their parents poses a potential threat to the parents' authority in the family in maintaining the parent–child dynamic and allows the kids, especially teens, to use this to their advantage. Families suffer when the youngsters learn English and the parents do not, thus causing great tension as the children become the interpreters and decision makers for the adults. We have heard a lot about Chinese and other immigrant parents complaining about their powerlessness in trying to maintain their authority over their children studying in public schools: "They no longer listen to us," said one of the Chinese workers we hired to paint our apartment, while he was on his lunch break. "We have totally lost our control of them. They talk less to us, thinking it is hard for us to understand them. It is true. Because we don't speak much English. We don't know what they are doing and how they are doing in school. Even if we know they are not doing well and need help, there is little we can do to help them." (Xu, 2012).

Educators must realize and understand the issues and cultural values of their English learners. Gathering as much information as possible about the student will help the teacher to determine the best teaching practices to employ. Realizing that many immigrants are accustomed to living in societies where self-disclosure is avoided due to ineffective or tyrannical governments, truthful answers may be withheld from the school. Ages or immigration documents may be falsified or in error, and educational history may be unattainable. In that case, the teacher must try to ascertain English language proficiency (and first language academic proficiency), to determine previous educational experience, and to evaluate the student for correct placement. Difficulty in communication can mask health or other problems.

Effective Communication

English learners may have difficulty with the subtleties of English modals (e.g., would, could, should, may, might, must). For example, English speakers use "You must" judiciously, and we know how to get the point across without using the imperative (e.g., command) form. English learners cannot discern when they sound rude, and they may unintentionally offend the native speaker. In another case, a native English speaker gets a private call and asks a nonnative speaker with whom he was having a conversation, "May I?" The non-native speaker may not realize that this grammatical structure is a polite request for some privacy, and may respond with something like "Sure, please go ahead." Ariza (2009) and Matsuda (1989) offer suggestions for educators to follow in trying to communicate effectively with the Asian American:

1. Do not hesitate in assuming the role of the authority. The teacher will be more respected.
2. Respect the beliefs of the Asian family.
3. Do not rush communication. Be patient and respect the silence of the parent.
4. Be very clear and provide step-by-step information, with details of each point. Make sure the parents know what you will do, what they will do, and what the family will do. Give comprehensible advice.
5. Compromise with the family.
6. Note body language. Nodding of the head does not mean agreement with what you are saying. The family may be saying no without verbalizing their disagreement.

Ms. Susan Hobgood, a teacher in Korea, writes about the Korean culture from her perspective. Although all Asian cultures are not the same, many similarities are discernible, especially if the individuals live under the guidance of Confucian or Buddhist principles. Additionally, many of the Asian languages have similarities; as a result, students of English display similar language interferences as learners transfer (positively or negatively) concepts from the native language to English. Therefore, although Ms. Hobgood refers to Korea, many of the idiosyncrasies she writes about can be related to Chinese, Japanese, and other Asian cultures.

Ms. Hobgood begins her rendition by describing a scenario that took place in her second-grade language arts class in the United States, which consisted of twenty students. One little girl from Seoul, Korea, Soo-Min Park, had been in the United States for six months. The following scenario shows how easily linguistic misunderstandings can occur when learning a new language.

In this scenario, it is clear the teacher has little information about Asian cultures. Obviously, the scene is exaggerated, as most teachers would be more sensitive, even without knowledge of Soo Min's culture. This incident, however, demonstrates some possible communication misunderstandings that can occur.

TEACHER: Everyone take out your reading books and turn to page 60. Sally, would you please read for the class?

(Sally begins to read. Soo Min looks confused.)

TEACHER: Soo Min, what's wrong?

SOOMIN: What page?

TEACHER: Page 60. Let me see. Soo Min, that's the wrong page; that is page 16. We are on 60.

SOOMIN: Oh, sorry.

(Class finishes reading the story.)

TEACHER: Let's talk about the story. Johnny, why was the boy in the story so sad?

JOHNNY: He was sad because his dog ran away.

TEACHER: Who helped him find his dog, Rosa?

ROSA: His mother, father, and his friend, Billy.

TEACHER: Who has a dog?

(Students raise hands.)

TEACHER: Soo Min, what is your dog's name?

SOO MIN: Nabi, but not my home. Older home.

TEACHER: Oh, so you had a dog in Korea?

SOO MIN: Yes.

TEACHER: But you don't have a dog here?

SOO MIN: Yes.

TEACHER: You do have a dog here?

SOO MIN: No, in Korea.

TEACHER: I'm confused; you don't have a dog here?

SOO MIN (looking down): Yes, my dog in Korea.

TEACHER: Soo Min, please look at me when I talk to you.

(Later at recess, three other girls are talking to Soo Min.)

YACHEN: Soo Min, we are going skating today after school. Do you want to come?

SOO MIN: I can't. I am go to math academy.

FATIMA: You mean you have to go to school again?

SOO MIN: Yes, Monday and Wednesday, I go math academy.

SARA: How terrible to have to go to school twice.

Implications for the Classroom

As we have shown, cross-cultural miscommunication can easily occur between the Asian student and the mainstream American. It can start when a teacher asks a student's age. East Asian age reckoning is a concept and belief that originated in China but is widely used by other cultures in East Asia and Vietnam, which share this traditional way of counting a person's age. Newborns are born one-year old, and each passing of a Lunar New Year, rather than the birthday, adds one year to the person's age. Therefore, if a Chinese, Japanese, or Korean student tells you he or she is 10 years old, it could mean 9 by the western way of calculating age. If school or grade placement is determined according to age, a problem can start from the moment the student enters the American school.

According to Byron (2006) and Lee (1996), indirectness is a big part of Korean culture, as well as other Asian cultures in general, and that can affect students in the classroom. Koreans are taught to practice *nunchi* before speaking and to modify their answers accordingly. *Nunchi* is the ability to grasp the unspoken word or intention of others (Kim, 2001), a subtle art of picking up all the visual clues to discern a Korean's pride, mood or state of mind, or to understand what a Korean really means when he or she is saying something. Therefore, responses to the teacher or to other children may be based on what they think the other person wants to hear, based on their observation and interpretation of body language and facial expression. Richardson and Smith (2007) and Hall (1990) explained this type of culture as being high context as opposed to the low context of American culture. Similarly, when you ask a Chinese student who does not speak much English "You are not Korean, are you?" She may most likely answer: "Yes, I am not."

In Asian countries, when a teacher or a person of power or respect is speaking to a student, we mentioned that the student is not supposed to make eye contact. Therefore, typically, when a student is being scolded, he or she looks down. Extended eye contact under the circumstances can be taken as an affront or a challenge of teacher's authority. This is contrary to the American expectation that children look at us when we are speaking to them. In speaking with several Asians who have studied in the United States, they have all said that at some point they got in trouble for not looking the teacher in the eye.

Asians also may use a smile or laughter in a difficult situation to express confusion, embarrassment or frustration. When a child is in trouble, the parents may smile. A U.S. teacher may perceive that as disrespect or not taking the problem seriously. That is probably not the case. The student is most likely just feeling confused or embarrassed (Huang, 1993). Often East Asians, Chinese, Japanese or Koreans included, will remain calm and polite during a conversation or disagreement. Therefore, Asian students' smiling and nodding in your class may not necessarily mean they have truly understood your question. On the contrary, unlike American students, Asian students in an American classroom are much less likely than their native English-speaking peers to ask their teachers to further explain or clarify something that they do not understand. Westerners may take their smile or nodding to mean everything is in accord; we may not see any warning signs of impending trouble. Then suddenly, they will become very hostile seemingly without reason. This is a perfect example of anthropologist Edward Hall's (1983) description of **high-context** culture (Richardson & Smith, 2007), which means that individuals do not verbally transmit information. The rules of the cultural expectations are implicit. As previously mentioned, this behavior is contrary to that which is found in the United States, which is a **low-context** culture because we are all so different and don't think the same way. Procedures, thoughts, ideas, and feelings are explicitly verbalized in U.S. culture. The United States is comprised of individuals from many cultures with a variety of dissimilar behaviors, whereas most of the populations of Asian countries are populated by the Asian from that country (e.g., Japanese in Japan, Koreans in Korea, and so on) who behave within a similar cultural paradigm.

As alluded to previously, the Korean concept of *nunchi* goes both ways. Asian people may assume that Westerners are reading their nonverbal signals, so they perceive that we are being insensitive (Huang, 1993). In not paying attention to the nonverbal signs, the Korean custom of *chaemyon* is being violated. Loosely translated, this means "dignity" or "face." Koreans are supposed to practice *nunchi* so they do not embarrass the other person or cause him or her to lose *chaemyon* (Lee, 1996). Koreans, as do the Chinese, have an indirect nonconfrontational approach to problem solving, so that all parties involved can save face.

Asian students place high pressure on themselves to achieve superior grades to avoid bringing shame to the family. They may receive a 90 or A– on a test and still get very upset. A 90 or A– is a good grade, so an American teacher may not understand the implication of receiving a less-than-perfect score. As previously mentioned, a fundamental value of the Confucian society is the importance of formal education. Asian parents sacrifice much for the student's education so a good grade or a less-than-desirable grade reflects on the whole family's integrity. Anything less than perfect may be perceived as undesirable. Therefore, much pressure is placed on the child to succeed, which can cause stress and conflict within the family (Huang, 1993; Lu, Gilmour, Kao, & Huang (2006).

Indians in the United States (Born in the United States or India)

KEY POINTS

- India is said to be the world's oldest culture
- For Indians, religion permeates every single aspect of Indian culture—surface or deep, tangible or intangible
- Indians show deep respect for teachers, family values, and education

I called upon Ms. Jini Heller, originally from India, to offer her insights regarding Indian students. Ms. Heller is one of those individuals who have had the experience of being able to step outside her culture and compare how she was raised with her life and environment today. Married to a Swiss man who speaks English, German, and French, Ms. Heller speaks English, Hindi, French, and several dialects from her native India. Her 4-year-old daughter, who has spent most of her life in Switzerland, speaks English, German, and Hindi. A master's student in education, Ms. Heller returns to India for several months every year. She is living in the United States because of her husband's job. I asked her to tell me about Indian students in the classroom and to explain what mainstream teachers should know. She researched the topic and shared her insight with me.

I am grateful to have the opportunity to share my thoughts with teachers in the United States. This presentation gave me the opportunity to research facts about my home country, as well as share my in-depth knowledge as an Indian woman who has experienced life in many countries and in the classrooms of the United States. India is a multifaceted country with intricate issues. What is perfectly understandable in my country often becomes a complex mystery to Americans. I hope to be able to shed some light on the complexities that teachers may encounter in the classroom situations.

The Federal Republic of India possesses a population of 1.04 billion people, 72 percent of whom are Indo-Aryan, 25 percent Dravidian, and about 3 percent of other lesser-known ethnic groups. We are multilingual and speak Hindi, Urdu, Tamil, Bengali, Kashmiri, and, of course, English. The core of our culture consists of historically traditional ideas and accompanying values that emphasize the intangible and symbolic aspects of group life. As Banks explains, India consists of a macroculture, the national or shared culture of the nation–state, or the big cultures, as well as the smaller cultures within that constitute the microculture (Banks, 2001, p. 72). Banks's categorization is perfect for a vast, diverse, and multicultural nation like India. As Banks depicts, India's macroculture is traditionalist, with freedom of religion and spirituality and belief in the family as an institution. The microcultures within would be the work ethic, literacy, material progress, and behavioral patterns influenced by cultural values, and so forth, including intense social issues like women's rights; *sati*, or bride-burning; and dowry systems (Banks, 2001, p. 73).

In my attempt to provide teachers with insights into the culture of immigrant student from India, it is important to note that "religion" permeates every single aspect of Indian culture—surface or deep, tangible or intangible. You see religion in art, devotional music, fashion, housing and decor (Vaastu Shastra, a type of Indian architecture), festivals, death, celebrations, marriage, birth, business, growth and development, material progress, ecology and environment, and so forth. Culture in India is a function of race, religion, region (urban or rural), and socioeconomic level. Respect for all elders is sacred, and the student will feel discordance in the classroom if other students disrespect the teacher. Additionally, the male child is favored, and being shy and reticent is considered a positive trait, especially for the female child. This should not be regarded as maladjustment.

India	
History	Thousands of years ago, India was home to the Indus Valley civilization, one of the world's oldest civilizations. In the 300s and 200s BC, the Maurya Empire ruled the land. It became one of the largest empires in the world. Years later, the Golden Age of India took place during the Gupta dynasty. Lasting from 320 to 520 AD, the Gupta dynasty produced new developments in science, great art, and advanced culture.
	With the rise of Islam in the Arab nations, it began to spread into India. During the 10th and 11th centuries the Turks and the Afghans invaded India and ruled as the Delhi Sultanate. Years later the Mughal Empire rose to power and ruled the land for over 300 years.
	In the 16th century, European explorers began to enter India. Britain eventually took control of India. In the early 1900s, India began to fight for independence from Britain. Led by Mohandas Gandhi, nonviolent protests were made against the British. After many years of struggling, India was granted independence from Britain in 1847.
	The country was later divided up into India and Pakistan. Later East Pakistan became a third country, Bangladesh. Despite significant problems including poverty, corruption, and overpopulation, India has recently seen strong economic and technology development (TSI, 2013d).
Cultural Tradition and Values	The culture of India is among the world's oldest, reaching back about 5,000 years. Joann S. Morris (2012) believes that traditional Indian culture places emphasis on the following: • Education • Devotion to the family • Trust in the institution of marriage (arranged marriage) • Respect for the elders • Group Harmony. The needs of the group are considered more important than those of the individual. • Cooperation and noncompetitiveness. Competition within the group is rare. There is security in being a member of the group and in not being singled out and placed in a position above or below others. • Modesty. Boasting and loud behavior that aim at drawing attention to oneself are discouraged. • Respect for individual's dignity • Nonviolence Religions: 80% Hindu, 13.5% Muslim, 2% Christian, 2% Sikh

Languages in India	Over 100 languages are spoken in India. Hindi is the national language and mother tongue of 30% of the population. English is also a major language for national, political, and commercial communication. There are 14 other official languages: Bengali, Telugu, Marathi, Tamil, Urdu, Gujarati, Malayalam, Kannada, Oriya, Punjabi, Assamese, Kashmiri, Sindhi, and Sanskrit. Hindustani is a popular variant of Hindi/Urdu spoken widely throughout northern India but is not an official language. Different states of India have different official languages. Some have more than one.

There's no "Indian" language per se, which is partly why English is still widely spoken almost half a century after the British departed India. Eighteen languages are officially recognized by the constitution, but over 1,600 minor languages and dialects were listed in the 1991 census. Major efforts have been made to promote Hindi as the national language and to gradually phase out English. But while Hindi is the predominant language in the north, it bears little relation to the Dravidian languages of the south. In the south, very few people speak Hindi.

The Indian upper class clings to English as the shared language of the educated elite, championing it as both a badge of their status and as a passport to the world of international business. In truth, only about 3 percent of Indians have a firm grasp of the language. |

Education in India

Traditionally, Indian culture regarded education as a holy duty that was linked to religion. *Mullahs* (a respectful name for one trained in holy Islam), *sadhus* (holy man), *gurus* (teachers), and saints taught the holy scriptures, languages, and sciences to the people in their community. The Hindu goddess Saraswati is the goddess of knowledge, widely revered and worshipped by the Hindus. Education was seen as a means to attain higher social status and spiritual well-being and was not available to all classes of society. Women of nobility and higher class had access to education through their priests.

Today, education is available to all in Indian society in the form of public schools, private schools, and religious schools. Convent and Muslim schools are attached to temples for Hindus and Buddhists, and all schools use English as the medium of education. Indian school schedules are based on a British format, that is, ten years of elementary and high school, two years for junior college, and three years of senior college, and post-graduation is another two or more years. Higher education is important, since professions such as medicine, engineering, and higher education are most sought after and augment the person's status in the marriage market. Literacy of females in India is over 63% percent, whereas literacy of males is 83 percent (Shah, 2013). Therefore, education is a vital factor in life positions, as arranged marriages are still prevalent, both in India and among Indians in the United States.

Currently, India is making headlines internationally for taking jobs from the West, rather than for its teeming slums and rural poor. At the same time, the burgeoning middle class in India of 250–300 million scampers to acquire education in the United States. The United States is by far the number-one choice for an Indian for migration and education. The typical Indian student in the United States is usually from a middle-to upper-class urban Indian family, has migrated to the United States at a young age with professional parents, was born in the United States, or was sent to the United States as an adult for higher education. The student will be totally dedicated to the pursuit of education, as the family will have spent much money and will have made a huge investment for the student to succeed. Meanwhile, the student will be strongly attached to an extended family back home in India or here within the United States.

More than 200,000 Indians attended an American college or university last year ("Census of India: Literacy and Level of Education", 2017). The United States has been the number one choice for higher education for Indian students because it has good universities that have led to good career prospects. However, since the Trump administration has indicated that U.S. citizens will be preferred for jobs, qualified Indian students who have already been accepted to American universities are looking at doing advanced studies in countries like Ireland, Canada, Germany and Australia, where they are welcome. They fear the United States will be a hostile environment and are unsure about what will happen with immigrations policies. (Sá & Sabzalieva, 2017). Some students who are still considering the United States as a place to study have changed their target institutions to those on the east or west coast, considering they would be safer in more democratic states.

Indian Immigrant Students

The Indian immigrant students will most likely possess common characteristics noticeable to the mainstream teacher. Students will have a good level of English literacy unless they are from the rural or urban poor society. Unlike in many other immigrant groups in the United States, parental involvement in education is the norm. Teachers work hard, along with the parents, to ensure academic success. Students are accustomed to rote and memorization strategies, and they are taught at a young age ways and means to enhance memory and concentration powers. Young students are not encouraged to ask questions.

Instruction methods in India are traditional with no audiovisual techniques. Reading, writing, and memorization are the preferred strategies. Finally, teachers will note that poverty or socioeconomic level is not an indicator of intellect and academic success in Indian society. Students of all socioeconomic levels will demonstrate the same commitment to educational attainment.

The Indian immigrant student	– Shows deep respect for teachers of any race, sex, or culture. – Believes that obedience and humility are the norm. – Is usually well-adjusted socially and psychologically. – Interacts with fellow students without much reserve, as they are used to diversity. – Will show respect for an older students and it is customary for the older ones to look out for the younger ones and to act as their mentor.
The mainstream teacher can expect	– To see a generally well-behaved, respectful, and academically focused Indian student. – To encourage the Indian student to work more independently and to ask questions. – To empower the Indian students by teaching them to become more responsible for their own learning, as the Indian student is used to following instructions and orders and does not voluntarily or proactively initiate learning. – To make the most of the Indian student's innate sense of "looking out for the younger ones," encouraging the student's natural empathy to form friendships with other students who have greater problems adjusting to a new cultural environment.

Impact on multicultural classrooms	– Family and parental participation in the child's academic life should be expected. – An Indian student would almost never assimilate or merge in the "melting pot," by losing his or her sense of identity and cultural belonging. He or she would acculturate relatively smoothly, and hence the multicultural educator would not have to grapple with "cultural and psychological interventions" in order to prepare the child for academic success (Igoa, 1995, p. 44). – Nonverbal communication such as not meeting the eye of the teacher should not be regarded as disrespectful. The educator needs to instruct the child that it is important to look the teacher in the eye when speaking.

For Indians, deep culture seems to have a tendency to change more slowly than surface culture. It would be easier for a modern Indian to change his or her dress style or food habits than other entrenched family values, social beliefs, and religion. Economic development, materialism, and consumerism lead to changes in values, culture, and social outlook. Although change is inevitably taking place as modern technology reaches further and further into the fabric of society, essentially rural India remains and will remain much the same as it has for thousands of years. Therefore, resilient are its social and religious institutions that it has absorbed, ignored, and eschewed all attempts to radically change or destroy them. This reluctance to change has been somewhat modified as more immigrants come to the United States; however, the basic tenets of Indian culture remain fixed.

I hope that I have clarified these cultural values to an extent that is helpful to the mainstream teacher in understanding the actions of the Indian student in the classroom.

- **Points to remember to facilitate instruction:**

Encourage children and older students to continue speaking their native language at home. Explain that it is exciting to know two languages (Ariza, 2009; Lee, 2003), and they will transfer knowledge easier.	Learn about the student's cultural background, as well as personal and family background. This is crucial to making the classroom a culturally sensitive environment (Ariza, 2009; Lee, 2003).
If possible, find Asian parent or community volunteers who can spend time interpreting and helping the student (Lee, 2003). Don't write a Korean student's name in red ink. This is the same as writing it in blood in Korean. Some believe that they or a family member will die (Wong & Teuben-Rowe, 1997).	Use music in the classroom. Students often love to sing, and it helps Asian students to become more comfortable with the English language. Group singing will help them feel less inhibited about pronouncing words. May be even ask the student to share a recording of a song in the native language or, if the student is outgoing, to sing a song for the class.
Use some stories and textbooks that have Asian language characters or stories in them. The Literacy Place series by Scholastic uses a variety of stories from different countries.	Have students write and illustrate a fairy tale from their countries. Encourage the Asian student to use native folktales such as "Hongbu and Nolbu," (Korean) or the story of how Korea (or other Asian countries) came to be.

Be careful how you pronounce your words, and speak slowly. Remember to stress sounds such as the short "a" sound. Be aware of the sounds that may cause the student trouble. Use fingers to demonstrate how the lips should use to form the sound (like a long e-the lips form a smile) Touch the throat for sounds that are made.

Use pairs and small groups to work on assignments. The student may take a little while to get used to it but eventually will be comfortable. The student may feel more comfortable speaking to one or two other people, than to the whole class.

FINAL POINTS

- All Asian cultures are different, but you will see some overarching similarities due to Confucianism, Buddhism, and other religious practices.
- In these cultures, individuals consider the good of the society as opposed to the individual.
- Family cultures appear to be the motivating factor that pushes for extensive education.
- It is important to notice what behavior Asian students are comfortable with.
- Use culturally relevant instruction whenever possible.
- Saving face is an important concept in all the Asian cultures.
- Learn your students as well as you can. Ask questions and usually they will be happy to tell you how they really feel, but only if they are comfortable with you.

Discussion Questions and Activities

1. Your new student, Jin Wu, focuses intently as you are giving instructions for the writing test. Students have 45 minutes to complete the exam. Students begin to work, and Jin Wu puts his head down and starts reading. Complete silence fills the room as students write furiously. After 30 minutes have elapsed, Jin Wu raises his hand to ask a question. You go to him, and he points to the first writing prompt and asks what it means. It reads, "Mr. Wagner's gross expenses far exceed his net salary and he can barely break even. Describe some ways for him to improve his lot." What do you think happened here?

2. Choi Soon Lee is a new Korean student in your class. He makes friends with other Koreans in class; soon you learn that he is carrying books, buying lunch, and doing homework for others who are a bit older. What do you think is happening, and how would you approach this sensitive cultural issue?

3. Akemi Kobayashi listens to her teacher talk and nods her head affirmatively. When asked if she understands, she says yes and leaves to do her homework. The next day she shows up with her assignment in hand. When her teacher corrects the paper, she discovers that the assignment is totally wrong. She talks to Akemi about being sure to ask questions when she doesn't understand. Akemi nods her head affirmatively, but the next day the same thing happens. What is the reason for this behavior?

4. Idris and Sabera Kumar, Indian students, are students in your class. Every time you ask Sabera a question, she lowers her eyes and puts her head down while Idris answers for her. You need to talk to Idris to tell him that he has to let Sabera answer her own questions. What is happening, and how will you approach this topic?

Resources

A China Family Adventure
http://www.china-family-adventure.com/chinese-culture.html

Chinese Culture for Children—Fun Facts, Food, Music, Language & More (Dino Lingo Blog)
http://dinolingo.com/blog/2011/05/04/chinese-culture-for-children/#.WO2XdvnyuM8

Chinese Culture and Traditions (documentary)
https://www.youtube.com/watch?v=uWA4S-wNSgs

China l National Geographic Kids
http://kids.nationalgeographic.com/explore/countries/china/#china-dragon.jpg

Culture and Cultural Differences l beyond Intractability
http://czechkid.eu/si1140.html

China l Time for Kids
http://www.timeforkids.com/destination/china

China l Activity Village
https://www.activityvillage.co.uk/china

China Fun Facts | Mocomi Kids (YouTube)
https://www.youtube.com/watch?v=u4H-x-j-shQ

China Highlights
http://www.chinahighlights.com/travelguide/article-things-not-to-do-in-china.htm

The Culturosity.com
http://www.culturosity.com/online_intercultural_resources.htm

Web Japan-All Things Japan
http://web-japan.org/factsheet/

National Geographics for Kids
http://kids.nationalgeographic.com/explore/countries/japan/#japan-gardens.jpg

The Japanese School System
http://web-jpn.org/kidsweb/explore/schools/index.html

Explore Japan Schools
http://web-japan.org/kidsweb/explore/schools/q5.html

Japanese Games for Ipads
http://www.digitaldialects.com/iPad/Japanese.htm

The 7 Best Videos for Japanese
http://takelessons.com/blog/japanese-videos-for-language-students-z05

10 Shocking Facts about Korean Schools
http://grrrltraveler.com/countries/asia/korea/teaching-english/10-facts-korean-school/

Time for Kids around the World
http://www.timeforkids.com/destination/south-korea

ESL and Culture Resources
http://sites.sandiego.edu/esl/korean/

Are Korean Students Really Learning English
https://www.gooverseas.com/blog/are-korean-students-really-learning-english

South Korea National Geographic for Kids
http://kids.nationalgeographic.com/explore/countries/south-korea/#south-korea-market.jpg

Observations of Korean Students Versus American Students
https://www.esl101.com/blogs/observations-american-students-versus-korean-students#.WPu5a4jyvIU

TIME: Teacher, Leave Those Kids Alone (Korean *hagwons*)
http://content.time.com/time/magazine/article/0,9171,2094427,00.html

Top Universities Blog for Indian Students
https://www.topuniversities.com/blog/33-useful-websites-students

Online Games and Activities/Interactive Indian for Kids
http://india.mrdonn.org/games.html

Best of India Websites
http://besthistorysites.net/ancient-biblical-history/india/

India, Time for Kids
http://www.timeforkids.com/destination/india

Super Teacher Tools for India
http://www.timeforkids.com/destination/india

Using Technology in the Multicultural Classroom
https://prezi.com/rlie4-zvhb3q/using-technology-in-the-multicultural-classroom/

Six Elements for Technology Integration in Multicultural Classrooms
http://www.tandfonline.com/doi/pdf/10.1080/14759399800200033

8 Best Apps for English Learners and ESL Students
http://www.fluentu.com/english/blog/best-apps-learning-english-esl-students/

Best iOS Apps for EL Students (AppCrawlr)
http://appcrawlr.com/ios-apps/best-apps-ell-students

Museum with Walls (cultureNOW)
http://www.culturenow.org/smart_phone_apps

Teaching Culture in the 21st Century Language Classroom
http://digitalcommons.unl.edu/cgi/viewcontent.cgi?article=1176&context=teachlearnfacpub

The Impact of New Social Media on Intercultural Adaptation
http://digitalcommons.uri.edu/cgi/viewcontent.cgi?article=1230&context=srhonorsprog

Culturally and Linguistically Driven Misunderstanding?
The Analysis of Intercultural Misunderstanding
http://comm.louisville.edu/iic/IF%20Journal/IF%201%20(2)%202008/if1(2)2008tsutsui.html

Resolve Cross-Cultural Misunderstandings
https://sielearning.tafensw.edu.au/MCS/9362/Sterilisation%20disk%203/lo/7374/7374_00.htm

EL Basics l Colorin Colorado
http://www.colorincolorado.org/ell-basics

From the Classroom: Working with Chinese ELs
http://www.colorincolorado.org/article/classroom-working-chinese-ells

The Impact of Biculturalism on Language and Literacy Development: Teaching Chinese English
Language Learners
http://citeseerx.ist.psu.edu/viewdoc/download?doi=10.1.1.518.2631&rep=rep1&type=pdf

Meeting the Needs of Chinese English Language Learners at Writing
Centers in America: A Proposed Culturally Responsive Model
http://files.eric.ed.gov/fulltext/EJ1060052.pdf

Top 10 Chinese-Westerner Cultural Misunderstandings
http://www.echinacities.com/china-media/Be-Warned-Top-10-Chinese-Westerner-Misunderstandings-According-to-Chinese

Cultural Misunderstandings
https://www.psychologytoday.com/blog/looking-in-the-cultural-mirror/201005/cultural-misunderstandings

Three Common Cultural Misunderstandings
https://www.thecambridgenetwork.com/3-cultural-misunderstandings/

Work with diverse people
http://etraining.communitydoor.org.au/mod/page/view.php?id=318

eChinacities
http://www.echinacities.com/expat-corner/9-Potentially-ExasperatingEmbarrassing-Moments-to-Avoid-in-China

References

Angloinfo (2013). *Cultural norms and transition in Japan.* Retrieved October 20, 2013, from http://tokyo.angloinfo.com/information/moving/country-file/culture/

Ariza, E. N. & Lapp, S. I. (2012). *Literacy, language, and culture, methods and strategies for mainstream teachers with not-so-mainstream learners.* Charlotte, North Carolina: Kona Publishing and Media Group.

Ariza, E., Yahya, N., Zainuddin, H., & Morales-Jones, C. (2015). *Fundamentals of teaching English to speakers of other languages in K-12 mainstream classrooms* (4th ed.). Dubuque, IA: Kendall/Hunt Publishing.

Ariza, E. N. (2009). *Not for ESOL teachers: What every classroom teacher needs to know about the linguistically, culturally, and ethnically diverse student* (2nd ed.). Boston, MA: Allyn and Bacon Publishing (Division of Pearson).

Bojang, A. B., & Barber, N. (2006). *Focus on China.* Milwaukee, WI: World Almanac Library. Hobber Wayland.

Bond, M. H. (2010). *The Oxford handbook of Chinese psychology.* Oxford University Press, USA.

Byon, A. S. (2006). The role of linguistic indirectness and honorifics in achieving linguistic politeness in Korean requests.

Castells, M. (2011). *The power of identity: The information age: Economy, society, and culture* (Vol. 2). Hoboken, NJ:John Wiley & Sons.

Census of India: Literacy and Level of Education (2017). *Censusindia.gov.in.* Retrieved April 22, 2017, from http://censusindia.gov.in/Census_And_You/literacy_and_level_of_education.aspx

Cummins, J. (2000). Putting language proficiency in its place: Responding to critiques of the conversational/academic language distinction. In *English in Europe: The acquisition of a third language* (pp. 54–83). Clevedon: Multilingual Matters.

Dam, P. (2010). *Linguistic considerations for English Language Learners.* Retrieved August 5, 2012, from http://www.viethoc.com/Ti-Liu/bien-khao/khaoluan/linguisticconsiderationsforenglishlanguage-learners.

Delpit, L., & Dowdy, J. K. (Eds.). (2008). *The skin that we speak: Thoughts on language and culture in the classroom.* New York: The New Press.

Freeman, D. E., & Freeman, Y. S. (2004). *Essential linguistics: What you need to know to teach reading, ESL, spelling, phonics, and grammar.* Phoenix, AZ:Education Review//Reseñas Educativas.

Furner, J. M., & Robison, S. (2004). Using TIMSS to improve the undergraduate preparation of mathematics teachers. *Issues in the undergraduate mathematics preparation of school teachers*, 4. Qualitative study. *Intercultural Communication Studies 20*(1), 141–157.

Gay, G. (2010). *Culturally responsive teaching: Theory, research, and practice.* Teachers College Press.

Guo, P. (2008). *Common English mistakes made by native Chinese speakers.* Retrieved August 6, 2012, from http://www.pgbovine.net/chinese-english-mistakes.htm.

Han, H. S., & Thomas, M. S. (2010). No child misunderstood: Enhancing early childhood teachers' multicultural responsiveness to the social competence of diverse children. *Early Childhood Education Journal, 37*(6), 469–476.

Holcombe, C. (2011). *A history of East Asia: From the origins of civilization to the twenty-first century.* Cambridge: Cambridge University Press.

Ikeda, M. (2010). *Teaching English to Japanese students.* Retrieved August 11, 2012, from http://humanities. byu.edu/elc/Teacher/japanesestudents.html

Kalman, B. (2009). *Japan: The culture.* New York, NY: Crabtree Publishing Company.

Klein, A. M. (2012). *Raising multicultural awareness in higher education.* Lanham, MD:University Press of America.

Kummer, P. K. (2008). *South Korea: Enchantment of the world.* New York, NY: Scholastic, Children's Press.

Kwintessential. (2004). *South Korea—Language, culture, customs and etiquitte.* Retrieved October 24, 2013, from http://www.kwintessential.co.uk/resources/global-etiquette/south-korea-country-profile.html.

Lai, E. Y. P., & Arguelles, D. (Eds.). (2003). *The new face of Asian Pacific America: Numbers, diversity & change in the 21st century.* Los Angeles, CA:Asian Week Books.

Langford, J. M. (2013). *Consoling ghosts: stories of medicine and mourning from Southeast Asians in exile.* Minneapolis, MN:University of Minnesota Press.

Lee, E., Mock, M. R., McGoldrick, M., Giordano, J., & Garcia-Preto, N. (2005). Asian families. *Ethnicity & family therapy* (pp. 269–289).

Lee, J. S., & Bowen, N. K. (2006). Parent involvement, cultural capital, and the achievement gap among elementary school children. *American Educational Research Journal, 43*(2), 193–218.

Lee, M. (2008). Mixed race peoples in the Korean national imaginary and family. *Korean Studies, 32*(1), 56–85.

Lee, S. J. (2015). *Unraveling the "model minority" stereotype: Listening to Asian American youth.* NY: Teachers College Press.

Li, G., & Wang, L. (2008). *Model minority myth revisited: An interdisciplinary approach to demystifying Asian American educational experiences.* UMichigan:IAP.

Lu, L., Gilmour, R., Kao, S. F., & Huang, M. T. (2006). A cross-cultural study of work/family demands, work/family conflict and wellbeing: the Taiwanese vs British. *Career Development International 11*(1), 9–27.

Mackerras, C. (Ed.). (2000). *Eastern Asia: An introductory history.* Australia: Longman.

Mason, C. (2000). *A short history of Asia: Stone Age to 2000 AD.* New York: St. Martin's Press.

Morris, J. S. (2012). Indian values, attitudes and behavior, and educational considerations. *HOME: Healing Ourselves & Mother Earth.* Retrieved September 15, 2013 from http://www.h-o-m-e.org/cultural-awareness/indian-values.html.

Murphey, R. (2003). *A history of Asia.* (4th ed.). New York: Longman.

Qian, X. (December 26, 2011). How to understand the core values of Chinese culture? *Liaoning Daily.* Retrieved September 13, 2013 from http://www.bjqx.org.cn/qxweb/n42499c7.aspx.

Richardson, R. M., & Smith, S. W. (2007). The influence of high/low-context culture and power distance on choice of communication media: Students' media choice to communicate with professors in Japan and America. *International Journal of Intercultural Relations 31*(4), 479–501.

Sá, C. M., & Sabzalieva, E. (2017). The politics of the great brain race: public policy and international student recruitment in Australia, Canada, England and the USA. Springer, Metherlands: *European Journal of Higher Education,* 1–23.

Scior, K., Kan, K. Y., McLoughlin, A., & Sheridan, J. (2010). Public attitudes toward people with intellectual disabilities: A cross-cultural study. *Intellectual and Developmental Disabilities 48*(4), 278–289.

Senge, P. M., Cambron-McCabe, N., Lucas, T., Smith, B., & Dutton, J. (2012). *Schools that learn (updated and revised): A fifth discipline fieldbook for educators, parents, and everyone who cares about education.* Danvers, MA: Crown Business.

Shah, N. R. (2013). Literacy rate in India. *International Journal of Research in all Subjects in Multi Languages.* 2321–2853.

Somervill, B. A. (2012). *Japan.* New York, NY: Children's Press.

State Demographics Data—NY. (2017). *migrationpolicy.org.* Retrieved April 22, 2017, from http://www.migrationpolicy.org/data/state-profiles/state/demographics/NY.

Sun, W. & Chen, G.-M. (1999). Dimensions of difficulties Mainland Chinese students encounter in the United States. Intercultural Communication Studies, 9(1), 19–30.

Takada, N. & Lampkin, R. L. (2011). *The Japanese way.* New York, NY: McGraw Hill.

Tillman, L. C., & Scheurich, J. J. (2013). *Handbook of research on educational leadership for equity and diversity.* NY: Routledge.

Trueba, H. T., Jacobs, L., & Kirton, E. (2014). *Cultural conflict & adaptation.* Routledge.

TSI (Technological Solutions, Inc.). (2013a). China. In *Ducksters.* Retrieved September 15, 2013, from http://www.ducksters.com/geography/country.php?country=China.

TSI (Technological Solutions, Inc.). (2013b). Japan. In *Ducksters.* Retrieved September 15, 2013, from http://www.ducksters.com/geography/country.php?country=Japan.

TSI (Technological Solutions, Inc.). (2013c). South Korea. In *Ducksters.* Retrieved September 15, 2013, from http://www.ducksters.com/geography/country.php?country=South Korea.

TSI (Technological Solutions, Inc.). (2013d). India. In *Ducksters.* Retrieved September 15, 2013, from http://www.ducksters.com/geography/country.php?country=India.

Tu, W. (Ed.) (1996). *Confucian traditions in East Asian modernity: Moral education and economic culture in Japan and the four min-dragons.* Cambridge, MA: Harvard University Press.

van de Kreeke, C. (2010). English speaking problems in Japanese classrooms. Retrieved August 10, 2012, from http://suite101.com/article/tefl-in-japan-a215687.

Xu, K. (2012). Chinese. In E. N. W. Ariza and S. I. Lapp (Eds.), *Literacy, language & culture* (pp. 229–224). Charlotte, North Carolina: Kona Publishing and Media Group.

Yao, X. (2000). *An introduction to Confucianism.* Cambridge University Press.

Yuan, W. (2011). Academic and cultural experiences of Chinese students at an American university: A qualitative study. *Intercultural Communication Studies 20*(1). 141–157.

Zimmermann, S. (1995). Perceptions of intercultural communication competence and international student adaptation to an American campus. *Communication Education 44*(4), 321–333.

CHAPTER 22

HAITIANS

Eileen N. Whelan Ariza

With contributions from Mr. Success Innocent,

and Mr. Evan Noel

KEY POINTS

- Haitians will go to extraordinary lengths to get a good education for their children.
- Haiti is the poorest nation in the Western Hemisphere, but the desire for education is probably one of the highest.
- Even if the Haitian parents are pre or semiliterate, they will go to great lengths to get their own children the best education possible.
- Haitian culture is a complex mix of cultures, religions, and ethnicities but is very family oriented and driven to become successful.

Being an educator in South Florida has given me the opportunity to learn much about Haitians and Haitian culture. The more my students from Haiti share about themselves, their beliefs, and their culture, the better I comprehend that Haiti is a historically rich, complex, fascinating country with citizens who are rightfully proud of their heritage. Mr. Success Innocent, Mr. Evan Noel, Mr. Joey Bautista, and Ms. Sheila Santiague have shared their perspectives on Haitian life and culture with me, which augments my personal experience with Haitian students and parents. Many mainstream teachers may not ever have the opportunity to know Haitians; therefore, I would like to share the delightful aspects of this culture, as well as clarify some unwarranted negative assumptions. People with whom we are culturally distant and have virtually no interaction often appear "mysterious" to mainstream Americans. Understanding a culture helps educators to provide a more amenable climate for instruction. However, realizing that research is not always current, may be inaccurate, and anecdotal experiences may appear to be hearsay, I will do my best to illuminate the richness and depth of this most fascinating society. I try to mix research with personal or anecdotal experience to capture a more accurate image.

Mr. Success Innocent, French teacher:

Educational opportunities in Haiti are among the lowest in the Western Hemisphere, and most kids do not have a chance to start school on time. However, the law says kids are supposed to begin school at six, but that never happens because most schools are private and parents cannot afford to send their kids at early age. About 90 percent of schools in Haiti are private schools. In addition, more than 55 percent of students drop out high school before they attended their senior year.

In Haiti, parents are sometimes required to act as educators. In certain cities, some schools only admit children who can already read and write. When parents are unable to afford to send all children to school, they either focus on one child who is interested in academics or alternate which year the kids get to go to school.

The level of poverty is very high in Haiti, and education is a means to gain prosperity, but the parents of students in your classroom may not have had the chance to attend school themselves. About 25 percent of Haitian parents have college degrees. They may not know how to interact with teachers and how the American school day is structured. But regardless of their own level of education, Haitian parents are diligent about their own children's education.

Family Culture/School Involvement

Teachers can welcome Haitian parents by shaking hands. This is a standard way to greet parents of all genders in Haitian culture. Parents will be very happy to see their children are going to school because children are extremely valued and parents do the best they can to educate their kids. Teachers need to teach the Haitian students the importance of being on time because it is not as important in the Haitian culture. More than 60 percent of Haitians live in a multi-generational house, where good manners are part of the culture. Children respect adults and are taught to politely greet visitors as good manners are tremendously important.

(*Note:* Mr. Innocent is a French teacher in the school district who is extremely intelligent. He speaks French, Kreyol, Spanish, and English. For two years, he has been allowed to work on a temporary teaching certificate (he already has a bachelor's degree) and needs to pass a series of exams [Florida Teaching Competency Exam] to get his permanent teaching certificate. He has passed all the exams, except the writing component. This is odd, because he is a very good writer in English, as I discovered while grading his papers in my Foreign Language Methodology class. We met to discuss the issue, and I began questioning him about the writing component. I was not surprised, but terribly disappointed when he told me that he could not pass the writing portion because he did not understand certain vocabulary words in either of the writing prompts. This validates my assertion about assessment needing to be authentic and reliable. How can you show you are capable of writing a three-paragraph essay if you do not understand the vocabulary in the prompt? No matter how well you write, you cannot answer the question if you don't know what they are asking, and the context did not give him enough clues. This is so unjust and actually invalid. He will lose his teaching job if he does not pass this essay.

Mr. Evan Noel, preservice teacher, undergraduate student:

Although, Haiti may be identified as one of the poorest nations in the world, their educational system is one of the highest in the world. If you could ask any Haitian about one positive aspect about education, they would probably say education is the key to success, or without education, the world would be a disaster. The value given in regard to education had been established many centuries ago when France colonized Haiti. We not only possess their native language, but we also have a similar educational system in which many individuals trust, including all Haitian parents. Parents are highly motivated about education. It is the primary reason why they push their kids so hard into getting a great education. Parents will put their own lives at risk in order to provide for the family, and come up with money to pay tuition for their kids. As a Haitian kid, you ought to be respectful to your parents because they want the best of everything for you. In other words, our parents are not used to the sweet life, nor the rich life, so they want their kids to experience the life they never had. They will sacrifice anything for their kids to get ahead, but they expect the kids to work hard for their education.

Haitian parents would rather hear any bad news about their sons and daughters, but they do not want to hear that they have a boyfriend or girlfriend. It would be a disaster if they ever found out about that, and they would say: "I pay my money to get you in school, and all you want to do is have a boyfriend or girlfriend." Your life will be a misery from this point on, because you just lost their trust. The only thing you should never do in life is to lose your parents' trust. They will make sure you get your life in order, to the point that they will make decisions about your life for you. Haitian parents will love you even more if you stay in school, but do not hurt them by having a boyfriend or girlfriend. Try to do the right thing.

Teachers are considered as a second family to a student because students listen to teachers a lot, and kids spend more time in school than home. Teachers will care for students in a way that will help them to facilitate their education. It is wonderful when a student has one or two teachers he or she can confide in, because these types of students will help the student encounter less pressure or stress. Teachers teach, students listen, and parents supervise. Parents have the most important job of all—the job to keep their kids on task, make sure their homework is done, and motivate them. Parents have high expectations for their kids no matter the circumstance. They will raise you to be kind, honest, respectful, optimistic, and valuable to your surroundings.

As already mentioned in the chapter, the Haitian educational system is derived from the French educational system. Before the Haitians fought a glorious battle to obtain their independence, they were colonized by France. One teacher made me realize that to know anyone's culture very well, you must learn about their history. Haitians are a very proud people.

Our educational system requires one more class than is necessary in the U.S. educational system. For instance, in the United States, students start from 1st grade through 12th grade, and we move to the university. In Haiti, students start from 1st grade through 6th grade (called "Primary School"), then we jump to 7th grade, 8th grade, 9th grade, 3eme, Segonde, Rheto, and Philo (and this stage is called "secondary school.") Before students are allowed to jump into 7th grade, there is a national official exam that all 6th graders must pass that we often called "certificate or sept kout Pikwa." If students do not meet the expectations, they will not be allowed in the secondary schools. If the students meet the expectations, they will receive a certificate from the department of education notifying them that they have succeeded in the exams.

Unfortunately, the educational budget of Haiti is usually the lowest amongst other nations. We encounter situations where parents are unable to send their kids to school due to lack of money. Also, some kids are orphans with no opportunity for them to access schools. Our last president, Michel Joseph Martelly, promised that he would include in his budget the right that all Haitian children would have free education. The schools that are led by the government are called "Lycee". In my hometown (Gonaives, Haiti), we had many schools from the government often called "lekol leta" and usually there is one Lycee for girls only, one for boys only, and the others are mixed gender. Those schools are affordable to many, but parents want their children to have the best education ever so they often chose a school with an extraordinary reputation. To enter a Lycee school, there is a test presented to all the possible new students, but the final decision is made like a lottery drawing. Either you have sufficient contacts, or you know an official person from the school to access your entry. Furthermore, we have schools led by religious organizations that would be for girls only or boys only, or mixed. Those schools have resources to create an educational atmosphere. They have better pay for teachers, which means their education level is at the top. Teachers should be better paid, because they are teaching kids who will shape the future, which is a future that seems bleak to us, but they are in charge of different minds. Religious organizations make their teachers happy in a way that can facilitate the education of students. They want to teach righteousness, and they are fighting for Haiti to have a prolific educational system.

Other schools often have problems in making their professors happy, which means teachers may not care enough to come to class if you are not paying them. This scenario happens frequently in Lycee schools, or local schools, due to lack of governmental funding. All the schools have their own uniforms, although sometimes it may appear that some uniforms are identical, but they are not. It is the only way to draw a difference between the schools. The schools with greatest achievement rate in the national exams are considered like a pot of gold because every parent would want their kids to be in that school in order for them to pass the national test. Inside we encounter situations where kids would rather want to stay on the streets rather than stay in school. The dropout rate is getting higher every day because of the hardship of life, and the fact that some families are not financially stable. Many students have parents living in the United States, meaning those students usually give signs of lacking interest in school because they know their parents will do their best to get them in the United States (the dreamland). However, we have students that believe, no matter whether their parents live in the United States or in Haiti, that they should take pride in their education, and they value the idea that education is essential.

Haitian History

Haitians proudly proclaim that they were the first Blacks to gain freedom from slavery when they fought against France in 1804. As descendants of African slaves, Haitians are predominately Black, with a small number of mulattos (a mix of Black and White) who often compose the more elite, privileged ruling class.

Haiti has two national languages, French and Haitian Creole, but the higher status language is French. Schooling has typically been through French. Although virtually everyone can speak or understand Haitian Creole, until recently it was easy to determine the educational status of individuals because anyone who had been to school spoke French. With the shift from teaching only French to the inclusion of Haitian Creole in the schools, it is now more difficult to determine educational backgrounds.

Because of its lower status, many Haitians deny their ability to speak Creole. On the other hand, because of its prestigious status, some individuals falsely claim to speak French.

Haiti's culture and society are complex, and they struggle with issues that are dualist in nature. Dualist characteristics include the following areas:

1. French language versus Haitian Creole.
2. European (or White) ethnic background versus African (Black) ethnic background.
3. Socioeconomic class differences between the mulatto elite and the majority population of poorer Blacks.
4. The wealthier urban versus the poorer rural population.
5. Christianity versus the Voodoo religions.
6. The inequity of the extremely wealthy versus the abject poorer masses.
7. Educational access of the rich versus the poor, who may be illiterate. (Civan, 1995; Lee, 2004).

As in many less advantaged countries, unskilled rural peasants have migrated into the cities in search of work, thus overpopulating the cities and contributing to urban problems and significant social changes. A prominent class system was typically marked by the distinction of the highly educated Haitians, who are extremely wealthy, and the very poor Haitians, who are illiterate or undereducated.

In the U.S. school systems, we see all types of Haitian students who reflect their educational and economic class, including a recently emerging middle class. As an educator, I am in awe when I meet Haitians from rural areas who could not afford to send their children to public schools (because they could not afford uniforms or books), yet they have triumphed over incredible odds to get to the United States. As I have learned from my students, many parents who have made it to the United States have found jobs and have sent money home to pay for their children's education, only to learn later that it was misused and the children never attended school. It is not uncommon for teachers in the American schools to have a new Haitian student, in any grade, who has never attended school. Or, in the case of one teacher, she found that the child in her class was obviously not the age the "birth certificate" states. False papers used to enter the country were shown when the student was registered in school; consequently, the student was incorrectly placed according to the stated age on the passport. Conversely, the reverse happens as well, when a student is placed in a class of age-related peers, yet is far more academically advanced than his or her American counterparts.

Religion and Vodou (or Voodoo)

Misconceptions about the Haitian religious practices abound and are as complex as they are distinct. One of the most salient and negative stereotypes about Haitians concerns the practice of Vodou (also known as Voodoo, Voudou, Bodoun, or Vodun) (Brown, 1998; Métraux, 2016). Although traditionally the population has been predominantly Roman Catholic, a small minority are Protestants, and many Haitians are converting to fundamentalist Christianity due to the proliferation of Protestant missionaries feeding and providing health care to the poor in Haiti. Some Haitians are exclusively Vodouists. This is not "black magic," but is a religion that combines African religious beliefs with rituals blended from Roman Catholic symbols, pictures of saints, and prayers and is similar to the Santeria beliefs of Cuba and Brazil. The amulets that are used in Catholicism may really represent saints or spirits in Vodou. Others observe a mixture of religious practices or practice no religion at all.

In actuality, this tradition of blending spiritualism with a traditional religion, such as Catholicism, is not limited to Haitians. I have seen this phenomenon in many Latin American countries. My own Colombian mother-in-law, a devout Roman Catholic, placed a glass of water and a votive candle in front of my deceased father-in-law's picture. She explained that his soul might return and be thirsty. Incorporated within the blend of rituals of traditional religion are beliefs in family spirits that may be ancestors of the living, intermediaries of God, human emotion, or natural forces. **Loas** (spirits) or **iwas**, can be called upon to help families, to bring fortune, to protect the family or loved ones, or to attack enemies in return for gifts of food, drink, or flowers. Drumming, dancing, and drinking near the family altar are usual components of Vodou ceremonies. Vodou beliefs do not encourage individual accountability for personal actions; therefore, the Roman Catholic clergy is more accepting of vodou practices than Protestant clergy, who think that the practices are diabolical (Civan, 1995; Desmangles, 2000; Michel & Bellegarde-Smith, 2006).

During illness or crisis, religion plays a major role in Haitian life. Vodou beliefs may include the ideas of the "living dead" (zombies) that bring misfortune. Craan (1988) and Pressley-Sanon, (2016) explain that zombification (catalepsy) results when an individual is poisoned with a neurotoxin (like that of a puffer fish) and is apparently dead. My students have explained to me that this is really a hoax to control the population. The person who appears dead has a funeral, and the family and friends mourn for the loved one. The apparent "deceased" is buried in a coffin that has holes or some way to let the individual continue breathing. Later the person is aroused, only to frighten the others into believing that he or she is a zombie. Uneducated individuals who are unaware of this scam are controlled by folk beliefs and superstitions. Practitioners of Vodou (Coriel, 1983; Cosgray, 1995; Rahill, Jean-Gilles, Thomlison, & Pinto-Lopez, 2011) may be the following:

- ❑ Readers or diviners
- ❑ *Hungan* (male priests), *mambo* (female priests), or *bokors* (black magic practitioners)
- ❑ *Docte fey* (folk healers)
- ❑ *Matronn* or *fam saj* (midwives)
- ❑ *Docte zo* (bonesetters)
- ❑ *Pikirist* (injectionists)

Health Practices

After looking at the Haitian perspectives of religion, it is easy to understand the connection between religion and health practices. Undereducated Haitians are likely to attribute illness to reasons that are not based on scientific sources. Cold, heat, winds, bodily imbalance, punishment from God, or bad spirits (Colin & Paperwalla, 1996; Martin, Rissmiller, & Beal, 1995; Pierre, Minn, Sterlin. Annoual. Jaimes, Raphaël, & Kirmayer, 2010) may be blamed for disease and afflictions. To a population whose beliefs and daily practices are shaped by a lack of basic healthcare (clean water, prenatal care, antibiotics, etc.), folk or spiritual healing may be the only options that have ever been available for treating disease. By learning about and understanding living conditions and the environment in Haiti, it is easier to understand why we might see Haitians who go to a doctor and also seek treatment from the herbalist, *docte fe,* and use magic or religious measures to prevent illness or harm (DeSantis & Thomas, 1990; Khoury, Kaiser, Keys, Brewster, & Kohrt, 2012). In fact, this occurs in many other societies, including the United States.

As in many cultures (Italian, Jamaican, and Greek, for example), Haitians recognize culture-bound illnesses such as **maldyok** (the evil eye, which is brought on as a result of an envious glance from another). Disease prevention (Colin & Paperwalla, 1996) may include being plump (as a result of eating well), sleeping well, keeping warm, exercising, and keeping clean to avoid weakness (*febles*). A balance between "hot" and "cold" factors such as hot and cold foods is believed to prevent illness. Enemas (*lavman*) for children and pregnant women are used to purify the inner body. Herbal teas, massage, and spiritual practice (including Catholic ritual and Vodou practices) are other ways to prevent illness. It may be frustrating to the U.S. educator when the Haitian does not comply with traditional doctors' prescribed medicine or treatment (Preston, Materson, Yoham, & Anapol, 1996). Noncompliance with conventional prescribed medicine may be a consequence of many causes, such as difficulty understanding the illness, difficulty maintaining ongoing relationship with the care providers, self-medication, or because the patient is listening to the spiritual healer instead of the doctor. In the case of a minor, this type of situation becomes delicate because U.S. educators, who are mandated to report child abuse, might misinterpret the actions of the Haitian parent and report the incident to the child welfare authorities.

According to my Haitian students, the most devastating prejudice they have experienced was the misconception that they all had AIDS. When they went to donate blood, they were denied and told it was because they were Haitian. In 1982, the U.S. Centers for Disease Control mistakenly assumed that AIDS began in Haiti. Later, in 1985 the classification was abandoned, but the damage was already done; Haitians everywhere have been ostracized and have felt like pariahs in U.S. society (Rose St. Clair, personal communication November 24, 2004). This fallacy is slowly losing ground, but many Haitians recall the mortification of living through this travesty.

Social Relations

Haitians usually live with the extended family, but this may not be possible after leaving their country. Although a matriarchal family structure is the norm, common law marriages (*plasaj*) are considered acceptable, and an individual might have more than one common law marriage in life (Coreil, Barnes-Josiah, & Cayemittes, 1996). The extended family includes half-brothers and half-sisters that are born to either the mother or father. They will live harmoniously in the same household. The man of the family is controlling and the highest authority, but both parents are authoritative, and discipline is corporal. When Haitians live in the United States, this attitude presents a problem because corporal punishment is considered child abuse. Haitian parents face true crises in the United States. Because they fear governmental authorities, they often lose control of their children to the negative influences of the U.S. culture. Without a strong ethnic enclave to support one another, Haitian families may not survive in the United States (Colin & Paperwalla, 1996; McCurdy, Gannon, & Daro, 2003).

Language:

Haitian students in the United States come to the classroom with a special language situation. All Haitians communicate in Creole, and it keeps the population connected. However, the schools in Haiti usually instruct in French, and students may have the opportunity to learn English. Formerly Creole was not a written language, and it suited the culture as Haiti has a strong oral culture and language, which promotes literacy through storytelling. Usually you can tell if the students have attended school in Haiti if they can read and write French. However, when students are in the U.S. classroom, it might be helpful to try to instruct through Creole scaffolding while trying to teach English academics (Dejean, 2010). Creole began to be the medium of instruction in Haiti, but French was still the official language of instruction, and reading and writing were conducted in French. A stigma existed for those who spoke Creole because French was the higher status language. To add English to the mix becomes even more difficult, so it might be a good strategy to continue to maintain literacy in Creole to facilitate learning in English.

Creole has 10 vowels and 3 semi-vowels, and 17 consonant sounds. When Creole became a standardized orthography, the sound symbol correspondence was kept so it could be acquired easier. In addition, there are different ways of speaking Creole, depending on what part of the island the person is from. Arts, acting, singing, drama, role-play, chorale singing, videos and cartoons, and language learning mobile apps are great choices to help students learn English.

Problems for Haitian Speakers Learning English:

Double negatives
No-ing on words
No subject–verb agreement
Trouble distinguishing subject and objects (he, I)
Nouns before a number are not pluralized

Implications for the U.S. Educator

Before beginning this section on education, I want to point out that in any teaching or learning situation the most difficult goal to achieve is trying to teach a concept that is nonexistent to the students. You are asking them to imagine something they have never seen. For example, most U.S. children know what a zoo is. But if they have never visited a zoo, how can you explain what it is? Some students do not know what I mean when I talk about an escalator. Why not? Think about where you would find an escalator—in a modern mall, maybe? If the parents shop only at a swap meet where tables are laden with goods or spread out on a blanket on the ground, you can see why they would not understand the concept of an escalator. This is true for Floridian students who have never seen a New York fire escape, a basement, an attic, a fireplace, or snow. Similarly, a child from Massachusetts may not know about central air conditioning or a Florida room. Even the most educated students may not know what culturally bound concepts are. Many Americans do not know what a bidet is. My own child made me realize this simple yet profound truth. One day when my daughter was five, I was ironing a blouse. Pointing to the iron, she said, "Mommy, what is that?" I was incredulous, and a little embarrassed. Had I not taught her what an iron was? It occurred to me that I ironed only at night when the children were asleep. But what would her teacher have thought if she had asked my daughter to label or describe an iron?

Haitian culture is vibrant and rich in oral tradition. Jokes, riddles, proverbs, folktales, games, and stories reflect their clever use of oral expression. Storytelling is an art and is performed for an appreciative audience. This expressive ability is quite a contrast to the literacy statistics; about 50 percent of Haitians can read and write (*The World Factbook*). Although the dropout rate is high, there is no age limit on returning to school. Therefore, an adult could be in a class of young children.

In U.S. schools and school supply stores, resources are unlimited and are governed only by the teacher's budget. The Haitian teacher, like many teachers all over the world, becomes adept at creating something out of nothing. However, what Americans recycle (such as a tire), might hold a different meaning for someone from another culture. Two students in my graduate class demonstrated this point vividly when we were examining a picture of a U.S. recycling center that showed used tires used as a planter for flowers and for a children's swing hanging on a tree. My Venezuelan student shared with the class that a tire would never be recycled as trash; they use tires to make shoes. However, my Haitian student said that in her country, in times of political unrest, the tire could be used as a burning barricade or a mode of execution known as "**Pe Lebren**" or "**Pere Lebrun**," named after a man who owned a tire store. We were all shocked to learn that tires were put around someone's neck and lit on fire as a deadly warning to others.

The educational system in Haiti is very different from that of the United States. The school system was modeled after the traditional French system with a rigorous, classical curriculum. In spite of recent reforms, receiving an education in Haiti remains an elusive goal for most citizens. A limited number of Haitians receive formal education. In 1987, the educational system was changed to include instruction through Haitian Creole, the prominent language originally shunned by the elite. Education remains a class privilege only afforded to the wealthy and the middle class.

Official transcripts might belie the amount or quantity of educational content the student from Haiti might possesses. Huge academic gaps may exist, and often the student must first learn to read or write. On the other hand, the student might be further advanced than his or her counterpart in the American school. Previous educational and life experiences will vary greatly; it is up to us as educators to determine, to the best of our ability, the individual needs of our students.

FINAL POINTS

- Haitian parents have gone through great sacrifices to put their children in school.

- Students are expected to do their best in school and will be severely punished for not doing well.

- Haitian parents are not accustomed to being partners in education and must be taught that they have a right to collaborate with the school.

- Haitian parents often will let the teacher be the "boss" because they have great respect for the teachers. They may ask the teacher to discipline (spank) the child for misbehaving or not studying enough.

- We must educate the parents to teach them what to expect in schools in the United States.

Discussion Questions and Activities

1. In Mrs. Brown's class, Pierre Frank, a student from Haiti, is having difficulty in a number of areas. He will not look at Mrs. Brown when she speaks to him, and she thinks he is very rude. What is the reason for Pierre's behavior, and how can Mrs. Brown learn about his culture?

2. Mrs. Brown needs to have a conference with Pierre's family; she has called his house several times, but she has gotten nowhere. She sends letters home only to find them in Pierre's book bag months later. He is having a difficult time taking multiple-choice tests. Describe ways that Mrs. Brown can help Pierre become more successful in school.

3. Pierre has been sick, and Mrs. Brown has noticed strange smells emanating from his clothes. He went to the doctor, who prescribed antibiotics, but he went to see a folk healer as well. What might be the reasons for this behavior?

4. The after school program for Haitian students is very well attended. Students love to come to the library where we offer books, video games, recordings, practice work sheets, and volunteer students work tutoring the kids with the homework. We notice that the parents come with the kids and seem to enjoy watching their children working with literacy games. Think of five ways we could include the parents in this after school center program. The parents speak very little English but we can tell they are very happy that their kids are here every day.

Resources

NYC Resource Department
http://schools.nyc.gov/Academics/ELL/FamilyResources/default.htm

Division of World Languages
https://clas.uiowa.edu/dwllc/allnet/haitian-creole-language-and-culture-resources

How to teach ESL to Haitian Children
http://www.eslteachersboard.com/cgi-bin/lessons/index.pl?read=5010

HaitiHub
https://www.haitihub.com/resources/

Stories from Haiti
http://www.oxfam.org.uk/education/resources/stories-from-haiti-11-14

Teaching for Haiti
http://www.teachingforchange.org/teacher-resources/haiti

English Learner Resource
https://www.readinga-z.com/ell/

Facts about Haiti
https://www.factretriever.com/haiti-facts

Eight Days: A Story of Haiti
http://www.colorincolorado.org/book/eight-days-story-haiti

Parent Tip sheet
http://www.colorincolorado.org/guide/parent-tip-sheets-haitian-creole

The Banza: A Haitian Story
http://www.colorincolorado.org/book/banza-haitian-story

Ten Ways to Support Displaced Students from Haiti
http://www.ldonline.org/article/36284

References

Dejean, Y. (2010). Creole and education in Haiti. *The Haitian Creole language: History, structure, use, and education*, 199–216.

Desmangles, L. G. (2000). *The faces of the gods: Vodou and Roman Catholicism in Haiti*. University of North Carolina Press.

Khoury, N. M., Kaiser, B. N., Keys, H. M., Brewster, A. R. T., & Kohrt, B. A. (2012). Explanatory models and mental health treatment: is vodou an obstacle to psychiatric treatment in rural Haiti?. *Culture, Medicine, and Psychiatry, 36*(3), 514–534.

Lee, W. O. (2004). *Equity and access to education: Themes, tensions, and policies.* Hong Kong: Asian Development Bank.

McCurdy, K., Gannon, R. A., & Daro, D. (2003). Participation patterns in home based family support programs: Ethnic variations. *Family Relations, 52*(1), 3–11.

Métraux, A. (2016). *Voodoo in Haiti.* Pickle Partners Publishing.

Michel, C., & Bellegarde-Smith, P. (Eds.). (2006). *Vodou in Haitian life and culture: invisible powers.* Springer.

Pressley-Sanon, T. (2016). *Zombifying a Nation: Race, Gender and the Haitian Loas on Screen.* McFarland.

Rahill, G., Jean-Gilles, M., Thomlison, B., & Pinto-Lopez, E. (2011). Metaphors as contextual evidence for engaging Haitian clients in practice: A case study. *American Journal of Psychotherapy, 65*(2), 133–149.

CHAPTER 23

NATIVE AMERICANS

Eileen N. Whelan Ariza

KEY POINTS

- It is important to respect the culture of Native Americans.
- There are over 566 Native American tribes in existence.
- Many people don't realize the religious significance of rituals and artifacts.
- Culturally relevant instruction is critical to these students.
- Numerous different Indian nations are found throughout the United States. For example, in the state of Florida alone we can find:
  Seminoles, Ais, Apalachee, Calusa, Creek, Miccosukee, Timucua, and Yemassee.
- Teachers can research the Native American students who are in their own states to determine the cultural values, beliefs, and matters of cultural relevance.

Native Americans or American Indians

I have always believed that Native American people were the closest people to royalty that the United States could claim. In writing this chapter, my plan was to research Native Americans, or Indians, so I could generalize what mainstream teachers could expect from students of this culture. I discovered that this was almost impossible, as I found over 500 indigenous tribal groups with distinctive cultural traits and over 2,200 languages spoken among them. Much mystery and misunderstanding surround the nation's first inhabitants. Interestingly, even Mormons have their own theories about Native Americans, believing that they are the ten lost tribes of Israel.

Every tribal nation has its own government and particular societal rules that govern and determine the wellbeing of the nation. These particular governments determine decisions concerning how rules should be enforced, how children should be disciplined, and how the tribal members should be taken care of it they are widows, orphans, sick, or indigent (Kunstadter, 2017; Reich, Patterson, Campbell, Tandon, Mazieres, & García, 2012).

Every tribe had its own language, sometimes related and mutually intelligible to other tribes, but usually not. Each has their own traditions, culture, mythology, and religions. Indian people were free citizens of their tribes when the people who would one day form the United States were the subjects of tyranny in lands far from here. Each tribe had citizens loyal and devoted to their nation, religion, language, society, and culture. Every state in the United States is home to Indian Nations and each population can be very different from one other. It is up to the teacher to determine which cultural groups their students are from, and what information is necessary to create culturally relevant instruction.

It is not easy to measure English language proficiency or the extent of mainstream acculturation found within the Native American tribes across North America (Baruth & Manning, 1992; Garrett & Pichette, 2000; Spring, 2016). I had read that members of Native American cultures were offended by being called Indians; however, according to my further research, books written by Native Americans claim this is not always true, and it truly depends on the individual's preference as to which is the more courteous and politically correct name (Axtell, 1988; King, 2012). Axtell suggests that reservation and urban Indians prefer the term "Indian" over Native American, but the term "Native American" is found on federal grants and college applications. Technically, all people who are born in the United States could refer to themselves as "Native American." The ideal situation is to study individual tribes and to refer to the individuals according to their tribes in this manner. "This semester we are going to study the Navaho and Hopi Indians (or whatever individual tribe is chosen as a topic of study)," as opposed to consolidating all Indians.

Another point I will add is that I kept finding different spellings for a certain tribe or word to describe an Indian object. I attribute this to many incorrect interpretations of pronunciation made by English speakers. Additionally, many words used in English today come from Indian origins or are a misconstruction of original Indian words. Table 14.1 shows examples from Watkins's book (1992; Watkins, 2001).

What is greatly offensive are racial stereotypes and terms such as: *Redman* or *Redskins*; the sidekick *Tonto* for the Lone Ranger; the requisite Indian statue outside of a store indicating that it is a trading post, and so on; Indians portrayed as sports mascots; trivialized spiritual ceremonies and inappropriate use of sacred items such as pipes, feathers, and body paint designs; and myths that are innocently passed on by teachers who read inaccurate history books. I suggest that all teachers read books such as *Lies My Teacher Told Me, Everything Your American History Textbook Got Wrong* by James W. Loewen (1995) and *Tribes and Tribulations, Misconceptions About American Indians and Their Histories* by Laurence M. Hauptman (1995).

Individuals of all cultures mirror the influence of community norms and values; imagine the miscommunication that can take place in the mainstream classroom when Indian children behave according to the rules and values of their home culture (Pewewardy & Hammer, 2003; Powers, 2006). An exploratory study of cultural identity and culture-based educational programs for urban American Indian students was performed, and researchers studied the community norms and socialization practices of tribal groups. Findings have shown that societal rules indeed do determine the behaviors of Native American students in the classroom. Although not all tribal nations are the same, often we can find overarching tendencies that might baffle the teacher who judges all students by cultural norms practiced by mainstream North Americans. The focus of this chapter is to examine some fundamental beliefs shared by many Indian tribes and to see how we can modify our classrooms to accommodate the different cultural, behavioral, and learning styles of Native American students.

TABLE 23.1 Words of Native American Origin
• *Athabaska* is also *Athapasca*.
• *Chippewa*, another pronunciation of *Ojibwa*, means "roasted until puckered."
• *Crazy Horse*, a Dakota warrior, was so named by English speakers because of a misinterpretation of his Indian name, which meant that he was so great that just the sight of his horses made people crazy with fear.
• *Eskimos* call themselves *Inuit* (the people). Eskimo means *raw meat eaters* in Eastern Canadian Algonquin. Some Inuit prefer *Eskimo* not be used (Damas, 1984).
• *Goyathlay* is the Apache name for *Geronimo*, which means *yawning* or *sleepy*.
• Hopi means *Hopitu* (peaceful ones) or *Hopitu-shinumu* (peaceful all people).
• *Igloo* (*igdler*) means "snow and ice house."

- *Iroquois* is Algonquin for *I'inakhoiw*, which means "real adders."
- *Kayak* is an Inuit man's boat.
- *Klondike* is Athapascan for *chendik* or *deer*.
- *Maize* (corn) originates from the Arawak, *marise*.
- *Manhattan* means "hilly island."
- *Missouri* is Algonquin for "Big Muddy."
- *Ojibaway* is also *Ojibway*, or *Ojibwa*.
- *Potlatch* means *giving* or *gift* and relates to the Chinook (Nootka Indian language) ceremony: the custom of giving away things, gifts of blankets, at the end of a ceremony, or the giving of valuable gifts so a man can increase his social prestige and standing (Pierre, 1971).
- *Wampum* originates from the word *wampampiak*, which approximates a meaning of a string of white shells used as money by Indians and early White settlers (Pierre, 1971).
- *Wigwam* is Algonquin for *wegiwa*.

Tharp (1989) and Cheng, Andrade, and Yan (2011) posit that two salient learning styles that contrast with each other are visual/verbal and holistic/analytic. Often schools value and reward the student who is verbal/analytical, as opposed to the student who has a visual learning style and prefers to learn through observation and practice. Typically, the Native American student demonstrates a more holistic thought process and may find the mainstream classroom incongruent with his or her cognitive learning style.

The Traditional Native American Classroom

Ms. Diane Y. Talley-Strike, a full-blooded Ojibwa Indian and member of the Sault Saint Marie Chippewa Indian nation, is a teacher who writes the following narrative about teaching Native American students. Her rendition of what being a Native American means illuminates the ideals, cultural characteristics, and learning styles of the Native American student. After reading her illustrious description, a mainstream teacher will be better prepared to teach the Native American in the classroom and will be able to adapt learning strategies to successfully reach students from Native American cultures.

I have had the fortune to see several of the classrooms on many reservations. Except for the different languages, each classroom is alike in its expectations with obvious similarities. On one of the reservations, the school is set up to house approximately 10 to 20 students. The school is circular with all the rooms leading to an atrium or a fire circle, and each room exits to a patio where group projects have a natural entrance to nature and the playground. There were ten rooms that started at the fire circle along the hall to each classroom and bathrooms were set between each classroom.

Each classroom has a different theme, depending on the age of the students who will inhabit the room. The younger ones have mats and pillows, and a rug in the middle of the room. A loom rests on one of the patios attached to the classroom; during the third-grade year, students learn how to weave in many different methods. A fire pit with the rules for fire makers is located on another patio. In this world, a fourth-grade class will boil the colors that are needed for the rug.

Once the students get to the fourth grade, they start to experience the different jobs within the complex system of the reservation and tribe. Some classroom patios have plants where students are learning medicine man ways from traditional old ways. Some of the patios had homes built from natural resources, for example, a tipi from skins, a hut from leaves and willow branches, and so forth. Each classroom focused on a different skill that the students would be learning for that year.

Today's society operates with computers, as they do on the reservations; they have one room complete with computers and a media center attached that even has a studio for television productions. The school has been equipped with all the latest conveniences. It is not the normal reservation school, but this tribe has seven casinos and a leader who has reinvested the profits in the tribe with acreage, schools, houses, and has promoted tribal support. This particular school goes to the ninth grade, but they recently learned that the ninth grade will be relocated to the high school the following year to make room for two new kindergarten classes.

Teachers carefully watch the students to see what their interests are, so they can start teaching the students an occupation within the tribe. Once the students' natural interests are determined, this is the work they will be dedicated to performing in the tribe. The students will begin to work with an elder who does the job the student wants to learn. These apprenticeships will last for the duration of the individual's membership with the tribe. When the person becomes an elder, he or she will take over the position at the time that it is needed. The older students also start teaching the younger students about the job they are doing. All students help the reservation out by picking up trash and building with the elders to make the reservation buildings better. Part of the day is spent with the elders; this is the highlight of the day for the children. The students are part of the community and are taught very early that they are responsible for the world around them.

The school day starts out the same; all the students get together at the fire circle with the elders, teachers, and staff. They watch announcements and discuss the day's assignments. They talk out problems and note the successes in a council fire setting. They do have fire pits so some of the students can learn to be keepers of the fire.

The students have mock council fires so that children can learn what position is right for them in the celebration setting of the circle of life. When the elders have a council fire, students are invited to learn how the elders reach agreements; the students are able to look on, but say nothing during an elders' council. Sometimes the elder council fires are at the school and other times they are held at the reservation council fire where the important tribal decisions are made.

Throughout the school, the most important concept the teachers try to promote is that of good manners so the students learn appropriate behavior from examples. The teachers talk to all the students, no matter what age or class that the student is in. This school is like a community with all eyes watching all the community members; no one can get away with bad behavior very easily. When an adult starts talking to the student, the young child's eyes move to the ground and you can actually see the child thinking about what is being said.

These are the children of the earth. They like to be outside with nature. The classroom is confining with four walls when one is used to being able to feel and touch nature. These are students who embrace the world around them. They believe everything has a spirit and every day, 24 hours a day, seven days a week, and 365 days a year, they are in God's country, being the keepers of the earth and skies. Every person is responsible for his or her own actions, rather than placing blame on good or evil, and the earth's force is all giving and loving to all. This goodness of earth will lead one in the straight path of life, if the choices for the good life are made.

These students will be the ones who learn by doing and experiencing the world around them. They may not sit in the chairs, but may choose to sit on the floor. They may be the ones who choose not to write, but will tell tales of the past and forecast the happenings of the future. Storytelling is an important skill that is taught to students so that the oral traditions are kept alive. The use of the hands to explain what is going on designates whether the student will be the researcher, a listener, or speaker. They will learn to listen and express their feelings and learn when it is their time to listen or be the talker. This is what you will see and feel with a Native American child in your classroom.

Cultural Beliefs

Native American culture and spirituality teach the group the value of living in harmony with the earth, honoring each other, and respecting the interdependence of all life. By looking back and rediscovering "The Old Ways," we can look forward to applying these constant truths to our modern dilemmas of today. Native American spirituality is based on an understanding of the fundamental organization of religion, for this is the basis of the culture. The spiritual approach gives the participant a chance for growth and to experience life.

Native American cultures look at life as a pathway that will lead them back to the whole life and to oneness with the creator. They are here to experience the love of life and to accept the great mystery of the seasons of maturity throughout the universe.

Throughout time, mankind has asked questions and has sought answers to the questions of existence, mortality, and immortality, what direction to follow, or how to find the answers that justify existence. Humans cling to the belief that there is a greater force in the universe and that there is a greater power than us. This belief system gives people comfort, logic, and order to the world they live in. In the Native American life, there is no death, only a passing that is celebrated for one year after what is considered to be the passing of the body to the pathway to the next world. Each individual tries to find a path to balance and understanding, to find his or her center and the meaning of life. The first lesson that was taught the Native Americans when the Europeans stepped foot on the land was that religion is a manmade institution, but the Creator gives spirituality to us. The Native Americans do not practice their way of life just on Sundays; they practice it every minute of the day, seven days a week, year in and year out.

Native Americans believe that we all possess the same spirit and energy. We may all have different qualities, gifts, and powers, but overall, we are all one. We are connected to the circle of life. Once these beliefs are understood, the mainstream teacher will connect with and understand the Native American; the child is taught to see the Creator in all living things: animals, birds, insects, plants, herbs, trees, rocks, air, water, fire, and earth. These are all part of the creation and life; they are their grandfathers, grandmothers, brothers, and sisters.

Cross-Cultural Communication Problems

The cross-cultural communication problems may not be apparent if the teacher does not realize he or she has Native American students, since many of these children have been Europeanized (Spring, 2016). Some tribes have returned to the old ways with the old languages. These students have been given their education on the reservations in both the old ways in the language of the tribe and in English with the new methods.

The tribes that have been able to survive and relish the culture they had previously have retained the past as much as possible in the new culture of today. The children may not be talkers but may be listeners, and they are concerned about nature and other fellow beings and spirits. These students live in a household where there is no yelling. If wrong decisions are made, they are asked to think about what was done right or wrong and to talk it over to correct a problem or to seek the wisdom that is needed to point one in the right direction. It is a different way that many people don't include in today's society.

Problems to Anticipate in the Classroom

The major problems that teachers can expect to see from the indigenous child is that of introverted feelings. At home, the indigenous children listen and learn, and they are not expected to talk back, to be rude, or to be belligerent. The tribal customs may not include talk about a God; however, they may talk about spirits, so the student might be confused if the teacher talks about the history of different cultures. Also, many of the tribes have a custom that the younger person looks down at the ground to show respect when an adult is speaking to him or her (Aragon, 2004).

The teacher might be from the mainstream culture that expects the child to look at the person talking, which conflicts with the indigenous culture. The tribal elders use a talking stick, and the person talking holds the stick; he or she passes the stick when the next person is to talk. As the person with the stick is talking, the others listen and look down, showing respect for the stick and person talking; they are listening, and the speaker's thoughts come easier. Therefore, if the teachers like the students to look at them, it might not happen, even though the students will be listening.

Teachers will also have trouble communicating the methods of learning if they are trying to obtain answers without using the hands-on method of instruction. These students learn from discovery and are taught that the world moves in a circle of life; thus, touching is a major learning experience.

Their Languages

The student's English language literacy and proficiency will vary, depending upon the acculturation of their tribe. The origins of each tribe's language can be traced back to about twelve original linguistic families of languages that have been identified. These languages are Eskimo-Aleut, Athapaskan, Algonquian, Iroquoian, Siouan, Muskogean, Caddoan, Shoshonean, Hokan, Shahaptian-Penutian, Salishan, and Wakashan. Languages are subdivided under the twelve larger language families. The languages have numerous derivatives, and each smaller tribal unit has defined itself over time by its own linguistic identity. Therefore, depending on the geographical location, the language will vary according to the individual tribe (Campbell, 2000).

Indigenous people feel that language is a valuable, living thing that is another special way of looking at the world. The Native American Indian languages are rich with connotation of man's natural relationship with the universe. Concepts and shades of meaning that cannot be expressed in English relate naturalistic and humanistic behavior. Although English may be the language of instruction and communication, the indigenous child should also be given the opportunity to study and learn his or her own language. When native language is recognized as an important part of the school curriculum, the student feels a sense of pride and security in his or her culture and in being a member of the tribe.

The indigenous languages are primarily oral, with an introduction of the written language in a simplified form. It names objects and builds simple sentence patterns. No grammar rules are stressed, but rather the emphasis is placed on learning the language through pattern and repetition. The general Indian language is a living symbol of the cultural heritage. Children must be given the opportunity to preserve the language both orally and in its written form; otherwise, in a few generations from now, language will be part of the past and irreplaceable. Too much of the knowledge of the customs and life values of the ancestors have already been lost.

Implications for the Classroom

The indigenous child will be a challenge if a teacher has a classroom that is not moving, up and around, adventurous and challenging. The indigenous child is always mannerly but needs to be in motion, not hyperactive but touching the surrounding world, exploring and asking questions after thinking about what is happening with the situation. The classroom has to be challenging, and everything learned is going to help the tribe in the future. The child being groomed as a chief will be learning different skills than the child that who will be a medicine man or hunter for the tribe. Each job in the tribe has different skills that need to be learned. The incongruity of the mainstream classroom with the Indian child's reality will be a challenge for a teacher.

The spiritual center of the indigenous student can be discovered in meditation and healing, as he or she seeks to "walk in balance" of spirit, mind, and body. The numbers four and seven are important in Native American cultures. Spiritual guidelines are given to the children of the tribe as the healing power from within. The children are taught to find their own pace, to be conscious of each breath, and to shed anything that might be hindering their journey. They are taught to stay tuned in to themselves and let experience be the guide to find the center of their being. Students are taught to ponder their experiences, and to show gratitude and reverence to the God who has walked with them. When the child is picking up an object and moving it to other places, he or she will tell Mother Earth his or her plans for the object, and thank her for producing the object to be used.

Students are taught to love tobacco, a product abhorrent to mainstream America. Tobacco may also be left as a thank you for something good in life happening, like a mother giving birth. Tobacco is revered as having high spiritual value and is thought to refurbish the earth. Many tribes have a giving tree where one ties a pouch of tobacco for thanks. These customs, although beautifully spiritual, may be contrary to what is found in the mainstream American classroom where days are organized, a schedule is fixed, and moments of silence or prayer are outlawed by the government.

What the Teacher Should Know

The first step is for the teacher to know the spiritualism of the tribe or nation the students come from in order to understand what values have been taught. Most students know the magic of an immediate, intimate, personal connection with the natural world; they usually will learn better with hands-on experiences. Animals are important to the tribes, and care must be taken not to be offensive or discourteous when talking about or studying animals. Each tribe has its own beliefs about the sacredness of animals. Therefore, teachers should know which nations the students come from to educate themselves about rituals and spirituality of the individual cultures.

Indigenous people believe in forbearance, charity, and helping one another; students are generous and giving. They are the ones who will give away their last supplies, which may be contrary to the American values that foster individualism and competition. When looking at the lifestyles of students, we see that they socialize in colorful gatherings where many different tribes came together, forming vast towns of other nations, where members wear different ceremonial outfits, and celebrate with dancing and singing, racing and playing, gambling games, trading stories, and bartering for goods. These meetings or events give the young men and women of different tribes the chance to meet, court, and fall in love. A person is held in high esteem not for his or her wealth but for the generosity the person has extended. Giving is an act of sacrifice; to give in any other way is not deemed as honorable.

In these nations, it is often surmised that men see more in the physical world and women see more in the spiritual or inner world. Native American culture in general has a great respect for age. Children might be raised more by their grandparents than their parents, who are busy being the providers for the clan. The elders, having lived long, full lives, are believed to have many lessons in survival to teach the youngsters. The elders are the guardians of wisdom, and they pass this wisdom down through the line of ancestors. Modern problems of inexperienced, heavily stressed parents rearing children in isolation do not exist, as these people enjoy an extended, supportive familial community. Children are not scolded and are allowed to be children; for example, children with imaginary play friends are not told to grow up, but are seen as potentially having the gift of vision. Teachers need to look at these qualities of life in the Native American culture to understand where the child is coming from, to understand how to help the student cross over into mainstream society and into the culture of learning in the non-native classroom.

The idea of the Native American warrior is a source of pride in this culture, and a child being raised in this light is learning compassion and tolerance along with the skill and courage of coping with the enemy upon whom he is advancing. He is taught that disputes are settled not by war but by sporting competitions that are often dangerous and require physical prowess and freedom from fear. These students accept life as fragile and short, as a transitory journey with the purpose of which is returning to the spirit world. One wonders how these teachings affect the interactions in a classroom of mainstream students. Does it create more tolerance for individuality?

These indigenous people are raised to sit in council, which is the tribe's organized body of government, where they prove their ability to think, act, and speak in the best interest of all. Balance and harmony are important to the community. The process of listening, thinking, and then talking when holding the stick is evident in the classroom as the teacher questions the student who does not answer immediately. This child will be the thinker first, then will react to the situation that is presented. Allowing extra wait time is crucial, and being comfortable in silence is a positive, explicit message that says it is acceptable to think before speaking. Many teachers might say, "Susie, can you help Johnny with the answer?" before Johnny has had a chance to formulate an answer.

The child who is slated to be the medicine man will be the entertainer, to show another side of life to the members of the community. This student acts with mythological vision. He shows the courage to plunge into the situation and get his feet wet, while being able to see the green of the world, the remedies of the world, and become the healer of the community.

The people of this culture realize that each individual brings a unique experience to the tribe or clan that all are expected to share, so each person is taught a different part of life. One mold is not for all people; the traditional teacher has to discover what mold that child comes from and encourage that student to move down the path of his or her individual destiny. Ideally, with a small class, the teacher can foster this individual growth. However, in reality, the teacher may have more than thirty students in the class, with a specified curriculum to follow within a given time, which makes individual attention very difficult.

More Effective Classrooms

It is easy to see why communication difficulties arise in the mainstream classroom. Native Americans are more comfortable with silence and longer periods of time without interaction, whereas typically mainstream American teachers expect quicker responses. High verbal activity is not necessarily a positive value in the Native American culture; in the traditional mainstream classroom, talking and participating are encouraged. In fact, teachers often base a grade on how often students respond in conversation. Native Americans usually speak more softly and are overall less verbally responsive.

Students are expected to be analytical and verbal, in the style of the mainstream American student; these cognitive styles are preferred to the visual, symbolic, and holistic thinking, which typically represent the Native American student (Cheng et al., 2011; Tharp, 1989). After learning about the tribal values, the teacher can weave the preferred style of learning into the class; for example, have students read the story through to the end before discussion, instead of taking it piece by piece (Tharp & Yamaguchi, 1994). Try to utilize materials that will be culturally relevant to the Native Americans. For more effective teaching, exploit the social organization preferences of Native learners, and use cooperative learning, hands-on activities, and group work with peer-oriented direction instead of adult supervision. Individual or group activities replicate the tribal circle of interaction. Manipulatives, group productions, and mental images are other strategies that the teacher can incorporate to create a more realistic learning experience for Native American students.

The Native American child needs to be looked at as a naturalist who loves the environment and everything in the natural world. If the teacher makes the learning environment feel like a real-world atmosphere, Native American students are bound to achieve.

The guidelines in Table 23.2 for teaching Native Americans were taken from the Ableza Institute website (1998) and were written by Native Americans (www.ableza.org/dodont.html). This website is one of the useful resources you can turn to for comprehensive information about the indigenous students in your classes.

TABLE 23.2 Appropriate Methods for Teaching Native Americans
• Understand that the term "Native American" includes all peoples indigenous to the Western Hemisphere.
• Present Native Americans as appropriate role models for children.
• Native American students should not be singled out and asked to describe their families' traditions or their peoples' culture(s).
• Avoid the assumption that there are no Native American students in your class.
• Use books and materials that are written and illustrated by Native American people as primary source materials, such as speeches, songs, poems, and writings that show the linguistic skill of a people who have come from an oral tradition.
• When teaching ABCs, avoid "I is for Indian" and "E is for Eskimo."
• Avoid rhymes or songs that use Native Americans as counting devices, e.g., "One little, two little, three little Indians . . ."
• Research the traditions and histories, oral and written, of Native Americans before attempting to teach them. Know the significance animals play in each nation. (Certain tribes may ascribe to complex cleansing or religious rituals after seeing animals, such as a bear.)
• Avoid referring to or using materials that depict Native Americans as "savages," "primitives," "The Noble Savage," "Red Man," "Red Race," "simple," or "extinct."
• Present Native Americans as having unique, separate, and distinct cultures, languages, beliefs, traditions, and customs.
• Avoid materials that use non–Native Americans or other characters dressed as "Indians."
• Avoid craft activities that trivialize Native American dress, dance, and beliefs (e.g., toilet-paper-roll kachinas or "Indian dolls," paper bag and construction paper costumes and headdresses). Research authentic methods and have the proper materials. Realize that many songs, dances, legends, and ceremonies of Native Americans are considered sacred and should not be "invented" or portrayed as an activity.
• If your educational institution employs images or references to Native American peoples as mascots (e.g., "Redskins," "Indians," "Chiefs," "Braves," etc.), urge your administration to abandon these offensive names.
• Correct and guide children when they "war whoop," use "jaw-breaker" jargon, or employ any other stereotypical mannerisms.
• Depict Native Americans, past and present, as heroes who are defending their people, rights, and lands.
• Avoid manipulative phrases and wording such as "massacre," "victory," and "conquest" that distort facts and history.

- Teach Native American history as a regular part of American History and discuss what went wrong or right.

- Avoid materials and texts that illustrate Native American heroes as only those who helped Europeans and Euro-Americans (e.g., Thanksgiving).

- Use materials and texts that outline the continuity of Native American societies from past to present.

- Use materials that show respect and understanding of the sophistication and complexities of Native American societies. Understand and impart that the spiritual beliefs of Native Americans are integral to the structure of our societies and are not "superstitions" or "heathen."

- Invite a Native American guest speaker/presenter to your class or for a school assembly. Contact a local Native American organization or your library for a list of these resources. Offer an honorarium or gift to those who visit your school.

- Avoid the assumption that a Native American person knows everything about all Native Americans.

- Use materials that show the value Native Americans place on our elders, children, and women. Avoid offensive terms such as "papoose" and "squaw." Use respectful language.

- Understand that not all Native Americans have "Indian" surnames, but many have familiar European and Hispanic names as well.

- Help children understand that Native Americans have a wide variety of physical features, attributes, and values, as do people of ALL cultures and races.

- Most of all, teach children about Native Americans in a manner that you would like used to depict YOUR culture and racial/ethnic origin.

Source: Ableza Native American Arts and Media Institute (1998).

- "Indian Country Diaries. Today's Challenges. Cultural Protocol | PBS", 2017
- According to the PBS website (http://www.pbs.org/indiancountry/challenges/protocol.html) There is proper protocol for attending a celebratory POW WOW. Whites and other visitors are welcome but need to follow the protocol:
- Arrive on time.
- Wear appropriate respectful clothing. You may dance if you wear dance clothing.
- At the arena benches, blankets are used to reserve space and benches are for dancers. Don't sit on someone's blanket.
- Be respectful and listen to the MC.
- When dancing, respect the Head man and Head woman dancers. They will start and stop each song.
- No alcohol or drugs.
- When not dancing, be quiet and show respect.
- Do not touch religious items if you are not qualified to.

FINAL POINTS

- Many tribes of Native Americans still exist across the nation.
- Each tribe has its own name, language, cultures, and customs.
- It is important to be respectful to Native Americans and their individuality.
- When teaching Native American students, it is important to understand which society your students are from.

- Study your students' cultures so you won't inadvertently offend, insult, or humiliate your students.
- Native American students may have different learning styles that are different from the culture of your classroom. Be sensitive to their needs, and differentiate instruction.

Discussion Questions and Activities

1. What steps can you take to determine whether you have Native American students in your classroom?
2. Understanding Native American cultural beliefs, describe what steps you would take to ensure that your students feel comfortable in the learning situations you create in your classrooms.
3. List ten cultural values of Native Americans, and discuss what teachers can do to make these values congruent with the values of the mainstream teacher.
4. What are some negative or incorrect stereotypes often associated with Native Americans? How do you think misconceptions came to be so prevalent?
5. How could you use an opportunity to rectify a mistake that someone may make about Native Americans in your classroom?

Resources

Teaching/understanding prejudice about Native American/Native American issues
http://www.understandingprejudice.org/teach/native.htm

Library of Congress: Native American information for students
http://www.loc.gov/teachers/classroommaterials/themes/native-americans/students.html
https://www.teachervision.com/native-american-heritage-month/teacher-resources/6648.html

Strategies for teaching Native Americans
http://literacynet.org/lp/namericans/strategies.html

Tips on teaching Native Americans
http://serc.carleton.edu/research_education/nativelands/tips.html

PBS online: Native American Myths
http://www.pbs.org/edens/yellowstone/teach2.html

Effective ways to teach Native American language and culture webinar:
http://www.youtube.com/watch?v=uxQrNf-spn4

George Washington University webinar
http://www.youtube.com/watch?v=xAkAAPN3o80

Tradition and culture
http://indianyouth.org/american-indian-life/traditions-culture

References

Aragon, S. R. (2004). Information processing patterns of postsecondary American Indian/Alaska native students. *Journal of American Indian Education*, 1–20.

Campbell, L. (2000). *American Indian languages: the historical linguistics of Native America*. Oxford University Press.

Cheng, H., Andrade, H. L., & Yan, Z. (2011). A cross-cultural study of learning behaviours in the classroom: From a thinking style perspective. *Educational Psychology, 31*(7), 825–841.

Garrett, M. T. & Pichette, E. F. (2000). Red as an apple: Native American acculturation and counseling with or without reservation. *Journal of Counseling and Development: JCD, 78*(1), 3.

Indian Country Diaries. Today's Challenges. Cultural Protocol|PBS. (2017). *Pbs.org*. Retrieved May 8, 2017, from http://www.pbs.org/indiancountry/challenges/protocol.html

King, T. (2012). *The inconvenient Indian: A curious account of native people in North America*. Doubleday Canada.

Kunstadter, P. (2017). *Southeast Asian tribes, minorities, and nations* (Vol. 1). Princeton University Press.

Pewewardy, C. & Hammer, P. C. (2003). Culturally responsive teaching for American Indian students. *ERIC Digest*.

Powers, K. M. (2006). An exploratory study of cultural identity and culture-based educational programs for urban American Indian students. *Urban Education, 41*(1), 20–49.

Reich, D., Patterson, N., Campbell, D., Tandon, A., Mazieres, S., Ray, N., & García, L. F. (2012). Reconstructing native American population history. *Nature, 488*(7411), 370–374.

Spring, J. (2016). *Deculturalization and the struggle for equality: A brief history of the education of dominated cultures in the United States*. Routledge.

Watkins, J. (2001). *Indigenous archaeology: American Indian values and scientific practice*. AltaMira Press.

APPENDICES

APPENDIX A

ESOL INSTRUCTIONAL STRATEGIES MATRIX

(*HOW* WE TEACH IS AS IMPORTANT AS *WHAT* WE TEACH)

A Accommodations	B Clear Communication	C Assessments	D Vocabulary	E Collaboration & Conversation	F Metacognitive & Metalinguistic	G Context Embedded Supports & Close Reading	H Multimodal & Multimedia	I Advance Organizers	J Additional Resources
A1 Heritage Dictionary	B1 Concise Language	C1 Rubrics	D1 Etymology/Cognates	**Grouping Configurations:** E1 Heterogeneous Grouping (Language/Content Readiness; Learner Profiles; Interests)	F1 L1 Transfer	G1 Activating and/or Building Prior Knowledge	H1 Audio-Visual Applications	I1 Charts (Flowcharts, T-Charts, etc.)	J1 Art Integration
A2 Heritage Language (L1) Support	B2 Clear Directions	C2 Presentation	D2 Semantic Feature Analysis	E2 Homogeneous Grouping (Language/Content Readiness; Learner Profiles; Interests)	F2 Mnemonic Devices	G2 Chunking Text	H2 Digital Books	I2 Anticipation Guide	J2 Community Resources
A3 Flexible Scheduling	B3 Enunciation	C3 Portfolio	D3 Context Clues	E3 Jigsaw	F3 Dialogue Journals	G3 Annotations & Symbols	H3 Computer Software	I3 Cornell Notes	J3 Cultural Sharing
A4 Flexible Setting	B4 Pauses & Pacing	C4 Checklist	D4 Tier II/Tier III Analysis	E4 Peer Pair	F4 Self-Correction	G4 Ask Inferential & HOT Questions	H4 Document Camera	I4 Digital Tools/Software	J4 Celebrations
A5 Flexible Timing	B5 Pointing	C5 Labeling	D5 Interactive Word Walls	E5 Reader's Theater	F5 Self-Evaluation	G5 Ask Clarifying Questions	H5 Interactive White Board	I5 Foldables	J5 Field Trips
	B6 Repeating/Paraphrasing	C6 Interview	D6 Vocabulary Games	E6 Think/Pair/Share	F6 Self-Monitor	G6 Modeling	H6 Tablet/Interactive Devices	I6 Graphs/Diagrams	J6 Guest Speakers
	B7 Gestures	C7 Response Cards	D7 Multiple Meanings	E7 Academic Games	F7 Peer Editing	G7 Read Aloud	H7 Language Master	I7 K-W-L	J7 Holiday Programs
	B8 Show Examples & Non-Examples	C8 Oral Assessment	D8 Phonology	E8 Group Presentations/Projects	F8 Associations	G8 Think Aloud	H8 Video/Film/CD/MP3	I8 Reading and Analyzing Non-Fiction (RAN)	J8 Multicultural Resources
	B9 Demonstrations	C9 Observation	D9 Vocabulary Banks	E9 Socratic Seminar		G9 Multimodal Texts	H9 Digital Simulations	I9 Notes TM	J9 Music/Songs/Jazz Chants
	B10 Anecdote/Storytelling	C10 Context-Embedded Text		E10 Panel Discussion		G10 Visualization/Illustrations	H10 Translation Devices	I10 Webbing/Mapping	
		C11 Voting Devices		E11 Debate/Defend with Evidence		G11 Summarizing		I11 Story Maps	
		C12 Cloze Test				G12 Dramatic Enactments/Role Play		I12 Timelines	
		C13 Visual Representations				G13 Identify Key Concepts		I13 Venn Diagrams	
		C14 Self/Peer Assessment				G14 Similarities & Differences		I14 Vocabulary Improvement Strategy (VIS)	
		C15 Samples				G15 Language Experience Approach			
		C16 Sentence Frames				G16 Note-Taking/Outline Notes			
						G17 Question-Answer-Relationship (QAR)			
						G18 Reading with Specific Purpose			
						G19 Reread Text			
						G20 Text Features & Structural Analysis			
						G21 Survey, Question, Read, Recite, Review (SQ3R)			
						G22 Text Connections			
						G23 Total Physical Response (TPR)			
						G24 Vary Complexity of Assignment			
						G25 Realia/Manipulatives			
						G26 Captioning			

APPENDIX B
LANGUAGE-LEVEL CLASSIFICATIONS AND DESCRIPTIONS

This level of classifications comes from the School Board of Broward County. However, you can find other classification on the WIDA website:

https://www.wida.us/standards/Resource_Guide_web.pdf

And at ACTFL (American Council of the Teaching of Foreign Languages
https://www.actfl.org/publications/guidelines-and-manuals/actfl-proficiency-guidelines-2012

Broward County

A[1] **Non-English Speaker (NES) or minimal knowledge of English:**
Demonstrates very little understanding.
Cannot communicate meaning orally.
Unable to participate in regular classroom instruction.

A[2] **Limited English Speaker (LES):**
Demonstrates limited understanding.
Communicates orally in English with one- or two-word responses.

B[1] **Intermediate English Speaker:**
Communicates orally in English, mostly with simple phrases and/or sentence responses.
Makes significant grammatical errors that interfere with understanding.

B[2] **Intermediate English Speaker:**
Communicates in English about everyday situations with little difficulty but lacks the academic language terminology.
Experiences some difficulty in following grade-level subject matter assignments.

C[1] **Advanced English Speaker:**
Understands and speaks English fairly well.
Makes occasional grammatical errors.
May read and write English with variant degrees of proficiency.

˙C² Full English Speaker (FES):
Understands and speaks English with near fluency.
Reads and writes English at a comparable level with native-English-speaking counterparts.
May read and write the native language with variant degrees of proficiency.

D   Full English Speaker:
Speaks English fluently.
Reads and writes English at a comparable level with English-speaking counter parts.

E   Monolingual English Speaker
No services required.

From the School Board of Broward County, Florida, Multicultural/Foreign Language/ESOL Education Department.

˙When students achieve C² status, they can be exited from the ESOL program. State guidelines require that all ELs' progress be monitored for two years after exiting the program.

APPENDIX C

SAMPLE OF MODIFIED LESSON PLAN—SCIENCE

Academic Achievement for ELLs
Lesson Plan Activity

Name: Katherine Kollitides   School: Driftwood Elementary

Grade/Class/Subject: 5th Grade Science

Standards: SC.5.P.11.1.

Objectives: Investigate and illustrate complete circuits using a battery, wires, and a light bulb

Key Vocabulary	Materials
Circuit Complete Loop Conductor Insulator	Battery Wires Light Bulb

ESOL Instructional Strategies:
-Provide definition and/or examples of each key vocabulary word.
-Translate the vocabulary word into L1
-Show or draw a picture of the word
-Repeat and paraphrase instructions for ELLs

Lesson Sequence: (Keep in mind presentation style, student practice, and review/assessment)
Students will be divided into pairs. They each receive a battery, 3 pieces of wire, and a light bulb. They will be given 15 mintues to work together to investigate how to make the light bulb light up. Students will not be told where to place the materials; instead, they will need to discover this naturally.
After the time has expired, the teacher will lead a share-out explaining the different arrangement of materials that worked and did not work. Two students will be selected to draw a complete loop and an incomplete looop on the board. Then, students will write an explanation of items other than a light bulb that can be put in a complete circuit (i.e. radio).

Differentiated Instruction:

Beginning:
-ELLs will be grouped with a student who speaks their language
-Students can draw a picture and verbally answer the prompts instead of writing

Intermediate:
-Encourage verbal explanation of the materials necessary to form a complete circuit, with an emphasis of content understanding over word prounuciation.

Advanced:
-Provide modeling and support for written explanations

341

APPENDIX D

CLASS ASSIGNMENT:
CONTENT AREA TEXTBOOK ANALYSIS FORM

This assignment asks the reader to examine the text to determine if it would be appropriate for English learners. Even with illustrations, students without background, or schema, will have difficulty making sense of the content. The teacher will have to adapt and modify the content to help the EL understand the text.

Name of Textbook:

Publisher:

Publication Date:

Content Area:

Grade Level:

1. Content Objectives of Entire Book—Scope and Sequence (Describe)

2. Unfamiliar Cultural Assumptions (Think beyond the box: Try to look at the text from the perspective of a non-native English speaker, as well as someone from another country. Look hard: There is always something.)

3. Higher Order Thinking Skills (Look at Bloom's taxonomy. Find and list exercises that call for higher order thinking skills and relate them to the skill.) Could you break the text into comprehensible language?

EXAMPLE	SKILL
Suppose the height of a right prism is doubled. What effect does it have on the surface area?	Predict, draw conclusions; Relate knowledge from several areas; Use previous knowledge to create new ideas . . .

4. Evaluation of Overall Text

(In three or four paragraphs, tell why you would or would not recommend this text, why, how it could be improved, and if you would use it to teach ELs.)

APPENDIX E

PROJECT RUBRIC FOR MODIFICATION
OF TEXTBOOK

Name/s _____ Subject modified _____ Grade level_____

Choose a chapter from a textbook. Please attach original chapter in hard copy. You may also submit the chapter electronically. Do not forget to cite your references using APA 6th edition style.

   Modification of text for ELs with language levels A (beginner), B (intermediate), and C (advanced). Using the language levels (see Appendix B) as your guide to the proficiency levels of your students, modify text for beginner, intermediate, and advanced speakers.

10 points possible _____	Attach a copy of the original text you are adapting.
10 points possible _____	Make three separate sections with dividers so it is clear which section is for each level. For beginning speakers . . . For intermediate speakers . . . For advanced speakers . . .
25 points possible _____	Modify the chapter in your chosen content area. (e.g.,Turn complex sentences into two simple sentences. Pre teach vocabulary. Avoid using the passive tense. Break complex topics into manageable chunks. Use templates and graphic organizers.)

Modify the content for A, B, and C language proficiency levels of project. Include questions for comprehension (at least one question for each level) for each level of proficiency. Try to use higher order thinking skills (see Bloom's Taxonomy).

10 points possible _____	Include Visual Representations (pictures/pictorial)
10 points possible _____	Outline Formats (Simple words)
10 points possible _____	Write instructions for teacher presenting the lesson.
10 points possible _____	Include the TESOL strategies applicable to teaching this chapter. (Strategies are found in the ESOL matrix in Appendix A) Explain your strategy choices.
15 points possible _____	Create three authentic alternative assessments, one for each language level. Make sure your instrument assesses your objectives. Beginner level Intermediate level Advanced level
Total points out of 100_____	

APPENDIX F

SIOP® LESSON PLANNING GUIDE

Center for Applied Linguistics

http://www.cal.org/siop/lesson-plans/

The SIOP® Lesson Planning Guide was developed by Jana Echevarria, Mary Ellen Vogt, Deborah Short, and Chris Montone, through research sponsored by the Center for Research on Education, Diversity, and Excellence (CREDE) with a grant from the U.S. Department of Education, Office of Educational Research and Improvement.

This guide was developed as an aid in planning sheltered lessons. The right column can be used for writing notes or as a checklist to ensure attention to each indicator.

Unit Plan Theme: _____

Preparation

1. Clearly defined *content objectives* for students	
2. Clearly defined *language objectives* for students	
3. *Content concepts* appropriate for age and educational background level of students	
4. *Supplementary materials* used to a high degree, making lesson clear and meaningful (e.g., graphs, models, visuals)	
5. *Adaptation of content* (e.g., text, assignment) to all levels of student proficiency	

6. *Meaningful activities* that integrate lesson concepts (e.g., surveys, letter writing, simulations, constructing models) with language practice opportunities for reading, writing, listening, and/or speaking

7. *Concepts explicitly linked* to students' background experiences

8. *Links explicitly made* between past learning and new concepts

9. *Key vocabulary emphasized* (e.g., introduced, written, repeated, and highlighted for students to see)

10. *Speech* appropriate for students' proficiency level (e.g., slower rate, enunciation, and simple sentence structure for beginners)

11. *Explanation* of academic task clear

12. Uses a variety of *techniques* to make content concepts clear (e.g., modeling, visuals, hands-on activities, gestures, body language)

13. Provides ample opportunities for students to use *strategies*

14. Consistent use of *scaffolding* techniques throughout lesson, assisting and supporting student understanding (e.g., think-alouds)

15. Teacher uses a variety of *question types, including those that promote higher order thinking skills* (e.g., literal, analytical, and interpretive questions)

16. Frequent opportunities for *interactions* and discussion between teacher/student and among students, which encourage elaborated responses about lesson concepts

17. *Grouping configurations* support language and content objectives of the lesson

18. Consistently provides sufficient *wait time for students' responses*

19. Ample opportunities for students to *clarify key concepts in L1* as needed with aide, peer, or L1 text

20. Provides **hands-on** materials and/or manipulatives for students to **apply content and language knowledge** in the classroom

21. Provides activities for students to **apply content and language knowledge** in the classroom

22. Uses activities that integrate all **language skills** (e.g., reading, writing, listening, and speaking)

23. **Content objectives** clearly supported by lesson delivery

24. **Language objectives** clearly supported by lesson delivery

25. **Students engaged** approximately 90% to 100% of the period

26. **Pacing** of the lesson appropriate to the students' ability level

27. **Content objectives** clearly supported by lesson delivery

28. **Language objectives** clearly supported by lesson delivery

29. **Students engaged** approximately 90% to 100% of the period

30. **Pacing** of the lesson appropriate to the students' ability level

31. Comprehensive **review** of key vocabulary

32. Comprehensive **review** of key content concepts

33. Regularly provide **feedback** to students on their output (e.g., language, content, work)

34. Conducts **assessment** of student comprehension and learning of all lesson objectives (e.g., spot checking, group response) throughout the lesson

APPENDIX G

RESOURCES: JOURNALS AND WEBSITES

Journals

(By no means a complete list: Hundreds of journals exist for the ESOL teacher.)

Annual Review of Applied Linguistics
Applied Language Learning
Applied Linguistics
Applied Psycholinguistics
College ESL
Cross Currents
Discourse Processes
DSH Abstracts (deafness, speech, and hearing)
ELR Journal (English research)
ELT Journal
English for Specific Purposes (ESP journal)
English Language Teacher
English Teacher Journal
English Teaching Forum
English Today
Guidelines
International Journal of American Linguistics
International Review of Applied Linguistics
IRAL (International Review of Applied Linguistics in Language Teaching)
ITL Review of Applied Linguistics
JALT Journal (Japan)
JETT (Journal of English Teaching Techniques)
Journal of Educational Research for Language Minority Students
Journal of Linguistics Journal of Memory and Language
Journal of Multilingual & Multicultural Development

Journal of Psycholinguistic Research
Journal of Research in Reading
Journal of Second Language Writing
Language
Language and Speech
Language in Society
Language Learning
Language Learning Journal
Language Research
Language Testing
Linguistics
Modern Language Journal
Modern Language Quarterly
Modern Language Review
NABE: Bilingual Research Journal
NYSABE Journal
Papers & Reports on Child Language Development
Reading in a Foreign Language
Reading Research Quarterly
Second Language Research
Studies in Second Language Acquisition
Sunshine State TESOL Journal
TESL Reporter
TESOL Journal
TESOL Quarterly
TESOL Matters (formerly)
TESOL Newsletters
TESOL Quarterly
TESOL Talk
The Canadian Modern Language Review
The Education Digest
The Language Teacher (Japan)
The Modern Language Journal
World Englishes

Websites

Dave's ESL Café: http://www.eslcafe.com/

Florida Educator Accomplished Practices: http://www.fldoe.org/teaching/professional-dev/the-fl-educator-accomplished-practices.stml

ESOL in Higher Education: https://www.esolinhighered.org/

TESOL Standards: http://www.tesol.org/advance-the-field/standards

Website for ESOL learners http://www.colorincolorado.org/

https://www.youtube.com/user/colorincolorado

https://sharemylesson.com/partner/colorin-colorado

Common ESOL/TESOL terms https://www.tesol.org/enhance-your-career/career-development/ beginning-your-career/a-guide-to-common-acronyms-in-the-tesol-profession

Glossary of EL terms http://www.colorincolorado.org/ell-basics/ell-glossary

English Learners http://www.fldoe.org/academics/eng-language-learners/

TESOL = Florida TESOL (Teaching English to Speakers of Other Languages): www.fldoe.org/aala/ perstand.asp

Stephen Krashen's webpages: http://www.sdkrashen.com/

http://www.sdkrashen.com/articles.php

http://esl.fis.edu/teachers/support/krashen.htm

https://www.facebook.com/SDKrashen/

Jim Cummins's webpage (BICS/CALP): https://www.youtube.com/watch?v=zCeWIA7lJUU

https://www.youtube.com/watch?v=N-JvqObf5qk http://esl.fis.edu/teachers/support/cummin.htm

TESOL International: www.tesol.org

California Association of Bilingual Education: www.bilingualeducation.org

U.S. Department of Education: https://www2.ed.gov/about/offices/list/oela/index.html

Teaching Tolerance: www.teachingtolerance.org

Massachusetts Department of Education: www.doe.mass.edu/ell

California Department of Education: http://www.cde.ca.gov/sp/el/

Webpages for Making Rubrics: http://rubistar.4teachers.org/index.php

http://rubric-maker.com/

https://www.quickrubric.com/

WIDA (World-class Instructional Design and Assessment): https://www.wida.us/

ESSA (Every Student Succeeds Act): https://www.ed.gov/esea
http://www.edweek.org/ew/issues/
every-student-succeeds-act/index.html

English Grammar: https://www.englishgrammar.org/

Topics for conversation: http://iteslj.org/questions/

Make ESL videos: http://www.eslvideo.com/

Activities and resources: http://www.brighthub.com/education/languages/topics/esl.aspx

Dictionary: http://www.dictionary.com/

Using English (idioms, etc.): https://www.usingenglish.com/reference/idioms/h.html

Make your own worksheets, etc.: http://busyteacher.org/

Fantastic website with unlimited resources: http://learnenglish.britishcouncil.org/en

Reading site for ELs: http://www.readingrockets.org/reading-topics/english-language-learners

Literacy for ELs: http://www.readingrockets.org/article/teaching-literacy-english-k-5-english-learners

GLOSSARY

Academic language   The vocabulary, phrases, and expressions used in academic texts and classes. Academic language has common terms and phrases across academic disciplines, but also has unique terminology and expressions to the field. Academic language tends to be formal, succinct, and abstract.

Acquisition versus learning hypothesis   Describes language acquisition as a process that does not require conscious grammatical rules or drills. Meaningful interaction in the target language produces natural communication. Learning a language, on the other hand, is a formal process through the use of grammar rules.

Active participation   When the student takes an active role in the classroom participation.

Affective filter hypotheses   States that only when learners feel secure and comfortable enough does the language acquisition process work. If learners are bored, angry, frustrated, unmotivated, or stressed out, they cannot be receptive to language input, and so they screen the input. This screen is referred to as the *affective filter*. Teachers need to try to maintain a low affective filter so that learning can take place.

Algorithmic process   The process used in calculating math, such as division or subtraction.

American paradigm   When, in true intercultural competence, one knows the rules of American culture and will avoid making inappropriate social or cultural mistakes.

Approximate (v)   When language learners cannot reproduce the sound perfectly (often because they cannot hear it correctly), they make the sound the best way they can. The sound is not exact, but it is approximate. So, the language learner *approximates* the sound that he or she interprets. (People who are deaf often approximate the sounds they cannot hear.)

Basic Interpersonal Communication Skills (BICS)   Often referred to as "playground English" or "survival English." It is the basic language ability required for face-to-face communication on a social level. Dr. Jim Cummins is the researcher who first coined this phrase, based on his research measuring native English speakers' standardized tests compared to English learners' test scores on standardized tests. He found that ELs can pick up social language pretty quickly and sound like native speakers, which is confusing when they cannot do well academically on standardized tests.

Behaviorist theory   A belief based on work by psychologist B. F. Skinner, who posited that behavior is learned by imitation. This theory was applied to language learning, where the belief was that language is learned by imitation.

Bidet (French, pronounced bee-day)   A bathroom fixture similar in design to a toilet with water faucets, straddled for bathing the genitals and the posterior parts.

***Bien educado* (Spanish)**   Cultured, ladylike, polite, and well mannered.

Body language   Describes gestures and facial expressions that show nonverbal communication.

Bottom up   The individual study of grammatical structures or sentence structures. It focuses on small components of the language (individual sounds, morphemes, or words) in order to interpret the whole message. This phrase is used in reading as well, as opposed to "top down," where you read the whole text and try to make global sense of what you are reading.

Brain-based research   Forwards the idea that adults and children use different parts of their brain to learn a second language.

Brain-based theories   Theories based on the belief that the structures and functions of the brain influence language acquisition and how language is used.

Brown v. the Board of Education of Topeka, Kansas   In 1954, the Supreme Court decision in case of *Brown v. Board of Education of Topeka, Kansas* provided the legal basis for equal educational opportunity. The Court ruled that "in the field of public education, the doctrine of 'separate but equal' has no place. Separate education facilities are inherently unequal. We hold that the plaintiffs and others similarly situated are by reason of the segregation complained of deprived of the equal protection of the laws guaranteed by the Fourteenth Amendment."

***Chaemyon* (Korean)**   Describes how Koreans keep their self-esteem according to the perspectives of others, or living up to the expectations of others. In social situations, there is an expectation of behavior that people must adhere to in order to save face in the culture.

Chronemics   The study of the use of time in nonverbal communication.

Close-end exercises   Activities that allow for one, or a small range of correct answers. Close-ended exercises defer from open-ended activities that allow learners multiple correct answers to express themselves in a wide range of language.

Code-switching   Any switching between languages in the course of a conversation. The speaker may start in one language and go back and forth between two languages.

Cognitive Academic Language Proficiency (CALP)   The language ability required for successful academic achievement. Dr. Jim Cummins researched the standardized test scores for native English speakers and compared them to English learners. He found that it can take 5 to 7 years for NNS to catch up to native English speakers in academic achievement. Without academic language, ELs are at risk of dropping out of high school since they speak English well socially but lack the academic vocabulary to be successful. *See also* BICS.

Cognitive process   The mental activities people's brains are engaging in when they are making intellectual sense of something. Each person's mental process is based on the person's own schema, background, or experience.

Cognitive styles Individual differences in mentally processing and analyzing information, in knowledge, and in reactions to teaching and learning styles.

Collocations Two, or more words, that often appear together in speak or writing. For example, hot tea, stone cold, dead wrong, right of way.

Common underlying proficiency (CUP) Cummins explains his theory by noting how the first language helps learners with skills in the second language. Once a task is learned in the native language, the knowledge will be transferred to the second language. The only problem may be new vocabulary or idioms, but not the concept.

Communicative competence The ability to communicate correctly in the target language and speaker know-how in using the language appropriately in all social and cultural contexts.

Compadrazgo In the Hispanic cultures, the idea of godparents or coparents "compadrazgo" carries a more significant meaning than the English "godparent."

Comprehensible content or input When learners acquire language by being given the appropriate, understandable input. The input should be easy enough that they can understand, but just beyond their level of competence. Krashen included this stage in his Monitor Model Theory and depicted it "I" + "i."

Confucianism The religion based on the teachings of Confucius that seeks to delineate the nature of a life worth living. It emphasizes the importance of human relationships—those within the family, between friends, and those between governments and their citizens. Confucius' ideas set out the desired ethical character of human beings and how they relate to others. Cultures that live under the beliefs of Confucianism showed this influence in all areas of life, such as government, education, and public relationships.

Context clues Sources of information that help students understand what they don't know by using clues to identify the answers.

Critical framing When learners evaluate what they have learned by critiquing their own work.

Critical period A concept proposed by G. H. Lennenberg that language can be acquired only within a certain time frame, usually from early infancy to puberty. Other language researchers have applied this hypothesis to L2 learners as well as Ll.

Cultural cues Information one receives that give one an idea about meaning in other cultures. With cultural clues, we are better able to negotiate within another culture.

Culture shock A sense of confusion and frustration with feelings of anxiety that may affect people who come from a different environment or culture without adequate preparation. Manifestations of culture shock can be physical, emotional, or mental.

de facto ESOL teachers Teachers who are not officially ESOL teachers but have English learners in a classroom and are responsible their academic success. Therefore, the teacher is a "de facto" ESOL teacher.

Deep culture Cultural norms that are not easily detected unless one is born and raised in that specific culture or spends an extended amount of time in the culture.

Don A term used with the first name of a man to show respect in Hispanic etiquette, as in *Don José*.

Doña The feminine equivalent of *Don*, as in *Doña Rosa*.

EL (English learner)   Student whose first language is not English and who is in the process of learning English.

Embedded   When an item is built into an idea or a concept. For example, context clues are embedded in the text. By reading the text, you can figure out the meaning.

English as a second language (ESL)   An educational approach in which English language learners are instructed in the use of the English language. Their instruction is based on a special curriculum that typically involves little or no use of the native language, focuses on language (as opposed to content), and is usually taught during specific school periods. Students may be in an ESL program or receive EL support while they are in a mainstream or bilingual class.

ESOL (English for speakers of other languages)   Another, more accurate, term for ESL.

ESSA (Every Student Succeeds Act, December 2015)   Formerly the No Child Left Behind Act (NCLB) is the law that modifies the periodic standardized tests administered to all children in the United States.

Ethnocentrism   When one feels one's ethnic group or culture is superior to all others.

Febles   Haitian Creole for "feeling weakness."

Feita   Diminutive in Spanish meaning "little ugly girl."

Field-dependent learners   Learners characterized as global, socially sensitive, and interpersonally oriented learners who like to work with others to achieve a common goal.

Field-independent learners   Learners characterized as being analytical self-reliant, and impersonal in orientation. They work well individually.

Five Pillars   One of the principal tenets of Islam, consisting of acceptance of the creed, prayers, almsgiving, fasting during Ramadan, and pilgrimage to Makkah (also known as Mecca).

Flaco   Spanish for "emaciated, shrunken, or skinny one."

Foreigner talk   The simplified way of talking native English speakers use with English learners to be sure they are understood.

Formalism   A concept that emphasizes accuracy in speaking rather than fluency. These students will not answer questions in another language for fear of making a mistake.

Formative assessment   A type of evaluative process that helps guide teachers in collecting and analyzing student work to determine that students understand.

Fossilized error   A language error becomes permanent if the student never gets corrective feedback. The error may not affect communication or comprehension.

Generation 1.5   Students who come from other countries and enter the U.S. school system while still learning English, usually in their teens or middle school age. Immigrants who are students educated in the U.S. educational system while they are still in the process of learning English. They share characteristics of both first- and second-generation immigrants.

Gordito or *Gordita*   In Spanish, adding "ito" (for a male) or "ita" (for a female) can soften the meaning of an adjective such as fat (*gordito/gordita*), ugly (*feito/feita*), or old (*viejito/viejita*).

Graphic organizer   A visual guide, graph, chart, or aid that helps prepare a student before, during, or after the lesson. It can provide prior knowledge for the lesson and offer cues to listen or look for to remind students of what they are learning.

Gurus   Teachers of the Holy Scripture, language, and science in Indian culture, regarding education as a holy duty.

Halal   Arabic for "lawful" or "permitted," referring to food that is permissible to consume during Ramadan.

Hands-on activites   Any instructional activities used when students work with objects relevant to the content being studied.

Hangul   Another name for the Korean language. It's alphabet is very different from the Romanic alphabet, which confuses Korean students trying to learn English.

Haptics   Refers to communicating through touch.

Heterogeneously   The grouping together of students who have varying abilities, interests, or ages.

High context   Refers to people of a certain culture who do not communicate verbally but understand each other by a look or a nod of the head.

High involvement with a low considerateness   When people of certain cultures talk and interrupt each other without being bothered by who interrupts them; they all talk at once.

High-stakes testing   The primary method of monitoring and improving school performance, usually gauged by grades students make on standardized tests.

Hijab or *Chador*   A scarf that covers the heads of some Muslim women.

Home culture   The culture one gets from the home and one's environment.

Incongruence   Discord or disharmony when people, cultures, or teacher and students are not in agreement.

Indigenous child   One who is native to the land. In the United States, indigenous children can be American Indian, Alaska Native, First Nations, Inuit, and Métis.

Input Hypothesis   The idea that language is acquired by receiving comprehensible input (one of the theories in Krashen's Monitor Model). That is, we have to receive input that is just beyond our competence but not beyond our understanding. According to Krashen, language is acquired through the learner's efforts to understand or comprehend the L2, rather than through trying to use the L2. Speaking and writing are simply the end products of the learner's attention to input.

Instructional Conversation   A manner to engage learners with academics through open-ended questions, scaffolding, and extended responses, which focuses learners on evidence in reading content, models academic language use and themes of instruction.

Jaw-breaker   Slang term for a word that is hard to pronounce.

Kafiyyeh   What some Muslim men wear as traditional headpieces to demonstrate pride in their cultural identity, usually carries no religious significance.

Kinesics   The study of body language; refers to nonverbal communication, including gestures, facial expressions, and stances.

Kinesthetic objective   An objective that utilizes the intelligence reflected in body movement or active participation.

KWL chart   A graphic organizer in the form of a chart. Teachers elicit information from the students by asking them to complete the following descriptions: *K* stands for what one knows about a subject; *W* stands for what one wants to know about a subject; and *L* is identifying what one has learned about the subject.

L1   The native language of the speaker.

L2   The second language that the speaker is trying to learn.

Language Experience Approach   An approach to reading and writing in which the teacher serves as a scribe, writing down the learners' language. Learners generate the language of story or personal experiences orally.

Language interference   The negative effect of language learners' first language on their production of the language they are learning.

Lau v. Nichols   A legal suit filed by Chinese parents in San Francisco in 1974 that led to a landmark Supreme Court ruling that identical education does not constitute equal education under the Civil Rights, and as a result, school systems must provide remedies that afford equal educational access regardless of native language.

Lavman   Haitian Creole for "enema," used to purify the inner body.

Learning style   An individual's preferred way of learning.

Lexicon   The words of a language, or its vocabulary.

***Loas* or *Iwas* (Haitian Creole, based on African origin)**   A spirit that can be called upon to help families, bring good fortune, and protect from or attack enemies. In return, families leave gifts such as food, drink, or flowers.

Low context   Cultures that are considered low context include those of North America and much of Western Europe. Communication is direct and verbalized so that the meaning of participants is absolutely clear.

Low involvement with high considerateness   Characterizes a culture in which one does not disrupt a person speaking, listens politely, will show interest, and speaks one at time.

Mainstream classroom   Typical classroom with native English speakers. No accommodations are made for ELs.

Mainstream culture   The majority culture of the mainstream population; in the United States this refers to native English speakers, usually Caucasian.

Maldyok   The Haitian Creole word for "evil eye," which is brought on a result of an envious glance from another.

Masjid   Mosque for midday prayers.

MATESOL   Master of Arts in Teaching English as a Second Language. A master's degree in the study of English as a second language.

Meyer v. Nebraska   Court case in which German Lutherans filed suit against Nebraska. The Supreme Court ruled in June 1923 that forbidding teaching non-English speakers until the eighth grade violated liberty under the 14th amendment.

Modals   Auxiliary verbs used with another word to indicate its mood. Words such as *can, may, might, must, should,* and *would* are modals.

Monitor Hypothesis   Principles of learning language according to Krashen. This hypothesis refers to a supposed error-correcting mechanism in the brain that edits the utterance of language learners and helps a learner to focus on the correct form. The "editing" or repair of the error takes place only when the learner knows the correct rules of the language.

Monochronic   Refers to a culture that prefers to make one sound or complete one action at a time.

Monolingual teacher   A teacher who has knowledge of only his or her native language.

Morphology   The study of how words are formed.

Motherese (or Parentese)   A social environment with truncated speech that is believed to promote an understanding of speech between parent and child.

Mullahs   Islamic clergy who teach religious law and doctrine.

Narrow, extensive reading   An approach to reading in which students read a lot of material on a narrow topic.

Nativist theory   Noam Chomsky's idea that children are born with the basic capacity to learn language biological patterned in the brain (LAD—language acquisition device).

Natural order hypothesis   According to Krashen, language is learned in a predictable sequence.

Negative transfer   The errors that language learners make when mistakenly transferring first language knowledge to the second language.

Nonmainstream culture   Refers to individuals coming from cultures other than the mainstream or dominant culture.

Nunchi   In Korean culture, the subtle art of listening and gauging another's mood.

Paralinguistics   The elements outside or beyond speech that affect and modify vocal speech.

Parallel distributed processing (PDP)   Language learning takes place in different parts of the brain.

Parentese   See *motherese.*

Participation structure   Class participation and interaction in the classroom. Each culture has different expectations about when, where, and how to speak in the classroom. Students must learn what expectations are acceptable in a U.S. classroom.

Pe Lebren or Pere Lebrun   In Haiti, refers to a tire being used as a burning barricade or a mode of execution. A tire is placed around the victim's neck and lit on fire, particularly during political unrest.

Personal independence   A trait that is prominent in U.S. culture and encouraged in U.S. students.

Phonology   The study of the sound system of a language.

Plasaj In Haitian cultures, the most common form of marriage among the lower socioeconomic class; it is a kind of common law marriage.

Pocket door A door that slides between the walls instead of opening in or out.

Polychromic cacophony Multiple sounds at once.

Polychronic When multiple tasks are done simultaneously.

Positive transfer When language learners successfully transfer knowledge of their first language to their second language. We will not be aware this is taking place because the student does not make an error.

Pragmatic rules The rules of a culture that determine the underlying meaning of communication or indirect speech.

Pragmatics How people use words and language within a culture.

Productive skills The language skills of speaking and writing in which a person produces language.

Project-based activities Activities, such as role playing or putting on a play, in which students show knowledge by creating the activity, often through their own research and writing.

Proxemics The study of personal distances maintained by speakers and their use of personal space both consciously and unconsciously.

Ramadan The Muslim religious holiday that takes place during the ninth month of the Islamic calendar. Observers fast and do not eat or drink anything from dawn until sunset.

Receptive skills The language skills of listening and reading in which a person receives language.

Reliable When a test is considered reliable, it means that the test consistently measures the same thing every time it is used; therefore, it is a reliable measure.

Sadhus Holy men of India.

Scaffold An instructional technique in which the teacher breaks a complex task into smaller manageable tasks, then models how they should be done. Students receive support until they are able to do the task alone. A scaffold helps the student until it is not needed, thus promoting success.

Schema An outline, diagram, plan, or preliminary draft. When referring to students, it is prior knowledge from the student's individual background. A student's schema will determine how he or she makes sense out of the world.

Semantics Word and phrase meanings in communication. People give meaning to words that often is not literal, that is, that has an "insider" meaning not obvious to the language learner.

Semitic A subfamily of the Afro-Asiatic language family that includes Hebrew, Aramaic, Arabic, and Amharic.

Sheltered English or Sheltered Instruction An instructional approach used to make academic instruction in English understandable to English language learners by using scaffolding and special instructional strategies.

Sheltered Instruction Observation Protocol (SIOP) A format that incorporates language and academic teaching in a specialized lesson plan. The SIOP plan incorporates language and content objectives.

Silent stage   An early stage in the second language acquisition process during which the learner is silent while listening and internalizing the sounds of the new language and which is part of a natural process that the learner goes through at his or her own speed.

Social interactionist theory   Refers to children who learn language by socially interacting with others.

Social language   The language of interpersonal communication for social purposes. Social language tends to be informal, repetitive, and contextualized.

Special education (or exceptional education)   Programs designed to help students with learning disabilities or exceptional students.

Stereotyping   Preconceived ideas about a particular social group or culture that are usually based on physical or verbal appearance.

Summative evaluation   The process of measuring learning achievement after a specified task that utilized specific objectives, materials, and methods.

Surface culture   Cultural differences that can be seen through native dress, food, music, and so on.

Syntax   The acceptable pattern of the parts of speech in a language; common grammatical patterns or word order.

Tag question   A form of question followed by a mini-question. The whole sentence is a "tag question," and the mini-question at the end is called a "question tag": For example, *You like candy, don't you? You didn't eat candy, did you?* English learners have problems forming or answering these types of questions because when the main part of the sentence is negative, the tag is positive. Conversely, when the sentence is positive, the tag part is negative.

Target language   The language that a student is learning as a second or additional language. For English language learners in the United States the target language is English.

Task-oriented   When a person is motivated to finish a project or task.

Thematic approach   The instruction of curriculum around themes. Thematic instruction integrates content such as reading, math, and science within the exploration of a broad subject.

Tirando piropos   The accepted common occurrence in some Hispanic cultures of making flattering remarks to women.

Top down   The studying of language (or in reading a text) as a whole without worrying about the individual components of language. The learner is trying to understand using cues such as intonation, tone of voice, or body language without focusing on specific words and structures.

Total Physical Response (TPR)   An approach to teaching a foreign language through physical actions. James Asher made this a popular method of teaching through commands.

****Translanguaging is the act performed by bilinguals of accessing different linguistic features or various modes of what are described as autonomous languages, in order to maximize communicative potential. Ofelia García (2009: 140)

Vaastu Shastra   In India a line of thought based on promoting harmony between physical and metaphysical flows of energy.

Valid   Refers to a test that measures what it is supposed to measure.

Viejito   A Spanish diminutive that means "little old man."

Vodou or Voodoo   A religion that combines African spiritual beliefs with rituals derived from Roman Catholic symbols.

Yut Nori   An ancient traditional Korean board game played during Korean New Year.

** García, O. (2009). Education, multilingualism and translanguaging in the 21st century. *Social justice through multilingual education*, 140–158.

REFERENCES

Ableza Native American Arts and Media Institute, San Jose, CA. (1998). *Tips for teachers.* Retrieved January 1, 2004, from www.ableza.org/index.shtml, and www.ableza.org/dodont.html

Adeed, P. & Smith, G. P. (1997). Arab Americans: Concepts and materials. In J. A. Banks (Ed.), *Teaching strategies for ethnic studies.* Boston: Allyn & Bacon.

American-Arab Anti-Discrimination Committee (ADC). (1993a). *Educational outreach and action guide: Working with school systems.* Washington, DC: Author.

American-Arab Anti-Discrimination Committee. (1997). *1996–1997 Report on hate crimes and discrimination against Arab Americans.* Washington, DC: Author.

Anderson, J. A. (1988). Cognitive styles and multicultural populations. *Journal of Teacher Education, 24* (1), 2–9.

Ariza, E. N. (2000). Actions speak louder than words—Or do they? Debunking the myth of apathetic immigrant parents in education. *Contemporary Education, 71*(3), 36–38.

Ariza, E. N. (2002). Cultural considerations: Immigrant parent involvement. *Kappa Delta Pi Record, 38*(3), 134–137.

Ariza, E. N., Morales-Jones, C., Yahya, N., & Zainuddin, H. (2002). *Why TESOL? Theories and issues in teaching English to speakers of other languages in K–12 classroom* (3rd ed.). Dubuque, IA: Kendall Hunt.

Asher, J. (1972). Children's first language as a model for second language learning. *Modern Language Journal, 56*, 133–139.

Asian American Almanac. (1995). Detroit, MI: Gale Research.

Axtell, J. (1988). *After Columbus: Essays in ethnohistory of colonial North America.* New York: Oxford University Press.

Axtell, R. E. (1998). *Gestures: The do's and taboos of body language around the world.* New York: John Wiley & Sons.

Bachman, L. F. (1990). *Fundamental considerations in language testing.* Reading, MA: Addison-Wesley.

Baik, Y. & Chung, J. Y. (1996, March). Family policy in Korea. *Journal of Family and Economic Issues, 17*(1), 93–112.

Baker, C. (1996). *Foundations of bilingual education and bilingualism.* Clevedon, England: Multilingual Matters.

Banks, J. A. (2001). *Cultural diversity and education* (4th ed.). Boston: Allyn & Bacon.

Banks, J. A. & Banks, C. A. (1993). *Multicultural education: Issues and perspective* (2nd ed.). Boston: Allyn & Bacon.

Baruth, L. G. & Manning, M. L. (1992). *Multicultural education of children and adolescents*. Boston: Allyn & Bacon.

Bennett, C. I. (Ed.). (1990). *Comprehensive multicultural education: Theory and practice*. Boston: Allyn & Bacon.

Bialystock, E. (1978). A theoretical model of second language learning. *Language Learning, 28*(1), 69–83.

Bloom, B.S., et al. (Eds.). (1984). *Taxonomy of educational objectives. Book 1: Cognitive domain*. White Plains, NY: Longman.

Brand, D. (1987, August 31). The new whiz kids. *Time, 130,* 42–51.

Brinton, D. M., Snow, M. A., & Wesch, M. B. (1989). Content-based second language instruction. New York: Newbury House.

Brown v. the Board of Education of Topeka, Kansas, 347 U.S. 483, 74 S. Ct. 686 (1954); 349 U.S. 294, 75 S. Ct. 853 (1955).

Brown, H. D. (1994). *Principles of language learning and teaching* (3rd ed.). Englewood Cliffs, NJ: Prentice Hall Regents.

Brown, P. L. (1998, December 31). Where the spirits of vodou feel at home. *New York Times,* B1, B18.

Burt, M., Peyton, J. K., & Adams, R. (2003). *Reading and adult English language learners: A review of the research.* Washington, DC: National Center for ESL Literacy Education & Center for Applied Linguistics.

Cadiero-Kaplan, K. (2004). *The literacy curriculum and bilingual education: A critical examination*. New York: Peter Lang.

Canale, M. & Swain, M. (1980). Theoretical bases of communicative language approaches to second language teaching and testing. *Applied Linguistics, 1,* 1–47.

Cantoni-Harvey, G. (1987). *Content-area language instruction: Approaches and strategies*. Reading, MA: Addison-Wesley.

Capps, L. R. & Gage, M. S. (1987). Mathematics spoken here. A case for language and vocabulary in mathematics (pp. 4–6). In Houghton Mifflin (Ed.), *Current issues in mathematics*. Boston: Houghton Mifflin.

Capps, L. R. & Pickreign, J. (1993). Language connections in mathematics: A critical part of mathematics instruction. *Arithmetic Teacher, 41*(1), 8–12.

Carrell, P. (1983). Some issues in studying the role of schemata, or background knowledge, in second language comprehension. *Reading in a Foreign Language, 1,* 81–92.

Chamot, A. & O'Malley, M. (1987). A cognitive academic language learning approach: A bridge to the mainstream. *TESOL Quarterly, 21,* 227–249.

Choi, S. (1991). Children's answers to yes-no questions, a developmental study in French and English [Electronic version]. *Developmental Psychology, 27,* 407–420.

Chomsky, N. (1979). *Language and responsibility*. New York: Pantheon.

Civan, M. B. (1995). *Haitians' history and culture*. Coconut Creek, FL: Educavision.

Coker, D. M. (1988). The Asian students in the classroom. *Education and Society, 1*(3), 19–20.

Colin, J. M. & Paperwalla, G. (1996). Haitians. In J. G. Lipson, S. L. Dibble, & P. A. Minarik (Eds.), *Culture and nursing care: A pocket guide* (pp. 139–154). San Francisco: UCSF Nursing Press.

Collier, V. P. (1989). How long? A synthesis of research on academic achievement in a second language. *TESOL Quarterly, 23,* 509–532.

Collier, V. P. (1992). A synthesis of studies examining long-term language minority student data on academic achievement. *Bilingual Research Journal, 16*(1–2), 187–212.

Comer, J. P. (1984). Home–school relationships as they affect the academic success of children. *Education and Urban Society, 71,* 323–337.

Coriel, J. (1983). Parallel structures in professional and folk health care: A model applied to rural Haiti. *Culture, Medicine and Psychiatry, 7*(2), 131–151.

Coriel, J., Barnes-Josiah, D. L., & Cayemittes, A. (1996). Arrested pregnancy syndrome in Haiti: Findings from a national survey. *Medical Anthropology Quarterly, 10*(3), 424–436.

Cosgray, R. E. (1995). Haitian Americans. In J. N. Giger & R. E. Davidhizar (Eds.), *Transcultural nursing: Assessment and intervention* (pp. 501–523). St. Louis, MO: Mosby.

Council of Chief State School Officers (CCSSO). (1992). *Recommendations for improving the assessment and monitoring of students with limited English proficiency.* Washington, DC: Author.

Council on American-Islamic Relations (CAIR). (1997). *An educator's guide to Islamic religious practices.* Washington, DC: Author.

Craan, A. G. (1988). Toxicologic aspects of vodou in Haiti. *Biomedical and Environmental Sciences, 1*(4), 372–381.

Crandall, J. A. (1993). Content-centered learning in the United States. *Annual Review of Applied Linguistics, 13,* 111–126.

Crawford, J. (1999) *Bilingual education: History, politics, theory, and practice* (4th ed.). Los Angeles, CA: Bilingual Education Services.

Crawford, J. & Krashen, S. (2007). *English learners in American classrooms: 101 questions, 101 answers.* New York: Scholastic.

CultureGrams. (2001). *CultureGrams 2002 Standard Edition* (2 vols). Chicago: Ferguson Publishing.

Cummins, J. (1981a). Age on arrival and immigrant second language learning in Canada: A reassessment. *Applied Linguistics, 2,* 132–149.

Cummins, J. (1981b). The role of primary language development in promoting educational success for language minority students. In C. F. Leyba (Ed.), *School and language minority students: A theoretical framework* (pp. 3–49). Los Angeles: Evaluation, Dissemination and Assessment Center, CSULA.

Cummins, J. (1982). *Tests, achievement and bilingual students.* Wheaton, MD: National Clearinghouse for Bilingual Education.

Cummins, J. (1984). Wanted: A theoretical framework for relating language proficiency to academic achievement among bilingual students. In C. Rivera (Ed.), *Language proficiency and academic achievement.* Clevedon, England: Multilingual Matters.

Cummins, J. (1994). The role of primary language development in promoting educational success for language minority students. In C. F. Leyba (Ed.), *Schooling and language minority students: A theoretical framework* (2nd ed., pp. 3–48). Los Angeles: California State University, National Evaluation, Dissemination and Assessment Center.

Dale, T. & Cuevas, G. (1992). Integrating mathematics and language learning. In P. Richard-Amato & M. Snow (Eds.), *The multicultural classroom.* White Plains, NY: Longman.

Damas, D. (Ed.). (1984). *Handbook of North American Indians—Arctic.* Washington, DC: Smithsonian Institution.

DeGeorge, G. P. (1988). Assessment and placement of language minority students: Procedures for mainstreaming. *Equity and Excellence, 23*(40), 44–56.

Delgado-Gaitan, C. (1991). School matters in the Mexican American home: Involving parents in the school: A process for empowerment. *American Journal of Education, 100*(1), 20–46.

dePaula, T., Lagana, K., & Gonzalez-Ramirez, L. (1996). Mexican Americans. In J. Lipson, S. Dibble, & P. Minarik (Eds.), *Culture and nursing care: A pocket guide* (pp. 203–221). San Francisco: UCSF Nursing Press.

DeSantis, L. & Thomas, J. T. (1990). The immigrant Haitian mother: Transcultural nursing perspective on preventive health care for children. *Journal of Transcultural Nursing, 2*(1), 2–15.

Diaz, C. (1989). Hispanic cultures and cognitive styles: Implications for teachers. *Multicultural Leader, 2*(4), 1–4.

Diaz-Rico, L. & Weed, K. (1995). *The cross-cultural language and academic handbook.* Boston: Allyn & Bacon.

Dunn, R. & Dunn, K., (1978). *Teaching students through their individual learning styles: A practical approach.* Reston, VA: Reston Publishing.

Dunn, R. & Griggs, S. (1990). Research on the learning style characteristics of selected racial and ethnic groups. *Reading, Writing, and Learning Disabilities, 6,* 261–280.

Echevarria, J., Vogt, M. E., & Short, D. (2004). *Making content comprehensible for English learners: The SIOP model.* Boston: Allyn & Bacon.

ESSA (2015). Every Student Succeeds Act of 2015, Pub. L. No. 114-95 § 114 Stat. 1177 (2015–2016).

Fillmore, L. W. & Snow, C. E. (2000). *What teachers need to know about language.* Retrieved August 1, 2004, from www.cal.org/resources/teachers/teachers.pdf

Fitz-Gibbon, J. & Garcia, E. (2003, July 15). Many Hispanics eschew racial categories, study finds. *The JournalNews.Com.* Retrieved November 10, 2003, from www.nyjournalnews.com/071503/a0115hispanicrace.html

Frank, M. & Jones, R. (2002). *Harcourt science.* Orlando, FL: Harcourt.

Freeman, Y., Freeman, D., & Mercuri, S. (2002). *Closing the achievement gap: How to reach limited formal schooling and long-term English learners.* Portsmouth, NH: Heinemann.

Garcia, S. & Malkin, D. (1993). Toward defining programs and services for culturally and linguistically diverse learners in special education. *Teaching Exceptional Children, 26*(1), 52–58.

Gardner, H. (1993). *Multiple intelligences: The theory in practice.* New York: Basic Books.

George, P. & Aronson, R. (2003). *How do educators' cultural belief systems affect underserved students' pursuit of postsecondary education?* The Pathways to College Network and Clearinghouse. Retrieved August 2, 2004, from www.pathwaystocollege.net/graphics/pathways_label.gif

Gollnick, D. M. & Chinn, P. (1990). *Multicultural education in a pluralistic society* (3rd ed.). New York: Merrill.

Goodman, A. (1997). *Korean Online. Korean grammar. I.* Retrieved on November 9, 2003, from www.sigmainstitute.com/koreanonline/grammar.shtml

Grant, C. A. & Sleeter, C. E. (1989). *Turning on learning: Five approaches for multicultural teaching plans for race, class, gender, and disability.* Columbus, OH: Merrill.

Hakuta, K. & Pease-Alvarez, C. (1992). Enriching our views of bilingualism and bilingual education. *Educational Researcher, 21,* 4–6.

Hall, E. T. (1959). *The silent language.* Garden City, NY: Anchor Press/Doubleday.

Hall, E. T. (1966). *The hidden dimension.* New York: Doubleday.

Hall, E. T. (1983). *The dance of life.* Garden City, NY: Anchor Press/Doubleday.

Hall, E. T. (1990). *Understanding cultural differences.* Yarmouth, ME: Intercultural Press.

Harklau, L., Losey, K. M, & Siegal, P. (Eds.). (1999). *Generation 1.5 meets college composition: Issues in the teaching of writing to US-educated learners of ESOL.* Mahwah, NJ: Lawrence Erlbaum.

Harris, W. J. & Schultz, P. N. B. (1986). *The special education resource program: Rationale and implementation.* Columbus, OH: Merrill.

Hauptman, L. (1995). *Tribes and tribulations, misconceptions about American Indians and their histories.* Albuquerque: University of New Mexico Press.

Herrera, S. G., Murry, K. G., & Morales Cabral, R. (2007). *Assessment accommodations for classroom teachers of culturally and linguistically diverse students.* Boston: Allyn & Bacon.

Hill, J. & Flynn, K. (2006). *Classroom instruction that works with English language learners.* Alexandria, VA: Association for Supervision and Curriculum Development.

Hoover, J. J. & Collier, C. (1989). Methods and materials for bilingual special education. In L. M. Baca & H. T. Cervantes (Eds.), *The bilingual special education interface* (pp. 231–255). Columbus, OH: Merrill.

Huang, G. (1993). Beyond culture: Communicating with Asian American children and families. *ERIC/CUE Digest Number 94* (ED366673).

Hvitfeldt, C. (1986). Traditional culture, perceptual style, and learning: The classroom behavior of Hmong adults. *Adult Education Quarterly, 36*, 65–77.

Hymes, D. (1972). Models of the interaction of language and social life. In J. J. Gumperz & D. Hymes (Eds.), *Directions in sociolinguistics: The ethnography of communication* (pp. 35–71). New York: Holt, Rinehart, & Winston.

Igoa, C. (1995). *The inner world of the immigrant child.* Mahwah, NJ: Lawrence Erlbaum.

Ishii-Jordan, S. & Peterson, R. (1994). Behavior disorders in culture and community. In R. Peterson & S., Ishii-Jordan (Eds.), *Multicultural issues in the education of students with behavioral disorders* (pp. 251–262). Cambridge, MA: Brookline Press.

Jackson, M. L. (1997). Counseling Arab Americans. In C. C. Lee (Ed.), *Multicultural issues in counseling* (2nd ed., pp. 333–352). Alexandria, VA: American Counseling Association.

Kayser, H. (1998). *Assessment and intervention resource for Hispanic children.* San Diego: Singular.

Kim, J. M. (1998). Korean children's concepts of adult and peer authority and moral reasoning [Electronic version]. *Developmental Psychology, 34*(5), 947–955.

Kim, P. H. (2001, June 8). [Korea business culture] Korea viewed by 7 cultural measures. *Digital Chosun-Ilbo.* Retrieved November 10, 2003, from http://english.chosun.com/w21data/html/news/200106/200106080184.html

Kim, Y. Y. (1985). Intercultural personhood: An integration of Eastern and Western perspectives. In L. A. Samovar & R. E. Porter (Eds.), *Intercultural communication: A reader* (4th ed.). Belmont, CA: Wadsworth.

Kim-Rupnow, W. S. (2001). A collaborative project between NTAC-AAPI and the Center for International Rehabilitation Research Information and Exchange (CIRRIE) at the State University of New York at Buffalo [Electronic version]. *Asian Culture Brief: Korea, 2*(1).

Kleinman, A. & Good, B. J. (1985). *Culture and depression.* Berkeley: University of California Press.

Kohls, R. (2001). *Survival kit for overseas living* (4th ed.). Yarmouth, ME: Intercultural Press.

Korean Overseas Information Service. (1997). *History of Hangul.* Retrieved November 9, 2003, from www.sigmainstitute.com/koreanonline/hangul_history3.shtml

Krashen, S. D. (1978). The monitor model for second language acquisition. In R. C. Gingras (Ed.), *Second language acquisition and foreign language teaching* (pp. 1–26). Arlington, VA: Center for Applied Linguistics.

Krashen, S. D. (1981). *Second language acquisition and second language learning.* Oxford: Pergamon Press.

Krashen, S. D. (1982). *Principles and practice in second language acquisition.* London: Pergamon Press.

Krashen, S. D. (1999). What the research really says about structured English immersion: A response to Keith Baker. *Phi Delta Kappan, 80*, 705–706.

Krashen, S. D. (2002a) The comprehension hypothesis and its rivals. In *Selected papers from the Eleventh International Symposium on English Teaching/Fourth Pan Asian Conference* (pp. 395–404). Taipei: Crane Publishing Company.

Krashen, S. D. (2002b). *Explorations in language acquisition and use: The Taipei lectures.* Taipei: Crane Publishing Company.

Krashen, S. D. & Terrell, T. D. (1983). *The natural approach: Language acquisition in the classroom.* Hayward, CA: Alemany Press.

Kreeft, J. (1984). Dialogue writing—Bridge from talk to essay writing. *Language Arts, 61*, 141–150.

Lambert, W. E. & Tucker, G. R. (1972). *Bilingual education of children.* Rowley, MA: Newbury House.

Lareau, J. (1987). Social class differences in family–school relationships: The importance of cultural capital. *Sociology of Education, 60,* 73–85.

Lau v. Nichols, 414, U.S. 563 (1974).

Lee, A. (1989). A socio-cultural framework for the assessment of Chinese children with special needs. *Topics in Language Disorders, 9*(30), 38–44.

Lee, G. L. (2003). Understanding immigrated Korean children's educational needs [Electronic version], *Kappa Delta Pi Record, 39*(4), 168–172.

Lee, J. Y. (1996). Some tips for teaching English to Korean students. Presented at the INTESOL Conference, Indiana University, Purdue University, Indianapolis, November 1, 2003. Retrieved November 8, 2003, from www.intesol.org/lee.html

Lennenberg, E. (1974). *Biologic foundations of language.* New York: Wiley.

Lewis, R. B. & Doorlag, D. J. (1987). *Teaching special students in the mainstream.* Columbus, OH: Merrill.

Loewen, J. (1995). *Lies my teacher told me: Everything your American history text got wrong.* New York: Touchstone, Simon & Schuster.

Logan, J. R., Stowell, J., & Vesselinov, V. (2001, October). *From many shores: Asians in Census 2000.* Albany: State University of New York, Albany, Lewis Mumford Center for Comparative Urban and Regional Research.

Los Angeles Times poll. April 13, 1998.

Mandell, C. J. & Gold, V. (1984). *Teaching handicapped students.* St. Paul, MN: West.

Martin, M. A., Rissmiller, P., & Beal, J. A. (1995). Health-illness beliefs and practices of Haitians with HIV disease living in Boston. *JANAC, 6*(6), 45–53.

Matsuda, M. (1989). Working with Asian parents: Some communication strategies. *Topics in Language Disorders, 9*(3), 45–53.

Mazurek, K. & Winzer, M. (2005). *Schooling around the world: Debates, challenges and practices.* Boston: Allyn & Bacon.

McDade, K. (1995). How we parent: Race and ethnic differences. In C. Jacobson (Ed.), *American families: Issues in race and ethnicity* (pp. 283–300). New York: Garland.

McIntyre, T. (1993). Reflections on the impact of the proposed definition for emotional and behavioral disorders: Who will still fall through the cracks and why. *Behavioral Disorders, 18*(2), 148–160.

McIntyre, T. (1995). *The McIntyre assessment of culture: An instrument for evaluating the influence of culture on behavior and learning.* Columbia, MO: Hawthorne Educational Services.

McLaughlin, B. (1980). Theory and research in second language learning: An emerging paradigm. *Language Learning, 30,* 331–350.

Meyer v. Nebraska, 262 U.S. 390 (1923).

Moon, I. (2001, August 27). For Korean kids, a long trip to school—Why parents are enrolling kids abroad [Electronic version]. *Business Week.* Retrieved October 14, 2008, from www.businessweek.com/magazine/content/01_35/b3746069.htm

National Clearinghouse for Bilingual Education (NCBE). (1990). *Two-way language development programs.* ERIC Digest. Washington, DC: ERIC/CLL.

National Council of Teachers of Mathematics (NCTM). (2000). *Principles and standards for school mathematics.* Reston, VA: Author.

National School Public Relations Association. (1993). *Capturing the best of the 1993 NSPRA seminar.* Arlington, VA: Author.

New London Group (NLG). (1996). A pedagogy of multiliteracies: Designing social futures. *Harvard Educational Review, 66*(1), 60–92.

No Child Left Behind Act of 2001. 107th Congress of the United States of America. Retrieved August 7, 2004, from www.ed.gov/policy/elsec/leg/esea02/107-110.pdf

Nunan, D. (1989). *Designing tasks for the communicative classroom*. Cambridge, UK: Cambridge University Press.

Nydell, M. (1987). *Understanding Arabs*. Yarmouth, ME: Intercultural Press.

Oberg, K. (1998). Culture shock and the problem of adjustment in new cultural environments. In G. R. Weaver (Ed.), *Culture, communication and conflict: Readings in intercultural relations* (2nd ed., pp. 185–186). Needham Heights, MA: Simon & Schuster.

Ogbu, J. (1988). Class stratification, racial stratification, and schooling. In L. Weiss (Ed.), *Class, race, and gender in American education* (p. 163). Albany: State University of New York Press.

Oh, Y., Koeske, G. F., & Sales, E. (2002). Acculturation, stress, and depressive symptoms among Korean immigrants in the United States. *Journal of Social Psychology, 142*(4), 511–526.

Olsen, L. & Jaramillo, A. (1999). *Turning the tides of exclusion: A guide for educators and advocates for immigrant students*. Oakland, CA: Coast Litho.

Onishi, N. (2003, September 21). Divorce in South Korea striking a new attitude [Electronic version]. *New York Times*. Retrieved October 14, 2008, from http://query.nytimes.com/gst/fullpage. htm/?res-9900E7DA113AF932A1575ACOA9659CBB63

Pajares, F. M. (1992). Teacher's beliefs and educational research: Cleaning up a messy construct. *Review of Educational Research, 62*(3), 307–322.

Pajewski, A. & Enriquez, L. (1996). *Teaching from a Hispanic perspective: A handbook for non-Hispanic adult educators*. Phoenix, AZ: Adult Literacy and Technology Resource Center. Retrieved on August 4, 2004, http://literacynet.org/lp/hperspectives/

Park, E. J. (1995). Voices of Korean-American students [Electronic version]. *Adolescence, 30*(120), 945–953.

Pease-Alvarez, C. (1993). *Moving in and out of bilingualism: Investigating native language maintenance and shift in Mexican-descent children*. Santa Cruz, CA: National Center for Research on Cultural Diversity and Second Language Learning.

Peregoy, S. F. & Boyle, O. F. (2001). *Reading, writing, and learning in ESOL: A resource book for K–12 teachers*. Longman: New York.

Perez, M., Pinzon, H., & Garza, R. (1997). Latino families: Partners for success in school settings. *Journal for School Health, 67*(5), 182–184.

Philips, S. U. (1983). *The invisible culture: Communication in classroom and community on the Warm Springs Indian Reservation*. White Plains, NY: Longman.

Pierre, G. (1971). *American Indian crisis*. San Antonio, TX: The Naylor Company.

Preston, R. A., Materson, B. J., Yoham, M. A., & Anapol, H. (1996). Hypertension in Haitians: Results of a pilot survey of a public teaching hospital multispecialty clinic. *Journal of Human Hypertension, 10*(11), 743–745.

Purcell-Gates, V. (2001). What we know about readers who struggle. In R. F. Flippo (Ed.), *Reading researchers in search of common ground* (pp. 118–143). Newark, DE: International Reading Association.

Ramirez, M. & Castaneda, A. (1974). *Cultural democracy, bicognitive development, and education*. New York: Academic Press.

Rueda, R. S. & Forness, S. R. (1994). Childhood depression: Ethnic and cultural issues in special education. In R. Peterson & S. Ishii-Jordan (Eds.), *Multicultural issues in the education of students with behavioral disorders* (pp. 40–62). Cambridge, MA: Brookline Press.

Rumbaut, R. G. & Ima, K. (1988, January). *The adaptation of Southeast Asian Refugee youth: A comparative study*. Final Report to the U.S. Department of Health and Human Services, Office of Refugee Resettlement. Washington, DC: U.S. Department of Health and Human Services.

Shen, W. & Mo, W. (1997). Parental involvement: A new challenge to Asian-American parents. In *Perspective of Chinese American education in the 21st century* (pp. 59–64). Houston, TX: Chinese American Educational Research and Development Association.

Short, D. J. (1991). *How to integrate language and content instruction: A training manual* (2nd ed.). Washington, DC: Center for Applied Linguistics.

Siu, S. F. (1992). *Taking no chances: Profile of a Chinese-American family's support for success.* Boston, MA: Wheelock College. (ERIC Document Reproduction Service No. ED 361446).

Skinner, B. F. (1957). *Verbal learning.* New York: Appleton-Century-Crofts.

Spolsky, B. (1989). *Conditions for second language learning: Introduction to a general theory.* Oxford, UK: Oxford University Press.

Tharp, R. (1989). Psychocultural variables and constants: Effects of teaching and learning in schools. *American Psychologist, 44*(2), 349–359.

Tharp, R. & Yamaguchi, L. A. (1994). *Effective instructional conversation in Native American classrooms (Educational Practice Report No. 10).* Santa Cruz, CA: National Center for Research on Cultural Diversity and Second Language Learning.

Thomas, W. P. & Collier, V. (2002). *A national study of school effectiveness for language-minority students' long-term academic achievement.* Santa Cruz, CA: Center of Research, Diversity and Excellence.

Tompkins, G. E. (2001). *Literacy for the 21st century: A balanced approach* (3rd ed.). Englewood Cliffs, NJ: Prentice Hall.

Trueba, H. T. & Cheng, L. (1993). *Myth or reality: Adaptive strategies of Asian Americans in California.* Bristol, PA: Falmer Press.

Utley, C. (1983). *A cross-cultural investigation of field-independence/field-dependence as a psychological variable in Menominee Native American and Euro-American grade school children.* Madison: Wisconsin Center for Education and Research.

Valdez, G. (1996). *Con respeto: Bridging the distances between culturally diverse families and schools.* New York: Teachers College Press.

van Kraayenoord, C. & Paris, S. G. (1996). Story construction from a picture book: An assessment activity for young learners. *Early Childhood Research Quarterly, 11*(1), 41–61.

Vogt, L. A., Jordan, C., & Tharp, R.G. (1987). Explaining school failure: Producing school success: Two cases. *Anthropology and Education Quarterly, 18,* 276–286.

Vygotsky, L. S. (1962). *Thought and language.* Cambridge, MA: MIT Press.

Vygotsky, L.S. (1978). *Mind in society.* Cambridge, MA: Harvard University Press.

Watkins, S. (1992). *Native American history, reference manual.* Beverly Hills, CA: Myles.

Wei, T. (1980). *Vietnamese refugee students: A handbook for school personnel.* Cambridge, MA: Lesley College (EDAC).

Wiggins, G. & McTighe, J. (2005). *Understanding by design* (2nd ed.). Alexandria, VA: Association for Supervision and Curriculum Development.

Willis, S. (1993). Multicultural teaching: Meeting the challenges that arise in practice. *Association for Supervision and Curriculum Development Curriculum Update,* September 1–3, 6.

Wong, S. & Teuben-Rowe, S. (1997). Honoring students' home languages and cultures in a multilingual classroom [Electronic version]. *Sunshine State TESOL Journal* (Fall 1997), 20–26.

Wong-Filmore, L. (1991). When learning a second language means losing the first. *Early Childhood Research Quarterly, 6,* 323–347.

Woo, J. (1985). *The Chinese-speaking student: A composite profile.* New York: Bilingual Education Multifunctional Support Center at Hunter College.

The World Factbook, CIA homepage, country profiles, Haiti. Central Intelligence Agency, Office of Public Affairs, Washington, DC. Retrieved August 6, 2008. www.cia.gov/cia/publications/factbook/index.html

Zemelman, S., Daniels, H., & Hyde, A. A. (1998). *Best practice: New standards for teaching and learning in America's schools.* Portsmouth, NH: Heinemann.

INDEX